Faith, War, and Violence

Faith, War, and Violence

Religion & Public Life

Volume 39

Gabriel R. Ricci
Editor

Transaction Publishers
New Brunswick (U.S.A.) and London (U.K.)

Copyright © 2014 by Transaction Publishers, New Brunswick, New Jersey.

All rights reserved under International and Pan-American Copyright Conventions. No part of this book may be reproduced or transmitted in any form or by any means, electronic or mechanical, including photocopy, recording, or any information storage and retrieval system, without prior permission in writing from the publisher. All inquiries should be addressed to Transaction Publishers, 10 Corporate Place South, Piscataway, New Jersey 08854. www.transactionpub.com

This book is printed on acid-free paper that meets the American National Standard for Permanence of Paper for Printed Library Materials.

ISSN: 1083-2270
ISBN: 978-1-4128-5499-3
Printed in the United States of America

Volumes 1 through 28 were originally published under the title *This World: An Annual of Religion and Public Life*.

Contents

Introduction
Gabriel R. Ricci ... vii

1. 'Abdullah 'Azzām—The Ideology behind Al-Qā'ida
   Asaf Maliach ... 1

2. The Arab Spring and the Religious Agenda
   Jonathan Fine ... 25

3. Sikhism, the Seduction of Modernism, and the Question
   of Violence
   Nicholas F. Gier ... 47

4. The Catholic Church, Violence, and the Nationalist Struggles
   in Ireland, 1798–1998
   Oliver Rafferty, SJ ... 65

5. Responsibility and Limitation: The Early Christian
   Church and War
   Darrell Cole ... 87

6. The Medieval Papacy and Holy War: General Crusading
   Letters and Papal Authority, 1145–1213
   Rebecca Rist ... 105

7. "Generosity . . . in the Slavery of This Brave Cavalier":
   Sanctity Honor and Religious Violence in the French
   Mediterranean
   Brian Sandberg ... 123

8. Deferral of War: The Religious Sign System of Ritual Violence
   Christopher S. Morrissey ... 133

9. Martyrs of Liberty: Open-Air Preaching and Popular
   Violence in Victorian Britain and Ireland
   Mark Doyle 149

10. Moral Injury: A Case Study in the Intersection of
    Religion and Violence
    Kathryn McClymond and Anthony F. Lemieux 165

11. Marshall McLuhan and the Machiavellian
    Use of Religious Violence
    Grant N. Havers 179

12. The Trenches of Capernaum, 1914–1918
    Yves Pourcher 205

Contributors 227

Introduction

Gabriel R. Ricci

In 1920 George Grosz produced a politically charged lithograph series titled *Gott mit Uns*. These were tumultuous days in Weimar Germany and Grosz intended to satirize conservative counter-revolutionary forces as well as the militaristic culture that had led Germany to a catastrophic war. Grosz had been declared unfit for military service because of his opposition to the war, and he was assigned to transportation duties away from the front. After an attempt at suicide the Germany military was prepared to execute the defiant Grosz, but intervention from an influential patron in 1917 saved him. The nine images in this series are a scathing rebuke of the brash militaristic ethos that violently abused the working class. One lithograph represents an aloof officer casually smoking a cigarette with a dead soldier at his feet; another depicts a group of soldiers suppressing protesters as a high-ranking officer and a war profiteer enjoy a lavish meal (Figure 1). Grosz's communist sentiments are clear to see but, along with his publisher, he was subsequently fined for insulting the military, not for being a communist. His portfolio was confiscated by the army and he would seek asylum in the United States in 1932.

The motto *Gott mit uns* had an entrenched cultural presence in Germany before it was inscribed on the belt buckle of German soldiers in World War I. The phrase first graced the Prussian Order of the Crown from its inception in 1861 and it later appeared on the imperial standard from 1870 to 1918, and on silver and gold coins from this period. The slogan was intended as a nationalistic cry to smite the enemy, and by the end of the nineteenth century it played a role in politically infusing the state with a romantic religious ideology. To some extent this took the form of making Lutheranism the state religion. This revitalized Christian spirit followed in the wake of Bismarck's challenge to the growing independence of the various Churches, particularly the Catholic Church and what was perceived as the growing threat of Judaism. In *Infected Christianity: A Study of Modern Racism*, Alan T. Davies interprets Bismarck's *Kulturkampf* as a subterfuge for a romantic nationalism that had been percolating since the rise of the organic conception of the state and the emergence of *Volkstudien* earlier in the nineteenth century. The Jews who had found some political relief in the Weimar moment, with its parliamentary procedures and liberal constitution, would lose their political foothold as the German nation became

Figure 1
George Grosz, *Die Kommunisten Fallen—und die Devisensteigen*, 1919

identified with the mystical body of Christ, thus equating German history with sacred history. In this moment of "unity of altar, throne and Volk," according to Davies, *Gott mit uns* became both a Protestant and an imperial slogan.

Wehrmacht soldiers in World War II continued to use the insignia on their uniforms, but the Germans were not alone in identifying their efforts with God's anagogical designs. The motto of the Russian Empire was a variation on this theme and the Order of St. Andrew established by Peter the Great had adapted the even more ancient Roman labarum by emblazoning the crucified St. Andrew, patron saint of Russia and first disciple, on the award. The labarum was the prototypical military standard that combined religious fervor and imperial ambitions. The spirit of this unity still has an ecclesiastical presence in the purple-clothed labara, decorated with the Chi-Rho, and imperceptibly blended with liturgical processions.

Constantine's use of the Chi-Rho as a rallying cry to his legions is legendary, and there are contemporary accounts of the battle at the Milvian Bridge where Constantine claimed to have had his vision of the new sign under which his army should conquer. Eusebius, an historian and biblical scholar, claimed to have received an account from Constantine himself. Whichever account one reads, it was clear that Constantine's new design for the Roman military standard meant that the religious zeal of early Christianity was well suited to the aims of Roman imperialism. The Roman standard had been revered since the time it was a simple spear sheathed in reeds. Constantine's institution of the religious labara sanctified these sacrosanct standards that much more. While there may be conflicting reports of what Constantine saw in the sky over the Milvian Bridge in 312 CE, the fact that his legions were paid in silver coins stamped with the Chi-Rho as early as 317 CE is good evidence that they had been fighting under this sign for some time. Now Roman soldiers could march under the new Christian symbolism at the same time that they exchanged currency embossed with the Chi-Rho. In battle a special cadre of Roman soldiers would guard the labarum and today the Order of Centurions survives as an association of Church militants dedicated to the memory of Cornelius of Capernaum, a paragon of Christian faith whose story is recounted in the Gospel of Matthew. This modern-day fellowship gathers under the symbolism of the labarum and the

Gladius-Vitis, a shield marked with crossed swords and the motto *Time Deum et Operare Iustitiam*.

In the Crusades initiated by Pope Urban II we have the most notorious nexus between religious authority and the justification for war and violence. Whether it took the form of recapturing territory in the Holy Land, fortifying borders in the Eastern Roman Empire, or subjugating idiosyncratic expressions of Christian theology within Europe, the High Middle Ages saw the papacy mount a campaign of military conquest and vigilant vindication of Christian doctrine. This particular unity of religious fervor and militaristic mobilization was resurrected during the Bush administration's campaign to suppress the contrived national security threat posed by Saddam Hussein's potential use of weapons of mass destruction.

Bush, who declared the war on terror a "crusade," was routinely sent intelligence updates from the then Secretary of Defense Rumsfeld, memoranda with cover sheets that combined biblical quotations with inspirational images. First disclosed by *GQ* in the spring of 2009, it was suspected that Rumsfeld was fueling Bush's commitment with a dose of homegrown fundamentalist zeal. The neoconservative think tanks had already been mobilized to preach that Bush's justification for war had solid religious roots. Rumsfeld's rousing memo campaign only fortified this religious justification for war. Among the illuminated intelligence updates there is one dated April 8, 2003, showing American tanks passing under one of the Swords of *Qādisīyah* or Victory Arch in Baghdad with the biblical lines "Open the gates that the righteous nation may enter, the nation that keeps faith" (Isaiah 26:2). No doubt we can easily imagine that the primary faith of the conquered territory would be inclined to counter with a personalized religious riposte for the gathering Western infidels. After all, these victory arches are named after a key battle in the Muslim expansion into Persia in 683 CE. Ironically the religious fundamentalism that fed the invasion of Iraq and instilled religious hostility placed an ancient indigenous Christian community at risk.

During the Iraq War, there were some in the military that did not conceal their belief that the war was a holy war sanctioned by their God. After the war Chris Kyle, the acclaimed sniper, gained notoriety for establishing an international business dedicated to honing military assault skills and for poignantly perishing at the hands of a fellow soldier with posttraumatic stress disorder. While in service in Iraq, he and his companions decorated their helmets with their personal version of the Totenkopf. Kyle would adapt this international symbol of death for the logo for Craft International by placing a Templar's cross, which is suggestive of sniper crosshairs, at the right eye. With a crusader's cross tattooed on his left bicep, Kyle went into battle shrouded in Christian symbolism (Figure 2).

William G. Boykin, because of his high-rank and high-profile status in the military, created a dustup when he couched his political and military views in religious terms. Boykin stirred controversy when he pitted his Judeo-Christian God against a lesser Islamic God who personified Satan, when he challenged the Somali warlord and dissident, Osman Atto. Even George W. Bush would distance himself from his Under Secretary of Defense for Intelligence. Boykin was found to have overstepped his boundaries by his military superiors in some of his public proclamations, but even after his retirement from the military in 2007 he continued to battle what he viewed as the threat of Sharia law to the American way of life.

x   Faith, War, and Violence

Figure 2
Craft International LLC Logo

While our intuitions and beliefs about religion tell us that spirituality has beneficent goals, our perceptions of the geopolitical landscape inform us that religion is too often connected to violence and war. This inescapable realism has produced theologically grounded political ideals, is woven into political rhetoric, and has been inflated into a cosmic struggle between the forces of good and evil. David Frum, Bush's speechwriter, after a close study of Roosevelt's speech to Congress on December 8, 1941, was able to revive the threat of the axis powers and enshrine it in a universal struggle against what Bush would pronounce as the axis of evil. In both cases, there was a clear justification for war and the presumption that the enemy was evil personified. Bush was only returning the insult that opposing religious forces had already leveled against the West and the United States; in particular, the enemy was Satan incarnate.

At loggerheads as to who was ultimately responsible for destabilizing the world, each side was confident that their aggression was spiritually justified and that the other was spearheading the forces of evil. When Bush conjured up a reincarnated axis of evil, political commentary characterized his dualistic mind-set as Manichean and/or Zoroastrian. However it is theologically parsed, this cosmic drama evoked Carl Schmitt's analysis of the true function of the state. Ever vigilant about delineating friends from enemies, Schmitt's core conception of the state meant that political unity required purging alien and potentially schismatic forces. Schmitt was responding to the unstable political situation in the Germany of the 1930s, but these dualisms are so culturally and religiously entrenched that they can be spontaneously retrieved to suit rhetoric of fear and anarchy. Bush's religious prejudices were revealed when he described the war on terror as a crusade. In doing so he also announced that even if the threat of terror was eliminated, his personal spiritual reality would demand a long line of perpetual dualisms, at least until an ultimate messianic moment eliminates the cosmic polarity. Bush audaciously created a messianic role for himself so he was not a Manichean. A truly Manichean interpretation of these dueling forces does not entail the elimination of the other, since in Manicheism the structure of reality originates in the strife and tension produced by these antagonistic forces.

Given the theatrical scope of the violence perpetrated by religious zealots of all stripes, following Mark Juergensmeyer's prevailing analysis, it is more the case that these acts of violence are not intended to accomplish tactical objectives as much as they are perpetrated for their symbolic significance. This only intensifies the pious quality of events that are already grounded in spiritual ideology, because as performance acts and spectacles they are logical extensions of liturgical rituals which are designed to spiritually and ideologically transform victims and perpetrators alike. As a drama steeped in patriotism, national pride, and liturgy, when Rumsfeld made good on his threat of "shock and awe," the night sky over Baghdad lit up in March 2003 like a fireworks display and provided TV viewers with the same feelings that one could reverently enjoy on July 4. After such a sight, it is no wonder that there followed a rush to commercially employ the trademark *shock and awe* and that fireworks companies would be the first to seek advantage on the very day of the Baghdad bombing. Likewise the attacks on the World Trade Center on September 11, 2001, were charged with symbolism intended to demonstrate that the United States, despite the imposing structures that housed global commercial networks, was indeed vulnerable. The fact that the United States had its own technology turned on itself lent the spectacle that much more ideological advantage.

Symbolically charged religious violence has a long history and its destructive consequences are variously addressed by contributors of this work. In "'Abdullah 'Azzām—The Ideology That Motivated Al-Qā'ida's Founder" and "The Arab Spring and the Religious Agenda," Asaf Maliach and Jonathan Fine, respectively, reveal the ideological and religious foundations that inspired the founders of the global militant group al-Qaeda and its role in the Arab Spring. While religious scholars may not have been on the front lines, these authors show the political and military influence they have in recruiting and producing waves of religious militants. The Arab Spring that might have first appeared to be a spontaneous expression of democracy soon proved to be another global instance of religion influencing politics. Nicholas Gier's "Sikhism, the Seduction of Modernism, and the Question of Violence" shows that this dangerous union is not restricted to Abrahamic religions or to one geographic region. Sikhism is just as vulnerable when national identity merges with religious sentiment and tradition is seduced by modern idols. The long history of religious conflict in Ireland that came to be known as the Troubles when violence erupted in the twentieth century receives a detailed analysis by Oliver Rafferty in "The Catholic Church, Violence, and the Nationalist Struggles in Ireland 1798–1998." Rafferty notes that the Irish situation was similarly fueled in the nineteenth century when nationalism conjoined with religious fervor, but it was the difficulty that the Catholic Church had translated traditional transcendental values into viable and practical ideas about participation in political life that hampered resolution to the centuries' long tensions with Britain.

Darrell Cole's essay "Responsibility and Limitation: The Early Christian Church and War" traces the evolution of the Christian approach to war from early pacifism, to Augustine's public struggle with the justification for war, and finally to the militancy of the crusades. This latter stage has been commemorated in literature and film, and Rebecca Rist's examination of papal correspondence in "The Medieval Papacy and Holy War: General Crusading Letters and Papal Authority, 1145–1213" demonstrates how the medieval popes asserted their authority to promote crusades and to reinforce their influence over the Christian faithful through their writing and letters. Rist argues that the medieval papacy has left a clear written record of the alliance between the pen and the sword. In a related theme, Brian Sandberg's "'Generosity . . . in the Slavery of This Brave Cavalier': Sanctity Honor and Religious Violence in the French Mediterranean" explores the participation of French nobles in religious warfare in the sixteenth and seventeenth centuries. Organized to combat the threat of the Muslim military, many of these nobles, following capture and enslavement, supplied a literary record of religious violence in the early modern Mediterranean world and chronicled the changing conceptions of honor among nobility. While the crusades were a moment in which religious aggression was overt and encouraged, Christopher Morrissey's application of the semiotic theory of the cultural anthropologist Eric Gans in "Deferral of War: The Religious Sign System of Ritual Violence" shows that religion, through the use of ritual systems, can actually perform the function of deferring war.

Mark Doyle's contribution "Martyrs of Liberty: Open-Air Preaching and Popular Violence in Victorian Britain and Ireland" reveals that aggression in the name of religion is not restricted to the battlefield and open combat. Doyle's account of the violence brought on by street preaching in Victorian Britain and Ireland is politically nuanced. Suppressed in Britain, the violence in Ireland was allowed to intensify for political display, revealing a country that was inherently more violent and thus in need of authoritarian rule. In challenging the practice of simplifying the relationship between religion and violence, McClymond and Lemieux present a psychological reading in their coauthored "Moral Injury: A Case Study in the Intersection of Religion and Violence." Placing aside the view that religion either reduces or encourages violence, they examine the experience of moral injury as a form of PTSD that originates in violence to others. Construed as a form of violence, they explore the ways in which moral injury is linked to religion in a military context.

Grant N. Havers in "Marshall McLuhan and the Machiavellian Use of Religious Violence" uncovers the relationship between religion and violence in an unlikely place, the communication theory of Marshall McLuhan. This discovery has come to light with McLuhan's posthumous publications on the role of Catholicism in the age of mass media. McLuhan who converted to Catholicism in the 1930s claimed that his communication theory explained Aquinas and Aristotle in modern terms. An examination of his body of work reveals a recurrent interest in the role of religion as well as its violent use and misuse in the modern era, particularly in the pervasive influence of Machiavelli and realpolitik. McLuhan considered the core tenet that rulers need only give the appearance of being pious and honorable to be the source of political evil in the modern age and that too often his fellow Christians, out of expediency, made Machiavelli's ideas more acceptable than they were.

Yves Pourcher's "The Trenches of Capernaum, 1914–1918" marks the one-hundredth anniversary of the beginning of World War I. Even though Pourcher's account of the war provides an intimate look at how his family was disrupted by the horrors of war, there is no waving of flags or inflated accounts of heroism and chivalry. When we experience war at a distance, as Pourcher did, we remember the color of a son's chestnut hair and a family farm that went idle after all the young men were called to the front; we discover the war through faded sepia photographs with the family name, the location, and the date scribbled on the reverse side. This is the memory of war that drifts through a house thanks to familial memories and locks of hair tucked away in old bureaus. Pourcher's thoughts

Figure 3
Albert Herter, *Le Départ des Poilus*, Aôut 1914
Gare de L'Est, Paris

about war are laced with reconstituted vignettes and physical descriptions taken from state archives, but it is not a recollection of dramatic trench warfare steeped in bravado and undaunted fearlessness. Pourcher's reflections on war do not ignore the ossuary and vast cemeteries of Verdun, the butchery of the Somme, and the epidemic of suicides in the Great War, but his account goes beyond his personal odyssey. By using the arc of history to frame his narrative, capably translated into English by Trevor Merrill, Pourcher provides a meditation on war. Thus he reaches back to a moment imbued with biblical imagery. The year 1914 is a resurgence of a scourge that reaches back to the Roman occupation of Capernaum and the beginnings of a new faith, and it will continue to spread "across the entire world, a filthy epidemic of Fourteen that reaches and infects Leningrad, Stalingrad, Berlin, China, Korea, Vietnam, Eritrea, Iraq, Syria. Fourteen means war, all wars, gathers them together, qualifies them. It's a global synonym, a number stronger than words." Pourcher's visits to Verdun make him want to put the war behind him, but he can always expect to be reminded of it every time he passes through the Gare de l'Est in Paris. There the painter Albert Herter has left an indelible memory of what departing for the front in World War I might have been like. A gift to France in 1926, Herter has placed his own son, Everit (Figure 3), triumphantly in the center of this composition. While serving with a camouflage unit, Everit Herter was killed at Château-Thierry in the last days of the war.

1

'Abdullah 'Azzām—The Ideology behind Al-Qā'ida[1]

Asaf Maliach

Background

After the Soviet Union's invasion of Afghanistan on December 25, 1979, the United States provided support for the Afghan Mujāhidīn, whose primary aim was to repel the Soviet Army from the country. Following the realization of this aim in February 1989, the Muslim volunteers who came to the aid of their Afghan brothers from all over the world, mainly Arab countries such as Egypt, Saudi Arabia, Syria, and Jordan, returned to their native countries and began "preaching" the theory of a worldwide Islamic Jihād as taught by 'Abdullah 'Azzām during the war in Afghanistan. These volunteers, commonly known as "Afghan Alumni" or the "Afghan Arabs," were recruited and trained, beginning in 1984 by the "Office of Services for the Mujāhidīn" (Maktab Khidamāt al-Mujāhidīn—MAK) founded by 'Abdullah 'Azzām and his disciple Usāma Bin Lādin. Today, they represent the spinal cord of the most Islamic terrorist organizations operating around the world, most notably "al-Qā'ida."

'Abdullah 'Azzām was born in 1941 in the West Bank village of Silat al-Harthiyyah, northwest of Jenin; today, this area is controlled by the Palestinian Authority. Following the Six-Day War, 'Azzām fled with his family to Jordan, and in 1969 joined the ranks of the Muslim Brotherhood. In 1973 he finished his doctorate in the Roots of Islamic Law department in the religious al-Azhar University in Cairo with honors. After that he returned to Jordan and taught at the Shari'ah college in the Jordanian University. In 1981, he began teaching at King 'Abd al-'Azīz University in Jeddah, Saudi Arabia. Shortly thereafter, he moved to Pakistan to teach at the International Islamic University in Islamabad, a move that afforded him access to the Afghan Jihād in which he was so interested. In 1984, 'Azzām relocated to the border town of Peshawar, where he founded, together with Usāma bin Lādin, the "House of Supporters" (Bayt al-Ansār), a guesthouse that in October 1984 transformed into the MAK. The MAK served as a center for both the financial and physical recruitment of Muslims from around the world for the Afghan Jihād. It was also active in various other fields, such as education, medicine, information, military aid, and the funding and establishment of training camps. Branches of the MAK were established in cities all over the world; the central one, known as the Al-Kifāh Refugee Center, Inc., was located in Brooklyn, New York, and even received economic aid from the Reagan administration.[2]

The paths of ʿAzzām and Bin Lādin crossed in a critical point in the lives of the two. ʿAzzām, a world renowned Muslim religious authority, linked with Afghan Mujāhidīn leaders, and a gracious speaker who was authoritative and charismatic, captured the heart of the young and ambitious Bin Lādin, who grew stronger in his faith and requested to widen his knowledge regarding Afghan Jihād. Bin Lādin granted ʿAzzām with immense financial support when ʿAzzām moved to Peshawar and began his attempt to recruit both Arab and non-Arab Muslim volunteers for the Afghan Jihād. After joining forces, the two were able to establish the MAK. ʿAzzām, also known as "the father of Arab and non-Arab Muslim volunteers," served not only as a father figure for Bin Lādin, taking the place of his dead father, but also as a source of religious wisdom and extreme Islamic ideology. Without a doubt, ʿAzzām and the war in Afghanistan shaped the character of Bin Lādin, as well as a complete generation of Muslims—the ones who came to fight in Afghanistan and the ones identifying with the warriors even though they were far away.

ʿAzzām was killed in Peshawar on November 24, 1989, together with his two sons, Muhammad (20) and Ibrāhīm (15), when a large bomb exploded next to a car they were riding on their way to the Friday prayer in the Sabʿ al-Layl mosque. In spite of the interest generated by the assassination of ʿAzzām in and out of Pakistan, the Pakistani leadership were unable to reach the assassinators, and as of the writing of these lines, there is no clue to their true identity. A few days after this assassination, Usāma bin Lādin announced the establishment of al-Qāʿida in Peshawar, based on the concept of al-Qāʿida al-Sulbah (The Solid Basis) created by ʿAzzām, which appeared in the April issue of *al-Jihād*, a bulletin published by the MAK.[3]

This article introduces the reader to the ideology of the man who is considered to have laid the foundations for the establishment of al-Qāʿida, the spiritual guide of Usāma Bin Lādin and many other radical Muslim ideologists of our generation, and the father of the theory of Global Islamic Jihād, which was the basis for bin Lādin's activities before he died and is the basis for the activities of many other al-Qāʿida activists and other radical Muslims identifying with the concept of global Jihād. This article deals with the major principles of ʿAzzām's belief, his concept of the Muslim state, and his link to the extreme Egyptian ideologist Sayyid Qutb, with the theory of Global Islamic Jihād he formed in Afghanistan and with his relation to the Jews and the State of Israel.

Never Questioning: How?

From an analysis of ʿAzzām's writings, it appears that he was striving to apply the primeval, pure Islam, as it existed in the days of the Prophet Muhammad, "Without questioning: How?" (in Arabic: *Bilā Kayfa*). He wished to limit the philosophic religious inquiry, especially regarding Allah and his titles:

> The enemies of the Salafiyyah are infidels, who are beyond the pale of Islam, because the Salafiyyah was brought about by the messenger of Allah and it represents the way in which the Sahābah (the Prophet Muhammad's Companions) and their followers validated the Muslim religion. [...] It is known that I am a Salafi from the enemies of the Sufism. [...] We believe in the unity of Allah [Tawhīd], and in the unity

of the names and titles [of Allah]. We accept the good names and the great titles listed in the Quran and in the Suna without distortion [Tahrīf], negation [Ta'tīl], personification [Tashbīh], allegorical exegesis [Ta'wīl] or analogize [Tamthīl]. We believe that the forefathers, may Allah bless them, believed in the titles of Allah and knew their meanings, and yet they never questioned: How?. We believe that he is creating, supporting, animating and killing, and everything returns to him, he is king of all.[4]

In a discussion regarding the unity of Allah's names and titles, 'Azzām declared that he supports the forefathers (the Salaf) who accepted the titles as they were, without questioning them. While those who support the personification of Allah and those who support the negation of his titles were defined by 'Azzām as "infidels beyond the pale of Islam," he was careful not to define as "infidels" the Khalaf, the generations following the Salaf, some of which used the allegorical exegesis, even though he did not support their position.[5]

The Belief in "Al-Wala' wa-al-Bara'"

'Azzām stressed that the belief in the unity of Allah, his names, and titles will not be complete without the belief in "al-Wala' wa-al-Bara'" [the display of loyalty and friendship (Wala') toward the believers, on the one hand, and that of hatred and disavowal (Bara') from the infidels, on the other]. For this purpose, he quoted from the Quran: "There is a goodly pattern for you in Abraham and those with him, when they told their folk: Lo! we are guiltless of you and all that ye worship beside Allah. We have done with you. And there hath arisen between us and you hostility and hate for ever until ye believe in Allah only" (Chapter 60, "Al-Mumtahina," Verse 4). However, with the term "infidels," 'Azzām and other Muslim religious leaders meant not only the pagans, but also the "People of the Book"—the Jews and the Christians—as they argued that the Jews and the Christians forged the sacred writings given to them, and therefore they should not be considered as Dhimmis (non-Muslim protégés) as was promised to them in the Quran.[6]

'Azzām argued that behind the obvious meaning of the belief in "al-Wala' wa-al-Bara'" hides another important significance which is the avoidance of selling the lands of Islam to the infidels. According to him, sticking to this faith is even more important in view of the empowerment of the slogans for the homeland, the nationality, the race, and the secularism. This led 'Azzām to emphasize that the Muslim ruler must be with religious knowledge and must be a Muslim jurisprudent (a Mufti), who fears of Allah, to whom at least forty of the Muslim jurisprudents of the generation shall swear allegiance.[7]

A Primordial Decree or Free Will

'Azzām sided with the concept of the primordial decree (Qadar), meaning that Allah decides the actions and the destiny of his creations in advance, and the human actions are a necessary outcome of this decree. His opinion was based on Verse 145 in Chapter 3 (Surat "Aāl 'Imrān") in the Quran: "Nor can a soul die except by Allah's leave, the term being fixed as by writing." In this aspect, 'Azzām was a part of the "Jabarīya" (an Islamic school of thought teaching the inescapability of fate). According to 'Azzām, the belief in the primordial decree grants the believer peace of mind, as he knows that his destiny is predetermined, and there is no way to change it. According to him, the most obvious expression to the primordial decree in the Afghan battlefield is the complete reliance of the Mujāhidīn on Allah ("al-Tawakkul") and the fact that they hand their destiny to him without questioning. In a lecture he held on April 14, 1989, apparently in Egypt, 'Azzām said, "History is comprised of events. These events are created by individuals which are a primordial decree (Qadar) of Allah. The Martyrs (Shuhadā') are a part of Allah's primordial decree on his nation. Allah motivates them to create the history of their nation."[8]

Dār al-Islām versus Dār al-Harb

The three schools of thoughts of Islam—the Hanafiyya, the Mālikiyya, and the Hanbaliyya—divide the world into two areas. The first area is called by them Dār al-Islām (the dwelling of Islam) or Dār al-'Adl (the dwelling of justice)—an area held by a Muslim ruler that applies the Muslim religious law (the Sharī'ah). The definition of an area as Dār al-Islām does not require a Muslim majority, and therefore the conversion to Islam is not a condition to make the area Dār al-Islām, and the ruler has no obligation to force such a conversion. The other area is called Dār al-Harb (the dwelling of the enemy) or Dār al-Kufr (the dwelling of infidelity)—an area in which the Muslim religious law does not apply. The area is also defined as Dār al-Harb if the majority of its citizens are Muslims.[9] Dār al-Islām and Dār al-Harb are constantly at war, with pauses of truces. At the end of this war, the entire world shall be united within Dār al-Islām.

The Shāfiitic school of thoughts, an additional (the fourth) school of Islam, and a few Hanbalitic religious scholars added a third area: Dār al-'Ahd—an area that holds a peace treaty between its residents and the Muslims, apparently due to the difficulty to take it over. In this area, the Muslim religious law does not apply, but it is signed on a peace treaty with Dār al-Islām in exchange for the payment of a land tax (Kharāj) or a head tax (Jizya) (the type of tax paid is set by the religious scholar which the Muslim community trusts). This treaty guarantees Dār al-'Ahd security from future Muslim attempts to take over it. 'Azzām made an example of the Christians in the city of Najran in the Arabian Peninsula during the days of the Prophet Muhammad, Armenia, during the conquests of Islam, and the Nubic areas in Sudan at the times of the army commander 'Abdullah Bin Sa'd Bin Abi Sarh, one of the Prophet's companions and the high commissioner of Egypt in the midst of the seventh century.[10]

An additional issue discussed by Muslim religious scholars, and also related to by 'Abdullah 'Azzām, was the terms that transform Dār al-Islām to Dār al-Harb. Apart from Na'mān Bin Thābit Abu Hanīfah, the founder of the Hanfitic school of thoughts, the three other school founders, as well as many of Abu Hanīfah's friends, argued that Dār al-Islām transforms into a Dār al-Harb when it is taken over by individuals who annul the rules of Allah and rule according to infidelity rules, or when Allah's laws are combined with infidelity laws. In contrast to this opinion, Abu Hanīfah argued that there are three terms to transform Dār al-Islām into Dār al-Harb: first, when the rules of the infidels are applied in Dār al-Islām; second, when the border between Dār al-Islām and Dār al-Harb is blurred; and third, when there is no Muslim or Dhimmi (a non-Muslim protégé) who gets security by Dār al-Islām, as determined in the Muslim religious laws.[11] 'Abdullah 'Azzām was supportive of the majority's stance. According to him, the land, in itself, has no worth if it is not governed by Allah's rules. "The protection of Dār al-Islām is not the protection of the land as it is the defense of the Islamic faith and society," he says. "The defense of Dār al-Islām is a means to implement Allah's kingdom on earth, and make it a basis for the expansion of the Da'wah (the Islamic propaganda) to the entire world. Dār al-Islām is a more urgent need than water or air."[12]

The Islamic State

While Dār al-Islām describes a territorial unit, the Islamic state (Al-Dawlah al-Islāmiyyah) is the political entity that will be established within Dār al-Islām.

'Azzām's concept regarding the Islamic state and its establishment was formed, to a great extent, during the Afghan war. 'Azzām argues that there is no escape from the establishment of an Islamic movement with faithful members, who, through the Daw'ah and the militant Jihād, will lead the Muslims toward the establishment of the Islamic state and the Islamic society. According to him, an Islamic movement that does not hold the militant Jihād shall eventually be busy with itself, and its lines will separate. However, the Islamic movement will not be able to achieve this without the full trust and assistance of the people, who "fuel the Jihād," and without which the Islamic movement is considered dead. 'Azzām further argued that a movement that does not consider the establishment of the Islamic state at the basis of its manifest cannot be considered as an Islamic movement, but as a charity foundation. Therefore, foundations dealing with the fight with smoking, building mosques, sponsoring orphans and widows, and teaching the Quran cannot be considered an Islamic movement, as they lack the major component—the establishment of an Islamic state in which the Muslims could live according to Allah's wishes.[13]

When 'Azzām was asked, "how one should operate in order to make sure that the world upholds Islam and that the Caliphate on earth shall be established—is such a thing even possible or is it merely a dream?" he answered,

> Arriving at a state of Caliphate shall be done in the way of the Prophet, Peace be upon him: there shall be a man calling for an amendment based on true faith and healthy thoughts, people shall gather around him, the Jāhiliyyah (the infidel society) shall confront with them and there shall be a verbal fight between this group and the Jāhiliyyah surrounding it. As time passes, one will hold on, and the other shall fall. Afterwards, this group shall ignite the Jihād against the enemies of Allah almighty, it shall win and progress from one location to another, conquer the locations of the Jāhiliyyah one by one, Allah shall grant it with victory and with the entire land.[14]

According to 'Azzām, the model of the Islamic movement is the Muslim Brotherhood Society that was founded in Egypt by Hasan al-Banna in March 1928. The Muslim Brotherhood was the first Islamic movement to be established after the abolition of the Ottoman Caliphate in 1924 and called to restore passed glory.[15] According to several studies, during the first decade of their existence the Muslim Brotherhood focused on education and the Da'wah, but in the end of the 1930s and in the beginning of the 1940s, they began to accumulate weapons and establish training camps in the desert. At the same time, Hasan al-Banna established the "special organization" (Al-Nithām al-Khāss, the secret terror organization of the movement). In the middle of the 1940s, the Muslim Brotherhood began practicing the militant Jihād to drive the British out of Egypt, and in the 1948 war, they volunteered to assist the Arabs fighting against Israel.[16]

According to 'Azzām, the head of the Islamic state will be Amīr al-Mu'minīna (the commander of the faithful) also called Khalīfat Rasūl Allah (the acting messenger of Allah, the Caliph). This leader shall be found within the members of the Islamic movement after its victory, and the Islamic nation shall vow allegiance to him. The Caliph must be a religious scholar and jurist, who is devout and decent, and during the conquests of Islam, he should have been the one with the most combat experience. The Caliph shall rule according to the Muslim religious law (the Sharī'ah) and shall protect the religious, the blood, the honor, and the property of the Muslims. After the Caliph's death, he shall be replaced by the most wise and decent of the forty Muslim jurisprudents (Muftis) of the generation.[17]

As time necessitates, the Islamic state shall declare Jihād for the sake of Allah and shall grant every Muslim immigrating to it from Dar al-Harb all the privileges of an ordinary citizen. It shall vouch for Muslims all over the world and shall come forward to save the Muslims suffering from oppressions in Dar al-Harb states. The Islamic state shall disconnect the diplomatic and commercial links with Dar al-Harb states—should such links exist.[18]

'Abdullah 'Azzām—"The Jordanian Sayyid Qutb"

'Abdullah 'Azzām and Sayyid Qutb never met. Qutb was hanged in Egypt in 1966 due to his political subversion, two years before 'Azzām arrived to Egypt to study for his master's degree. However, during the period of 1971–1973, when 'Azzām was in Egypt for his doctoral studies, he became friends with Sayyid's sister, Hamīda Qutb, other members of his family, and his close acquaintances.[19]

Following the events of "Black September" in Jordan (1970), 'Azzām began teaching in the Sharī'ah college in Amman, the capital city of Jordan. However, after a short time, in 1971, he left Amman to study for a doctorate in Al-Azhar University in Cairo. He graduated cum laude in 1973. During the time he spent with his family in Egypt, 'Azzām became friends with Sayyid Qutb's family and Zaynab al-Ghazāli, who was Qutb's confidante and the head of the women's organization in the Muslim Brotherhood Society. He paid plenty of visits in the Qutb home, where he listened to stories about Sayyid, his arrest, and his execution.

'Azzām and his family had no fixed address in Egypt. They moved around a lot due to the oppressions of the Egyptian intelligence, going after them due to a piece of intelligence, arguing that the anonymous letter, sent about five years before to President Jamāl 'Abd al-Nāsir, denouncing the execution of Qutb and his friends in the Muslim Brotherhood, and even hinting at a revenge, was written by the doctoral candidate 'Abdullah 'Azzām.[20]

In 1973, 'Azzām returned to Jordan, and after a short time, he began lecturing about the Da'wah and the Islam in the Sharī'ah college in the Jordanian University. Soon he preached students into penitence. Abu Mujāhid, 'Azzām's nephew, who studied at the university at that time, talked about his students' admiration of him. According to his nephew, 'Azzām was called "the Jordanian Sayyid Qutb," due to his extreme political views reminiscent of Qutb's, which challenged the legitimacy of the Arab rulings in the Arab states that abandoned the laws of Allah and harmed one of the special qualities of Allah—the Hākimiyyah (Allah's sovereignty on earth). Abu Mujāhid added that the tense relationship created between 'Azzām and the Jordanian regime following his extreme sayings in general, and regarding the regime in particular, his reluctance to "keep a low profile," and finally, the limitations imposed on his influence and his activity within the Da'wah, and the confiscation of his Jordanian passport all these contributed to the comparison between him and Qutb by the Jordanian students.[21]

And indeed, this comparison had a basis. 'Azzām considered Qutb as a competent authority and quoted him in order to strengthen his words. He even compared the period during which Qutb was locked behind bars, writing books for his generation, and the time he ('Azzām) sat in Afghanistan during "dark" nights, writing books for his own generation.[22] In an article in memory of Qutb, which was published in *Al-Jihād* magazine in October 1986, 'Azzām declared that in his life he was influenced by four individuals, but the one who influenced him the most was Sayyid Qutb:

> To be honest, I was not influenced by any writer dealing with Islamic thought as I was influenced by Sayyid Qutb. I feel the mercy of Allah upon me, when he made me like the writings of Sayyid Qutb, and opened my heart to learn them. Sayyid Qutb was my ideological guide, [Taqī al-Dīn] Ibn Taymiyyah was guiding my faith, Ibn Qayyim [al-Jawziyyah] was guiding my spirit, and the Imam al-Nawawī was guiding me juristically. Sayyid Qutb's martyrdom had a greater influence on the awakening of the Muslim world, than his entire life [. . .]. He was right when saying: "our sayings shall remain as wax dolls until we die for them, and then it shall awake and live amongst the living."[23]

'Azzām's admiration to Qutb was expressed in 1981, when he wrote his biography titled *The Giant of Islamic Thought—The Martyr Sayyid Qutb*. This biography, much like other books written by 'Azzām, was only published after his death, by the information center named after him—Markaz al-Shahīd 'Azzām al-I'lāmī—which is in Peshawar, Pakistan. In this biography, 'Azzām described in detail Qutb's life story from his birth to his death, described his character, clarified him from the "false accusation" told by Sheikh Muhammad Nasr al-Dīn al-Albānī, which was considered by many as the greatest scholar of the Hadīth of his time, and expressed his admiration toward Qutb many times. Here follows an example of the things 'Azzām wrote in Qutb's praise:

> It shall not be considered an exaggeration to say that Sayyid Qutb had a greater influence than anybody else on the generations after the second half of the twentieth century. We do not know any individual marking the young spirits with a more significant mark. I believe that I do not exaggerate saying that there is no Muslim group that influenced its society and that Sayyid Qutb's influence is not seen in it—in large scale or even in small scale.[24]

'Azzām went even further and presented Qutb as one of individuals who alter the face of complete societies, and that complete societies revolve around them:

> The great individuals who alter the faces of complete societies are of three types: the religious scholar, the honorable man, and the man fighting Jihād. These three are the axis of the societies revolving around them, they are their foundations, and they are capable of carrying the entire society. Therefore, if they are acting in faith, the society shall be purified, clean and united, but if their intentions are malicious and their conscience corrupt, the society shall become a pile of dirt. [. . .] I shall provide two examples from the ancient and modern Muslim history: the Sheikh of Islam Ibn Taymiyyah [. . .] and Sayyid Qutb.[25]

Qutb's influence on 'Azzām was obvious not only by writing about him but also in 'Azzām's views, as was testified by 'Azzām himself. From reading the writings of the two, and additional writings about Qutb, it appears that there is indeed a wide common denominator between the two. I shall focus on three prominent terms in the writings of the two: First, the Muslim society representing the new Jāhiliyyah or the Jāhiliyyah of the twentieth century and the need to "immigrate" from it; second, the Hākimiyyah—applying the complete sovereignty of Allah on earth, which is, in fact, the objective of the establishment of the Islamic state—and from which the third term derives—the permission to label the Muslim ruler who does not go by the laws of the Sharī'ah, an infidel.

The term "Jāhiliyyah" was originally meant to describe the period before the appearance of Islam that was characterized by ignorance and not knowing Allah. The new Jāhiliyyah (al-Jāhiliyyah al-Muʿāsirah) or in its other name, the Jāhiliyyah of the twentieth century (Jāhiliyyat al-Qarn al-ʿAshrīn), was perceived as worse and far more impious than the old Jāhiliyyah. It is perceived not only as the period of ignorance toward Allah, but also as a period in which the human laws rule, a period during which secular ideologies that oppose religion, such as nationalism, liberalism, and socialism are ruling, and there is hostility toward the uniqueness of Allah and his sovereignty.

Much like Qutb, ʿAzzām defined all the societies not living according to Islamic law, such as Jāhili societies, and urged withdrawal from them immediately, acting toward their annihilation and the establishment of Islamic societies that will replace them. According to him, keeping silence about the existence of the Jāhili society or making an armistice agreement with it are in contrast to the laws of Allah. However, if such a thing is necessary for the existence of the true Islamic society, then an interest-based relationship with the Jāhili society can be held for a short time. However, immediately following, one should act for its removal and the establishment of an Islamic society in its place. In any event, ʿAzzām argued that one should not be overly patient with the corrupt Jāhili society since such treatment sabotages the soul and might make the Muslims accustomed to it, and even friendly toward it.[26]

According to ʿAzzām, at the beginning the battle with the Jāhili society will be conducted with words, and only afterward will it be an armed battle. "The battle against the Jāhiliyyah with weapon and sword," according to ʿAzzām, "shall not be made possible if a propaganda campaign did not precede it."[27] ʿAzzām used to quote Qutb's saying uttered minutes before he was executed: "the finger designating the uniqueness of Allah in prayer shall refuse to write a single letter qualifying the rule of the tyrants."[28]

The Hākimiyyah issue was first mentioned by ʿAzzām in 1975, when he spoke at a pilgrim camp near Mecca during the Hajj season (the pilgrim season). ʿAzzām challenged the legitimacy of the Arab rulers in the Arab states and argued that the battle against the Shirk (polytheism), which was promoted by religious scholars such as the Imam Muhammad Bin ʿAbd al-Wahhāb, was replaced by a battle against a new kind of Shirk. This is a Shirk not by sharing gods other than Allah, but in the way of making rules by humans and abandoning the rules of Allah. According to him, this harms one of the most unique traits of Allah—the Hākimiyyah, and therefore the religious scholars are obliged to preach for the application of the rules of Allah instead of the rules of human beings.[29]

As Qutb did, ʿAzzām relied on Verse 40 in Chapter 7 (Surat "Yusuf") in the Quran as the source for the Hākimiyyah. About this, he wrote,

> Allah's sovereignty is expressed by the true subordination of the human being to the desire of his maker, and by holding the religion and its values. Removing the religious ruling from life means removing the subordination of the human being to his maker, and removing the religion, even if the religious rites were kept and the minarets and stages were built. [. . .] Removing Allah's religion from life and allowing the rules of the human being in its place are a terrible step and a squelcher to the Muslim nation from east to west. Humanity was never struck by a greater disaster.[30]

ʿAzzām derived the permission to define a Muslim who hurts the Hākimiyyah as an infidel Qutb from Verse 44 in Chapter 5 (Surat "al-Māʾida") in the Quran: "he who does not want to rule according to Allah's rules is an infidel."³¹ 'Azzām explained the verdict of one who granted priority to the human rules, over the rules of Allah:

> He who thought that the rules of the human being are better for society, and shall decrease its problems, or that one should rule according to the rules of the human being—is an infidel beyond the pale of Islam. If the ruler, in any state, shall not act according to Allah's laws, he is an infidel beyond the pale of Islam, and the legislator and the parliament confirming the rules of the human being shall be beyond the pale of Islam.³²

'Azzām was against those who argued that due to the blood or national relationship one Muslim cannot kill another Muslim, even if the other one chose to neglect the rules of Allah, thus harming the Hākimiyyah. According to him, the blood or national relationship is irrelevant in this matter, as what holds the Muslims together is only the link of faith. 'Azzām made an example of the Prophet Muhammad who fought his tribe and killed them.³³

According to 'Azzām, permission was granted to kill not only the Muslim harming the Hākimiyyah but also a faithful Muslim, who intends to harm the honor of other Muslims. Honor is the most important asset of the Muslims, and therefore it should be protected at all costs. The most known example 'Azzām used is that of a faithful Muslim cop in one of the Muslim states arresting another Muslim, and in the process harming the dignity of his wife, the homeowner. The question arises, "Is it permitted to kill the cop even though he is praying, feasting and worshipping Allah?" 'Azzām answers this question in the affirmative.³⁴

The Theory of Global Islamic Jihād—Thus the Lands of Islam Shall Return to Their Owners

In contrast to fundamentalist Islamic movements praising, first and foremost, the overthrow of infidel regimes in their states blocking the establishment of the Islamic Caliphate, 'Abdullah 'Azzām formed, throughout the Afghan war, the Global Islamic Jihād theory. This theory, which has been preached by 'Azzām since 1984 and inspired his disciple and follower Usāma bin Lādin, derives from two sources. The first source is Verse 97 in Chapter 4 (Surat "al-Nisā'") in the Quran: "Lo! As for those refusers who sin to their souls, they will be asked by the angels when they die: In what were ye engaged? They will say: We were oppressed in the land. [The angels] will say: Was not Allah's earth spacious that ye could have migrated therein and joined the war? These sinners, their habitation will be hell, an evil journey's end." The second source is the individual duty (Fard 'Ayn), which Islam has imposed on its followers since its earliest days, to repel foreign incursions into Islamic territory.³⁵

The Global Islamic Jihād theory determined that all Arabs have the individual duty to embrace the Jihād for the liberation of Palestine, as a first step toward the liberation of all Islamic lands and the establishment of the Kingdom of Allah on the earth. However, because 'Azzām believed that this objective cannot be implemented in his time, he argued that they are individually obligated to apply the second part of Verse 97 in Surat "al-Nisā'" mentioned above, that is, to immigrate to Afghanistan, where the Jihād for the sake of Allah took place and where there was the best chance of defeating the aggressive infidels and establishing Dār al-Islām. About other Muslims around the world—they are obliged to skip Palestine and start directly in Afghanistan. After the establishment of Dār al-Islām in Afghanistan, the Muslims shall continue to liberate the next Islamic land, and the first priority is Palestine. They shall continue in this path until the liberation of all Islamic lands and the establishment of the Islamic Caliphate, from Indonesia in the east and up to Morocco and Spain in the west.[36] 'Azzām took a classic example from the Prophet Muhammad, arguing that the Prophet acted in a similar way: "[after being forced to run away from Mecca] the Prophet Muhammad began to search for a piece of land. After he found Yathrib [later on named al-Madina] he started to establish the religion of Allah and educate his followers in its spirit. As the time passed, his kingdom spread, until he established a central powerful state, and the residents of the Arabian Peninsula surrendered and accepted Islam."[37]

It should be noted that 'Azzām emphasized the fact that the Jihād for the liberation of Afghanistan started against the infidel Muslim rulers, rather than the Soviets.[38] This emphasis is important as it signals the regimes in the Arab and Muslim states, which do not reign according to the Sharī'ah (Muslim religious law) and thus harm the concept of the Hākimiyyah, that the mere fact of being Muslim does not grant them immunity from the Global Islamic Jihād, and that the legitimacy for their forceful overthrow exists at any time.

Since Islam does not acknowledge the Islamic land division by borders, 'Azzām did not differentiate between the Muslim states in their current version. As far as he was concerned, there is no difference among Saudi Arabia, Syria, Egypt, Turkey, Palestine, Afghanistan, Azerbaijan, Uganda, Somalia, Eritrea, the Philippines, and Andalusia (part of Spain)—they are all a single land. Therefore, there is an individual duty to liberate them all (from the non-Muslim infidels and from the secular Muslim regimes that are also considered infidels) and cancel the borders between them. In addition, 'Azzām argued that the Muslim minorities suffering from the oppressing regime of the non-Muslim rulers in states such as the Philippines and Bulgaria should be liberated too. Therefore, 'Azzām encouraged the Muslim individuals who cannot reach Afghanistan to immigrate to any place in the world where there is a conflict between the Muslim believers and their secular Muslim rulers, or between them and the non-Muslim rulers.[39]

'Azzām divided the Global Islamic Jihād into two paths: primary and secondary. One must focus on the bulk of Muslims' efforts on liberating one Islamic territory (such as Afghanistan), and later move on to another location where "Jihād for the sake of Allah" was under way and where the highest probability existed of defeating the "infidels" (the first priority being Palestine); this would be repeated in different locations until such time as all Islamic lands have been liberated. In parallel, as much strength as possible must be invested in the rest of the Islamic lands that need to be liberated (such as Egypt and Algeria), as well as any place in which there exists a confrontation between "oppressed" Muslims and their non-Muslim rulers (such as the Philippines).

In a sermon delivered in Islamabad on February 24, 1989, nine days after the withdrawal of Soviet forces from Afghanistan, 'Azzām described the *modus operandi* of the Global Islamic Jihād theory. In his description, he presented a pan-Islamic approach, according to which, eventually, a single Muslim state shall be established on all the Muslim lands:

> We shall force the world to acknowledge us. If it does—it is welcome, and if not—it is the world's problem. We shall fight, win over our enemies and establish an Islamic state on a piece of land, such as Afghanistan.

Afghanistan shall expand, the Jihād shall spread, Islam shall fight in other locations, Islam shall fight the Jews in Palestine and establish an Islamic state in Palestine and an Islamic state in Afghanistan and in other locations. Later on, these states shall be united into a [single] Islamic state.[40]

The religious justification to this *modus operandi* exists in the writings of Tāqī al-Dīn Ibn Taymiyyah, the well-known fourteenth-century neo-Hanabli scholar, who argued that when historical circumstances oblige the Muslims to establish a few Islamic states simultaneously, an Imam or Caliph can be appointed in each one, on the condition that he is found to be suitable.[41]

The Global Islamic Jihād was perceived by 'Azzām as a religious conflict between Islam and those who opposed it, between the rule of Allah and the rule of Satan, and between the Islamic faith and infidelity.[42] This theory is actually applied in two parallel levels. The first is that of militant Jihād (the holy war), which is composed of four stages, each of which depends on the previous one and none of which can be skipped: *migration for the sake of Allah* (Al-Hijra fī sabīl Allah), which is a migration to an attacked Islamic land or to a place where an oppressed Muslim minority exists; *preparation* (I'dād), both mentally and physically; *camping along the enemy's border* (Ribāt), that is, waiting by the enemy until contact with it is made; and *fighting* (Qitāl). This level realizes the transformation the Muslim undergoes from being an immigrant until becoming a fighter in the holy war of the Global Islamic Jihād. The second level, which is parallel to the first one, is that of the Da'wah (propaganda). This level realizes the changes that the Muslim preacher undergoes during the Global Islamic Jihād. This level is also composed of four stages, each of which depends on the previous one and none of which can be skipped: the call to adhere to Allah, the "cold war" (a verbal war), the "warm war" (the actual fighting), and the final victory. During the stage of war, the Da'wah level unites with the militant Jihād level.

'Azzām argued that the unification of Militant Jihād and Da'wah was an essential step toward the triumph of Global Islamic Jihād. On the one hand, 'Azzām argued that the Da'wah cannot unite the Islamic nation on its own, and in fact could even pose a major threat if not accompanied by sweat, blood, and martyrs. The evidence to this is the Prophet Muhammad in its flesh, who could not unite the Arabian Peninsula using only propaganda and preaching, and had to win battles in order to guide people under the wings of Islam. On the other hand, 'Azzām argued that the carrying of arms—without the power to overcome the desires, without the power to deliver the truth through education, and without fear of Allah—shall not unite the nation in itself. Moreover, the one who carries arms prior to experiencing an exhaustive Islamic education is no different from a criminal and a suicidal individual. Therefore, the level of militant Jihād and the Da'wah must exist simultaneously and, during the war, be united with each other. According to him, in times of need and test, it is the Da'wah that receives the largest trust from the Muslim people.[43] 'Azzām allegorically described the necessity of the integration between the militant Jihād and the Da'wah:

> The lives of the Muslim nation depend only on the ink of the 'Ulamā (religious scholars) and the blood of the Shuhadā (martyrs), and therefore the Islamic historical map is colored in two colors: One is black—from the pen of the religious scholar, and the other is red—from the blood of the martyrs. What is more beautiful than writing the history of the Islamic nation with the ink and the blood of the religious scholar? What is more beautiful than having the hand that pours the ink and operates the pen be the same hand that

spills the blood and drives the Ummah? The larger the number of religious scholar Martyrs (*Shuhadā*), the larger the awakening of the Ummah from its slumber and the larger its salvation.[44]

The Conflict with the West Is a Religious Conflict

In 1996, Samuel Huntington, the Director of Harvard's Center for International Affairs, published *The Clash of Civilizations*. In his book, Huntington argued that the conflicts that took place in the world at the end of the twentieth century were set, first and foremost, on a cultural background (such as an ethnic or religious background) and not on an ideological or an economic background. Unlike the followers of Samuel Huntington's theory, 'Azzām saw the conflict between Islam and the West as an exclusive religious conflict, and not as an inclusive cultural conflict.[45] In one of his lectures, 'Azzām explicitly said, "the battle that continues since the dawn of time until our own days is the battle with the People of the Book—the Jews and the Christians—and the Jews are the spearhead which stick in the Muslims hearts."[46] In another place, he wrote, "the battle between Islam and its enemies—the Jews and the Christians—did not cease since the battle against Banu Qaynuqā', Banu al-Nadīr and Banu Quraytha and until these days."[47]

Another expression for seeing the conflict with the West as a religious conflict can be seen in 'Azzām's recurring use of the terms such as "the Crusader West," "the Crusader western states," "the Jewish–Crusader hatred," "the Global Judaism," and "the Jewish state," describing the West, led by the United States and Israel. 'Azzām argued that in fact there was no cultural conflict between the Islamic culture and the "Crusader" western culture. According to him, the neglect of Islam by the Muslims during the last three centuries enabled the "Crusader" West to easily insert its culture and values to the crumbling Ottoman Empire, and afterward to secular Muslim states, which requested, to a great extent, to adopt the culture and values of the West. However, when Islam was required to prove its supremacy over the other religions, he proved it. The evidence to this are as follows: Muhammad's victory over the hostile Jewish clans in al-Madīna; the conflict between the Muslim East and the "Crusader" West during the Crusader wars, which led to the victory of the Muslims and the return of the Crusaders to their countries; and the victory of the Islamic Jihād in Afghanistan.[48] According to 'Azzām, "religion drives the nations, making them willing to pay the highest price." In other words, Islam is the solution.[49]

'Azzām argued that Judaism and Christianity, which are represented by the West, have been fighting against Islam since its establishment, out of a religious motive and not out of a cultural one. He referenced his argument from the Quran: "Never will the Jews or the Christians be satisfied with thee unless thou follow their form of religion. Say: the guidance of God, that is the (only) guidance" (Chapter 2, "al-Baqara," Verse 120).[50] Additional evidence to the religious motive behind the ancient conflict between the West and Islam, according to 'Azzām, is the great fear of the West from the expansion of Islam[51]:

> This demon, as the enemies of Allah refer to it, is out of the bottle. Islam returns once more to confront the world. You are Islam, you are the gigantic demon held captive for three hundred years and thought of as rested. [. . .] The problem frightening the world is found in Afghanistan, in Palestine, in Chad, in Somalia, In Lebanon, in the Philippines and in every place in which Islam wishes to revive the religion of Allah. [. . .] They fear that Islam shall take over a piece of land, express the religion of Allah, and returning mankind to Allah's religion.[52]

In order to strengthen his argument and show that the fear of the West from Islam is not temporary and passing, but a real and lasting fear, 'Azzām quoted western figures from various historic periods, who, according to him, openly expressed their fear of Islam. For instance, he quoted the words of the British Colonel Thomas Lawrence: "we have threatened Zionism but found the Zionists our friends; we have threatened Bolshevism, but found the Bolsheviks our allies in war. [. . .] Our only enemy is Islam who stood as a wall against the European Imperialism for three hundred years."[53] In addition, 'Azzām quoted a statement of Zbigniew Brzezinski, US national security advisor to President Jimmy Carter: "The American government is very worried in the face of the growing activity of the Islamic movements around the Muslim world. The United States works to neutralize Islam and prevent it from fulfilling an influencing role in the international politics."[54] 'Azzām argued that proofs to the religious conflict are also evident in the western states coming forward to solve conflicts in places that hold a risk to Christian individuals on behalf of Muslim enemies and also in places where there is fear that Islam shall take over, for instance, in Ethiopia, Eritrea, and Sudan.[55]

According to 'Azzām, the West planned to eliminate Islam and the Jihād. According to his description, in order to bring about the elimination of Islam, the "Crusader" West saw, first and foremost, the need to prevent its expansion using a few measurements: physically encircling Islam by the "Crusaders" so that it is only necessary to tighten the hold in order to suffocate it and kill it; making Islam responsible for the retrogression of the Muslims; denouncing Islam and creating a negative image of it as a violent, blood-spilling, retrograde, offensive religion; calling upon world peace; and calling to bring the various religions closer and to gap the differences between them. Another way to eliminate Islam is to affect it directly through the inflammation of the religious conflicts between the Muslims: contesting the faith among the Muslims, encouraging Arab nationalism, preferring the Christian Arab over the Muslim Arab and over the non-Arab Muslim, and also establishing and supporting Muslim movements that oppose Islam.[56]

From the analysis of 'Azzām's writing and doctrine, it can be established that had he been alive, he would surely disagree with Huntington's forecast that the future conflict with the West is about to be a cultural one, and that in order to avoid great wars between the civilizations it is obligatory for the "core states" of the West to avoid interfering in conflicts within other civilizations. According to 'Azzām, even if the West avoids interventions in conflicts within the "Islamic civilization," the Muslims shall not stop demanding that the West returns the lands of Islam to their original owners. Also, according to him, the future conflict with the West is expected to be a religious conflict rather than a cultural one. The reason is that western culture is already disintegrating, and it shall not survive. This culture does not provide its members with peace of mind, values, principles, and standards, but only with materialism, which leads to crime, self-destruction, devastation, and civil wars. Therefore, 'Azzām argued that there is no danger from the western culture, which is not based on religion, and its fall is known. However, Judaism and Christianity, religions seeking to harm Islam and take over its lands, shall continue to exist until Islam comes to banish them.[57] According to him, the solution to the ailments of the West and the salvation of the entire humankind exists only in the Quran and the Sunna, which are the walls protecting Islam from the fierce power of the West.[58]

The Jews Provoke a Quarrel and the State of Israel Has No Right to Exist

'Azzām considered the conflict between the Jews and Judaism and Islam and the Muslims distinctly religious. According to him, this conflict began during the period before the appearance of Islam. He granted much weight to the consequences of the Jews' deportation a few times in history, and as a result of the church haunting them during the first centuries of the Common Era. In his opinion, these circumstances sewed great hatred in the hearts of the Jew toward all those who are not Jews, and made them want to avenge and to "spill the blood of the 'gentiles.'"[59] 'Azzām mentioned that this determination grew stronger as the Jews understood that Muhammad is a real threat on their national, financial, and religious leadership in al-Madina. In response, the Jews told false tales about Muhammad and threw "hard blows" on him and all the Muslims who just entered Islam.[60] According to him, ever since that day, the war between Islam and the Jewish forces has continued unabated.[61]

Based on his reading of the Quran, 'Azzām argued that the Jews are indeed the source of confrontation with the Muslims. They are the ones leading this religious war, from the dawn of Islam to the present. According to him, Allah, who knew the secret ways of the Jews, also knew that they are about to fulfill a central role in the religious confrontation with Islam and serve as a tool to wreck all the values and principles on the earth, and that is the reason in the Quran for which he warned the Muslims: "Strongest among men in enmity to the believers wilt thou find the Jews and Pagans" (Chapter 5, "Al-Mā'idah," Verse 82); "Never will the Jews or the Christians be satisfied with thee unless thou follow their form of religion. say: the guidance of God, that is the (only) guidance" (Chapter 2, "al-Baqara," Verse 120); "O ye who believe! take not the Jews and the Christians for your friends and protectors: They are but friends and protectors to each other. And he amongst you that turns to them (for friendship) is of them. Verily Allah guideth not a people unjust" (Chapter 5, "Al-Mā'idah," Verse 51).[62]

These and other verses led 'Azzām to three major conclusions. The first one is that since the dawn of Islam and until our days, there has been a battle with the "people of the book"—the Jews and the Christians—and the Jews are the spearhead that sticks in the Muslims' hearts.[63] The second one is that the desire of the "people of the book" cannot be satisfied, unless the Muslims shall convert their religion. The third one is that the "people of faith" (the Muslims) cannot meet the "people of infidelity" (the Jews and the Christians) halfway.[64] 'Azzām stressed that this is true not only because the Jews provoke a quarrel, and merchants of battles,[65] but also because Allah sentenced an eternal struggle between the truth and the lie ever since man was banished from heaven, and this struggle shall not cease until the victory of the "truth": "(God) said: Get ye down, with enmity between yourself. On earth will be your dwelling place and your means of livelihood, for a time" (Chapter 7, "Al-A'rāf," Verse 24).[66]

According to 'Azzām, unlike the divine truth in the Quran, the Jews and the Christians falsified the Bible and the New Testament to meet their interests. He quoted verses from the Quran pointing at the falsification of the holy writs in order to warn the Jews and the Christians: "Then woe to those who write the book with their own hands, and then say: this is from God, to traffic with it for a miserable price! woe to them for what their hands do write, and for the gain they make thereby" (Chapter 2, "al-Baqara," Verse 79). He further argued that if they were bold enough to falsify Allah and lie to him, they are sure to falsify the truth about Islam and the Muslims in our days to serve their own interests in the religious conflict with Islam.[67]

'Azzām's hatred toward the Jews, which was nurtured ever since he was a child, was also fed by stories of the Prophet's life, in which the Jews are described as bribers and as supporting "the hypocrites," meaning, the Muslims who seem to be believers though deep down defying the lord and his messenger.[68]

In order to not lean only on the past when describing the hatred, the Jews show Islam, and in order to show that their hatred still exists these days, 'Azzām quoted sayings, he attributed to Israeli leaders, in which they show great fear of the awakening of Islam. Thus, for instance, 'Azzām argued that David Ben Gurion, the first prime minister of the State of Israel, allegedly said, "we do not fear of socialism, of nationalism and of monarchism in our area. We fear of Islam, the demon which was asleep for a long time and starts to roam the area." In other circumstances, Ben Gurion allegedly said, "I fear of the appearance of a new Muhammad in the area"[69]; an additional saying is attributed to Moshe Dayan, the former minister of Defense of the State of Israel: "The West, led by the United States, should grant a greater attention to Israel being the defense of western culture in the face of the wheels of the Islamic revolution, that started in Iran, and that may spread quickly and surprisingly through other regions in the Arab world, perhaps even in Turkey or Afghanistan."[70]

In his writings, 'Azzām discussed the terms for temporal reconciliation or for a temporal treaty with the Jews. He refers to them as infidels even though they were not defined as such in the Quran, which regards them as protégés who may continue to practice their religion in return for tax payment (Jizya) and the recognition that they are superior to Islam. Since the Jews were defined as infidels by him, the rule for a temporary treaty with them is similar to that of a temporary treaty with infidels.[71] In other words, according to 'Azzām it is possible to make a temporary treaty with the infidel Jews as long as this treaty serves the interests of the Muslims and does not induce a threat to them, and as long as it does not include items such as the recognition on their rights to a piece of the Muslim lands, as the land of Islam belongs to Allah, and to Allah alone, and no one has the right to negotiate it. However, since the current situation, the existence of the State of Israel on the land of Palestine, contradicts the prohibition to acknowledge the infidels' privileges on a piece of Muslim land, it is definitely forbidden, according to 'Azzām, to make a temporary peace treaty with the Jews on the land of Palestine, as long as the State of Israel exists.[72]

'Azzām supported his words using three juristic rulings (*Fatwā*). The first is the undated *Fatwā* of Muhammad Rashīd rida, the undisputed intellectual leader of the Salafiyyah movement, dealing with the prohibition to sell the land of Palestine to the Jews and the British. The *Fatwā*, as it was brought by 'Azzām, determines that one who sells the land of Palestine to the Jews or the British is similar to the one who sells Al-Aqsa mosque and the entire homeland and to the one who betrays Allah, his messenger, and the loyalty to Islam.[73] The second *Fatwā*, published by Hājj Amīn al-Husaynī, the Mufti of Jerusalem and the chair of the Supreme Muslim Council in Palestine, in 1935, deals with the prohibition to sell the Muslim lands to the Jews. In the *Fatwā*, as it was brought by 'Azzām, Islam defines as infidels those who sell the Muslim lands to the Jews, or even mediates in the deal.[74] The third *Fatwā* brought by 'Azzām to support his sayings was published in 1956 by the juristic ruling committee of the Al-Azhar University and deals with the prohibition to reconcile with the State of Israel. The *Fatwā*, as it was brought by 'Azzām, determines

> The reconciliation with Israel is forbidden according to the Muslim law since it recognizes its continuing exploitation and aggressiveness. Muslims cannot reconcile with the Jews who exploited Palestine land and attacked its residents and their properties. Moreover, all Muslims should work together in order to return this land to its residents.[75]

An additional issue raised by 'Azzām in the context of religious confrontation between the Jews and Islam and the Muslims—which is also relevant today in view of the Islamic terror attacks in the world and in Israel—is, What is the verdict for infidel women and children who do not take part in the battle against the Muslims? Basing himself on a few traditions of the Hadīth literature and on the Hanafitic and the Shāfiitic schools of thoughts, 'Azzām mentioned three cases in which it is allowed to kill women, children, and even Muslim captives. The first case is when there are attacks from the air on the infidels' concentrations, and it is impossible to discern the women, the children, and the Muslim captives from the infidel warriors. The second case is when the women, the children, and the Muslim captives serve as a human defense shield to the infidel warriors; in any case, it should not be done on purpose. The third case is when the women and the children actively participated in the war, through assisting the warriors and/or through active participation in the battles.[76] Suicide terrorism, for instance, depends on these three exceptions in order to justify the killing of women and children on the opposite side.

Summary

Abdullah 'Azzām was a pious Muslim, a Salafī, who believed in the primordial decree and who considered the establishment of the Islamic state as the primary source of life. He granted much importance to the belief in "al-Wala' wa-al-Bara'" and considered it a barrier in front of selling the lands of Islam to the infidels. Also during the time he devoted himself to the Afghan Jihād, he remained religion and led a strict Muslim life. In order to religiously validate his articles and speeches, he relied on verses from the Quran, traditions about the Prophet, things he said, and sayings of scholars of Islam. Due to his radical sayings, including his challenge to the legitimacy of the Arab regimes in the Arab states and his provocative behavior when he was in Jordan, he was nicknamed "The Jordanian Sayyid Qutb."

We can argue that the first stirrings of Global Islamic Jihād already appeared with the territorial spread of Islam out of the Arabian Peninsula. However, it can be said that 'Azzām renewed this Global Islamic Jihād and developed it into a theory and inserted it—in a practical manner, and not a mere theoretical one as Abu al-A'lā al-Mawdūdī did—into the awareness of Muslims around the world. He was the first one, in the Arab and Muslim world, to rule that the Global Islamic Jihād for the liberation of Afghanistan and the other conquered Muslim lands is an individual duty of all those who are Muslims. Through the recruitment and the unity of the thousands of both Arab and non-Arab Muslim volunteers under a single roof, he and Bin Lādin were the first to successively implement, and not only to renew, the concept of Global Islamic Jihād. 'Azzām presented Bin Lādin with an ideological and practical infrastructure which he took with him after 'Azzām's death in November 1989.

The theory of the Global Islamic Jihād was perceived by 'Azzām as a battle between religions. This theory is implemented in two parallel levels: the militant Jihād (the holy war) and the Da'wah (the Islamic propaganda). The unity of these two levels was a guiding principle for 'Azzām and was defined as a precondition to the victory of Global Islamic Jihād. Through understanding the two levels and the need to combine them, it is possible to understand the way that the Global Islamic Terrorism of the last two decades works. Its practical meaning is that a terror attack does not occur surprisingly, but following a long process, which is necessary for its realization.

The emphasis 'Azzām granted to the religious nature of the conflict with the West did not minimize it to the faith that the foreign attendance on Muslim lands is a modern crusade against Islam, and Jews play a major role in it. The religious emphasis also expressed an intense desire to make the Islamic Jihād against the West into a Global Islamic Jihād. Through accessing the most basic common denominator of all Muslims—the Islam religion—'Azzām sought to unite all the Muslims in the world against the infidel West. According to him, only a religious conflict shall turn the tables and bring about the reign of Allah on the earth, due to the supremacy of Islam over the two other religions joined together in the "Zionist–Crusader Alliance." Therefore, he emphasized the importance of the Muslim scholars and preachers in the conflict with this alliance and argued that this is the reason that the "Zionist–Crusader Alliance" leads a campaign for their arrest and murder.

Dealing with the religious conflict with the West, 'Azzām focused especially on the Jews. First of all, 'Azzām negated the Jew's alleged historic privilege over the land of Israel and therefore did not acknowledge the State of Israel's right to exist. Therefore, he rejected any option of a temporary treaty with the Jews on the land of Palestine, as long as the State of Israel exists.[77] Second, according to him, the plan to harm Islam was deriving out of the religious hatred of the Jews to this religion, and they were the ones leading the hatred campaign against Islam since the dawn of times.[78]

Because he is a world renowned Muslim figure, 'Azzām's statements, as are the statements of other religious authorities in his status, might be considered as juristic rulings for radical Muslims. Therefore, when an individual of such a religious status calls upon the annihilation of the State of Israel, the United States and other western states, and even for the overthrowal of the secular Arab regimes, this is not merely rhetoric, but a command for the believers to implement the word of Allah coming from his representatives on the earth—the religious scholars.[79] Even if 'Azzām and other religious scholars are not pulling the trigger themselves, they are responsible for the Islamic terror no less than its perpetrators, and even more they use their religious authority and their far-reaching influence in order to produce more and more radicals, as in a factory production line.

Notes

1. This chapter is based on the author's doctoral dissertation, entitled 'Abdullah 'Azzām and the Ideological Origins of Usāma bin Lādin's Worldwide Islamic Terrorism, written in the framework of the Department of Middle Eastern History at Bar-Ilan University under the supervision of Professor Rami Ginat from the Department of Political Studies in March 2006.
2. Asaf Maliach and Shaul Shay, *From Kabul to Jerusalem—Al-Qa'ida, the Worldwide Islamic Jihād and the Israeli-Palestinian Conflict* (Tel Aviv: Matar Publication, 2009), 22–33 (Hebrew).
3. 'Abdullah 'Azzām, "Al-Qā'ida al-Sulbah" [The Solid Basis], *Al-Jihād* 41 (1988): 4–6.

4. 'Abdullah 'Azzām, *Al-As'ila wal-Ajwiba al-Jihādiyya* [Questions and Answers Regarding Jihād] (Peshawar: Maktab Khadamāt al-Mujāhidīn, year unavailable), 19. The word *Salafiyyah* (from Salaf—the forefathers) denotes the return to the ways of the Prophet, the Prophet's companions (Sahābah), and the Muslims in the first centuries of Islam, when the Islam was pure, and the Arab Caliphate was at its prime; Sufism is a mystic movement with roots at the beginning of Islam—the Zuhād (the ascetics). The Sufism emphasized the spiritual religious experience of religion while the mainstream orthodox movement emphasized the keeping of the virtues. The indifference about keeping the virtues of Islam and postponing them, as well as the statement about the annulment of the values of the religious laws, created harsh attacks of this movement by the representatives of the acceptable theology, who considered it an infidel movement; the concept of the unity of Allah (Tawhīd) connects with the general nature of Allah. Some argued that the personification of Allah (Tashbīh or Tajsīm) through his titles includes sharing Allah ("Shirk") and harms the concept of his pure unity. In other words, it is impossible that Allah will share common traits with human beings. This led to an allegorical exegesis (Ta'wīl), for instance, when the Quran talks about the "hand" of Allah, it does not mean a physical hand, but "Allah's grace." Their opposition accused them in negating the titles (Ta'tīl al-Sifāt), the negation of Allah's ability to see, to talk, to hear, etc. The compromise was found by Abu-Hassan al-Ash'arī (874–936), who argued that Allah has entities which are a part of his nature, and therefore he is not obliged to negate these titles. He argued that they should be accepted without questioning: How? ("Bilā Kayfa").
5. 'Abdullah 'Azzām, *Al-'Aqīda wa-Atharuhā fī Binā' al-Jīl* [The Faith and Its Influence on the Generation] (Beirut: Dār Ibn Hazm, 1990), 58–66.
6. Abu 'Ubāda al-Ansārī, *Mafhūm al-Hākimiyyah fī Fikr al-Shahīd 'Abdullah 'Azzām* [The Term Hākimiyyah as Was Coined by the Martyr 'Abdullah 'Azzām] (Peshawar: Markaz al-Shahīd 'Azzām al-I'lāmī, not dated), 11; 'Abd al-'Azīz Bin Bāz, "Hawla al-Wala' wa-al-Bara'ah [About the Faith of Loyalty and Disavowal]," in *Majmū' Fatāwā Samāhat al-Shaykh 'Abd al-'Azīz Bin 'Abdullah Bin Bāz* [The Religious Rulings Collection by the Honorable Sheikh 'Abd al-'Azīz Bin 'Abdullah Bin Bāz], ed. 'Abd al-'Azīz Bin Bāz and 'Abdullah al-tayyār, 3 (Riyadh: Dār al-watan, 1416 AH: May 1995–1996), 1021–22.
7. Al-Ansārī, ibid.; 'Azzām, "Al-Qā'ida al-Sulbah," 6.
8. 'Abdullah 'Azzām, *Al-Jihād wa-Atharuhu fī Binā' al-Jīl al-Rabbānī* [The Jihād and Its Influence on the Building of the Divine Generation], audio tape; 'Abdullah 'Azzām, "Hakadhā 'Allamanī al-Jihād" [This is What the Jihād Taught Me], *Al-Jihād* 37 (December 1987): 4–6, 4; 'Abdullah 'Azzām, *Sa'ādat al-Bashariyyah* [The Bliss of Humanity] (Peshawar: Markaz al-Shahīd 'Azzām al-I'lāmī, not dated), 4; 'Abdullah 'Azzām, *Al-Tahrīd al-'Ālamī Didd al-Wujūd al-'Arabī wa-al-Shuhadā' al-Thalāthah* [The Universal Incitement against the Arab Presence and the Three Martyrs] (Peshawar: Maktab Khidamāt al-Mujāhidīn, 1989), video tape.
9. 'Abdullah 'Azzām, *I'lān al-Jihād* [Declaration of Jihād] (Peshawar: Maktab Khidamāt al-Mujāhidīn, 1990), 41–43, 45; 'Abdullah 'Azzām, *Muqaddimah fī al-Hijra wal-I'dād* [Preface to Migration and Preparation], 25.
10. 'Azzām, *I'lān al-Jihād* [Declaration of Jihād], 43–45.
11. Ibid., 44–47.
12. 'Azzām, *Al-Jihād wa-Atharuhu fī Binā' al-Jīl al-Rabbānī* [The Jihād and Its Influence on the Building of the Divine Generation], audio tape.
13. 'Abdullah 'Azzām, *Intisār al-Haqq* [The Victory of the Truth] (Peshawar: Maktab Khidamāt al-Mujāhidīn, 1988), video tape; 'Abdullah 'Azzām, *Bashā'ir al-Nasr* [The Good News of Victory] (Peshawar: Markaz al-Shahīd 'Azzām al-I'lāmī), 5; 'Abdullah 'Azzām, *Kalimāt min Khatt al-Nār al-Awwal* [Words from the Battle Front Line], 100; 'Abdullah 'Azzām, *Fī al-Ta'ammur al-'Ālamī* [Concerning the Worldwide Conspiracy] (Peshawar: Markaz al-Shahīd 'Azzām al-I'lāmī), 26; 'Azzām, "Hakadhā 'Allamanī al-Jihād" [This Is What the Jihād Taught Me], 5; 'Azzām, *Muqaddimah fī al-Hijra wal-I'dād* [Preface to Migration and Preparation], 82.
14. 'Azzām, *Al-As'ila wal-Ajwiba al-Jihādiyya* [Questions and Answers Regarding Jihād], 8–9. The review of the way bin Lādin has gone through since he left Afghanistan for the first time, at the beginning of the 1990s until he was killed in May 2011, shows that he acted according to the *modus operandi* presented by 'Azzām.
15. 'Azzām, *Fī al-Ta'ammur al-'Ālamī* [Concerning the Worldwide Conspiracy], 26; 'Azzām, *Intisār al-Haqq* [The Victory of the Truth], video tape.
16. 'Uthmān Raslān, *Al-Tarbiyah al-Siyāsiyyah 'inda Jamā'at "al-Ikhwān al-Muslimūna"* [The Political Education among the "Muslim Brotherhhod" Group) (Cairo: Dār al-Nashr wa-al-Tawzī' al-Islāmiyyah, 1989), 153; Chris Horrie and Peter Chippindale, *Islam Mahu?* [What Is Islam?] (Tel Aviv: Ahi-Asaf, 1991), 96–97; Hasan al-Bana, *Majmū'at Rasā'il al-Imām al-Shahīd Hasan al-Bana* [The Letters Collection of the Martyr Imam Hasan al-Bana] (Al-Mansura: Dār al-Wafā', 1988), 204–5.

17. 'Azzām, *Hakadhā 'Allamanī al-Jihād* [This Is What the Jihād Taught Me], 5; 'Azzām, *I'lān al-Jihād* [Declaration of Jihād], 71.
18. 'Azzām, *Muqaddimah fī al-Hijra wal-I'dād* [Preface to Migration and Preparation], 25.
19. 'Abdullah 'Azzām, *Al-Tarbiyah al-Jihādiyyah wa-al-Bināʾ* [Education for Jihād and Reconstruction] (Peshawar: Maktab Khidamāt al-Mujāhidīn), 131; 'Abdullah 'Azzām, *'Imlāq al-Fikr al-Islāmī—al-Shahīd Sayyid Qutb* [The Islamic Thinking Giant—The Martyr Sayyid Qutb] (Peshawar: Markaz al-Shahīd 'Azzām al-I'lāmī), 7; Abu Mujāhid, *Al-shahīd 'Abdullah 'Azzām Bayna al-Milād wa-al-Istishhād* [The Martyr 'Abdullah 'Azzām between Birth and Martyrdom] (Peshawar: Markaz al-Shahīd 'Azzām al-I'lāmī), 13; Husnī Jarār, *Al-Shahīd 'Abdullah 'Azzām—rajul Da'wa wa-madrasat Jihād* [The Martyr 'Abdullah 'Azzām—Propaganda Man and Jihād School] (Amman: Dar al-Diyāʾ, 1990), 23.
20. 'Abdullah 'Azzām, "'Ashrūna 'Āman 'alā al-Shahādah" [Twenty Years for the Martyrdom], *Al-Jihād* 23 (October 1986): 4–7, 4; Abu Mujāhid, *Al-shahīd 'Abdullah 'Azzām Bayna al-Milād wa-al-Istishhād* [The Martyr 'Abdullah 'Azzām between Birth and Martyrdom], 13–14; Jarār, *Al-Shahīd 'Abdullah 'Azzām—rajul Da'wa wa-madrasat Jihād* [The Martyr 'Abdullah 'Azzām—Propaganda Man and Jihād School], 22–23; Peter L. Bergen, *Holy War, Inc.* (New York: The Free Press, 2001), 52; "Hiwār ma'a al-Khunasāʾ—Umm Muhammad" [A Conversation with al-Khunasāʾ—Umm Muhammad], *Al-Bunyān al-Marsūs* 30 (February 1990): 64–67, 65.
21. Abu Mujāhid, *Al-shahīd 'Abdullah 'Azzām Bayna al-Milād wa-al-Istishhād* [The Martyr 'Abdullah 'Azzām between Birth and Martyrdom], 6, 14; Bashīr Abu Rummān and 'Abdullah al-Sa'īd, *Al-'Ālim wa-al-Mujāhid wa-al-Shahīd al-Shaykh 'Abdullah 'Azzām* [The Scholar, the Holy Warrior, the Sheikh 'Abdullah 'Azzām] (1990), 33–34.
22. 'Abdullah 'Azzām, *Fī al-Jihād . . . Fiqh wa-Ijtihād* [In Jihād: Jurisprudence and Intellectual Effort to Infer Law] (Peshawar: Maktab Khidamāt al-Mujāhidīn), 137; 'Abdullah 'Azzām, "Tahtīm al-Quyūd" [Crushing the Chains], *Al-Jihād* 33 (August 1987): 4–9, 6; 'Azzām, *'Ashrūna 'Āman 'alā al-Shahādah* [Twenty Years from the Martyrdom], 4; 'Azzām, *Al-Tarbiyah al-Jihādiyyah wa-al-Bināʾ* [Education for Jihād and Reconstruction], 9–10; 'Azzām, *Kalimāt min Khatt al-Nār al-Awwal* [Words from the Battle Front Line], 17, 47; 'Azzām, *Hakadhā 'Allamanī al-Jihād* [This Is What the Jihād Taught Me], 5.
23. 'Azzām, *'Ashrūna 'Āman 'alā al-Shahādah* [Twenty Years from the Martyrdom], 7.
24. 'Azzām, *'Imlāq al-Fikr al-Islāmī—al-Shahīd Sayyid Qutb* [The Islamic Thinking Giant—The Martyr Sayyid Qutb], 7.
25. 'Azzām, *Al-Tarbiyah al-Jihādiyyah wa-al-Bināʾ* [Education for Jihād and Reconstruction], 81–82, 85, 87.
26. 'Abdullah 'Azzām, *'Ibar wa-Basāʾir lil-Jihād fī al-'Asr al-Hādir* [Lessons and Approaches to the Holy War in the Modern Era] (Amman: Maktabat al-Risālah al-Hadīthah, 1987), 44–46.
27. 'Abdullah 'Azzām, *Al-Jihād wa-Atharuhu fī Bināʾ al-Jīl al-Rabbānī* [The Jihād and Its Influence on the Building of the Divine Generation], audio tape.
28. 'Abdullah 'Azzām, *Al-Tarbiyah al-Jihādiyyah wa-al-Bināʾ* [Education for Jihād and Reconstruction], 88.
29. Abu Rummān and al-Sa'īd, Ibid.
30. 'Abdullah 'Azzām, "Inna al-Hukm Illā li-llah" [The Decision Is for Allah Only], *Al-Jihād* 40 (March 1988): 4–5.
31. 'Azzām, *I'lān al-Jihād* [Declaration of Jihād], 46; Sayyid Qutb, *Ma'ālim fī al-Tarīq* [Landmarks] (Beirut: Dār al-Shurūq), 92.
32. 'Azzām, *I'lān al-Jihād* [Declaration of Jihād], 54.
33. 'Abdullah 'Azzām, *Khatar al-Qawmiyya 'alā al-Jihād al-Afghānī* [The Danger of Nationalism vis-à-vis the Afghan Jihād] (Peshawar: Maktab Khidamāt al-Mujāhidīn, 1989), video tape; 'Azzām, *Kalimāt min Khatt al-Nār al-Awwal* [Words from the Battle Front Line], 26.
34. 'Azzām, *Al-Jihād wa-Atharuhu fī Bināʾ al-Jīl al-Rabbānī* [The Jihād and Its Influence on the Building of the Divine Generation], 7; 'Azzām, *Al-Tahrīd al-'Ālamī Didd al-Wujūd al-'Arabī wa-al-Shuhadāʾ al-Thalāthah* [The Universal Incitement against the Arab Presence and the Three Martyrs], video tape.
35. 'Abdullah 'Azzām, *Jihād Sha'b Muslim* [Holy War of a Muslim Nation], 54; 'Azzām, *Fī al-Jihād . . . Fiqh wa-Ijtihād* [In Jihād: Jurisprudence and Intellectual Effort to Infer Law], 135.
36. 'Abdullah 'Azzām, *Fī Khidamm al-Ma'rakah* [In the Spacious Battlefield] (Peshawar: Maktab Khadamāt al-Mujāhidīn, 1989), 44; 'Abdullah 'Azzām, *Al-Difā' 'an Arādi al-Muslimīna Ahamm Furūd al-A'yān* [The Defense of Muslim Lands—The Most Important of Individual Obligations] (Amman: Maktabat al-Risālah al-Hadīthah, 1987), 36 (the long version); 'Abdullah 'Azzām, *Bashāʾir al-Nasr* [The Good News of Victory], 5; 'Abdullah 'Azzām, *Tahqīq al-'Ubūdiyya* [Fulfilling the Servitude] (Kuwait: Home video tape, 1989); it should be mentioned that every state that once held an Islamic regime, even for

a short period of time, becomes religiously Dār al-Islām forever, and it is forbidden to relinquish or replace it, give it away, or sell it to the infidels. In the case of Andalusia (al-Andalus, a large territory in Spain), 'Azzām and Bin-Lādin, along with many other Muslim radicals, encouraged a return to Islam.

37. 'Abdullah 'Azzām, "Madha Turīdūna?" [What Do You Want?], *Al-Jihād* 63 (January 1990): 8.
38. 'Abdullah 'Azzām, *Fī Khidamm al-Ma'rakah* [In the Spacious Battlefield] (Peshawar: Maktab Khidamāt al-Mujāhidīn, 1989), 29.
39. 'Abdullah 'Azzām, *'Abdullah 'Azzām* (Oklahoma: IAP, 1988), video tape; 'Abdullah 'Azzām, *Afghānistān wal-Mu'āmarah al-Dawliyya* [Afghanistan and the International Conspiracy] (al-Sharika al-I'lāmiyyah lil-Khadamāt, 1989), video tape; 'Azzām, *I'lān al-Jihād* [Declaration of Jihād], 67; 'Azzām, *Fī al-Jihād . . . Fiqh wa-Ijtihād* [In Jihād: Jurisprudence and Intellectual Effort to Infer Law], 53, 57, 134; 'Azzām, *Al-Difā' 'an Arādi al-Muslimīna Ahamm Furūd al-A'yān* [The Defense of Muslim Lands—The Most Important of Individual Obligations], 83–133; 'Azzām, *Bashā'ir al-Nasr* [The Good News of Victory], 5; 'Abdullah 'Azzām, *Samām al-Amān* [The Security Valve] (Peshawar: Maktab Khidamāt al-Mujāhidīn, 1989), video tape.
40. 'Azzām, *Samām al-Amān* [The Security Valve], video tape.
41. Imanuel Sivan, *Qanaei ha-Islām* [The Fanatics of Islam] (Tel Aviv: 'Am 'Oved, 1994), 94. Paraphrased by the author.
42. 'Abdullah 'Azzām, *Khatar al-Qawmiyya 'alá al-Jihād al-Afghānī* [The Danger of Nationalism vis-à-vis the Afghan Jihād], video tape.
43. 'Azzām, *Fī al-Ta'ammur al-'Ālamī* [Concerning the Worldwide Conspiracy], 4, 8; 'Abdullah 'Azzām, *Dhikrayāt Falastīn* [Palestine Memories] (Peshawar: Markaz al-Shahīd 'Azzām al-I'lāmī), 12; 'Azzām, *Samām al-Amān* [The Security Valve], video tape; 'Azzām, *Kalimāt min Khatt al-Nār al-Awwal* [Words from the Battle Front Line], 100–101.
44. 'Azzām, *Kalimāt min Khatt al-Nār al-Awwal* [Words from the Battle Front Line], 134.
45. Samuel Huntington, *The Clash of Civilizations and the Remaking of World Order* (New York: Simon & Schuster, 1996).
46. *Shahīd al-Ummah al-Islāmiyyah al-Duktūr 'Abdullah 'Azzām* [The Martyr of the Islamic Nation the Doctor 'Abdullah 'Azzām] (Peshawar: Maktab Khidamāt al-Mujāhidīn), video tape. The tape documents a memorial service for Azzam and features videoclips of Azzam.
47. 'Abdullah 'Azzām, *Hamās—al-Judhūr al-Ta'rīkhiyyah wa-al-Mithāq* [Hamās—The Historical Roots and the Charter] (Peshawar: Maktab Khidamāt al-Mujāhidīn, 1990), 103.
48. 'Abdullah 'Azzām, *Khat al-Tahawwul al-Ta'rīkhī* [The Turning Point of History] (Peshawar: Markaz al-Shahīd 'Azzām al-I'lāmī), 1, 16; 'Abdullah 'Azzām, "Li-Ayyam al-Shadā'id" [For the Calamities Days], *Al-Jihād* 28 (March 1987), 4–7, 5; 'Azzām, *Kalimāt min Khatt al-Nār al-Awwal* [Words from the Battle Front Line], 28.
49. 'Azzām, *Muqaddimah fī al-Hijra wal-I'dād* [Preface to Migration and Preparation], 73.
50. 'Abdullah 'Azzām, *Al-Jihād al-Islāmī fī Afghānistān* [The Islamic Jihad in Afghanistan], (Al-Sharikah al-'Arabiyyah al-Markaziyyah—al-Fīdiyū wa-al-Tawzī'), video tape.
51. 'Abdullah 'Azzām, "Jā'a al-Haqq wa-Zahaqa al-Bātil" [The Truth Came and the Lie Consumed], *Al-Jihād* 52 (February–March 1989), 4–7, 6; 'Abdullah 'Azzām, *Tujār al-Hurūb* [Merchants of War], 10.
52. 'Abdullah 'Azzām, *Al-As'ila wal-Ajwiba al-Jihādiyya* [Questions and Answers Regarding Jihād], 27.
53. 'Abdullah 'Azzām, *Ayāt al-Rahmān fī Jihād al-Afghān* [The Merciful Verses about the Afghans' Jihād] (Amman: Maktabat al-Risālah al-Hadīthah, 1986), 30.
54. 'Abdullah 'Azzām, "Wa-Allah Ghālib 'alā Amrihi" [Allah Wins], *Al-Jihād* 51, (January–February 1989), 4–7, 6. The author of this text believes that this citation is fabricated.
55. 'Abdullah 'Azzām, "Aa Hashafan wa-Sū' Kīlah?" [Are There Spoilt Dates and Defect Measurements?]," *Al-Jihād* 62 (December 1989), 6–9, 9; 'Azzām, *Al-Tahrīd al-'Ālamī Didd al-Wujūd al-'Arabī wa-al-Shuhadā' al-Thalāthah* [The Universal Incitement against the Arab Presence and the Three Martyrs], video tape; 'Abdullah 'Azzām, "Hatā Lā Tamūtu al-Ummah al-Islāmiyyah Ilā al-Abad" [So That the Islamic Nation Will Never Die], *Al-Jihād* 63 (January 1990), 29.
56. 'Abdullah 'Azzām, "Jihād . . . Lā Irhāb" [Holy War . . . Not Terrorism], *Al-Jihād* 27 (February 1987), 6; 'Abdullah 'Azzām, *Tujār al-Hurūb* [Merchants of War], 10–11.
57. 'Abdullah 'Azzām, *Al-Islām wa-Mustaqbal al-Bashariyyah* [Islam and the Future of Humanity] (Jerusalem: Maktabat al-Sadaqāt al-Islāmiyyah), 13–14, 26–27; 'Azzām, *Samām al-Amān* [The Security Valve], video tape; Samuel Huntington, *The Clash of Civilizations and the Remaking of World Order* (Jerusalem: Shalem Publication, 2003), 432 (Hebrew).
58. 'Azzām, *Al-Islām wa-Mustaqbal al-Bashariyyah* [Islam and the Future of Humanity], 18; 'Azzām, *Samām al-Amān* [The Security Valve], video tape.

59. 'Azzām, *Hamās—al-Judhūr al-Ta'rīkhiyyah wa-al-Mithāq* [Hamas—The Historical Roots and the Charter], 12–13; 'Azzām argued that many pogroms that the Jews underwent during a later period in Europe, mostly in Spain, Russia, and Italy, fueled the fire of religious hatred toward those who are not Jewish.
60. 'Azzām, *Fī al-Ta'ammur al-'Ālamī* [Concerning the Worldwide Conspiracy], 42.
61. 'Azzām, *Hamās—al-Judhūr al-Ta'rīkhiyyah wa-al-Mithāq* [Hamas—The Historical Roots and the Charter], 103.
62. 'Azzām, *Al-Jihād al-Islāmī fī Afghānistān* [The Islamic Jihad in Afghanistan], video tape; 'Azzām, *Fī Khidamm al-Ma'rakah* [In the Spacious Battlefield], 28; 'Azzām, *Hamās—al-Judhūr al-Ta'rīkhiyyah wa-al-Mithāq* [Hamas—The Historical Roots and the Charter], 11–12.
63. *Shahīd al-Ummah al-Islāmiyyah al-Duktūr 'Abdullah 'Azzām* [The Martyr of the Islamic Nation the Doctor 'Abdullah 'Azzām], video tape.
64. 'Abdullah 'Azzām, *'Ibar wa-Basā'ir lil-Jihād fī al-'Asr al-Hādir* [Lessons and Approaches to the Holy War in the Modern Era] (Amman: Maktabat al-Risālah al-Hadīthah, 1987), 106.
65. 'Azzām, *Tujār al-Hurūb* [Merchants of War], 1.
66. 'Azzām, *Fī al-Ta'ammur al-'Ālamī* [Concerning the Worldwide Conspiracy], 43. This verse relates to the banishment of Adam and Eve and the Satan from the Garden of Eden.
67. 'Abdullah 'Azzām, "Hasabana Allah wa-ni'am al-wakīl" [Enough That the Creator Will Help Us and Grace Us], *Al-Jihād* 61 (November 1989): 6–9, 9; 'Azzām, *Al-'Aqīda wa-Atharuhā fī Binā' al-Jīl* [Faith and Its Influence on the Generation], 37–38.
68. Muhammad Na'īm Yāsīn, *Al-Jihād—Mayādīnuhu wa-Asālībuhu* [The Holy War—Its fields and Its Methods] (Amman: Maktabat al-Aqsā, 1981), 113. Yassin mentions that the danger the Islam considers in the "hypocrites" derives from their ability to assimilate in the Muslim society and to harm the Daw'ah from within. They strive to ruin Islam, and since they appear to be believers, they are acting while the environment does not understand the nature of their acts. Therefore, the "hypocrites" are considered the most dangerous enemies of the Daw'ah, even more than the infidels, which are obvious and can be coped with; 'Abdullah 'Azzām, "Tahtīm al-Quyūd" [Smashing the Cords], *Al-Jihād* 33 (August 1987): 4–5.
69. 'Azzām, *Al-Islām wa-Mustaqbal al-Bashariyyah* [Islam and the Future of Humanity], 54.
70. 'Azzām, *Wa-Allah Ghālib 'alā Amrihi* [Allah Wins], 6.
71. 'Azzām, *Hamās—al-Judhūr al-Ta'rīkhiyyah wa-al-Mithāq* [Hamas—The Historical Roots and the Charter], 90; 'Azzām, *I'lān al-Jihād* [Declaration of Jihād], 20.
72. Ibid., 90–93.
73. Ibid., 97.
74. Ibid., 93.
75. Ibid., 98.
76. 'Azzām, *I'lān al-Jihād* [Declaration of Jihād], 113–14, 120–23.
77. 'Azzām, *Samām al-Amān* [The Security Valve], video tape.
78. 'Azzām, *Tujār al-Hurūb* [Merchants of War], 1.
79. 'Azzām and Bin Lādin assumed that the regimes of the Arab states and the Muslim states surrender to the United States, and that their ruling is not based on the laws of Allah, and therefore they harm the concept of the Hākimiyyah. Accordingly, they are infidel regimes, and there is a complete religious legitimacy to forcefully overthrow them, in accordance with the theory of Global Islamic Jihad. Hence, the fact that these regimes are Muslim does not grant them immunity from radical Islam, and their cooperation with the West regarding the Global Islamic Terrorism entails a great risk for their stability, certainly not less, and even more, than the West and the State of Israel.

Works Cited

'Abd al-'Azīz Bin Bāz, "Hawla al-Wala' wa-al-Bara'ah" [About the Faith of Loyalty and Disavowal], in *Majmū' Fatāwā Samāhat al-Shaykh 'Abd al-'Azīz Bin 'Abdullah Bin Bāz* [The Religious Rulings Collection by the Honorable Sheikh 'Abd al-'Azīz Bin 'Abdullah Bin Bāz], ed. 'Abd al-'Azīz Bin Bāz and 'Abdullah al-tayyār, 3 (Riyadh: Dār al-watan, 1416 AH: May 1995–1996), 1021–22.

'Abdullah 'Azzām, *'Abdullah 'Azzām* (Oklahoma: IAP, 1988), video tape.

'Abdullah 'Azzām, *Afghānistān wal-Mu'āmarah al-Dawliyya* [Afghanistan and the International Conspiracy] (al-Sharika al-I'lāmiyyah lil-Khadamāt, 1989), video tape.

'Abdullah 'Azzām, *Al-As'ila wal-Ajwiba al-Jihādiyya* [Questions and Answers Regarding Jihād] (Peshawar: Maktab Khidamāt al-Mujāhidīn).

'Abdullah 'Azzām, *Al-'Aqīda wa-Atharuhā fī Binā' al-Jīl* (Faith and Its Influence on the Generation) (Beirut: Dār Ibn Hazm, 1990).

'Abdullah 'Azzām, *Al-Difā' 'an Arādi al-Muslimīna Ahamm Furūd al-A'yān* [The Defense of Muslim Lands—The Most Important of Individual Obligations] (Amman: Maktabat al-Risālah al-Hadīthah, 1987).
'Abdullah 'Azzām, *Al-Islām wa-Mustaqbal al-Bashariyyah* [Islam and the Future of Humanity] (Jerusalem: Maktabat al-Sadaqāt al-Islāmiyyah).
'Abdullah 'Azzām, *Al-Jihād al-Islāmī fī Afghānistān* [The Islamic Jihad in Afghanistan] (Al-Sharikah al-'Arabiyyah al-Markaziyyah—al-Fīdiyū wa-al-Tawzī'), video tape.
'Abdullah 'Azzām, *Al-Jihād wa-Atharuhu fī Binā' al-Jīl al-Rabbānī* [The Jihād and Its Influence on the Building of the Divine Generation], audio tape.
'Abdullah 'Azzām, "Al-Qā'ida al-Sulbah" [The Solid Basis], *Al-Jihād* 41 (1988): 4–6.
'Abdullah 'Azzām, *Al-Tahrīd al-'Ālamī Didd al-Wujūd al-'Arabī wa-al-Shuhadā' al-Thalāthah* [The Universal Incitement against the Arab Presence and the Three Martyrs] (Peshawar: Maktab Khidamāt al-Mujāhidīn, 1989), video tape.
'Abdullah 'Azzām, *Al-Tarbiyah al-Jihādiyyah wa-al-Binā'* [Education for Jihād and Reconstruction] (Peshawar: Maktab Khidamāt al-Mujāhidīn).
'Abdullah 'Azzām, "Aa Hashafan wa-Sū' Kīlah?" [Are There Spoilt Dates and Defect Measurements?], *Al-Jihād* 62 (December 1989): 6–9.
'Abdullah 'Azzām, "'Ashrūna 'Āman 'alā al-Shahādah" [Twenty Years from the Martyrdom], *Al-Jihād* 23 (October 1986): 4–7.
'Abdullah 'Azzām, *Ayāt al-Rahmān fī Jihād al-Afghān* [The Merciful Verses about the Afghans' Jihad] (Amman: Maktabat al-Risālah al-Hadīthah, 1986).
'Abdullah 'Azzām, *Dhikrayāt Falastīn* [Palestine Memories] (Peshawar: Markaz al-Shahīd 'Azzām al-I'lāmī).
'Abdullah 'Azzām, *Fī al-Jihād . . . Fiqh wa-Ijtihād* [In Jihād: Jurisprudence and Intellectual Effort to Infer Law] (Peshawar: Maktab Khidamāt al-Mujāhidīn).
'Abdullah 'Azzām, *Fī Khidamm al-Ma'rakah* [In the Spacious Battlefield] (Peshawar: Maktab Khidamāt al-Mujāhidīn, 1989).
'Abdullah 'Azzām, *Fī al-Ta'ammur al-'Ālamī* [Concerning the Worldwide Conspiracy] (Peshawar: Markaz al-Shahīd 'Azzām al-I'lāmī).
'Abdullah 'Azzām, "Hakadhā 'Allamanī al-Jihād" [This Is What the Jihād Taught Me], *Al-Jihād* 37 (December 1987): 4–6.
'Abdullah 'Azzām, *Hamās—al-Judhūr al-Ta'rīkhiyyah wa-al-Mithāq* [Hamās—The Historical Roots and the Charter] (Peshawar: Maktab Khidamāt al-Mujāhidīn, 1990).
'Abdullah 'Azzām, "Hasabana Allah wa-ni'am al-wakīl" [Enough That the Creator Will Help Us and Grace Us], *Al-Jihād* 61 (November 1989): 6–9.
'Abdullah 'Azzām, "Hatā Lā Tamūtu al-Ummah al-Islāmiyyah Ilā al-Abad" [So That the Islamic Nation Will Never Die], *Al-Jihād* 63 (January 1990): 29.
'Abdullah 'Azzām, *I'lān al-Jihād* [Declaration of Jihād] (Peshawar: Maktab Khadamāt al-Mujāhidīn, 1990).
'Abdullah 'Azzām, *'Ibar wa-Basā'ir lil-Jihād fī al-'Asr al-Hādir* [Lessons and Approaches to the Holy War in the Modern Era] (Amman: Maktabat al-Risālah al-Hadīthah, 1987).
'Abdullah 'Azzām, *'Imlāq al-Fikr al-Islāmī—al-Shahīd Sayyid Qutb* [The Islamic Thinking Giant—The Martyr Sayyid Qutb] (Peshawar: Markaz al-Shahīd 'Azzām al-I'lāmī).
'Abdullah 'Azzām, "Inna al-Hukm Illā li-llah" [The Decision Is for Allah Only], *Al-Jihād* 40 (March 1988): 4–6.
'Abdullah 'Azzām, *Intisār al-Haqq* [The Victory of the Truth] (Peshawar: Maktab Khidamāt al-Mujāhidīn, 1988), video tape.
'Abdullah 'Azzām, "Jā'a al-Haqq wa-Zahaqa al-Bātil" [The Truth Came and the Lie Consumed], *Al-Jihād* 52 (February–March 1989): 4–7.
'Abdullah 'Azzām, *Jihād Sha'b Muslim* [Holy War of a Muslim Nation].
'Abdullah 'Azzām, *Kalimāt min Khatt al-Nār al-Awwal* [Words from the Battle Front Line].
'Abdullah 'Azzām, *Khat al-Tahawwul al-Ta'rīkhī* [The Turning Point of History] (Peshawar: Markaz al-Shahīd 'Azzām al-I'lāmī).
'Abdullah 'Azzām, *Khatar al-Qawmiyya 'alā al-Jihād al-Afghānī* [The Danger of Nationalism vis-à-vis the Afghan Jihād] (Peshawar: Maktab Khidamāt al-Mujāhidīn, 1989), video tape.
'Abdullah 'Azzām, "Li-Ayyam al-Shadā'id" [For the Calamities Days], *Al-Jihād* 28 (March 1987): 4–7.
'Abdullah 'Azzām, *Muqaddimah fī al-Hijra wal-I'dād* [Preface to Migration and Preparation].
'Abdullah 'Azzām, *Sa'ādat al-Bashariyyah* [The Bliss of Humanity] (Peshawar: Markaz al-Shahīd 'Azzām al-I'lāmī).
'Abdullah 'Azzām, *Samām al-Amān* [The Security Valve] (Peshawar: Maktab Khidamāt al-Mujāhidīn, 1989), video tape.
'Abdullah 'Azzām, *Tahqīq al-'Ubūdiyya* [Fulfilling the Servitude] (Kuwait: Home video tape, 1989).

'Abdullah 'Azzām, "Tahtīm al-Quyūd" [Smashing the Cords], *Al-Jihād* 33 (August 1987): 4–9.
'Abdullah 'Azzām, *Tujār al-Hurūb* [Merchants of War].
'Abdullah 'Azzām, "Wa-Allah Ghālib 'alā Amrihi" [Allah Wins], *Al-Jihād* 51 (January–February 1989): 4–7.
Abu Mujāhid, *Al-shahīd 'Abdullah 'Azzām Bayna al-Milād wa-al-Istishhād* [The Martyr 'Abdullah 'Azzām between Birth and Martyrdom] (Peshawar: Markaz al-Shahīd 'Azzām al-I'lāmī).
Abu 'Ubāda al-Ansārī, *Mafhūm al-Hākimiyyah fī fikr al-Shahīd 'Abdullah 'Azzām* [The Term Hākimiyyah as Was Coined by the Martyr 'Abdullah 'Azzām] (Peshawar: Markaz al-Shahīd 'Azzām al-I'lāmi).
Asaf Maliach and Shaul Shay, *From Kabul to Jerusalem—Al-Qa'ida, the Worldwide Islamic Jihād and the Israeli-Palestinian Conflict* (Tel Aviv: Matar Publication, 2009) (Hebrew).
Bashīr Abu Rummān and 'Abdullah al-Sa'īd, *Al-'Ālim wa-al-Mujāhid wa-al-Shahīd al-Shaykh 'Abdullah 'Azzām* [The Scholar, the Holy Warrior, the Sheikh 'Abdullah 'Azzām] (1990).
Chris Horrie and Peter Chippindale, *Islam Mahu?* [What Is Islam?] (Tel Aviv: Ahi-Asaf, 1991).
Hasan al-Bana, *Majmū'at Rasā'il al-Imām al-Shahīd Hasan al-Bana* [The Letters Collection of the Martyr Imam Hasan al-Bana] (Al-Mansura: Dār al-Wafā', 1988).
Husnī Jarār, *Al-Shahīd 'Abdullah 'Azzām—rajul Da'wa wa-madrasat Jihād* [The Martyr 'Abdullah 'Azzām—Propaganda Man and Jihād School] (Amman: Dar al-Diyā', 1990).
Muhammad Na'īm Yāsīn, *Al-Jihād—Mayādīnuhu wa-Asālībuhu* [The Holy War—Its Fields and Its Methods] (Amman: Maktabat al-Aqsā, 1981).
Samuel Huntington, *The Clash of Civilizations and the Remaking of World Order* (Jerusalem: Shalem Publication, 2003).
'Uthmān Raslān, *Al-Tarbiyah al-Siyāsiyyah 'inda Jamā'at "al-Ikhwān al-Muslimūna"* [The Political Education among the "Muslim Brotherhood" Group] (Cairo: Dār al-Nashr wa-al-Tawzī' al-Islāmiyyah, 1989).
"Hiwār ma'a al-Khunasā'—Umm Muhammad" [A Conversation with al-Khunasā'—Umm Muhammad], *Al-Bunyān al-Marsūs* 30 (February 1990): 64–67.
Shahīd al-Ummah al-Islāmiyyah al-Duktūr 'Abdullah 'Azzām [The Martyr of the Islamic Nation the Doctor 'Abdullah 'Azzām] (Peshawar: Maktab Khidamāt al-Mujāhidīn), video tape.

2

The Arab Spring and the Religious Agenda

Jonathan Fine

Introduction

Three years ago, a series of demonstrations, sparked initially in Tunisia and followed by massive protests in Egypt, Yemen, Lybia, Algeria, Bahrain, Syria, Jordan, Kuwait, and Morocco, were coined by western commentators as "The Arab Spring" (*al-rabi'al-arabi* in Arabic).[1] On January 6, 2011, following the protests in Tunisia, Mark Lynch posted in *Foreign Policy* an article entitled "Obama's Arab Spring":

> Noted the spread of seemingly unrelated protests and clashes through a diverse array of Arab states [...] Tunisia, Jordan, Kuwait, Egypt. Last night protests spread to Algeria, partly in response to rising prices on basic food items but more deeply by the same combination of economic desperation, fury over perceived corruption, and blocked political order [...] Are we seeing the beginnings of the Obama administrations equivalent of the 2005 "Arab Spring"?[2]

On June 2, 2011, the German magazine *Der Spiegel* quoted former Egyptian International Atomic Energy Agency director Mohamed ElBaradei as saying: "Perhaps we are currently experiencing the first sign of an Arab Spring."[3] At the time, some scholars described these events as "the Middle Eastern version of the American and French Revolutions," whereas others went so far as to compare them to similar changes that had taken place in Eastern Europe during the disintegration of the USSR in the late 1980s.[4] Some even said that the 1979 Islamic revolution in Iran had been the harbinger of what was to come, for better or for worse.[5]

From an international perspective, these events looked dramatic indeed: the sight of thousands of young Arabs rushing to Tahrir Square in Cairo, while their counterparts in Tunisia, Libya, and Yemen stormed government and military compounds, unafraid of getting shot, was unprecedented in the modern Arab world. They protested against corrupt dictatorships, untenable social–economic conditions, and ongoing abuses of human rights. Many Western scholars pointing to the fact that much of this surprising social–political activity was due to the massive use of social media, as one indicated:

> Given the "youth bulge" in the Middle East—where between 55 and 70 percent of the population of any given country is under the age of thirty—the fact that social media and modern technology have been used to bring political change should come as no surprise [...]. The youth are now being hailed as the "Facebook Generation," the "Internet Generation" and the "miracle Generation" because they have accomplished in less than two months in some places what previous generations had not been able to achieve in over thirty years.[6]

Other Western observers perceived these events as a late stage of the so-called third wave of global democratization that began in April 1974, when a group of young officers led a coup against Portuguese dictator, Marcello Caetano, which resulted in the transformation of Portugal into a democracy.[7] However, despite these positive dramatic events, one should also remember that other political forces are also playing a major role in this unfolding drama, and not all of them strive for a moderate Western democratic model. The most important of these are the radical Muslim groups, both Sunni and Shiite.

The Impact of Religion on Politics as a Global Phenomenon

Since the mid-1970s, we have witnessed a global increase in the impact of religion on politics. This has become very apparent in Judaism, Christianity, and Islam.[8]

Some of those groups espoused violence, such as the "Jewish Underground" in Israel, which planned to blow up the mosques on the Temple Mount in Jerusalem in the early 1980s.[9] The American Christian "Army of God" blew up abortion clinics and murdered gynecologists in the United States as part of their antiabortion campaign during the 1990s,[10] while various Christian identity advocators were branded domestic terrorists, for example, Timothy McVeigh, who blew up the Alfred P. Murrah Federal Building in Oklahoma City in 1995.[11] That being said, there is little room for comparison between these acts, horrible as they may be, and the scope and magnitude of violence carried out by radical fundamental Muslim groups such as al-Qaeda, Hezbollah, Hamas, and al-Shabaab, over the past twenty years.[12] It is also important to note that the religious violent agenda is distinct, in ideologies, strategies, and tactics, from secular political violence.[13]

Since the Enlightenment and the rise of secular ideologies, followed by the American and French revolutions, all of the three monotheistic religions went through crises and internal struggles, both spiritual and violent. Christianity and Judaism paid their toll to these changes over the past three hundred years, and Islam is paying it today.[14]

Since the Islamic revolution in Iran in 1979, and up to the recent events still broiling in the Middle East, radical religious Islamic ideologies and movements have won the hearts of many, and in some cases have been expressed by violence and coercion, as in the case of Iran,[15] or in violent attacks against Western targets, as in the case of al-Qaeda and other organizations. These developments have necessitated changes as well in the field of counterterrorism and the need to deal with phenomena ranging from apocalyptic visions advocating World War III to massive suicide attacks against civilian targets.[16] Although Israel was the first country to deal with this phenomenon in mass, very quickly many other countries found themselves confronting the same problem, as demonstrated in the United States in September 2001, Madrid in March 2004, London in July 2005, Boston in April 2013, and, most recently, the West Gate Mall in Nairobi, Kenya, in October 2013 and Volgograd, Russia, in December 2013.[17]

In order to understand what the Muslim world is going through at present, it might be helpful to take the image of a long train: while the locomotive is trying to dash into the twenty-first century at a speed of 160 miles per hour and is manned by many moderate Arab and Muslim forces who are willing to cooperate with the West and have nothing to do with radical Islam, at the same time, the Caboose is manned by radical Sunni and Shiite leaders who advocate very strong anti-Western policies, and cling to radical Islamic ideologies that are slowing the train down to a speed of seventy miles an hour. The most influential leaders among these were Ayatollah Khomeini in the Shiite case,[18] Sunni intellectuals such as Hassan al-Banna, the founder of the Egyptian Muslim Brotherhood (Al-Ikhwan al-Muslimeen and Sayyid Qutb of the second generation of leadership of the Muslim Brotherhood,[19] followed by Abdullah Yusuf Azam, Osama bin Laden's mentor and the forefather of Global Jihad.[20] More contemporary influential radical Sunni leaders are Sheikh Yussuf Cardawi,[21] Sheikh Mir Hamza, secretary of the Jamiat-ul-Ulema-e-Pakistan, and Sheikh Fazlul Rahman, leader of the Jihad movement in Bangladesh. Hamza and Rahman are also signed on al-Qaeda's famous Fatwa from February 1998 declaring war against the "Crusaders and Jews."[22] Consequently, what we are witnessing today is an internal struggle in the Muslim–Arab world, between more moderate and secular elements and their radical religious counterparts, which has yet to be decided.[23]

Where Is the Arab Spring Heading?

Although it is hard to tell at this point what the Middle East will look like ten years from now, this chapter will try to portray the current situation in the region, emphasizing the major challenges that lie ahead and arguing that the manner in which these challenges will be addressed will determine what the region will look like in the near future. The order of the discussion does not necessarily reflect the chronological sequence of events that led to the Arab Spring. Rather it presents a thematic analysis of the potential dangers that various countries face: those that were effected directly by the Arab Spring or less so, those who either possess or are pursuing to obtain weapons of mass destruction (that in addition of being involved in a deep religious strife), those who are of major importance for the region's future, and so forth.

Pakistan and Afghanistan

The US President Barak Obama's decision to withdraw the International Security Assistance Force from Afghanistan by November 2014 confronts the Afghan people with some very complex challenges in the near future.[24] However, without diminishing the tragedy of Afghanistan, it is the political future of Pakistan that worries the international community even more. Why is that so? Pakistan is a diverse Islamic republic with 180 million inhabitants, which both the Taliban and al-Qaeda have been trying to destabilize from within for years.[25] That in itself might not have drawn much attention, were it not for the fact that Pakistan has an estimated arsenal of about 90–110 nuclear warheads, whereas its major strategic rival, India, has about 280.[26] The combination of an unstable political system, influenced by radical Islamic ideas, and possessing hundreds of nuclear warheads, should put the West and its allies on guard, concerning the possibility of uncontrolled leaks of expertise and materials from Pakistan's nuclear program.[27] For unlike the Cold War era following the Cuban missile crisis in 1962, when all could rest assured that despite global tensions neither the United States or the USSR were inclined to launch a nuclear war, there is no similar guarantee today should several nuclear warheads in Pakistan fall into the wrong hands as the result of internal political strife. For example, as the United States prepared to attack the Afghan Taliban following the events of 9/11, then Pakistani president, Pervez Musharraf, was reported to have ordered the redeployment of Pakistan's nuclear arsenal as uncertainty grew concerning the future of the region, including the direction of US–Pakistan relations, especially in the event that the United States would decide to attack Pakistan's nuclear assets, should Pakistan refuse to assist the United States in its war against the Taliban.[28] Consequently, the same safeguards that applied during the Cold War no longer applied in the case of one global Jihad cell who may try to initiate a limited unconventional attack such as a "dirty bomb" scenario in Western Europe.[29] The same rationale may be applied should Iran get the bomb, or should Hezbollah or pro-al-Qaeda groups among the Syrian opposition (such as the Jabhat al-Nusra get their hands on Bashar al-Assad's conventional and biological weapons stockpiles, which are also equipped with long-range ballistic capabilities.[30]

Finally, the fact that US intelligence was reluctant to cooperate with its Pakistani counterpart, the Inter-Service Intelligence, while planning and executing the targeting of al-Qaeda commander Osama bin Laden on May 2, 2011, at his hideaway one block away from what one can be defined as the "Pakistan Military Academy," reflects the US government and its intelligence community's growing mistrust toward that country's government.[31]

Iran and the Bomb

Why does Iran need the bomb? First of all it needs the bomb as an insurance policy.[32] What does this mean? It is no secret today that the Islamic revolution in Iran has been a socioeconomic failure, and there are growing signs that many young Iranians are very discontented with the Ayatollah's regime and policies as expressed in the failed coup of 2009 in which hundreds of Iranians were killed by the regime.[33] This trend intensified with the cumulative impact of US-led international sanctions, which literally paralyzed the Iranian economy.[34] In order to prevent internal and external pressures, the regime needed an insurance policy, and what better such policy than acquiring military nuclear capability? In this case the Iranians have a good role model: North Korea. Since North Korea obtained military nuclear capabilities and subsequently conducted three nuclear tests between 2006 and 2013, no US president has dared take the risk of deactivating them by initiating a military strike, for the simple reason that North Korea can easily bomb Seoul or Tokyo, and has already threatened to do so during times of crisis with South Korea and the United States.[35] Regardless of the seriousness of those threats, no one is willing to risk the consequences involved in attacking North Korea. If one recalls the recent threats coming out of Pyongyang to nuke the United States, one can understand how dangerous it would be were Iran to attain nuclear weapons, and why Iran looks up to North Korea as a role model.[36] The two maintain close military relations with a special emphasis on the development of nuclear and ballistic missile capabilities.[37]

Of late, in October 2013, Iran agreed to begin negotiations with the United States and the international community. This was the first time the sides had spoken to one another since the 1980 US embassy takeover in Tehran. While the Iranians are determined to ease the West's strangling economic sanctions, they are no less determined to preserve their nuclear military capabilities, and the US-led coalition must insist on first deactivating its military nuclear program. For if Iran should get the bomb, there will be no "spring" in the region for a very long time, due to the fatal combination of radical Shiite Islamic ideology, with unconventional weapons capabilities, which would not only lead to a total change in the region's strategic balance, but also result in an accelerated nuclear arms race. For this reason political pressure to attack Iran's nuclear infrastructure has come not only from Israel, but also from the Sunni Gulf States, led by the Saudis, a fact that led to rumors of possible Saudi–Israeli military cooperation against Iran's nuclear facilities.[38] The recent Saudi refusal to become a member of the UN Security Council was only one of many signs of growing discontent on the part of former Middle Eastern Arab allies of the United States concerning President Obama's appeasement policy toward Iran, followed by the deteriorating image of the United States on both the international and the regional level.[39] However, on November 24, 2013, Iran and the US-led international coalition signed an interim agreement which should lead to a permanent agreement within six months.[40] The agreement has many flaw, and has come under severe criticism, in both the United States and the Middle East, because it does not abolish the Iranian nuclear program, but rather freezes it, while at the same time eases the economic sanctions, which provided the only practical leverage to stop Iran from achieving nuclear military capabilities in the first place.[41]

Egypt

Egypt was and remains the cornerstone of the Arab world, and whatever happens there will eventually spill over to the entire region. Moreover, Egypt's political history is a good example for the entire region, and should give us pause as to the outcome of the Arab Spring: since their advent after World War II, none of the modern Arab States has had what one could define as a Western democratic civil society. Egypt, for example, transitioned in 1952 from monarchy under King Farouk to three successive military dictatorships under Nasser, Sadat, and Hosni Mubarak, respectively.[42] When that political system was abolished following the events of January 2011, it was the Egyptian Muslim Brotherhood led by Mohamed Mursi that took over Egypt in 2012, and not the American and French revolutionary mode of democracy.[43] For those not familiar with the Brotherhood's ideology, it is useful to read a short book entitled *Milestones of the Road*.[44] In this book, written by the second-generation leader of the movement, Sayyid Qutb (1906–1966), the author among other things defines all nondevout Muslims as well as all of Judeo-Christian civilization as a *Jahili* society, meaning "heretic" and "ignorant of the true word of God."[45] It is also important to remember that it was both Qutb in Egypt and the young Khomeini in Iran during the early 1960s, who declared a Jihad to the finish against the West, a step that eventually paved the way for the mode of radical Islamic violence we see today. One cannot understand the contemporary religious mind-set of the Egyptian Muslim Brotherhood (or al-Qaeda and Hamas) without reading

Qutb.[46] His most important follower was Azam (1947–1989), a Palestinian who became Osama bin Laden's ideological mentor during the war against the Soviets in Afghanistan and helped him establish al-Qaeda. In 1984, Azam published two fatwas: In Defense of Muslim Lands and Join the Caravan. These fatwas, on top of Qutb's writings, became the major textual inspiration for the entire global Jihad movement.[47]

After a year in power, Mursi managed to antagonize many Egyptian government officials, from various institutions—civil, judicial, and military—by imposing the Brotherhood's religious ideology through the appointment of Brotherhood members to positions of power. For example, he appointed eight new members to the presidential office, seven new governors, twelve governorate assistants, thirteen governorate councilors, and twelve city mayors. These changes were accompanied by purges in the Egyptian judiciary system, beginning with the dismissal of Public Prosecutor Abdel Meguid Mahmoud, a step that was ruled unconstitutional by the Egyptian court. Furthermore, the president's "power grab" in November 2012 was considered a step that weakened the court system and shielded his decrees from judicial oversight.[48] But his biggest mistake was the way he dealt with the military and security services: it began with the dismissal of former defense secretary, Field General Mohammed Tantawy, a step that resulted in deep mistrust on behalf of the armed forces. It is important to remember that Tantawy and several other high-ranking officers from Egypt's Supreme Council of Armed Forces were those who helped Mursi initially by convincing Mubarak to resign. In addition, the Brotherhood insulted the army several times, replacing secular-oriented officers and members of the Egypt security services with Brotherhood sympathizers. Mursi also led a crackdown against the country's media, from the dismissal of leading editors, through the confiscation of a number of newspapers, through the questioning of 200 journalists by the general prosecutor.[49] The presidential office also filed one hundred suits against media figures and journalists, among them the media personality Bassem Youssef. On the economic front, the Brotherhood failed to improve Egypt's harsh economic conditions, leading to 514 strikes and 558 demonstrations during their short-lived reign, and although Mursi tried to initiate a tax reform last November, this ended in an increase in prices of essential commodities, whereas wages remained lower than ever.[50] As for foreign policy, Mursi's visits to Tehran and Moscow affected the perception of his position on the Syrian crisis, especially in light of the fact that he had come to power following a popular revolution, which had inspired the Syrian people, and now he was talking to those who suppressed them. Furthermore, the fact that leading Muslim Brotherhood clerics were making statements on state affairs gave the impression that they were the real decision makers and not the president. Mursi's attempt to enforce a state of emergency in three cities near the Suez Canal was a failure, placing both his judicial and political authorities into question. His decision to pardon former drug dealers and murderers from Wadi al-Natrun Prison didn't help improve his image in the eyes of the Egyptian public. Finally, his ongoing backlash against leading Egyptian opposition figures such as ElBaradei, Hamdeen Sabahi, and Amr Moussa, resulted in a big decrease in his popularity.[51]

On July 3, 2013, General Abdel Fattah el-Sisi, the commander of the Egyptian army, backed by masses of opposition activists, removed Mursi and the Brotherhood from power.[52] El-Sisi declared the Brotherhood an "illegal organization" and imprisoned many of its key leaders, including Mursi himself, who was recently brought to trial.[53] Although it is still too early to predict what direction Egypt is heading, the recent reshuffling of political power in Egypt constitutes the first successful attempt to halt the takeover by radical Islamic forces of an Arab state in the midst of the ongoing struggle between moderate Muslim and secular pro-Western activists, on the one hand, and radical Muslim forces, on the other. Although many in the West and especially in the United States are very critical of el-Sisi's military takeover, one should be more patient when judging the very complex internal political structure of Egyptian society, and not judge this military coup in the same manner as one would judge such an event in the context of a well-established Western democracy. It is also important to remember that despite its sometimes pragmatic appearance, the Egyptian Muslim Brotherhood has a very clear vision of what Egypt and the entire region should look like in due time under Shari'ah law. Here is Sayyed Qutb's understanding of Shari'ah's role in all walks of modern life: "Shari'ah is not limited to mere legal institutions, but includes the principles of administration, its system and its modes [. . .] By the Shari'ah of God is meant everything legislated by God for ordering man's life, it includes the principles of belief, principles of administration and justice, principles of morality and human relationships, and principles of knowledge."[54] As Egypt is the key country for the region's future, these recent events might encourage other moderate activists who have played an important role in the Arab Spring to take more decisive action against local radical Islamists. However, at the same time it is also important to note that the Middle East is very diverse and heterogeneous, and each county has its own unique social, demographic, and political structure, and therefore each should be approached separately.

The Maghreb and Africa

On December 17, 2010, a series of protests broke out in the Tunisian town of Sidi Bouzid, following the self-immolation of a young Tunisian named Mohamed Bouazizi in front of a local police station; in protest of local corruption and harsh social economic conditions. This act began the tide of protest that swept through the Arab world, and which came to be known as the Arab Spring. The Tunisians called it the "Jasmine Revolution."[55] Following the unrest in Sidi Bouzid, demonstrations spread to the capital, where the protesters called for the resignation of President Zine el-Abedin Ben Ali, who fled the country on January 14, 2011. This was the first time that an Arab dictator was removed from power by a civil revolution and not a military coup d'état. As a result of the subsequent election campaign that began on October 1, 2011, the Islamist party *Ennahda* won 41.47 percent of the votes and therefore secured eighty-nine seats in the 217-member constituent assembly. The new Tunisian government's first session was held on November 22, 2011, thus constituting the first democratically elected government in the Arab World as a result of the Arab Spring.[56]

Since then, the entire Maghreb, as well as parts of sub-Saharan Africa, has been rocked by a series of dramatic violent events: on March 22, 2011, following UN Security Council Resolution 1970, NATO began imposing a no-fly zone and weapons embargo on Libya. The operation was called Operation Unified Protector (OUP) and ended in October with the overthrow of the country's dictator, Muammar al-Gaddafi.[57]

On July 17, 2012, Libyans went to their first elections following the overthrow of Gaddafi: the secular National Forces Alliance, led by ex-interim Prime Minister Mahmoud Jibril, won thirty-nine out of eighty seats reserved for political parties, whereas the Muslim Brotherhood's Justice and Construction Party gained seventeen seats. The two hundred-member General Assembly also includes dozens of independent candidates.[58] Although a big change since Gaddafi's dictatorship, one of Libya's major challenges today is imbedded in its very complex and heterogenic clan structure, which may result in much instability in the future.[59] A good example illustrating this trend is the increasing involvement of pro-al-Qaeda and Global Jihad activists in the country as demonstrated by the recent assassination of US Ambassador J. Christopher Stevens and three members of his staff on September 11, 2012, at the US embassy compound in Benghazi.[60]

The direct outcome of the Arab Spring in the Maghreb was the fact that two new regimes emerged in Tunisia and Libya: one is secular and the other is religious oriented.[61] At the same time, one cannot ignore the growing violence of Global Jihad-affiliated groups in both North and sub-Saharan Africa, such as *AQIM* (al-Qaeda in the Islamic Maghreb, *Boko-Haram* in Nigeria, and *al-Shabaab* in Somalia.[62] Recently, France has been involved in two UN-backed military operations in Africa to halt a radical Islamic takeover: In January 2013 it deployed forces in Mali in order to drive out Islamist groups who were threatening to take over the country, and in December 2013 it deployed forces in the Central African Republic to prevent civil war between Muslim and Christians.[63] All these events indicate that the Maghreb and parts of Africa are still going through very difficult times, in terms of religious strife.

The recent assassination of the secular Tunisian opposition leader Chokri Belaid (head of the Unified Democratic Nationalist Party), a leading defender of human rights and a consistent critic of the ruling Tunisian Islamic Ennahda party, in February 2013 by Islamist activists, should remind us how fragile the situation is.[64]

However, both Algerian and Moroccan security services are waging an ongoing military campaign against radical Islamic groups, and not without success. Nonetheless, Islamist terror activities have slowed down reforms in Morocco, and the Algerian government is also challenged by similar activities on a frequent basis.[65]

Syria

The bloody civil war that has been tearing Syria apart over the past three years is far from over.[66] Aided by Iran and Hezbollah in both Lebanon and Syria, al-Assad's regime is apparently still holding strong and the "Tehran–Damascus–Beirut axis" seems stronger than ever.[67]

As for Syria's future, the country is going through major changes, but it is exactly in such transition phases that the gravest danger lies: if and when President al-Assad is removed, who will take over?[68] Since the Syrian opposition is so heterogenic, it is hard to foresee who will lead it: the more moderate pro-Western factions, who are trying to rebuff the Islamist groups and which both the United States and Europe wish to assist but hesitate in doing so,[69] or the pro-al-Qaeda *Jabhat al-Nusrah li-Ahl al-Sham*, who promise to turn Syria into a Shari'ah state, and at the same time may aim their guns against Israel in the

Golan Heights after al-Assad is gone.[70] From a Western point of view, the question is both morally and practically agonizing: Whom to support? The brutal secular quasi-fascist regime of al-Assad, or the radical al-Qaeda-affiliated Islamic coalition, whose methods of governing as seen in the northeastern Syrian city of Raqqa, can give some idea what Syria might look like under Islamist rule.[71] It therefore seems that the choice is not one of "good or bad," but rather one of the lesser of two evils. In the meantime, on August 21, al-Assad's military forces launched a chemical attack killing 1,400 civilians, many of them women and children, in one of Damascus's crowded neighborhoods.[72] This atrocity was followed by a US threat to attack Syria's chemical stockpiles, which finally led the Syrian government to begin dismantling its chemical arsenal under the supervision of a UN disarmament delegation sponsored by the US and the Russian Federation. To date, about 70 percent of it has been destroyed.[73] Although losing one of its major strategic weapons, al-Assad's regime paradoxically gained more time and breathing space for its ongoing confrontation against the rebels. On November 25, 2013, UN General Secretary Ban Ki-moon announced that an international conference including all rival Syrian factions would convene in Geneva on January 22, 2014. Yet, there are still many obstacles to overcome. Although no one knows how this conflict will end, one thing is for certain: the Levant is undergoing a political transformation that promises a long period of instability and an uncertain future.[74]

In the meantime, Lebanon's fragile sectarian structure is paying a heavy toll, since Iran and Syria involved Hezbollah in the fighting, which in the past year has been spilling over into Lebanon as well, resulting in a high toll in lives and physical destruction.

Yemen

Protests in Yemen began in January 2011, and by the beginning of 2012 it was clear that the old regime led by President Ali Abdullah Saleh was coming to an end.[75] General elections were held on February 21 of that year, and Abd Rabbuh Mansur al-Hadi was sworn in as Yemen's new president on February 25, 2012.[76] But unlike Egypt and Tunisia, Yemen's tribal structure has made its transition to democracy very difficult. Why is this so? The large and strongest Hashid tribal federation is concentrated in the modern northern half of the country, and also makes up the army's officer corps.[77] It was this group that dominated local politics following Yemen's unification under President Saleh during the 1990s.[78] A good illustration of the tribal complexity in the north of the country can be seen in the government's policy of denying the Shiite Bakil tribe of their autonomy. Recently, this has led to bloodshed, with violence breaking out on October 30, 2013 in the town of Damaj over the Sunni religious school there. This resulted in two hundred dead and more than five hundred wounded. The town is located forty kilometers from the Saudi border, and the Shiites are blaming radical Sunni activists, including many foreigners, of continuing the longstanding Sunni aggression toward them.[79]

Although Yemen has gas and oil deposits, 70 percent of its people still make a living from agriculture. Unemployment among university graduates and high levels of illiteracy don't make socioeconomic reforms any easier.[80] Added to this already complex situation are chronic shortages of water and food supplies, not to mention increased inflation, which rose from 5.5 percent in 2011 to nearly 20 percent in late 2012.[81]

Another problem that casts a dark shadow on Yemen's future has to do with the growing presence of al-Qaeda-affiliated groups, who initiate terror attacks in and outside the country. In fact, after Syria, Yemen has become al-Qaeda's most important stronghold.[82] For example, on December 5, 2013, al-Qaeda-affiliated groups attacked Yemen's Ministry of Defense, killing fifty-two people and injuring about 167.[83]

In addition to their desire to overthrow the elected government and replace it with an Islamist one, the ongoing attacks by the Islamist groups have harmed Yemen's economy. In the meantime, the United States has accelerated its unmanned aerial vehicle (UAV) operations; during November and the beginning of December 2013 alone, the United States conducted five UAV attacks, killing twenty-one terrorists, but leaving several government soldiers dead as well.[84]

Another example of the involvement of Yemeni al-Qaeda operatives in Global Jihad operations is found in the following US statistic: today, about 166 of these operatives are detained in Guantanamo Bay. The US concern regarding the Yemeni branch of al-Qaeda grew because the al-Qaeda in the Arabian Peninsula (AQAP) tried to blow up a US airline on its descent to a Detroit airport in 2009.[85] This campaign is thus far from being over, and both the Yemeni and the US governments are concerned about the growing cooperation between Yemeni-based al-Qaeda and its counterparts in the African Horn in general, and the Somalia-based al-Shabaab in particular. This cooperation can harm both commercial and naval traffic in the Red Sea and neighboring African states, such as Kenya and Tanzania.[86]

The Gulf States

Iraq

What role does Iraq play in the Arab Spring? Some scholars, for example, Professor Kanan Makiya of Brandeis University, argue that some of the causes that triggered the Arab Spring were rooted in the US overthrow of Saddam Hussein in 2003.[87] First of all, after 2003, the edifice of the Arab state system began to fall apart elsewhere: In 2005 many Lebanese organized demonstrations against the occupying Syrian army[88]; in 2006 the Palestinians led a democratic election campaign in the West Bank and Gaza[89]; and in the same year the US government put pressure on Egyptian President Hosni Mubarak to initiate some reforms toward the new election campaign in Egypt.[90] Second, the traditional political concepts that dominated the Arab world after the 1967 war, such as Pan-Arabism, anti-imperialism, anti-Zionism, and the armed struggle, made way for self-criticism and a greater focus on internal socioeconomic problems, accompanied by a growing demand for democracy.[91] In the words of Professor Makiya:

> No Arab Spring protester today, however much he or she might identify with the plight of the Palestinians or decry the cruel policies of Israeli occupation in the West Bank as I do, would think today to attribute all the ills of Arab polities to empty abstractions like "imperialism" and "Zionism." They understand in their bones that those phrases were tools of a language designed to prop up nasty regimes and distract people like them from the struggle for a better life. [...] In the place of these illusions, the young revolutionaries made the struggle against their own dictatorships their political priority, just as their Iraqi counterparts had done in vain 20 years earlier after the first Gulf war.[92]

But Iraq today, just like other countries in the region, continues to suffer from severe sectarian divisions. This policy was intensified following the 2003 war, when the United States placed in power the Shiite political class, which still advocates an ideology of victimhood and sectarian politics.[93] Following the complete US evacuation from Iraq in 2011,[94] al-Qaeda has been recuperating from the 2007–2008 surges, and gradually regaining its former capabilities. Since August 2013, the war between al-Qaeda-affiliated Sunni supporters and the Iraqi Shiite community is escalating on a daily basis, and the organization is growing stronger in the Western part of the country.[95] If one adds to this the increasing Iranian involvement in the country since 2003, and the former's ongoing attempts to influence the Iraqi Shiite population, Iraq's political instability is bound to continue.[96]

Bahrain and Saudi Arabia

The preliminary impact of the Arab Spring on the Gulf States was felt in February 2011, when the Shiite minorities in both Bahrain and Saudi Arabia began to demonstrate and demand political reform. The protests in Bahrain came to be known as the "Pearl Revolution" or the "February 14th Revolution."[97] Bahrain has a Shiite majority of between 60 and 70 percent, whereas the ruling family is Sunni. The country has been ruled since 1999 by King Hamad al-Khalifa, who has close ties with Saudi Arabia and the United States, for which his country also serves as a port base (for the United States' Fifth Fleet).[98]

On March 14, 2011, Saudi troops crossed the border between Saudi Arabia and Bahrain, in order to support the ruling Sunni government which declared a state of emergency due to the Shiite uprising.[99] Martial law was declared and about sixty-five people have been killed since the beginning of the unrest.[100] Both Saudi and Bahraini authorities blamed Iran's intelligence agencies and its proxy, Hezbollah, for instigating these demonstrations in order to overthrow their Sunni regimes.[101] But some scholars, such as Toby Matthiesen, argue that the use of sectarian politics against the "Shiite threat" was deliberately exaggerated in order to prevent any internal political reform in the Gulf states.[102] A similar strategy was also used concerning the Egyptian Muslim Brotherhood; with the exception of Qatar, no Gulf state is supporting the Brotherhood or any other Islamist group. In fact, Saudi Arabia, the United Arab Emirates, and Kuwait pledged a sum of $12 billion to aid the new military government headed by General el-Sisi. One of the major motivations behind this policy was to preclude the rise of any political Sunni alternative to their own.[103]

Kuwait

Unlike Bahrain, Kuwait does not suffer from sectarian divisions and has a more stable relationship with Iran. The demonstrations that broke out in 2011 and led to its government's resignation were not about sectarian or socioeconomic issues, but rather about democratic reform.[104] Kuwait also has a relatively functioning parliament, to which its present ruler, Sheikh Sabah al-Ahmad al-Sabah, partly owes his position.[105] However, just like the Saudis, they also support General el-Sisi's takeover in Egypt and oppose the attempts by radical Brotherhood activists to undermine governments in the region.[106] The major problem for the current Kuwaiti government is that the local opposition is made up of not only radical Islamists but also liberals. Therefore, the general assumption that the unrest in the Gulf derives primarily from the Sunni–Shia division or from poverty does not apply in the case of Kuwait.[107]

Qatar

Until the Arab Spring, this small but wealthy kingdom tried its best to maintain good relations with all the countries in the region. As Sheikh Hamad bin Khalifa al-Thani came to power in 1995, he has tried to enhance Qatar's international status in the region by first moving away from its strong neighbor and patron, Saudi Arabia.

Qatar also maintained good relations with Iran due to their shared huge gas fields and, of course, with the United States. As Qatar sees its strategic relations with the United States as vital for its national security, it allows the US navy to use its port as a base for its Fifth Fleet, while the Al Udeid Air Base serves as one of the most important US air bases in the Gulf. To become a more influential regional player, Qatar was also involved in mediating efforts to solve conflicts in Yemen, Sudan, Lebanon, and Palestine. Owning the al-Jazeera satellite TV network has resulted in occasional tensions with its neighbors, due to its unprecedented open political criticism of the Arab world, though generally speaking things have been stable.[108]

During the dramatic events in the region since 2011, Qatar was the only Gulf state to support the pro-Islamist Brotherhood-affiliated groups in general, and in Egypt and Syria in particular. This trend was rooted in Qatar's policy during the 1990s, when it granted asylum to the Brotherhood activists and leaders, among them the Egyptian religious scholar and influential Sunni cleric, Sheikh Yusuf al-Qaradawi, who was expelled by President Mubarak and used the al-Jazeera network to spread the Brotherhood ideology to the Arab world in his weekly program entitled "Shari'ah and Life."[109] When the Arab Spring began, many of the Qatari-based Islamists began playing an important role in Tunisia, Libya, Egypt, Yemen, and Syria, and also in the West Bank and Gaza. Why is this so? Qatar's policy is mainly driven by pragmatism: Emir Thani's major understanding was that Brotherhood-affiliated groups would play a major role in both African and Middle East politics, and that because their radical approach to politics was a direct result of the dictatorships that persecuted them, in time they would become more moderate. At the same time, they supported the Western NATO attack on Libya.[110]

Today it seems that Thani's optimism concerning the influence of Brotherhood-affiliated groups was premature. The events of 9/11, followed by the wars in Afghanistan and Iraq, the recent French operation in Mali, the overthrow of Mursi in Egypt, the deteriorating relations with Iran due to Qatar's support of the Syrian opposition, and the weakening of Hamas in Gaza are by no means an indication that Qatar's pro-Islamist Brotherhood policy has proven beneficial. But as far as stability in the Gulf matters, although not having any internal problematic opposition,as in Bahrain, it is worried about the Gulf's stability; therefore, it cooperates with allies in the Gulf Cooperation Council (GCC) including the Saudis, fearing very much from a growing Iranian intervention in the Gulf and any other potential causes of instability.[111]

At the end of the day, Qatar has to come to terms with its own limitations despite the weakening of major regional actors such as Egypt and Syria, and must think very carefully about the future of the region. While calling for military intervention in Syria in order to remove al-Assad and advocating the support of radical Islamists, it should be wary of colliding with Iran, Syria, Egypt, and the West, a collision it cannot afford.

Turkey

Where is Turkey heading? Turkey is the only Muslim member of NATO and for many years was considered a key factor for regional stability due to its pro-Western policies and strength.[112] But following the rise of the Islamic Justice and Development Party—AKP (*Adalet ve Kalkinma Partisi*) during the past decade, led by Recep Tayyip Erdogan, its government has begun advocating a pro-Islamic ideology similar to that of the Egyptian Muslim Brotherhood.[113] Following the European Union's ongoing refusal to admit Turkey into its ranks after eight years of negotiations, Turkey began changing its foreign policy.[114]

In addition to Erdogan's rhetoric declaring "the comeback of the Ottoman Empire," Turkey decided to forgo its strategic alliance with Israel a long time before the tragic events that took place aboard the Mavi Marmara in May 2010 in order to play a more pro-Hamas and regional leadership role.[115] This trend has been proved recently, following the decision of Turkey's National Intelligence Agency's (MIT) director, Hakan Fidan, to expose an Israeli-sponsored *Mossad* spying network in Iran to the Iranian authorities.[116] Turkey also tries to position itself as a legitimate competitor for regional hegemony, and by doing so, it confronts Iran and Egypt, a step that does not necessarily add to the region's stability.[117] Also, Erdogan's boasting of "Zero problems with neighbors" (*Komshularla Sifir Sorun Politikasi*) has proved unfounded, if one takes into consideration that there is not a neighbor in the region that Turkey does not have problems with today, in addition to Israel.[118] For example, Turkey's deteriorating relations with what it considered not long ago to be her "best friends": Iran and Syria, not to mention older problems such as the Kurds and the Partiya Karkerên Kurdistan, Cyprus, and Greece.[119]

Although it seemed that Erdogan's domestic policies proved to be successful by purging secular factors in the government, military, and security services, in May 2013, a series of demonstrations broke out in the *Taksim* square in Istanbul, following an attempt to uproot old trees at the famous Gezi Park. What began as a local environmental "green" protest turned very quickly into a countrywide anti-government campaign, following the police's attempts to evacuate them from the square on May 31.[120] The demonstrations were led by thousands of students and other representatives of Turkey's vast secular sector against Erdogan's party and policies. The demonstrations ultimately ceased, but this has been the first broad-based popular warning sign for Erdogan since coming to power, from many secular Turks who are accusing his government of becoming increasingly authoritarian and trying to impose conservative Islamic values on a secular society. Similar concern was expressed by both the European Union and the United States following the harsh methods used by the Turkish police while dealing with the demonstrators.[121] The most recent allegations (December 2013) concerning massive corruption among some of Erdogan's ministers and their sons, including Erdogan's son as well, might lead to more serious internal political instability, because now these allegations come not only from Turkey's secular opposition, but also from one of Turkey's most popular Muslim leaders, Fethulla Gelan, who once helped Erdogan reach power, and then became his sworn enemy from his US residence.

Jordan

Unlike most of its neighboring Arab states, which went through a series of harsh political shocks, Jordan has remained relatively stable and peaceful since the beginning of the Arab Spring, and also enjoys close ties with the United States and the United Kingdom.[122] Although the country suffers from chronic socioeconomic problems such as low wages, lack of labor rights, high electricity prices, and scarcity of water, most demonstrations and protests went by without any extraordinary violence. The main demand coming out from the first wave of protests on January 2011 was to amend the constitution made by King Abdullah. This resulted in the establishment of a genuine constitutional court system. However, it did have several flaws: First, the government was able to keep the state security courts intact, arguing that this does not contradict the constitution, and second, civilians may be tried in these courts if they are accused of committing terrorist attacks against the state, smuggling weapons or drugs, or even insulting the King.[123]

Although one should not underestimate Jordan's domestic socioeconomic problems, most of its serious problems have to do with external, first and foremost the Civil War in Syria. Since the beginning of the war, more than 500,000 Syrian refugees (out of an estimated six million dispossessed Syrians) have been concentrated at the Zaatari refugee camp in northern Jordan, equaling 10 percent of Jordan's population.[124] The effect on Jordan of this tragedy is twofold: First, the Syrian refugees create a heavy financial and demographic burden on Jordan's fragile economy, and second, the local Jordanian society is split between the supporters of al-Assad's regime on the one hand and the Muslim Brotherhood supporters on the other.[125] If one adds to this the significant presence of the Brotherhood in Jordan, one cannot rule out the possibility of violence and a threat to the monarchy. The late King Hussein and subsequently his son, King Abdullah, knew how to defuse these pressures by incorporating the Brotherhood members into both parliament and government. However, the recent foiled plan by al-Qaeda to attack government and Western targets in Amman in October 2012 proves that the threat is real.[126]

Because 60 percent of Jordan's population is Palestinian, some of them refugees descending from the 1948 Israeli–Arab war, the Hashemite ruling Bedouin minority is under constant pressure to intervene against Israel on the Palestinians' behalf, emphasizing in particular the issue of West Bank settlements.[127] As long as the Israeli–Palestinian conflict is not resolved, the monarchy will find itself under continuous pressure coming from both sides.[128]

The Israeli–Palestinian Conflict

Although many think that the Palestinians' well-being depends mainly on Israeli polices, it is also important to remember that at the same time they are also an integral part of the Arab–Muslim world, and whatever happens there it influences them as well. For example, the impact of radical Sunni Islam in Palestinian society goes back to the rise of the Egyptian Muslim Brotherhood in 1928, followed by the close links between its founding leader Hassan al-Banna and the Grand Mufti of Jerusalem, Haj Amin al-Husseini, during the British Mandate. Both supported Nazi Germany, hoping that Germany would drive the British out of the region, and also expressed strong anti-Semitic sentiments.[129] This eventually led to al-Banna's decision to begin preparations for a Jihad against the Jews in Palestine in October 1947.[130] Between 1949 and 1967, Palestinians who adhered to the Brotherhood ideology found themselves split geographically between Egyptian rule under Nasser in Gaza, and Jordanian rule under King Hussein in the West Bank. While Nasser advocated a harsh policy of repression against the Brotherhood in Egypt and Gaza, King Hussein incorporated the Brotherhood supporters in the Jordanian establishment, and thus defused their impact on the Kingdom's politics. In any case, during that period Palestinian radical Islamist activity was low.[131]

While all Palestinian groups affiliated with the Palestine Liberation Organization since its establishment in 1964 had been secular oriented, since 1967, the Israeli occupation in both Gaza and the West Bank has brought all Palestinian Brotherhood supporters under one geographic roof. Also, following the 1973 war, we have witnessed a steady increase in the impact of religious ideologies in Palestinian society, due to *dawa* money invested by international Islamic charity organizations in Gaza and in East Jerusalem, coming mainly from Saudi Arabia and Kuwait. This trend also diminished the popularity of Arafat's PLO, which at the time was involved in the Lebanese civil war, giving the impression that he and the Fatah organization were disconnected from the harsh socioeconomic realities in the occupied territories.[132]

Shortly after the Islamic revolution in Iran (1979), one could detect growing support for Iran among many young Palestinian students in the West Bank, simply saying that "where Arafat has failed to deliver the goods, Khomeini might prevail." In 1981 this led to the foundation of the first Palestinian Jihadist terrorist organization—the PIJ, or Palestinian Islamic Jihad.[133] It is also important to note that while the earlier generation of Palestinian Brotherhood activists was influenced by al-Banna's more passive strategies, which focused on charitable and educational missionary activities, the younger generation of the early 1980s was influenced by more militant Jihadist attitudes, such as those advocated by Qutb, Khomeini, and Azam.[134]

Since Israel's evacuation from Gaza in 2005, Hamas has succeeded in pushing the Fatah out, ultimately gaining total control of the Gaza Strip and evoking Shari'ah law since 2007.[135] From an ideological point of view, Hamas adopted much of the Brotherhood's guidelines, including its anti-Semitic views. This can be seen in Article 22 of the Hamas Treaty from August 1988, which literally quotes Nazi propaganda, including quotations from *The Protocols of the Elders of Zion*, with a special emphasis on "the international Jewish conspiracy that wants to dominate the world."[136] Recently, Hamas has gained enormous popularity following the Gilad Shalit deal, when Israel swapped more than 1,000 Hamas and Palestinian Islamic Jihad (PIJ) terrorists from prison for one abducted Israeli Defense Forces (IDF) soldier.[137] However, the military takeover in Egypt, followed by the banishment of the Brotherhood from the government in July 2013, in addition to Iran and Syria's harsh criticism of Hamas's refusal to back al-Assad's regime against the rebels, has brought Hamas to its worst political and economic crisis, losing its most important political and military supporters: the Egyptian Muslim Brotherhood, Syria, and Iran.[138]

In the meantime, US Secretary of State John Kerry has been trying to bridge the gap between the Israeli government and the Palestinian Authority through an intensive shuttle-negotiating process, taking place in Washington, Jerusalem, Ramallah, and Amman. The general idea is to reach an agreement on a two-state solution. While Israel's major concern is focused on security and defense arrangements, with a special emphasis on the Jordan valley, the Palestinians' major concern is focused on the removal of Israeli settlements in the West Bank. In any case, it is still early to speculate if these negotiations will be successful.[139] For the time being, recent hostilities mean that negotiations have failed.

Conclusion

Three years after the beginning of events leading to the Arab Spring, many experts are much more cautious and reserved with regard to the enthusiasm and optimism they had expressed in 2011. Although there is no doubt that the Middle East is going through a very dramatic change, it is still too early to determine whether the outcome of that change is a moderate version of Middle Eastern democracy or a setback to local ethnic-tribal-clan-style conflicts, motivated mainly by a radical religious current.

Adding to this confusion is the fact that the Arab Spring itself is characterized by a paradox: On the one hand, one sees a genuine desire to overthrow corrupted dictatorships and a sincere crave for democracy, such as in the cases of Egypt, Tunisia, Libya, and Yemen; on the other hand, however, some of the forces that are trying to lead that change are not advocating democracy but rather radical Islamist ideologies, such as in the cases of Egypt, Tunisia, and the ongoing division between Hamas in Gaza and the Palestinian Authority in the West Bank. Others are advocating the use of violence and terror, such as in the cases of Syria, Lebanon, Yemen, Libya, and sub-Saharan Africa, driven by al-Qaeda-affiliated groups. Also, religious sectarian divisions will continue to play a major role in countries such as Syria, Lebanon, Iraq, Bahrain, and parts of both northern and sub-Saharan Africa. Consequently, the religious factor will remain an important one, which no side will be able to ignore in any future political arrangement for the region.

On the international level, one should take into consideration the recent US–Russian agreement to rid al-Assad of his chemical arsenal, the upcoming UN-sponsored international conference on the Syrian war, and the recent intensified negotiations with Iran to stop its military nuclear program. As for the Israeli–Palestinian conflict, Secretary of State Kerry is trying to bridge the gap between the Israeli government and the Palestinian Authority, although in all these cases, it is still early to assess the outcome of those negotiations. Also, many pro-US regional allies, such as the Gulf states, Egypt under General el-Sisi, Jordan, and Israel, are worried about the apparent weakening of US global power and the growing potential intervention of the Russian Federation and China.

Notes

1. This was not the first time in modern history that the word "spring" has been used to describe a reformist political uprising. Following the political upheavals that swept Europe during spring 1848, the German term *Volkerfruhling* and the French *Printemps des Peuples* were used to describe the "Spring of Nations," and later, the word was used to name the short-lived "Prague Spring" in Czechoslovakia, led by Alexander Dubcek, until its suppression by the Soviet invasion.
2. Mark Lynch, "Obama's Arab Spring?," *Foreign Policy* (January 6, 2011), http://www.foreignpolicy.com/posts/2011/01/06/obamas_arab_spring.

3. "El Baradei on Democracy's Chances in Egypt," *Der Spiegel* (June 2, 2011), http://www.spiegel.de/international/world/elbaradei-on-democracy-s-chances-in-egypt.
4. Sven Biscop, Rosa Balfour, and Michael Emerson, eds., *An Arab Springboard for EU Foreign Policy* (Brussels: Egmont, The Royal Institute for International Relations, 2012), 5.
5. Raymond Ibrahim, "Parallel Betrayals: Iranian Revolution and the Arab Spring," *Middle East Forum* (June 12, 2012), http://www.meforum.org/3264/iranian-revolution-arab-spring. See also Richard Bulliet, "Aftermath-Iranian Revolution, Arab Spring," *Middle East Online* (February 12, 2012), http://midle-east-online.com/ENGLISH/?id=56941.
6. Natana J. DeLong-Bas, "The New Social Media and the Arab Spring," *Oxford Islamic Studies Online* (June 2011), http://www.oxfordislamicstudies.com/public/focus/essay0611_social_media.html.
7. Council on Foreign Relations, *The New Arab Revolt: What Happened, What It Means, and What Comes Next* (Washington, DC: Council of Foreign Affairs, 2011), 1.
8. Mark Juergensmeyer, *Terror in the Mind of God: The Global Rise of Religious Violence* (Berkeley, Los Angeles, London: University of California Press, 2003), xi.
9. Motti Inbari, *Jewish Fundamentalism and the Temple Mount* [Hebrew] (Jerusalem: Magnes & Eshkolot Series, Hebrew University of Jerusalem, 2008), 68.
10. Juergensmeyer, *Terror in the Mind of God*, 20–22.
11. Charles Selengut, *Sacred Fury: Understanding Religious Violence* (New York: Rowman & Littlefield Publishers, Inc., 2008), 78.
12. Bernard Lewis, *The Crisis of Islam: Holy War and Unholy Terror*, trans. Menashe Arbel (Or Yehuda: Kineret, Zemora Bitan, Dvir Publishers, 2006), 149–73.
13. Jonathan Fine, "Contrasting Secular and Religious Terrorism," *Middle East Quarterly* 15, no. 1 (Winter 2008): 62–67.
14. Hector Avalos, *Fighting Words: The Origins of Religious Violence* (New York: Prometheus, 2005), 111.
15. For example, between 1980 and 1999, Iran carried out 260 terrorist attacks in the international arena. See Shaul Shai, *Terror in the Name of the Imam: Twenty Years of Shiite Terrorism, 1979–1999* [Hebrew] (Herzliya: IDC, Mifalot, 2001), 5–7.
16. Boaz Ganor, *The Counter-Terrorism Puzzle: A Guide for Decision Makers* (New Brunswick and London: Transaction Publishers, 2005), 112–29.
17. Daniel Howden, "Terror in Nairobi: The Full Story Behind al-Shabaab's Mall Attack," *The Guardian* (October 4, 2013), http://www.theguardian.com/world/2013/oct/04/westgate-mall-attacks-kenya. See also "15 Fatalities in a Second Attack in Southern Russia in 2 days" [Hebrew], *Haarez* (December 31, 2013).
18. Martin Zonis and Daniel Blumberg, "Shiisim as Interpreted by Khomeini: An Ideology of Revolutionary Violence," in *Shiisim and Resistance*, ed. Martin Kramer (Boulder, CO: West View Press, 1987), 49–59.
19. For the history of the movement, see Richard P. Mitchel, *The Society of the Muslim Brothers* (New York and Oxford: Oxford University Press, 1993).
20. For Azam's impact and legacy, see Asaf Maliach and Shaul Shai, "The Concept of Jihad and Dawa' in Azam's Thought," in *From Kabul to Jerusalem: Al-Qaeda, the Worldwide Islamic Jihad and the Israeli Palestinian Conflict* [Hebrew] (Tel-Aviv: Matar Publications, 2009), 79–125.
21. Alexander Smoltczyk, "Islam's Spiritual 'Dear Abby': The Voice of Egypt's Brotherhood," *Spiegel Online International* (February 15, 2011), http://www.spiegel.de/international/world/islam-s-spiritual-dear-abby-the-voice-of-egypt-s-muslim-brotherhood-a-745526.html.
22. Rohan Gunaratna, *Inside Al-Qaeda: Global Network of Terror* (New York: Berkeley Books, 2003), 61.
23. Emmanuel Sivan, *The Crash within Islam* [Hebrew] (Tel-Aviv: Am-Oved Publishing, 2005), 18–22. See also Bernard Lewis, *What Went Wrong? Western Impact and Middle Eastern Response* (New York: Oxford University Press, 2002); Bernard Lewis, *The Crisis of Islam: Holy War and Unholy Terror* (New York: Random House Ballantine Publishing, 2003).
24. Sven Minsker, "NATO Parliamentary Assembly: Afghanistan: Towards 2014 and Beyond – General Report" (November 2012), 11–14, www.tbmm.gov.tr/ul_kom/natopa/dosc/raporlar_2012/sa1.pdf. See also Richard W. Weitz, *Dilemmas for US Strategy: Transition in Afghanistan* (2013), 37–8, www.startegicstudiesinstitute.army.mil/pubs/parameters/.../3_weitz.pdf.
25. Syed Manzar Abas Zaidi, "Geographic Trajectories of Al-Qaida and Taliban Groups in Pakistan," *Journal of Strategic Security* 3, no. 1 (March 2010). See also Sayed Salim Shazhad, *Inside Al-Qaeda and the Taliban: Beyond Bin Laden and 9/11* (London: Pluto Press, 2011).
26. Paul K. Kerr and Mary Beth Nikitin, *Pakistan's Nuclear Weapons: Proliferation and Security Issues* (Washington, DC: Congressional Research Service, 2013), 7.
27. Bruno Tertrais, "Pakistan's Nuclear and WMD Programs: Status, Evolution and Risks," *Non-Proliferation Papers* 19 (July 2012), 12.

28. Ibid., 15.
29. Boaz Ganor, "The Feasibility of Post-Modern Terrorism," in *Post Modern Terrorism: Trends, Scenarios and Future Threats*, ed. Boaz Ganor (Herzliya: IDC, Mifalot Projects, 2005), 19.
30. Jill Belamy van Aaist and Oliver Guitta, "Syria's Real Threat: Biological Weapons," *The National Interest* (September 19, 2013), http://nationalinterest.org/commentary/syrias-real-threat-biological-weapons-9093. See also "Design Characteristics of Syria's Ballistic Missiles," *Nuclear Threat Initiative* (September 2013), http://www.nti.org/country-profiles/syria/delivery-systems/.
31. For the targeting of bin Laden, see Chuck Pfarrer, *SEAL Target Geronimo: The Inside Story of the Mission to Kill Osama Bin Laden* (New York: St. Martin's Press, 2011).
32. For the evolution of Iran's nuclear program, see Ephraim Kam, *From Terror to Nuclear Bombs: The Significance of the Iranian Threat* [Hebrew] (Tel Aviv: Tel Aviv University and JCSS, 2004), 176–234.
33. Yahaya R. Kamalipour, *Power and Politics in the Digital Age: The 2009 Presidential Election Uprising Iran* (Lanham, MD: Rowman & Littlefield Publishers, 2010), 3–15. See also "Iran Human Rights Documentation Center: Violent Aftermath: The 2009 Election and Suppression of Dissent in Iran," http://www.iranhrdc.org/english/publications/reports/3161-violent-aftermath-the-2009-election-and-suppression-of-dissent-in-iran.html#.U5OkcnlOU5t
34. "The Lengthening List of Iran Sanctions," *Council on Foreign Relations* (October 2013), http://www.cfr.org/iran/lenghthening-list-iran-sanctions/p20258?cid=ppc-google-iran_.
35. Mary Beth Nikitin, "North Korea's Nuclear Weapons," Congressional Research Service, Report for Congress, April 3, 2013, 13–18.
36. "North Korea Threatens Preemptive Attack on US, South Korea," *Nuclear Threat Initiative* (October 7, 2013), http://www.nti.org/gsn/article/n-korea-threatens-carry-out-preemptive-attack-us-s-korea/.
37. James Martin, "North-Korea-Iran Nuclear Cooperation," Council on Foreign Relations (December 14, 2010), http://www.cfr.org/proliferation/north-korea-iran-nuclear-cooperation/p23625. See also Yonah Jeremy Bob, "The Nuclear Diplomacy of North Korea and Iran," *The Jerusalem Post* (August 19, 2013), http://www.jpost.com/LandedPages/PrintArticle.aspx?id=323609.
38. Kurt Nimo, "Nuclear Agreement May Result in Israel and Saudi Arabia Attacking Iran," *Global Research* (November 24, 2013), http://www.globalresearch.ca/nuclear-agreement-may-result-in-israel-and-saudi-arabia-attacking-iran/5359521. See also Bruce Riedel, "Saudi-Israeli Cooperation Unlikely to Go Beyond Iran," *Al-Monitor* (November 29, 2013), http://www.al-monitor.com/pulse/originals/2013/11/jerusalem-riyadh-axis-not-likely.html#.
39. Robert F. Worth, "Saudi Arabia Rejects U.N. Security Council Seat in Protest Move," *New York Times* (October 18, 2013), http://www.nytimes.com/2013/10/19/world/middleeast/saudi-arabia-rejects-security-council-seat.html?_r=0.
40. For the agreement draft: "Breaking down the Iran Nuclear Deal – 'Joint Plan of Action'" (November 24, 2013), http://edition.cnn.com/2013/11/23/world/meast/iran-nuclear-deal-details/.
41. Ibid., 1–4.
42. Maye Kassem, "Governance from Nasser to Mubarak," in *Egyptian Politics: The Dynamics of Authoritarian Rule* (Boulder, CO and London: Lynne Reiner, 2004), 11–49.
43. Steven A. Cook, *The Struggle for Egypt: From Nasser to Tahrir Square* (New York: Oxford University Press, 2012), 39–64.
44. Sayyid Qutb, *Milestones of the Road* (New Delhi: Islamic Book Service, 2005).
45. Ibid., 96.
46. Zachary Laub, "Egypt's Muslim Brotherhood," Council for Foreign Affairs (November 2013), http://www.cfr.org/egypt/egypts-muslim-brotherhood/p23991.
47. Maliach and Shai, *From Kabul to Jerusalem*, 65–66.
48. "Top Ten Mistakes That Led to Morsi's Ouster," *Al-Arabiya News* (July 2013), http://english.alarabya.net/en/news/middle-east/2013/07/05/top-ten-mistakes-that-le. See also James M. Dorsey, *Facing One's Demons: The Egyptian Military and the Brotherhood at a Crossroads* (The Middle East Institute – National University of Singapore, 2013), http://www.mei.nus.edu.sg/publications/mei-insights/facing-one%e2%80%99s-demo.
49. Ibid.
50. Ibid.
51. Ibid.
52. Jacques Neriah, "Egypt after Mursi: The Defeat of Political Islam?" *Jerusalem Center for Public Affairs* (July 12, 2013), http://jcpa.org/researcher/jacques-neriah/.
53. David D. Kirkpatrick, "Army Ousts Egypt's President; Mursi is Taken into Military Custody," *New York Times* (July 3, 2013), http://www.nytimes.com/2013/07/04/world/middleeast/egypt.html?hp&_r=o&a.

54. Qutb, *Milestones*, 107.
55. "The Spark That Started It All," in *Arab Spring: A Research & Study Guide* (Cornel University), http://guides.library.cornell.edu/content.php?pid=259276&sid=2163144. See also "Tunisia, Birthplace of the Arab Spring, Struggles to Reset its Democracy," *PBS News Hour* (November 25, 2013), http://www.pbs.org/neshour/bb/wor;d/july-dec13/tunisia_11-25.html?print.
56. *Arab Spring: A Research and Study Guide.*
57. "NATO and Libya," NATO website (October 2011), http://www.nato.int/cps/en/natolive/topics_71652.htm.
58. "Libya Election Success for Secularist Jibril's Bloc," *BBC News Africa* (July 18, 2012), http://www.bbc.co.uk/news/world-africa-18880908?print=tru.
59. Martin W. Lewis, "Libya's Tribal Divisions and the Nation-State," *GeoCurrents* (February 27, 2011), http://www.geocurrents.info/geopolitics/libyas-tribal-divisions-and-the-nation-state.
60. David D. Kirkpatrick and Steven Lee Myers, "Libya Attack Brings Challenges for US," *New York Times* (September 2012), http://www.nytimes.com/2012/09/13/world/midddleeast/us-envoy-to-libya-is-reported-.
61. Shafeeq Choucair, "The Arab Maghreb and Current Regional Transformations: Position Paper," *Al-Jazeera Center for Studies* (2013), 6.
62. Abdelkérim Ousman, "The Power of Radical Islamist Ideas in Fragile States in Parts of Sub-Saharan Africa," *OECD Development Cooperation Working Papers* 7 (2012), 5–16.
63. Major General Oliver Tramond and Lt. Col. Philippe Seigneur, "Early Lessons from France's Operation 'Serval' in Mali," *Army* (June 2013), http://www.ausa.org/publications/armymagazine/.../tramond_june2013.pdf. See also Emmanuel Braun, "French Army Battles Militias in Central African Republic's Capital," *Reuters* (December 9, 2013), http://www.news.yahoo.com/french-troops-disarm-fighters-central-african-republic-153629.
64. Monica Marks and Kareem Fahim, "Tunisia Moves to Contain Fallout after Opposition Figure is Assassinated," *New York Times* (February 6, 2013), http://www.nytimes.com/2013/02/07/world/africa/chkri-belaid-tunisian-opposition-fi. See also "Chokri Belaid, 1964–2013: Fierce Opponent of Tunisia's Islamists," *Ahram Online* (February 6, 2013), http://english.ahram.org.eg/NewsContentPrint/2/0/64204/world/0/Chokri-Belaid,--fie.
65. Steven Erlanger and Souad Mekhnnet, "Islamic Radicalism Slows Moroccan Reforms," *New York Times* (August 27, 2009), http://www.nytimes.com/2009/08/27/world/Africa/27morocco.html?_r=0&pagew. See also William Mark Habeeb, "The Maghreb," in idem, *The Middle East in Turmoil: Conflict, Revolution and Change* (Santa Barbara, CA: Greenwood Press, 2012), 143–61.
66. On Bashar al-Assad's regime, see Nicolas Van Dam, *The Struggle for Power in Syria: Politics and Society under Assad and the Ba'th Party* (New York: McMillan, 2011). See also Raymond Hinnebusch, *Syria: Revolution from Above* (London: Routledge, 2004).
67. "Iran and Hezbollah Have Built 50,000 Strong Force to Help Syrian Regime," *The Guardian* (March 13, 2013), http://www.theguardian.com/world/2013/mar/14/iran-hezbollah-force-syrian-regime.
68. Eyal Ziser, *Commanding Syria: Bashar al-Assad and the First Years in Power* (New York: I. B. Tauris, 2006), 77–99.
69. "Syria's Moderate Rebel Groups Launch 'Soft Power' Plan to Beat Islamists," *The Independent* (December 9, 2013), http://www.independent.co.uk/news/world/middle-east/syrias-moderate-rebel-groups-. See also Josh Rogin, "How the USA Lost Its Syrian Allies," *The Daily Beast* (December 8, 2013), http://www.thedailybeast.com/articles/2013/12/08/how-the-usa-lost-its-syrian-allies.ht.
70. "The Al-Nusra Front (Jabhat al-Nusra) – An al-Qaeda Salafist Jihadi Network," The Meir Amit Intelligence and Terrorism Information Center at the Israeli Intelligence & Heritage Commemoration Center, 1–7, http://www.terrorism-info.org.il/en/articleprint.aspx?id=20573.
71. Chris Looney, "Al-Qaeda's Governance Strategy in Raqqa," *Syria Comment* (December 8, 2013), http://www.joshualandis.com.blog.
72. Reihan Salam, "Brief Note on the Use of Chemical Weapons in Syria," *National Review Online* (December 9, 2013), http://www.nationalreview.com/node/365885/print.
73. "Syria Chemical Weapons Agreement Reached between United States, Russia," *CBS/AP* (September 14, 2013), http://www.cbsnews.com/news/syria-chemical-weapons-agreement-reached-between-. See also "Syrian Chemical Weapons Facilities Destroyed," *Al-Jazeera* (November 1, 2013), http://www.aljazeera.com/news/middleeast/2013/10/syria-chemical-weapons-facilities.
74. "Geneva Conference on Syria Set for January, UN Chief Announces," *UN News Center* (November 25, 2013), http://www.un.org/apps/news/printnews.asp?nid=46575.
75. On the evolution of modern Yemen, see Paul Dresch, *A History of Modern Yemen* (Cambridge: Cambridge University Press, 2000), 89–108.

76. "Yemen's Elections: One Vote, One Man," *The Economist* (February 25, 2012), http://www.economist.com/node/21548292.
77. Stephen W. Day, *Nationalism and Rebellion in Yemen: A Troubled National Union* (New York: Cambridge University Press, 2012), 60–71.
78. "The Yemeni Revolution: Historical Background, Local Specificity and Future Prospects" (February 26, 2012), http://english.dohainstitute.org/palbum/9bdfed97-9a4e-4f5e-a6b8-ba4da6940ef1.
79. James Dunnigan, "Yemen: Al-Qaeda Desperate to Stop American UAV's," *Strategy Page* (December 28, 2013), http://www.strategypage.com/dls/articles/Al-Qaeda-Desperate-To-Stop-American-UAVs-12-28-2013.asp.
80. Ibid., 79.
81. Ibid., 79.
82. Gregory D. Johnsen, *The Last Refuge: Yemen, Al-Qaeda, and the Battle for Arabia* (US: Oneworld Publications, 2013), 19–35.
83. "Al-Qaida Linked Group Claims Responsibility for Yemen Ministry Attack," *The Jerusalem Post* (December 6, 2013), http://www.jpost.com/landedpages/printarticle.aspx?id=334188.
84. Ibid., 79.
85. Neil MacFarquhar, "Yemen Making Strides in Transition to Democracy after Arab Spring," *New York Times* (May 25, 2013), http://www.nytimes.com/2013/05/26/world/asia/yemen-makes-strides-in-transition-to.
86. Christopher Anzalone, "Dangerous Liaison? Relations between Al-Shabaab and Al Qaeda," *Open Security* (August 13, 2011), http://www.opendemocracy.net. See also "Al-Qaeda Weapons Reaching al-Shabaab," *IPT* (August 3, 2011).
87. Kanan Makiya, "The Arab Spring Started in Iraq," *New York Times* (April 6, 2013), http://www.nytimes.com/2013/04/07/opinion/sunday/the-arab-spring-started-in-iraq.ht.
88. Neil MacFarquhar, "Huge Demonstrations in Lebanon Demands End of Syrian Control," *New York Times* (March 15, 2005), http://www.nytimes.com/2005/03/15/international/middleeast/15lebanon.html?_r=0.
89. Scott Wilson, "Hamas Sweeps Palestinian Election, Complicating Peace Efforts in Mideast," *The Washington Post* (January 27, 2006), http://www.washingtonpost.com/wp-dyn/content/article/2006/01/26/ar20060126003.
90. Lisa Blaydes, *Elections and Distributive Politics in Mubarak's Egypt* (Cambridge: Cambridge University Press, 2011), 192–210.
91. Ibid., 87. Makiya, "The Arab Spring Started in Iraq."
92. Ibid.
93. Kenneth Katzman, "The Persian Gulf States: Post-War Issues for U.S. Policy, 2003," Congressional Research Service (July 14, 2003), 17–18. Order Code: RL31533.
94. On the impact of the US evacuation from Iraq, see Kenneth M. Polack and Irena L. Sargsyan, "The Other Side of the COIN: Perils of Premature Evacuation from Iraq," *The Washington Quarterly* 33, no. 2 (2010): 17–32.
95. Jessica D. Lewis, *Al-Qaeda in Iraq Resurgent* (Washington, DC: Institute for the Study of War, 2013). See also Daniel L. Byman, "The Resurgence of Al-Qaeda in Iraq. Testimony," *Brooking Institute Website* (December 12, 2013), http://www.brookings.edu/research/testimomy/2013/12/12-resurgence-al-qaeda-iraq-b.
96. Lionel Beehner and Greg Bruno, "Iran's Involvement in Iraq," *Council on Foreign Relations* (March 3, 2008), 2–6. See also Geoffrey Kemp, *Iran and Iraq: The Shia Connection, and the Nuclear Factor* (United States Institute of Peace, November 2005), 1–2.
97. "Arab Spring: A Research Guide & Study Guide: Bahrain," http://www.guides.library.cornell.edu/content.php?pid=259276&sid=2163172.
98. Ian Black, "Bahrain: A Special Case among the Arab Spring Uprisings," *The Guardian* (June 19, 2012), http://www.theguardian.com/world/2012/jun/19/bahrain-special-case-arab-spring.
99. James Kirkup, "Saudi Troops Sent to Crush Bahrain Protesters 'Had British Training.'" *The Telegraph* (May 25, 2011), http://www.telegraph.co.uk/news/worldnews/middleeast/saudiarabia/8536037/saudi-t.
100. Ibid., 98. I. Black, *The Guardian*.
101. Kevin Downs, "A Theoretical Analysis of the Saudi-Iranian Rivalry in Bahrain," *Journal of Politics & International Studies* 8 (Winter 2012/2013): 203–6. See also "Bahrain Hints at Iranian Role over Country's Shia Uprising," *The Guardian* (March 21, 2011), http://www.theguardian.com/world/2011/mar/21/bahrain-iran-role-uprising-shia.
102. Toby Matthiesen, *Sectarian Gulf: Bahrain, Saudi Arabia, and the Arab Spring That Wasn't* (Redwood City, CA: Stanford University Press, 2013).

103. Toby Matthiesen, "The Sectarian Gulf vs. the Arab Spring," *The Middle East Channel* (October 8, 2013), http://www.mideastforeignpolicy.com/posts/2013/10/08/the_sectarian_gulf_vs_the-arab_s.
104. David Hearst, "Kuwait's Protests Remind Us of the Arab Spring's True Spirit," *The Guardian* (November 2, 2012), http://www.theguardian.com/commentisefree/2012/nov/02/kuwait-protests-arab-spring.
105. For the internal politics in Kuwait, see Abdulkarim al-Dekhayel, *Kuwait: Oil, State and Political Legitimation* (New York: Ithaca Press, 2000).
106. Ibid., 87. Makiya.
107. Doug Bandow, "The Arab Spring Comes to Kuwait: Will Democracy Arrive and Liberty Thrive?" *Forbes* (December 10, 2012), http://www.forbes.com/sites/dougbandow/2012/12/10/the-arab-spring-comes-to-kuwait-will-democracy-arrive-and-liberty-thrive/.
108. Guido Stenberg, "Qatar and the Arab Spring – Support for Islamists and New Anti-Syrian Policy," *German Institute for International and Security Affairs* (February 2012), 1–3.
109. Ibid., 4.
110. Ibid.
111. Ibid., 6.
112. For the evolution of Turkey's foreign policy, see F. Stephen Larrabee and Ian Lesser, *Turkish Foreign Policy in an Age of Uncertainty* (Santa Monica, CA: RAND Cooperation, 2003).
113. Ehud Toledano, "The AKP's New Turkey," Hudson Institute website (April 22, 2011), 1, http://www.currenttrends.org/research/detail/the-akps-new-turkey.
114. Vincent L. Morelli, "European Union Enlargement: A Status Report on Turkey's Accession Negotiations," Congressional Research Service, August 5, 2013, RS22517, www.fas.org/sgp/crs/row/rs22517.pdf.
115. Hay Eytan Cohen Yanarocak, "Israel: A Micro-Component of a Turkish Macro-Foreign Policy, *Tel Aviv Notes: An Update on Middle Eastern Developments* 7, no. 20 (October 27, 2013).
116. Yossi Melman, "Analysis: Turkey's Unprecedented Act of Betrayal against Israel," *The Jerusalem Post* (October 17, 2013). See also David Ingnatius, *The Washington Post* (October 16, 2013).
117. Zvi Barel, "Turkey's Greatest Threat: Its Own Foreign Policy," *Haaretz* (October 1, 2013), http://www.haaretz.com/misc/article-print-page/.premium-1.549756?trailingPath=2.1.
118. Toledano, "AKP," 6.
119. Gonul Tol, "Erdogan's Syria Frustrations," *Foreign Policy* (October 2, 2013), http://www.mideastafrica.foreignpolicy.com/posts/2013/09/26/erdogan_s_syria_frustrations.
120. "Police Clear Istanbul's Gezi Park after Erdogan Warning," *BBC News, Europe* (June 16, 2013), http://www.bbc.co.uk/news/world-22922697?print=true.
121. Ibid.
122. Hayley Slier, "Jordan Living under Shadow of Potential Arab Spring," *Channel News Asia* (November 4, 2013), http://www.channelnewsasia.com/news/world/jordan-living-under/873598.html.
123. Jonathan Schinberg, "Enough Compromise: Jordanians Are Tired of Being the Good Kids on the Block," *Foreign Policy* (August 20, 2013), http://www.foreignpolicy.com/articles/2013/08/14/jordan_s_simmering_spring.
124. Ibid.
125. Mohamed Olwan and Ahmad Shiyab, *Forced Immigration of Syrians to Jordan: An Exploratory Study* (MPC—Migration Policy Center, June 2012), 1–5.
126. Joby Warrick and Taylor Luck, "Jordan Disrupts Major Al-Qaeda Terrorist Plot," *The Washington Post* (October 21, 2012), http://www.articles.washintonpost.com/2012-10-21/world/35501513_1_terrorist-plot-jorda.
127. Robert Satloff and David Schenker, "Political Instability in Jordan," Council on Foreign Relations, Contingency Planning Memorandum No. 19 (May 2013), http://www.cfr.org/jordan/political-instability-jordan/p30698.
128. See Luisa Gandolfo, *Palestinians in Jordan: The Politics of Identity* (New York: I. B. Taurus, 2012).
129. Matthias Kuntzel, *Jew and Jihad – Hatred, Islamism, Nazism and the Roots of 9/11* [Hebrew] trans. Zur Erlich (Jerusalem: Tobi Publishers, 2006), 27–65.
130. Mitchel, *The Society of the Muslim Brothers*, 55–56.
131. Yifrach Zilberman, "The Evolution of Radical Islam in the Territories Since 1967," in *The Palestinian National Movement: From Confrontation to Reconciliation?* [Hebrew], ed. Moshe Maoz and B. Z. Keidar (Tel Aviv: Ministry of Defense, 1997), 321–22.
132. Ibid., 325–26.
133. Ibid., 326–27.
134. Ibid., 328–29.
135. Shaul Mishal and Avrahan Sela, *The Hamas Wind – Violence and Coexistence* [Hebrew] (Tel Aviv: Yediot Achronot, 2007), i–xv.

136. "The Covenant of the Islamic Resistance Movement, August 18, 1988," Yale Law School: Lillian Goldman Law Library: The Avalon Project – Documents in Law, History and Diplomacy, Article 22, http://avalon.law.yale.edu/20th'_century/hamas.asp.
137. "Gilad Schalit Prisoner Swap Deal Reached," *The Guardian* (October 11, 2013), http://www.theguardian.com/world/2011/oct/11/gilad-shalit-prisoner-swap-deal. See also Gershon Baskin, *The Negotiator: Freeing Gilad Schalit from Hamas* (Jerusalem: Toby Press, 2013).
138. Ehud Yaari, "Hamas in Crisis: Isolation and Internal Strife," *The Washington Institute for Near East Policy* (July 30, 2013), http://www.washingtoninstitute.org/policy-analysis/view/hamas-in-crisis-isolation-an.
139. Karen De Young and William Booth, "Kerry Works to Keep Israeli-Palestinian Peace Talks on Track," *The Washington Post* (November 6, 2013), http://www.washingtonpost.com/world/middle_east/kerry-tries-to-steady-wavering-israeli-palestinian-peace-talks/2013/11/06/650fdc52-46ea-11e3-b6f8-3782ff-6cb769_story.html.

3

Sikhism, the Seduction of Modernism, and the Question of Violence*

Nicholas F. Gier

*In the beginning was the Word, and the Word was with the
Guru, and the Guru was God.*
—Adapted from Singh Sabhā theology[1]

The strains of martial music [of the dhādhī jathās*] would be
the last thing one would expect to hear [from] a quietistic
teacher who preached a doctrine of liberation based upon
nām simran, meditation on the* nām *of Akal Purakh.*
—Louis E. French, *Martyrdom in the Sikh Tradition*[2]

*When all efforts to restore peace prove useless and no
words avail, lawful is the flash of steel, it is right to draw
the sword.*
—Guru Gobind Singh, *Zafarnāma*

*One can only say "my religion" . . . in a
Christian-European manner, through a process of
"conversion to modernity."*
—Arvind-Pal S. Mandair, *Religion and the Specter of West*

At first glance Sikhism appears to join the Abrahamic religions in having a record of religiously motivated violence. In previous work I have proposed that a number of theological doctrines might be responsible for violence in Judaism, Christianity, and Islam, and, while it appears that Sikhism might conform to several if not all of these beliefs, an in-depth analysis proves this to be mistaken. This means that Sikhism joins its South Asia counterparts—except for Hindu, Muslim, and Buddhist fundamentalists—in producing very little religiously motivated violence.

In the first section I lay out the evidence that suggests that the Sikhs have committed religiously motivated violence. In the second section I discuss the Abrahamic focus on the divine Word, which in the form of explicit declarations and commands (e.g., kill all the infidels, wipe out the Midianites) have led to violence committed in the name of God. We shall see that, even after colonial influences encouraged Sikhs to separate from Hindus and view their scriptures more like the Bible, very little religiously motivated violence was the result. Abrahamic religions are primarily religions of obedience to creeds, whereas the Asian religions are either religions of *gnosis* (Jainism and some schools of Buddhism and Hinduism) or religions of *praxis* (Sikhism, Confucianism, Daoism, and Zen). Even among modern Sikh fundamentalists the emphasis is much more on right conduct and emulating the deeds of the Gurus than on conforming to a set of theological doctrines.

The topic of the third section is the general Abrahamic demand for the purity of revelation and a firm rejection of religious syncretism. Here again we will see the precolonial Sikhs participated in Hindu rituals (even animal sacrifices to Durgā) and the scripture Guru Granth Sahib contains hymns and poetry from non-Sikhs. We shall see that the Sikhs actually claimed to be Hindus until the British offered them a modern idea of religion that allowed them to draw clean and sometimes antagonizing distinctions between themselves and their Hindu and Muslim neighbors. The precolonial situation is aptly described by Louis French: "It is now well known that it was only after the 1870 that the boundaries of categories such as 'Hindu,' 'Muslim,' and 'Sikh' were established."[3] For the many Sikhs this unfortunately led to a religious nationalism that included beliefs in one place (*gurdwaras* whitewashed of previous Hindu influence), one people (Sikhs living in a Punjabi-speaking state), one pure scripture (the *Ādi Granth* but not the syncretistic *Dasam Granth*), and one immutable, transcendent God (purged of pantheistic implications). These beliefs were bound to produce some religiously motivated violence.

In the fourth section I will discuss how divine transcendence in the Abrahamic religions may have desacralized the world to the point where any activity could be permitted—even the liquation of enemies or natives whose land and resources were much desired. Once again we will find that the Sikhs have a strong belief in divine immanence, which is characteristic of the Asian religions in general. I propose that the relative transcendence found in panentheism is the best way to solve the problems related to a wholly other God.

In the fifth and final section I will argue that what fundamentalist tendencies the Sikhs have developed are primarily due to their attempts to conform to colonialist and thoroughly modernist conceptions of self, religion, and nationhood. Instead of the Derridean interpretative framework that Arvind-Pal Mandair proposes, I prefer the constructive postmodernism of the process theologians. I also suggest that the "deep" religious pluralism that these thinkers have developed is an option that many Sikhs would find attractive as a religious minority in a Hindu majority nation. Swami Vivekananda described this position beautifully: "The Christian is not to become a Hindu or a Buddhist, nor a Hindu or a Buddhist to become a Christian. But each must assimilate the spirit of the others and yet preserve his individuality and grow according to his own law of growth."[4]

Recent Sikh Militants versus the Non-Violent Akali Dal

Sikh militants of the 1980s and 1990s declared that their organizations were a "righteous force," and that they had had just as much right as Pakistanis and Bangladeshis to use violence to establish a separate state of Khalistan—literally the "Land of the Pure." Sikh militants claimed the authority of their first Guru Nānak, who, perhaps, in comparison with Muslim martyrs, promised that "fighting for the right cause . . . [leads] straight to liberation."[5] The Sikh daily prayer contains blessings for all people but it ends with "May the Khālsā rule!" The Khālsā was established by Guru Gobind Singh in 1699 for the purpose of centralizing his authority in a paramilitary organization loyal to him, and it became the main vehicle for Sikh nationalism. Gurinder Singh Mann describes Gobind Singh's poets as "reciting the name of Vahiguru [=God] while preparing for a holy war."[6]

The *Bachitar Natak* of the *Dasam Granth* begins with what appears to be an identification of the Creator and the Sword: "Thee I invoke, All-conquering Sword, Destroyer of evil, Ornament of the brave. Powerful your arm and radiant your glory, your splendor as dazzling as the brightness of the sun. . . . Hail to the world's Creator and Sustainer, my invincible Protector the Sword."[7] The implication seems clear: it is God's powerful arm that holds the "All-conquering Sword." (One is reminded of the Angel of the Lord [1 Chron. 21:16; Num. 22:23] with a drawn sword leading the Israelite armies.) When the British defeated the Sikh army and annexed Panjab, Lord Dalhousie wrote to the directors of the East India Company about the disposition of some weapons belonging to the deposed Maharaja Ranjit Singh. He argued that as the weapons were "sacred and warlike symbols of a warlike faith,"[8] and as it was known that Ranjit Singh did *puja* before the "Raikot" sword every morning, it was essential that they be kept from the Sikhs. Just as the so-called Emerald Buddha was the symbol of the Thai king's right to rule, so, too, did these sacred objects represent the sovereignty of the Sikh nation. Removing them from the Maharaja's possession amounted to a "symbolic disarming and unmanning" of the militant Sikhs. The weapons were not returned until 1966 when the Panjab was recognized as one of the "linguistic" twenty-four Indian states. The weapons went on a tour of the entire province, marking out the boundaries of what many Sikhs celebrated as the sovereign state of Khalistan.

The government of Indira Gandhi may have regretted the reappearance of these sacred relics. In the late 1970s and 1980s, the Congress Party saw trouble on two fronts—the rise of Hindu nationalism and the demands of the Akālī Dal, a nonviolent Sikh political party that was insisting on more political autonomy in the Punjab. Congress decided to support Sikh extremists in the same way that the Central Intelligence Agency and Israel financed the militant Hamas against the Palestine Liberation Organization (PLO). The main difference, of course, from the PLO was that the Akālī Dal had no history of violence. Many in Congress portrayed all Sikhs as terrorists just as the Bharatiya Janata Party and far too many Americans and Europeans condemn all Muslims. Initially, Congress supported Sikh militant Jarnail Singh Bhindranwale, but he quickly realized that he was being used. Eventually Bhindranwale became the main target for the Indian military's attack on the Golden Temple in 1984. As Mandair explains, "Through the neat conflation of the image of Bhindranwale as the arch-'Sikh terrorist' with the 'Punjab problem' within India, the Sikh community as a whole came to be perceived as the 'enemy within.'"[9]

The battle for Khalistan involved targeted assassinations by Sikh militants. The government of Indira Gandhi was legitimately concerned, but in desperation she committed one of the greatest blunders of her already controversial career: on the night of June 5, 1984, she ordered the storming of the Harmandir Sahib, more widely known as the Golden

Temple in Amritsar. Incredibly enough, the commanding general chose Baisakhi, the holy day when the Sikhs celebrate the founding of the Khālsā. In addition to hundreds of heavily armed militants inside, there were thousands of pilgrims in and around the temple complex. Also incredible was the fact that tanks and artillery were used by the Indian army in a "shock and awe" attack. Government accounts of civilian deaths were in the hundreds but thousands were most likely killed. A sacred library containing manuscripts with the Gurus' signatures was also destroyed.

After the assassination of Indira Gandhi by her Sikh bodyguards later that month, an estimated 5,000 Sikhs lost their lives in pogroms across the country, mostly in New Delhi, where two hundred gurudwaras were also burned down. Nine commissions were set up to bring the perpetrators to justice, but there was no action until 2005, when Prime Minister Manmohan Singh, himself a Sikh, declared, "On behalf of our government, on behalf of the entire people of this country, I bow my head in shame that such a thing took place . . . I have no hesitation in apologizing to the Sikh community." A large majority of Sikhs do not support militant action, and they are frustrated and embarrassed by Sikh extremists, many with much foreign support, who still try to stir up trouble.

Sikh militants declared that Indira Gandhi's murder was declared a "holy act" and the execution of her two killers elevated them to martyr status. The Sikhs have a long tradition of honoring Guru Arjan, Guru Tegh Bahadur, and many others who were tortured and executed by post-Akbar Mughal emperors. The following is a decree by Emperor Bahadur Shah: "The disciples of Nānak [they are not yet called Sikhs] are to be slaughtered in every place that they are found."[10] A Sikh head was worth twenty-five rupees and the reward for a live Sikh was four times as much. Contemporary Sikhs will argue that the violence that they have committed is justified self-defense in the face of oppression by the Mughals, the Afghans, the British, and the Indian government. The Golden Temple was destroyed twice before the 1984 attack—by Mughal armies in 1736 and the Afghans in 1757 both during Baisakhi—so it is easy to sympathize with this claim.

Louis French states that "tradition maintains that Sikhs must always be defenders, not aggressors," and that a just war (*dharam yudh*) must be one that "is fought while keeping the principles of *dharma* foremost [in one's mind and heart]. A war in which deception, betrayal and falsehoods are not used; a war fought in order to protect the principles of *dharam*."[11] Some of the battles that were fought to consolidate Ranjit Singh's empire were not described as *dharma yudh*, which, as French surmises, "clearly suggests" that this was a "war of expansion" not defense.[12] Nevertheless, Sikh armies and later militants never attacked Hindu temples or Muslim mosques. Religious motivations for violence are sometimes very difficult to ascertain, but the destruction of holy sites, relics, and books are the best evidence that we have. The victims of these attacks certainly perceive them as such.

The Word of God: Abrahamic *Gnosis* and Sikh *Praxis*

Abrahamic patriarchs and prophets claimed to have had direct communication with God and they exhorted their followers to obey divine commands. By contrast Asian devotees rarely spoke about what God actually *said* for us to do. Guru Nānak claimed to have been lifted up into the presence of God and, following the Hindu tradition of an *avatāra*, God commanded him to return to the world to save humankind for the evils of the Kali Age. While taking his morning bath in Sultanpur, Nānak disappeared in the waters of the Vein River. After three days and nights he returned, and his first words were "there is neither Hindu nor Muslim."[13] (This most definitely did not mean that there were only Sikhs, because that religious identity did not exist until colonial times.) While in the God's presence, Guru Nānak drank the waters of immortality (*amṛta*) and then was told to return to the earth to preach a nonsectarian message. Much like the Hebrew prophets, Nānak said that he was unworthy and that he preferred to stay prostrated at the feet of God. Reluctantly he finally agreed to undertake the divine commission.

Mohammed called the Abrahamic faiths "Religions of the Book," and it is here that we can find a clue for our inquiry. Jews, Christians, and Moslems all claim to have received a linguistic revelation, that is, direct words of God. Moses claimed to have talked to God "as a friend," and the angel Gabriel's first ironic command to the illiterate Mohammed was "Read!" As we shall see, the Guru's Word was originally and primarily esthetic and nondiscursive, and not very conducive to systematic theology let alone divine directive.

The first epigraph above is derived from Mandair's exposition of the Sikh concept of *śabda-guru* as "the Guru exists *as* Word, that the Guru *is* Word, and that the Guru is revealed by the Word."[14] (In my own Christian adaptation above the imputation of divinity to both the Word and the Guru is correct.) Mandair submits that the Sikh reformists (the modernizing Singh Sabhā) "transcendentalized" *śabda-guru* "for the purpose of removing any traces of 'Hindu signification,'"[15] so that Sikhism could become an autonomous religion and have a proper theology in the eyes of British authorities.

The premodern Sikh idea of the divine Word, however, is very different from the Christian Logos, which was a Hellenistic concept of divine reason operating in the cosmos. Significantly enough, this is what *śabda-guru* becomes for Singh Sabhā theologians such as Jodh Singh, who rejects the *avatāra* theory of the Gurus and concomitantly rejects the Hindu idea of guru. As Mandair explains, Nānak is now a prophet, "God's personal messenger," who made a clean break with Hinduism, "to whom God spoke and revealed his Word" and "the path of True Religion."[16] Although it is difficult for them to do so, Sikh modernizers also wanted to distance themselves from the Vedic principle of sacred sound. In what appears to be an allusion to Christian theology, Jodh Singh believes that the Divine Word "mediates knowledge of God to man,"[17] and only the Punjabi language can carry this sacred communication. Mandair demonstrates that a modernist separation of distinct religions also led to the assumption that speaking Hindi, Urdu, or Punjabi went hand in hand with identifying oneself as Hindu, Muslim, or Sikh.

Most of the text of the *Guru Granth*—the last Guru embodied in words of the Sikh scripture the *Ādi Granth*—is poetry set to the musical meters of the Indian raga. Just like the Hindu *Vedas*, the Sikh scripture contains divine sounds created to evoke harmonious human emotions. They are not propositions by which one can produce a systematic theology and therefore lay out doctrines that devotees cognize as truths. Mandair argues that the key themes of the *Ādi Granth* "do not obey any theological or transcendental structure"[18]; rather, the musical structure is designed to lead to a mystical union with God as immanent in humans and nature. The typical Hindu worshipper does not understand the Sanskrit their priests recite, just as most Catholics do not understand the words of the Latin Mass. It is a performative experience but not a cognitive one in which a creed is cited and presumably affirmed. However, one could argue that the recitation of the Nicene

Creed is for many Christians an empty ritual not tied to either doctrine or a tradition of sacred sound. Mandair warns us not to assume that the esthetic component of the *Ādi Granth* is simply a supplementary ornament to scripture; rather, it is the very essence of the Gurus' experience of God.

As Luther and the Protestant Reformers did, the Sikh gurus wrote in the vernacular Sant Bhasa, a poetic language used in the fifteenth and sixteenth centuries. Most Sikhs can therefore understand Sant Bhasa and can read it in the Gurmukhi script of modern Punjabi. Sikhism joins Buddhism in its initial use of the Pāli, which established a clean break with the Vedic principle of sacred sound embodied solely in Sanskrit. Early Buddhist philosophy was sophisticated enough to propose a linguistic nominalism in which words were simply names given to things—including the human self—that were transient elements of human experience. As far as I know, no Sikh thinker expressed himself in this way, and Mandair is confident that the Gurus did not subscribe to a theology of sacred sound based on precise pronunciation of a sacred Punjabi language.

In any case modernizing colonial influences did not turn the *Guru Granth* into a set of propositions to be manipulated by fundamentalist theologians. South Asian *dharmas* are rarely ever connected to divine will and commands in the propositional form. The *Ādi Guru Granth* does not contain a single divine declaration or command; rather, the text is primarily praise for God in poetic hymns. It is mostly first person Guru sayings rather than divine speech. (In fact, Mandair makes the provocative claims that it is the Guru talking to himself; more on this later.) Furthermore, in most instances it is misleading to translate the Punjabi word *hakum* as divine "will"; it is more accurately rendered as cosmic order. W. H. M. McLeod, who labored with great frustration (and with incredible presumption) to write a systematic Sikh theology, states, "Here, in the divine Order (*kukam*), is the inscription of His will for all who are able to read it," but Mandair notes that he was never able to explain how an ineffable formless deity (*nirguṇa*) could be experienced except as a mystical union with an immanent divine (*saguṇa*). As opposed to the Abrahamic religions in which scripture contains the distinct divine sayings and commands, the Sikhs are unable to join this tradition with a doctrine of divine communication. McLeod concludes that Sikh theologians are never able to "give a satisfactory, coherent answer to the question of how . . . God communicates with man. The question has been allowed to remain a mystery."[19] This imponderable may well be viewed as a great advantage, because some many religious fundamentalists are very confident about what God has said to them and sometimes commanded them to do (see Cole, 274).[20]

This means that Sikhism primarily has a doctrine of general providence rather than the special providence we find in the Abrahamic religions. The Sikh deity is impartial, not showing favor to one people or the other. None of the Gurus claimed that the Sikhs have a special dispensation from God. Owen Cole points out that Guru Amar Das never encouraged petitionary prayer, and certainly not a prayer that would request divine guidance in war.[21] Much like the Stoic deity, the Sikh God works his will in the world without words and without partiality.

Abrahamic Revelational Purity versus Sikh Religious Syncretism

Religions of the Book have been more concerned with maintaining the purity of divine revelation. Even though the integrity of the Abrahamic faiths has been compromised by religious syncretism and cultural accretions, most of their followers find it very difficult to believe that their faiths have been adulterated in such a manner. Mandair phrases the inevitability of syncretism succinctly: "Cocontamination is the original condition of all cultures."[22] In Asia religious syncretism has been not only accepted, but in some cases celebrated. For example, the Rev. Sunyung Moon claims to be a good Buddhist, a Confucian, a Korean shaman as well as a good Presbyterian. Here and elsewhere in Asia there has been no fetish about revelational purity. This may be a key to widespread religious tolerance in Asia and less religiously motivated violence than in the Middle East and Europe.

With the compilation of *Ādi Granth* in 1604 and coming to its final form in 1706, one could say that Sikhism had become a Religion of the Book. One arguing for a connection between religion and violence could point to the apparent correlation between this written scripture, the martyrdom of Gurus Arjan and Tegh Bahadur, and Sikhs arming themselves to battle the Mughals. No distinct Sikh religious identity, however, grew up around *Ādi Granth*; and, as we shall see, the Mughal persecution was not religiously motivated. The followers of Guru Nānak continued to act as if they were just another expression of the South Asian *sanātana dharma*, from which later Singh Sabhā theologians wished to separate. Even in the nineteenth century those attending the Golden Temple in Amritsar believed that they, surrounded by walls depicting Hindu mythology, were tapping into the Eternal Sound of the Vedic tradition by reciting the hymns of the *Ādi Granth* and *Dasam Granth*, the latter filled with praise of the Hindu Goddess.

While on tour of South Asia, Guru Nānak traveled with a Muslim musician and there was never a time when the Guru required that he "convert." Eleanor Nesbitt relates that "a Muslim saint Mian Mir laid the foundation stone of the Harmandir Sahib."[23] The Mughal Emperor Jahangir (1605–1627) ordered the Fifth Guru Arjan's arrest not because he was a Sikh, but because he was supporting Jahangir's rival Khusrau. Muslim and Hindu rebels were arrested and executed for the same reason, not only by Jahangir but throughout the Mughal period.

It is significant that Jahangir did not order the persecution of Guru's followers, whom he considered to be Hindus. As Louis French points out, Jahangir was on good terms with the Hindu majority and that Guru Hargobind, even in the wake of Arjan's death, was able to establish a friendship with the emperor.[24] When Hargobind found it necessary to go to war with Jahangir, he still built a mosque for his Muslim friends in Kiratpur, making clear that his enemy was not the religion of Islam. When Gobind Singh went to war with the Mughals, five hundred Muslim soldiers joined his army, but he then turned around and sent his troops to the Deccan to aid the Mughal armies there.[25]

Up until the time of Emperor Aurangzeb (1658–1707), conflict in the empire was not primarily the result of religious differences. Contemporary Sikhs might argue that the Mughal authorities required that their coreligionists become Muslims, but Louis French argues that conversion "would have obviated the execution[s] seems highly implausible. From the perspective of the Mughal authorities, Sikhs in this period were rebels, bandits, and thieves.... The defiance of imperial authority, whether from a Muslim, Hindu, or Sikh ... was thus mercilessly crushed. This was politics pure and simple."[26]

The *Dasam Granth*, written by Guru Gobind Singh, explains, with the assumption that the Sikhs are included, that someone is Hindu and someone a Muslim, . . . , but all the human beings . . . are recognized as one and the same. . . . Thus worship the one Lord, who is the common enlightener of all; all have been created in His Image and amongst all comprehend the same one light. The temple and the mosque are the same, there is no difference between a Hindu worship and Muslim prayer.[27]

The *Ādi Granth* contains songs of divine praise from both Hindu and Muslim authors. Hindus consider Sikhism just another legitimate *sampradaya*, that is, one of many guru-led movements that have arisen in South Asia, and there is no reason to believe that Guru Nānak did not see himself in this light.

Nānak's successor Guru Angad (1539–1552) declared that Nānak's path was just one among many, and his daughter was not required to give up her "Sikh" faith when she married a Muslim?[28] Guru Tegh Bahadur (1664–1675) claimed to have died "for the protection of the sacred thread and the frontal mark" of the Hindu princes imprisoned with him.[29] A nineteenth-century text contains a declaration by Tegh Bahadur that "ours is the Hindu faith."[30] The tenth Guru Gobind Singh (1675–1708) held that all religions are united in a quest for truth and that, as we have seen above, the mosque and the temple are equally holy. During the lifetime of Ratan Singh Bhangu (d. 1846), the Sikhs were still considered Hindus, and they started calling themselves Sikhs only under colonial rule later in the century. It is ironic that the British recognized Sikhism as a separate religion before the Sikhs themselves did.

Hindus worshipped at the Golden Temple during the reign of Ranjit Singh and its walls are covered with frescos depicting Hindu mythology. In the twentieth century Sikhs associated with the Golden Temple were criticized by Sikh fundamentalists in Lahore for their syncretistic ways. They are called Sanātan Sikhs, those who followed *sanatana dharma*, the South Asian universal religion that makes no distinctions among Buddhists, Jains, Hindus, and Sikhs. This ideology of dharmic hegemony still leads many in South Asia to declare that "Everyone is a Hindu."

Until 1930 Mahatma Gandhi embraced *sanātana dharma* and he defined it as the religion that "transcends Hinduism, Islam, and Christianity, etc. It does not supersede them. It harmonizes them and gives them reality."[31] After 1930 Gandhi assumed a position more in line with Swami Vivekananda, who, while assuming fluid boundaries among them, acknowledged that no religion should be merged with the other. The Swami explains, "The Christian is not to become a Hindu or a Buddhist, nor a Hindu or a Buddhist to become a Christian. But each must assimilate the spirit of the others and yet preserve his individuality and grow according to his own law of growth."[32] I would hope that contemporary Sikhs would find this model of religious pluralism helpful in defending their distinctive religious identity and at the same time encourage them not to follow the exclusivism of their militant brothers and sisters.

Sanātan Sikhs were particularly attracted to Viṣṇu and his avatars, and the fact that there are the same number of avatars as gurus may not be just coincidental. The Sikh gurus came to save humankind from the extreme depredations of the *kaliyuga* just as Kalki, the tenth incarnation of Viṣṇu, is predicted to do so. Kalki is mounted on a white horse brandishing a sword, the weapon of choice for Sikh warriors and an honorific for God himself. As the Guru Gobind Singh states in his *Akāl Ustat*, "May we have the protection of All-Steel; may we have protection of All-Death."[33] The *Dasam Granth*—scripture held by some as equal to the *Ādi Granth*—calls Goddess "Durgā" and he sacrificed buffaloes—just as

Hindus do at Dasain—to her. He also worshipped the goddess Chandī, so the divine title of "All-Death" may be derived from this Kali-like goddess of death. (A word search of an online *Dasam Granth* listed 309 references to the goddess—most often Durgā and Chandī—and many times in acts of violence.) The *Dasam Granth* came under attack because of its references to the goddess and Hindu mythology. (Parts of it, however, are still part of the morning prayers of all good Sikhs.) It is significant that in the early twentieth century, Vir Singh, who founded the Khalsā Text Society and was a member of the modernizing Singh Sabhā, edited out references to goddess worship in Ratan Singh Bhangu's 1841 epic *Gur-panth Prakāś*.[34] For him and his colleagues the Sikh religion was unique and Guru Nānak's revelation was pure and superior to all others.

It is correct that Guru Nānak criticized Hindus, but not because their tradition was wrong; rather that they did not have the correct view of the *Vedas*. As he clearly states, "In the Vedas, the ultimate objective is the Nām, the Name of the Lord, but they do not hear this, and they wander around like demons." Nānak is placing himself within the *sanātana dharma* not outside of it. It is roughly similar to Christians saying that the Jews do not recognize all the alleged prophecies of the coming of Christ in the Hebrew scriptures. Guru Amar Das found that chanting the name Rāma did not bring union with God, but he still continued to use Rāma as the name of God.[35] The discrepancy here may be due to the fact that Nānak called on his disciples to reject Hindu rituals but did not expect for them to leave the Vedic tradition. By contrast modernizing Sikhs wished to have a complete break from Hinduism, a schism that would make Nānak's revelation pure and distinct and have a "real" religion worthy in the eyes of the British and historians of religion.

Abrahamic Divine Transcendence versus Sikh Immanence

Except for their minority mystical traditions, the Abrahamic religions have viewed God as a transcendent "Other," whereas Asian divinities have generally been viewed as immanent in each person and the world. The authors of *The Reenchantment of Science* have argued that the modern distinction between religion and science arose because of the concept of a transcendent deity. The neo-Platonic idea of the Great Chain of Being was very prominent in the early Renaissance, and Catholic theologians countered its paganism and pantheism by emphasizing the transcendence of God. The result was an unspoken truce between church authorities and the early scientists in which divine and worldly realms were separated and safeguarded by each side. The authors argue that both religion and science would have been much better off if they had agreed to share a resacralized world in which a "reenchanted" science would be more open to the paranormal and Christian theologians would reconceptualize the divine immanence in their own tradition. The authors submit that a constructive postmodern process philosophy best serves this goal.

Many have joined these authors in arguing that a transcendent deity makes way for secularism and a desacralized world that can be exploited for its natural resources. (If the earth is a goddess, how could you possibly agree to breaking open her body?) The American Puritan fathers, who accepted John Calvin's principle of the radical separation of God and the world, considered the wild tracts of their adopted country Satan's domain and the native inhabitants as cursed by God and less than human. Clearing the wilderness of trees, game, and Indians was therefore viewed as a divine mandate. As Carol Behrman states, "Clearing that wilderness, colonialists felt, meant clearing it of Indians as well."[36]

Not only did this theology make nature an alien other, but it also arguably led to human alienation in the modern world. Process theologian Catherine Keller argues that "the atomic ego is created in the image of the separate God."[37] (I believe that Democritean atomism must also have played a role in the rise of the modern autonomous self—one that is self-legislating in Kantian morality and libertarian political philosophy.) In Western philosophy and theology the ideal self is modeled on the concept of God as a self-contained, self-sufficient being of pure thought. If God is viewed as wholly other, then it may be easier for atomistic selves to see each other in the same way. Racism, intolerance, and violence may be the result. As Christopher Chapple observes, "When the other stands opposed to self, violence can proceed. When other is seen as self, nonviolence can prevail."[38]

As we turn back to Sikhism, it is significant to note that the modernizing Singh Sabhā theologians argued that God as a pure being must be fully actualized, much like Thomas Aquinas's God of pure act devoid of potentiality. For Christians who read their Bibles and discover a God who relates to his creatures on an intimate basis, this abstract philosophical theology makes relations between God and the world highly problematic. When M. A. Macauliffe maintained that no Sikh guru "has succeeded in logically dissociating theism from pantheism," he should have included his own faith as well. To make sense of the human religious experience one should not separate the two but combine them. The only theology that has arguably made divine transcendence and immanence intelligible is the panentheism of Alfred North Whitehead and Charles Hartshorne.

Without addressing this problem and unconsciously following Aristotle and Aquinas, Vir Singh proposed that God as *nirguṇa*—a no-thinged-ness that is potentially all things—had to be fully actualized. As a defensive move against Christian objections, the Sikh God could have no deficiencies. Mandair uses a passage from a commentary on early Christianity to demonstrate how far Sikh modernizers went in the direction of "extreme transcendence," a state in which there could be no residue of worldly things or sensation. This wholly other God cannot have anything other than its own thought as an object of knowledge. Mandair must know that it was Aristotle who first argued that the eternal form "can be presented only by thinking in and through form itself."[39] As I always joked with my ancient philosophy students, this is pure "*nous* nousing *nous*."

Mandair states that this radically transcendent deity—absolutely different from anything in the world and beyond time and space—was the price the Sikhs had to pay to join the elite club of the monotheistic religions. In order to meet Ernest Trumpp's charge that the Sikhs did not have "a sufficiently exalted idea of God," the Singh Sabhā had to prove a clean break with Hindu pantheism, which Christian theologians believed dissolved both divinity and human individuals into nothingness—the reason for which Meister Eckhart and other Christian mystics were condemned.

Many Sikhs fiercely objected to Trumpp's preface to his translation (the first) of the *Ādi Granth*. Trumpp rejected the description of Sikhism as a "moralizing deism" as inaccurate because ethics requires a robust concept of the self that Sikh pantheism could not support. Sikh scripture, he claimed, had no "leading principle"; it was "a mere promiscuous heap of verses"; and it was an "exceedingly incoherent and wearisome book."[40] (I wonder what Trumpp thought about making his way through some of the books of the Hebrew Bible?) He further offended many Sikhs in placing them further down the religious hierarchy—below Hindu pantheism and just above atheistic and "nihilistic"

Buddhism. Trumpp's outrage made modernizing Sikhs even more determined to conform to the Christian model of systematic theology.

Budding Sikh "theologians" were encouraged by the 1909 publication of M. A. Macauliffe's six-volume work *The Sikh Religion*, in which the author praised Sikhism as the Indian religion that, despite Nānak's inability to logically distinguish pantheism from monotheism, had made the most progress toward religion's "monotheistic consummation."[41] Mandair demonstrates, however, that even Macauliffe imposed an English model of translation and meaning on a Punjabi text that he and others could not trust the Sikhs to understand properly. This colonial subjugation parallels the creation of Hindi from the amorphous Hindustani of Northern India, whose native speakers were judged by British linguists as totally unreliable collaborators. Such examples totally destroy the notion that Euro-Americans in all walks of life are capable of mutual dialog with their foreign counterparts.

Mandair devotes numerous pages to an analysis of Vir Singh's gallant attempts to give the *mul mantar*, the first twelve words of the *Ādi Granth*, a monotheistic interpretation. The Sanātan Sikhs had always read these words from the standpoint of Vedāntist philosophy. The esthetic form of scripture does not easily lend itself to clear interpretation, but I side with the traditional Sikhs on this issue. I have neither inclination nor linguistic skill to offer my own interpretation, but passage after passage clearly indicates a God of immanence not radical transcendence.

Satinām, the third word of the *mul mantar*, may be interpreted as "Truth is the Name of God," where *nām* is not just a name as in the Latin *nomen* and theological nominalism; rather, *nām*, and therefore Truth, is the very essence and substance of deity. One, of course, is reminded of Gandhi's declaration that "Truth is God" and that a virtue ethics of living right and truthfully fits not only Gandhi but also the Sikh Gurus. Mandair, however, sees a disturbing trend in contemporary Sikhism in which "locking the discourse of ethics into a belief system" has prevented "individual Sikhs from adequately responding to the complex variety of ethical questions now being raised." I have argued that Gandhi's ethics of nonviolence is best interpreted as a virtue ethics and that this moral theory actually offers much more flexibility in moral action and judgment than generally believed.[42] I also agree with B. K. Matilal, "By the term *dharma* . . . I understand nothing short of moral virtue,"[43] and I have expanded on this proposition in other work.[44]

Mandair offers his own interpretation of how the Sikh Gurus dealt with the divine nature and its relation to human individuals. He begins with the provocative but persuasive thesis that Nānak's hymns are basically a dialogue with himself, what today's therapists refer to as analyzing one's "self-talk." Mandair explains, "Nānak almost always speaks to *his own mind*, addressing it at times through tender love, as when he says 'my beloved mind,' at times by cajoling it, as in 'my foolish mind,' and at other times beseeching it as a lover beseeches her beloved not to leave her."[45] When Nānak overcomes his foolish ego mind, he experiences God as an ineffable formlessness (*nirguṇa*), but simultaneously—because he is always embodied and in the world—as an immanent divine with qualities (*saguṇa*). That means that *nām*, as Mandair contends, is the proper name for God as both *nirguṇa-sarguṇa* in which the devotee experiences the "meeting of time and eternity, the absolute and finite."[46] *Nām* also provides the link between self and others, and chanting *nām simaraṇ* not only brings the person in union with the divine but allows love to be experienced between people. Meditating on *nām simaraṇ* is, as Mandair proposes, is a "concrete sacrificial practice" that sacralizes time and space.

What I call a both-and/synthetic dialectic is not unique to either Asia or Europe. Heraclitus set the conceptual stage with epigrams such as "the way up and the way down are one and the same," and his concept of *logos* as the guiding principle for reconciling opposites in the world. Most Christian theologians have followed an either/or dialectic drawn from formal logic, but Nicholas of Cusa's dialectical method of *coincidentia oppositorum* is the only way to make sense of the claim that Jesus Christ is *both* fully human *and* fully God. The Christian doctrine of liberty, as phrased by the evangelical J. I. Packer, is that "man is *both* free *and* controlled."[47] Luther expressed the Protestant doctrine of justification as *simul iustus et peccator* (simultaneously justified and sinful), and with his concept of "the masks of God" he revived the Hebrew concept of deity as both God and Satan (divine wrath). Most Christians are not aware of the verse from the Second Isaiah where Yahweh declares that "I form the light, and create darkness: I make peace, and create evil: I the Lord do all these things" (45:7).

In his exposition of Sikh theology, Mandair maintains that the Sikh Gurus also rejected "either/or oppositions" such as "good/evil."[48] Please note that, as far as I know, the Gurus' deity never speaks in Yahweh's direct manner of self-revelation—a fact that supports Mandair's theory of Guru-self-talk. Note also that, although called a creator, the Gurus' deity is not described as "doing all things" or as an omnipotent coercive power. The Sikhs have an immanental doctrine of creation (creation out of *nirguṇa*) similar to neo-Platonism rather than a transcendent God who, avoiding the heresy of pantheism, does not create out of himself, but as Aquinas explains, creates matter that is a mixture of being and nonbeing.

The other significant comparison that comes to mind is the dialectical coincidence of *nirvana* and *saṃsara* in Mahayāna Buddhism. Just as liberation for the Sikh Gurus is not a complete annihilation of the self, so, too, is *nirvana* not a total dissolution into the Dharmakāya. In the famous Ox-Herding story, it is significant that the story does not end with the eighth image "Ox and Self Transcended"; rather, the boy returns in the ninth image as a tiny figure in a sublime nature "seeing mountains as mountains for the first time," and then in the tenth image the boy is back in society in dialogue with an iterant monk/sage. One can also imagine Guru Nānak coming back from his divine encounter first to nature and then back to his fellow humans. The simultaneity of *nirguṇa/saguṇa*, as Mandair states, is "evident in the lives of the Sikh Gurus, for whom there was no contradiction between mystical experience and the life of a soldier, householder, or political leader."[49] Although there is no mention of Buddhism in the Sikh scripture, it is no exaggeration to say that the Sikh Gurus were Punjabi Bodhisattvas.

Mandair describes the Gurus' experience as a Zen-like "spontaneity of speech-thought-action," which is also expressed as a "wonder at the nature of existence," and a concept of natural (rather than supranatural) grace. Mandair phrases nature's grace beautifully: "Just as all creation simply happens without asking why, so the unspoken Word arises without connection to intention, desire, or will."[50] As in the Ox-Herding story, there is "no annihilation of the ego" and no "struggle against the world but a struggle to exist within the world." Rather than a Derridean "erasure" of the self, which still suggests dissolution, I would rather see this as a discovery of the social–relational self that one finds in the Buddha, Confucius, Heidegger, Merleau-Ponty, and Buber. When Mandair speaks of love appearing in the relation between the self and others, I think of Buber's *I and Thou* and his brilliant suggestion that God is that which happens in between—the deity as *Mitmenschlichkeit*. Is this what Mandair means in this rather cryptic statement: "[For Sikhism] monotheism in a strict sense becomes almost redundant in the movement and crossings of love." When Mandair suggests that Guru Nānak wanted his "beloved mind back," this must be a shared experience with others and the *nirguṇa/saguṇa*. Gandhi's village republic and Martin Luther King's "beloved community" also come to mind.

Rather than a deconstruction of the self, I propose what Buber has done is a constructive postmodern revival of a relational, social self. (The adjectives are not redundant because the Daoist sage's self is relational but antisocial.) When Mandair states that Guru Nānak "at once refines and negates the monotheistic concept of self/God as a relationship of inside and outside,"[51] I would reverse the order of this process by negating the self-contained God first and then reconstructing (or refining) a concept of deity that does justice to our experience, just as the Sikhs Gurus did in their own time. (Just as the isolated self is an abstraction, so is a radically transcendent deity; and I include in this category the isolated *puruṣas* of the Sāṃkya-Yoga tradition.) In other words, instead of the "death of God" of Mark Taylor's theology of Derridean deconstruction, one should instead think of a constructive postmodern retrieval of the sacred. Just as the relational self replaces the deconstructed autonomous self, the Gurus' God—aptly reconstructed by Mandair himself—replaces the self-contained isolated deity of Christian orthodoxy. Between radical transcendence, where God and the world never meet, and total immanence, where the world, God, and selves dissolve into one another, we can embrace the relative transcendence/immanence of panentheism. I like the Mandair's characterization of Sikh theology as "posttheistic," but I would affirm this in Whiteheadian rather than Derridean terms.

Sikh Fundamentalism: From Premodernism to Modernist Nationalism

The premodern vision of the world is one of totality, unity, and, above all, purpose. These values were celebrated in ritual and myth, the effect of which was to sacralize the cycles of seasons and the generations of animal and human procreation. Sikh scholar Harjot Oberoi refers to the cosmos of the Sanātan Sikhs as "enchanted,"[52] and it is significant that constructive postmodern philosophers call for the "reenchantment" of science. The human self is an integral part of the sacred whole, which is greater than and more valuable than its parts. And, as Mircea Eliade has shown in *Cosmos and History*, premodern people sought to escape the meaningless momentariness of history (Eliade called it the "terror of history") by immersing themselves in an Eternal Now. Myth and ritual facilitated the painful passage through personal and social crises, rationalized death and violence, and controlled the power of sexuality. One could say that contemporary humankind is left to cope with their crises with far less successful therapies or helpful institutions.

Following Descartes' insistence on a method of reducing to simples and focusing on clear and distinct ideas, modern humans have made great strides conceptually and theoretically. The practical application of modernism has extended the rule of science and conceptual analysis to all areas of life: personal machines of all sorts, a fully mechanized industry, and centralized bureaucratic administration. Modern philosophy generally separates the outer from the inner, the subject and the object, fact from value, the *is* from the *ought*, science from faith, politics from religion, the public from the private, and theory from practice. With regard to India specifically European Orientalists, as Michael Hawley explains, "reflected the binaries of stagnation/progress, superstitious/rational, barbaric/civilized, child/parent, disloyal/loyal, cowardly/brave, and lazy/industrious, just to name a few." The modern mind loves to dichotomize.

With regard to separating the inner and the outer, let us look again at Mandair's insight just above that Guru Nānak "at once refines and negates the monotheistic concept of self/God as a relationship of inside and outside." The transcendent God of Christian orthodoxy is totally outside the world, but the relative transcendence of panentheism brings God and the world back together. Process theologians, the primary proponents of constructive postmodernism, see the relationship of God and the world as analogous to the embodied self, which transcends the body in every conscious thought but is fully immanent in it at the same time. I do not think it would be inaccurate to say, especially as Mandair's exposition is very similar, that this is the Sikh view as well.

Constructive postmodernists wish to reestablish the premodern harmony of humans, society, and God without losing the integrity of the individual, the possibility of meaning, an affirmation of history, and the intrinsic value of nature. They believe that French deconstructionists are throwing out the proverbial baby with the bath water. The latter wish to reject not only the modern worldview but any worldview whatsoever. Constructive postmodernists want to preserve the concept of worldview and propose to reconstruct one that avoids the liabilities of both premodernism and modernism.

Constructive postmodernists would be very comfortable with Graham Parkes' interpretation of Nietzsche's Three Metamorphoses—a section of *Thus Spake Zarathustra*—as representing immersion, detachment, and reintegration. They could take the camel stage as symbolizing the premodern self-immersed in its society; the modern lion as protesting the oppressive elements of premodernism but offering nothing constructive or meaningful in return; and the child as representing the reintegrative task of constructive postmodernism. As Parkes explains, "The third stage involves a reappropriation of the appropriate elements of the tradition that has been rejected. . . . The creativity symbolized by the child does not issue in a creation *ex nihilo*, but rather in a reconstruction or reconstrual of selected elements from the tradition into something uniquely original."[53] It must be stressed that Parkes is attributing this view to Nietzsche, who is generally taken to be the nineteenth century's leading prophet of deconstructive postmodernism.

Mandair warns us that some attempts at reappropriating the past can lead to a false premodernism, which is only the illusion of recapturing a lost paradise. Following the lead of Orientalists who proposed that there was once a Golden Age of Hinduism that had been lost by a gradual devolution to the current state of Hindu deprivation, contemporary Sikhs are trying to recreate the Golden Age of Nānak and the Gurus. In what might be called a "reverse" Orientalism, many Hindu scholars in the last century have claimed that Sanskrit is not only the original Aryan language but also the only language that contains the eternal sounds of God. The orthodox *brahmins* were shocked to see the *Vedas* printed in English translation and European scholars presuming to understand them as a text read by private readers. Europeans did, however, agree with the *brahmins* that orality was indeed superior to textuality. (Socrates was a long forgotten advocate of this view.) Brahmanical orthodoxy not only reasserted the traditional priority of *śruti* (that which is heard) over *smṛti* (that which is remembered) but also rejected both Christian and Sikh textual authority. Mandair contends that in reaction against two violent textual religions (first Islam and then Christianity), Hindus orthodoxy assumed that "orality is synonymous with nativeness, ahistoricality, pacifism, and plurality, whereas textuality is foreign, violent, bringing with it a linear history of decline and the construction of boundaries."[54]

The contemporary Sikh response to this slight (one among many of course) is fascinating. Drawing on its own rich oral tradition and the power of modern technology, Sikhs around the world can tune their computers to "24/7" recitations of the Gurus' Word, which conjures up a grand the illusion that they are original sacred sounds. Enforcing this deceit is the Internet's ability to erase the sense time, space, and culture by simultaneous communication. Dedicated satellite TV stations allow millions of Sikhs to watch dozens of simultaneous complete readings of *Ādi Granth* (called the *akaṇḍ pāth*) at the Golden Temple. Mandair argues successfully that all of these Indian attempts at Reverse Orientalism are aping the false univeralism of a European idea of religion, reinforcing distinct religious identities that foster intolerance and violence.

Just as the modern media has facilitated the rise of Hindu, Buddhist, and Tamil fundamentalism and its attendant violence, the same technology certainly reinforces Sikh nationalism and sectarianism. Mandair points out that the idea of a Sikh Golden Age has yet another danger: "Sikh subjectivity or repetition will already have been defined in terms of quietist detachment from worldly politics through constant remembrance of the Name (*nām simaraṇ*) performed in conformity with a timeless Indian universal."[55] It was only appropriate for President George Bush to declare that Islam is a religion of peace in the aftermath of the September 11, 2011, attacks, but millions of moderate Muslims may have taken a pass in not being proactive enough against militants in their midst. Mandair submits that claims of Sikh pacifism also plays right into the hands of the reigning brahmanical and European universal, namely, that all the native South Asian religions are nonviolent and this assumption may well have justified government attempts to punish Sikh rebels who did not conform to the dominant Indian *sanātana dharma*. Punjabis who do not behave like nonviolent Hindus, Jains, and Buddhists are not true Sikhs and they therefore cannot claim any special religious consideration. As Michael Hawley states, "Modernity postulates a division between religion and violence," a distinction he correctly believes that Gandhi accepted. While religions are presumed to be nonviolent, it is assumed that modern nation state has a monopoly on the sometimes violent enforcement of law.

The foregoing analysis is truly ironic when we consider that fact that Singh Sabhā theologians assumed that Sikhism could become a legitimate faith only by purging itself of everything that was premodern. As Mandair observes, "The Singh Sabhā scholars could not easily avoid using the language of sonic monism even as they were eradicating 'Hindu' influence from the prior exegesis of the *Ādi Granth*."[56] But the ideology of sacred sound was used in a modernized theological framework, in which the Word is "directly revealed by as monotheistic God ... an eternal cosmic Wisdom, an eternal vibration from beginning to end."[57] One might argue that this is a legitimate integration of premodern and modern to construct a postmodern Sikh theology, but not if it is used to promote Sikh nationalism and sectarianism. As I have argued elsewhere with regard to Gandhi,[58] a constructive postmodern view of religious pluralism would not support an ideology of a special and exclusive revelation; rather, it would be similar to Swami Vivekananda's proposal mentioned above. To their credit, however, Sikh nationalists never claimed that Sikhism and Punjabi be the exclusive religion and language of India (or even of the Punjab), as Hindu fundamentalists have insisted about Hinduism and Hindi, and Sri Lankan Buddhists did for Buddhism and Sinhalese. It is not an exaggeration to claim that Hindu, Buddhist, and Sikh fundamentalism would not have been possible without British linguistic and religious imperialism.

It is significant to note that during the reign of Ranjit Singh (1799–1839) Muslims and Hindus were members of his administration and Sikhism was not the official religion of his forty-year reign. (Hindus were also found in great numbers as officials and soldiers during Mughal times.) After the Ranjit Singh's final victory in Lahore, no Muslims were executed in retribution for the liquidation of thousands of Sikhs during the period of the post-Akbar Mughal emperors. This is truly remarkable given the fact that Ranjit Singh was considered to be the reincarnation of the famous Sikh martyr Gurbahsh Singh Nihang.[59] As opposed to the practice of many Hindu and Muslim militants (today or centuries past), no temples or mosques were destroyed during that time. This is evidence of religiously motivated violence as I define it.

Mandair demonstrates how British linguists, frustrated by the fact that Indians did not seem to care about speaking a consistent and coherent language, constructed Hindi for them. Devoid of Persian and Arabic vocabulary (now found in Urdu), Hindi fostered a separate Hindu identity ready-made for the rise of Hindutva. A modernist project of language making went hand in hand with religion making, and with regard to the Sikhs, the creation of a theology based on a Christian model. Alluding to Heidegger's principle that "language is the house of Being," Mandair suggests that as a result the Sikhs took on a British self and a British worldview. This is not just idle speculation on Mandair's part, because in his book *On the Education of the People of India* Charles Trevelyan wrote, "They are about to have a new character imprinted on them" and they will end up "more English than Hindu."[60]

Yet another important contribution of Mandair's monumental project is to reject the notion that the British were in mutual dialog with their native colleagues. Long after the introduction of Hindi in English medium schools, students were still complaining about learning two foreign languages: the Empress's mother tongue and a national language that Victoria had created for them. The British "manufactured the consent" of their subjects and, drawing on Jacque Lacan, Mandair submits that "one does not master language; rather, one is mastered *by* language."[61] This dynamic leads me to question Mandair's claim that South Asians underwent a "conversion to modernity," a term that assumes conscious effort. Rather than freely accepting a British worldview, Indians, especially the Sikhs, were "seduced" by the appeal of modernism and the advantages that it gave them to establish a pseudo-national identity as a minority among a huge Hindu majority.

Whenever religious and national identities are fused, one will find religiously motivated violence. This is of course true for the Abrahamic religions, but also the case for Buddhist and Hindu fundamentalists, as well as Tibetan and Japanese nationalists and militarists. Shinto and Japanese national identity go back to the fifteenth century (only to be intensified by the Meiji Restoration), and Tibetan Buddhist imperialism became aggressively expansionist with the aid of Mongolian troops in the sixteenth and seventeenth centuries. Sri Lankan Buddhist, Hindu, and Sikh nationalism arose only after European intrusion into South Asia. Only these movements could be said to have been seduced by the false attractions of modernism.

Notes

*Editor's Note: This chapter as been reprinted with permission from N. F. Gier, *The Origins of Religious Violence: An Asian Perspective* (Lanham, MD: Lexington Books, 2014), chap. 8.

1. See Arvind-Pal S. Mandair, *Religion and the Specter of the West: Sikhism, India, Postcoloniality, and the Politics of Translation* (New York: Columbia University Press, 2009), 36.
2. Louis E. French, *Martyrdom in the Sikh Tradition* (New Delhi: Oxford University Press, 2000), 33–34.
3. French, 3.
4. Vivekananda's final address at the 1983 World Parliament of Religions found in *The Complete Works of Swami Vivekananda* at <www.ramakrishnavivekananda.info/vivekananda/volume_1/vol_1_frame.htm>
5. Quoted in Gurinder Singh Mann, *Sikhism* (Upper Saddle River, NY: Prentice Hall, 2004), 83.
6. Ibid.
7. Cited in W. H. McLeod, ed., *Textual Sources for the Study of Sikhism* (Manchester: Manchester University Press, 1984), 58.
8. Ann Murphy, "The Guru's Weapons," *Journal of the American Academy of Religion* 77, no. 2 (June 2009): 316. The author points out that this was not unique in the Indian tradition. Viṣṇu's discus (*chakra*) and his divine power are identified in the Hindu epics.
9. Mandair, 303.
10. Cited in French, 28n44.
11. Ibid., 91, 147.
12. Ibid., 99.
13. Cited in McLeod, *Textual Sources for the Study of Sikhism*, 21.
14. Mandair, 36.
15. Ibid.
16. Ibid., 211, 266.
17. Ibid., 267.
18. Ibid., 361.
19. McLeod, *GNSR*, 191.
20. W. Owen Cole, *Understanding Sikhism* or with P. S. Sambhi, *The Sikhs: The Religious Beliefs and Practices*, 229, 260.
21. Ibid.
22. Mandair, 431.
23. Eleanor Nesbitt, *Sikhism: A Very Short Introduction* (Oxford: Oxford University Press, 2005), 122.
24. French, 120.
25. Cole, 261, 263.
26. French, 131.
27. *Dasam Granth* at www.sridasam.org/dasam?Action=Page&p=51&english=t&id=64882, 51.
28. Cole, 225.
29. Quoted in French, 152.
30. Ibid., 153.
31. M. K. Gandhi, *All Men Are Brothers* (Ahmedabad: Navajivan Publishing House, 1960), 77.
32. Vivekananda's final address at the 1983 World Parliament of Religions found in *The Complete Works of Swami Vivekananda* at <www.ramakrishnavivekananda.info/vivekananda/volume_1/vol_1_frame.htm>
33. Quoted in Peggy Morgan and Clive A. Lawton, eds., *Ethical Issues in Six Religious Traditions* (Edinburgh: Edinburgh University Press, 2007), 154.
34. Gian Singh, *Panth Prakāś*, 79, cited in French, 190.
35. Cole, 229, 263.
36. Carol H. Behrman, *The Indian Wars: Chronicles of America's Wars* (Minneapolis, MN: Learner Publications, 2005), 13.
37. Catherine Keller, "Warriors, Women, and the Nuclear Complex" in *Sacred Interconnections: Postmodern Spirituality, Political Economy, and Art*, ed. David R. Griffin (Albany, NY: SUNY Press, 1990), 72.
38. Christopher Key Chapple, *Nonviolence to Animals, Earth, and Self in Asian Traditions* (Albany, NY: State University of New York Press, 1993).

39. Mandair, 232.
40. Ibid., 193.
41. M. A. Macauliffe, *The Sikh Religion: Its Gurus, Sacred Writings, and Authors* (Oxford: Chand and Company, reprinted, 1983), lviii.
42. See N. F. Gier, *The Virtue of Non-Violence: From Gautama to Gandhi* (Albany, NY: State University of New York Press, 2004), passim.
43. *The Collected Essays of Bimal Krishna Matilal: Ethics and Epics*, ed. Jonardon Ganeri (New Delhi: Oxford University Press, 2002), 50.
44. N. F. Gier, "Dharma Morality as Virtue Ethics" in *Indian Ethics: Classical Traditions and Contemporary Challenges*, vol. 2, ed. Purusottama Bilimoria and Joseph Prabuhu (Springer, 2013), forthcoming.
45. Mandair, 371.
46. Ibid., 375–76.
47. J. I. Packer, *Fundamentalism and the Word of God* (Grand Rapids, MI: Eerdmans, 1958), 117; my emphasis.
48. Mandair, 372.
49. Ibid., 378.
50. Ibid., 375.
51. Ibid., 372.
52. Harjot Oberoi, *The Construction of Religious Boundaries*; quoted in Mandair, 330.
53. Graham Parkes, *Composing the Soul*, 332.
54. Mandair, 354.
55. Ibid., 355.
56. Ibid., 330.
57. Ibid., 332–33.
58. N. F. Gier, "Gandhi, Deep Religious Pluralism, and Multicultrualism," forthcoming in *Philosophy East and West* (2015).
59. See French, 150.
60. Cited in Mandair, 96.
61. Mandair, 101.

4

The Catholic Church, Violence, and the Nationalist Struggles in Ireland, 1798–1998

Oliver Rafferty, SJ

Introduction

For a great deal of the period here surveyed, the Catholic Church in Ireland lived under a government not always sympathetic to its existence and outlook. This was true for the whole country in the period 1801–1921, and then in Northern Ireland since the inception of that state and its Protestant hegemony. After the introduction of partition in the early 1920s, the church existed in two jurisdictions. Independent Ireland was, for the most part, sycophantic in its deference to institutionalized Catholicism. This ensured Catholic support for the state even though independent Ireland had been born out of a violent revolutionary struggle that had, at best, dubious claims to be just according to Catholic moral theology.[1] Northern Ireland by contrast harbored barely concealed hostility toward the Catholic Church. But even here the Northern Ireland state had to deal with Catholicism as a social reality that commanded the respect, affection, and obedience of one-third of the state's citizens.

For the most part institutional Catholicism sought to inculcate in its adherents a respect for the structure of the state. This was true, from an early stage and despite lingering antipathy, even in the case of Protestant Northern Ireland. As early as 1926 Cardinal Patrick O'Donnell, Archbishop of Armagh, could say of the desire of Irish nationalists for an Ireland free of British rule: "All speculations belong to the past. The area of the Six Counties is now fixed as the area of Northern Ireland . . . and we must work for the general good of the community."[2] This should not come as a surprise. After all, throughout most of the nineteenth century the Irish hierarchy was in an analogous position—living under a government that ruled Ireland in the Protestant interest and which, for much of the century, sought to maintain Protestant privilege and ascendancy.[3] Bishop Patrick Leahy could thus complain that in the mid-1860s Catholic Ireland lived under a "wicked anti-Catholic, anti-Irish, anti-everything dear to us government."[4]

Despite protestations of loyalty to the state by bishops, and as we shall see these were subject to fluctuation, the Catholic community harbored within itself, in the whole period here considered, numbers of individuals whose aim was to overthrow the state by violent means. Even at the beginning of the most recent Troubles, the Irish Republican Army (IRA) claimed that its outlook and methods were based on "Irish and Christian values."[5] Some historians have argued that nationalism in the context of Catholic Ireland was not intrinsically violent, and this is, in general, a reasonable analysis.[6] Equally others have drawn attention to the fact that Catholic nationalism had clear sectarian undertones that worked to the exclusion of the Protestant Irish,[7] and this despite the fact that some of the leaders of nationalist Ireland such as Isaac Butt and Charles Stewart Parnell were themselves Protestants. The main point, however, is that Irish nationalism in the nineteenth century became inextricably linked with Catholicism and periodically exhibited dangerous violent tendencies.

That violence was at times the product of frustration at the perceived lack of political advancement for Irish Catholics and the slow pace of reform on the part of the London government. Violence could also be the result of a deliberate ideology. On a number of occasions between 1798 and 1998 militant Irish nationalists took up arms against the lawful authority of the state in a struggle to free Ireland from British rule. These instances were clearly contrary to Catholic teaching on the legitimacy of revolution.[8] And if by and large the bishops, as the hierarchical leaders of the church, adhered to a strict interpretation of the church's teaching and theology on the issue of political violence, the same cannot always be said of the lower clergy. Indeed this was the charge leveled against the generality of priests by the lord lieutenant, the Earl of Clarendon. Writing in mid-century to John MacHale, the Archbishop of Tuam, Clarendon declared that "the exercise of spiritual authority is doubted and the press asserts that the public believes that the Catholic clergy are the irresponsible promoters of disaffection and disorder."[9]

Even bishops would, occasionally, permit themselves to express an unguarded hostility to the operations of the British state in Ireland in a manner that appeared to give support to those whose aim was to separate Ireland from the United Kingdom by violent means. Thus, Archbishop MacHale not only sent three portraits of himself to be sold at the Fenian fair in Chicago in 1863, describing the Fenians[10] as a benevolent brotherhood, but he could also drink toasts to "the People, the source of all legitimate power."[11] Perhaps the latter is no more than an echo of the sentiments Alex de Tocqueville recorded when he had dinner with five bishops, including Archbishop Michael Slattery of Cashel, and some priests on July 20, 1835. The conversation was such that de Tocqueville recorded the sentiments of the clergy as being:

[E]xtremely democratic. Distrust and hatred of the great landlords . . . Bitter memories of past oppression. An air of exaltation at present of approaching victory. A profound hatred of the Protestants and above all of their clergy. Little impartiality apparent. Clearly as much the leaders of a Party as the representatives of the Church.[12]

Be that as it may, such sentiments are nonetheless far removed from the explicit instructions sent by Pope Pius VI to the Irish bishops in 1793, warning them that the aim of radical and revolutionary ideology would lead to the destruction of "the fundamental bases of religion and the throne."[13] The Irish bishops themselves in any case were all too keyed to the need to dissuade their flocks from any flirtation with revolutionary sentiment. As Bishop Francis Moylan of Cork noted in the aftermath of the 1798 rebellion, the church authorities had amended the catechism in Ireland so as to "impress our people with a due sense of the social and political duties of good citizens & with sentiments of loyalty and attachment to His Majesties person and government."[14]

One issue that preoccupied bishops in relation to revolutionary violence was the fear that in any revolutionary situation they might suffer the same fate as their episcopal colleagues in France. This was given explicit expression by Archbishop John Troy of Dublin in his pastoral letter condemning the United Irishmen's rebellion in 1798. Indeed he claimed that at least one aim of revolutionary propaganda was

> To destroy or diminish the salutary influence of our clergy in this kingdom, [and to achieve this] some ignorant and unsuspecting persons of our Communion, have been practiced on to consider the Roman Catholic Prelates as their enemies, or as mercenaries prostituting their venal pens and exhortations for pensions and bribes.[15]

By 1848 Archbishop Daniel Murray, in that revolutionary year, feared that the lesson of the French revolution was that throne and altar stood or fell together. And at a later stage in the face of the Fenian threat Cardinal Paul Cullen believed that in any revolutionary outbreak he would be one of the first to go to the wall.[16]

Antirevolutionary and antiviolence denunciations although welcome by the government could place the church in a difficult position. A priest was murdered in Kildare town in December 1797 for "having exhorted his congregation to abstain from disloyalty."[17] There was a decided danger for the church if ecclesiastics took a too antirevolutionary line. As Donal Kerr indicated, critics were only too ready to point to the fact that in the face of violence churchmen's "reluctance to loose influence over the faithful . . . made [priests and bishops] shrink from total opposition to the political demands of a people suspicious of government manipulation of the clergy."[18] Even the pronouncements of the highest ecclesiastic authority could attract widespread opprobrium, if the sentiments expressed did not resonate with the political antenna of the Irish people. Hence the rejection by both the laity and the clergy of Pope Leo XIII's condemnation of the sometimes violent activities of the Land League in the 1880s.[19]

Daniel O'Connell had already in the 1840s indicated the limits of clerical direction in politics when he asserted that Irish Catholics would take dictation in political matters as soon from Constantinople as from Rome. Subsequently some churchmen could not bring themselves to believe that O'Connell, the faithful Catholic, had uttered any such words, and in any case decided that the sentiment was a formal heresy.[20] Other ecclesiastical leaders thought it simply best that the clergy should refrain from political interference, and this was also the thinking exhibited by the Holy See at various points in the nineteenth century. For some government ministers the spectacle of the priest in politics represented the most acute problem in trying to govern Ireland. Robert Peel, when he was chief secretary for Ireland, was convinced that much of the unrest in the country was as a result of priestly activity and described the clergy as "the real offenders" against "order and stability."[21] Equally the perceptions of British statesmen were not always consistent in the matter, and hence Lord Russell's infamous declaration that Britain had tried to govern Ireland by force and failed: "[w]e have tried to govern by conciliation and failed also. No other means are now open to us except those we are now resolved on using, namely, to govern Ireland through Rome."[22]

In particular politicians sought from the clergy what they themselves were, at times, incapable of doing and that was to instill in the fractious Irish a sense of order. This remained a fairly consistent element in British government policy through the last two hundred years. Some ecclesiastics needed no encouragement in the matter. In 1883 the Holy See issued an epitome of Cardinal Cullen's condemnations of violent revolutionary groups so as to "disabuse those ignorant persons who think that they can remain good Catholics while they join secret, seditious associations which the church has never ceased to condemn."[23] At the same time a continuing problem for bishops was the difficulty in forming a policy that demanded the redress of grievances and that commanded the respect of the lower clergy, but that did not seem to encourage the more militant and violent tendency within some sections of the Catholic population. Bishop David Moriarty of Kerry well expressed it by observing that some of the bishops, "by our abuse of Gov[ernmen]t, drive the people into disaffection and the spirit of rebellion."[24]

By the time of the 1916 Rising, the dynamic had changed somewhat. Although several bishops and a number of the lower clergy were sympathetic to Sinn Féin, in the aftermath of the Rising the attempted revolution was condemned by individual priests and bishops. While the bishops had considered a collective pronouncement against the rebels, the action of the government in the execution of the leaders of the Rising and the internment without trial of many hundreds of men changed the political climate and made the church's officials less disposed to strong counterrevolutionary assertions.[25] The relative silence of the hierarchy about the Rising before the government reprisals, even on the part of the avowed nationalist Archbishop William Walsh of Dublin, gave the impression that the church was not as allied with the people as it ought to be. In 1918 when the British government tried to introduce conscription in Ireland, the Catholic Church itself joined Sinn Féin, the party of revolution, to defeat the will of parliament on the matter. The Church of Ireland Archbishop of Dublin, J. H. C. Bernard, wrote to the archbishop of Canterbury that the Catholic bishops' actions were only intelligible in the context of their "dominant motive . . . the desire to keep control over their people."[26] Their actions in the conscription crisis were then determined by the need to regain the confidence of Catholic Ireland which to some extent they had forfeited in 1916.

The anticonscription drive was, in one sense, an aberration on the part of the Irish Church in its relationship with authority. As Peter Donnelly has pointed out, for Irish bishops and theologians "power rather than justice was the essential constitutive and determining factor in legitimating established political authority."[27] In almost all circumstances, the church demanded of its subjects' reverence and respect for the constituted authority of the state since this was a manifestation of the divine will. This is certainly the attitude the bishops took in the face of the IRA border campaign of the 1950s, when they defended the integrity of Northern Ireland against the insurgents. Certain vestiges of that approach would survive into the era of the Troubles from 1969 to 1998. Although the bishops were careful to draw attention to what they saw as defects of government policy and complaining bitterly about outrages committed by the security forces against the Catholic population, they nevertheless warned that a resort violence even to achieve just ends was incompatible with Catholic thinking.[28] They also stressed that from the start of the IRA campaign they had consistently condemned it as "utterly immoral."[29]

Precisely, because of government policies on internment, the Bloody Sunday killings, and the general harassment by the army of the Catholic population, the official church found it necessary to castigate government in Belfast and London. Such criticism provoked hostility on the part of the government and its officials in their dealings with the church. This was a rerun of a nineteenth-century phenomenon, as indicated by the English Catholic aristocrat Aubrey de Vere, whereby in Ireland

> The Catholic Church is the only power capable of resisting Revolutionary ideas; yet hostility to the cause of the Catholic religion on the part of government would eventually render it impossible for the Catholic party to aid, as they would wish to aid, the party of order.[30]

We can begin to see a broad pattern in the official church's response to the violent proclivities within the Catholic body in Ireland in the last two centuries. In general bishops opposed violence, but they also expressed sympathy for the sufferings of their people. Violence was often a response to that suffering. The empathy of bishops was construed by politicians, and others, as an indication of ecclesiastical support for the men (and later also women) of violence.[31] In what follows I would like to look at a number of violent episodes in the evolution of Irish nationalism and the church's response to these. The aim is to try and discern whether the ecclesiastical reaction was always consistent, and if it was one of principled moral rectitude.

1798 and Its Aftermath

In the face of the United Irishmen's rebellion, the bloodiest in Irish history in which it is estimated that between 30,000 and 100,000 lost their lives, the bishops repudiated the "deluded" individuals who took part in it. They also expressed horror at the fact that not only were the rebels engaged in treason against King George III but they had "given their designs a colour of zeal for the religion they professed."[32] This was not simply because in some parts of the country the rising had deteriorated into sectarian slaughter, but that in some instances the insurgents had been led by priests.[33] Protestant opinion in Ireland fixed on this to berate the Catholic Church as an instrument of rebellion, treason, and disorder.

Although bishops poured opprobrium on the rebellion and its principles, they also feared the extent of French revolutionary ideas that were being prorogated by the United Irishmen and the deleterious effects such ideas were having on Irish Catholics.[34] The great problem for institutional Catholicism was that such ideas had indeed found an echo in the hearts of some of the clergy. As one Dublin newspaper of distinctly Protestant tastes acutely, if melodramatically, observed of priests caught up in revolutionary designs,

> The superior clergy know that the same renegade priest who would urge his blind and miserable flocks to the murder of heretics would not scruple to bathe his impious hands in the blood of his bishop.[35]

As Bishop Patrick Plunkett of Meath put it, the example of France was such that "if our nominal *Catholics* look the same way, if the sacred rights of religion are to form the phantom of political liberty . . . should not the ministers of religion of every rank take alarm and stand on their guard."[36]

This was part of a general difficulty that Plunkett had identified. Under the impulse of democratic ideas, the laity were less disposed to take direction from the higher ranks of the clergy. They had also indicated "an inclination to become our masters, and to dictate to us even in the line of our profession."[37] Some of the bishops such as the primate Archbishop Patrick Kelly of Armagh had a profound desire to keep out of politics altogether. He told one of his priests to "mention nothing to me in your letters of the politics of the time," and moreover it was dangerous even "to report the conduct or sentiments of others as regards to such topics."[38] Given, however, the circumstances of the rebellion and the widespread perception that many priests sided with the rebellion, it was impossible for the bishops to be silent. They rallied to the support of government even to the extent of supporting the Union with Great Britain and of agreeing to concede the right of veto to government over the appointment of Catholic bishops in Ireland.[39]

Their support for the Union placed them at variance with the political sentiments of certain portions of their flocks, especially the middle classes in counties Dublin and Meath, and they suffered accordingly. Bishops were accused of being the "tool of government" and of being well paid for their services to the state.[40] This last criticism might be related to the fact that they had also agreed to state provision for the Catholic Church in Ireland. Although the bishops were rebuked by the Holy See for their stance in admitting a government veto, nevertheless they insisted that a demonstration of loyalty to government was necessary in view of 1798.[41] Eventually, the issue of the veto and state payment were shelved, but Rome now also took the view that manifestations of loyalty to the British crown did not detract from loyalty to the pope. Indeed the need for loyalty to the state, despite its Protestant constitution, had been stressed in earlier papal correspondence with the Irish bishops.[42]

One other factor in determining the antirevolutionary stance of the hierarchy was that the attempted rebellion had produced a sectarian backlash. Reports of the burning of Catholic places of worship were widespread in some areas of the country. Only the London government had the military capacity and the disposition to protect the infrastructure of the Catholic Church.[43] But self-interest could go hand in hand with issues of principle. As late as 1803 the Church of Ireland Archbishop of Cashel, Charles Broderick, could write to the lord chief justice, Lord Redesdale, that once again fear of what happened in France gave rise on the part of Irish Catholic bishops to the sincere resolve to prevent the Catholic community from in anyway countenancing a French invasion.[44] The year is significant because of another attempt at rebellion that was easily repressed. But the suspicion of the Catholic Church as an instrument of disorder had not abated. The day after the attempted rising Archbishop Troy of Dublin issued a pastoral letter denouncing the entire escapade. The speed of his response was proof positive, for some, that Troy had advanced knowledge of the rebellion but had not communicated this intelligence to the authorities.[45]

Already in the context of 1798 the characteristics of the church's reaction to revolutionary violence were being elaborated and laid down. The need to oppose violence, the fear that in a revolutionary context the church itself would suffer, the specter of sectarianism, and the question of the church's influence over its people all emerged as factors that would shape the political and religious debate for the rest of the century and beyond. Along with these issues there was the emerging contention of Catholic political aspirations in the shape of demands for Catholic Emancipation and then the repeal of the Act of Union. These factors would condition the response of the church to the tensions and violence of Ireland during the middle decades of the nineteenth century.

Mid-Century Politics and Violence

At times violence in Ireland seemed endemic. It came in three forms: rural and ad hoc, intentional and directed against the landlords, and politically inspired. Given that many people were desperately poor, there seemed little to lose in violent encounters with authority.[46] The campaigns by Daniel O'Connell first for Catholic political rights, in the shape of emancipation, and then for Repeal of the Union, although heralded as instance of peaceful political agitation, could lend themselves to a climate that created disorder teetering on violence. The fact that the bishops declared themselves in favor of O'Connell in the 1820s meant that the church had thrown in its lot with popular political agitation. This perfectly fitted O'Connell's aims and desires and aligned Catholicism with the emerging political nation. Further O'Connell expected that the clergy would follow lay direction in secular politics.[47] But it was the possibility of violence that forced the government to concede emancipation in 1829. It was said of one parish priest Dr. England of Charleston, County Mayo, that he had the pledges of 40,000 men to fight in the event that emancipation would not be carried.[48] It is difficult to believe that the number is anything other than an exaggeration.

The Court of Rome treated with a degree of skepticism socioreligious developments in Ireland and intervened on a number of occasions to urge bishops and priests to refrain from political agitation. Thus, Cardinal Philip Fransoni wrote to the Irish bishops on behalf of Pope Pius IX warning them not to get involved in secular affairs. He also exhorted the bishops and priests to lead by example in "a due submission to the temporal power in those matters which pertain to civil affairs."[49]

Occasionally bishops would say things that seemed to lend support to radicalism. Bishop James Doyle of Kildare and Leighlin had warned in the 1820s that if rebellion broke out in Ireland, the bishops would be reluctant to excommunicate those who were involved. It must be said that this outburst produced a howl of protest issued from his fellow bishops and from the professors at St. Patrick's College, Maynooth.[50] The so-called Sorbonne manifesto made clear that the Maynooth professors saw it as their duty to inculcate in their students the New Testament teaching on obedience to kings and others in authority.[51]

O'Connell's posturing tested the church's room for maneuver to the limit in its ability to direct the course of Catholic Ireland in a peaceful direction. Its moral influence was stretched to breaking point by the Great Famine of 1845–1850.[52] There were allegations that priests urged violence, and even death, against landlords who were not doing enough for famine relief.[53] Archbishop William Crolly of Armagh denied that priests incited their parishioners to murder. He did concede however, in writing to Rome in February 1848, that other allegations of the use of churches for political meetings and the harangues of priests against individual landlords were unfortunately, *nimis verae* (only too true).[54] Even some bishops could speak and write in the most provocative tones. Edward Maginn, bishop of Derry, imagined that

> [T]here is no means under heaven that I would not cheerfully resort to, to redeem my people from their present misery; and sooner than allow it to continue . . . I would rather grasp the cross and the green flag of Ireland and rescue my country or perish with its people.[55]

And this from a bishop who could write of Irish Catholic loyalty to "the best of English queens", that such loyalty stood "unimpeached before the world."[56]

Other priests confirmed that "in the case of an outbreak the clergy would be with the people to a man."[57] When, however, the outbreak did come in the shape of the Young Ireland Rebellion on July 30, 1848, hopelessly organized as it was, it fizzled out largely under clerical condemnation.[58] Participants in the attempt were not slow to blame priests for opposing "the liberation of Ireland."[59] Bishop John Cantwell of Meath had, well before the rebellion, articulated the episcopal view that any recourse to physical violence would only "prove fatal to the temporal and eternal welfare of the flocks committed to our care."[60] One factor in the attitude of the Irish clergy in 1848 may well have been the fate of Archbishop Denys-Augusta Affre who was shot dead by the revolutionaries in Paris on June 25. His death in that year of revolution caused horror among the Irish clergy. Lord Clarendon, the lord lieutenant, was delighted and declared that Affre "never did a better thing in his life than getting himself murdered."[61]

The arrival of Paul Cullen in Ireland as Archbishop of Armagh in 1850, and subsequently archbishop of Dublin in 1852–1878, marks a new phase in Irish ecclesiastical politics. Although only too aware of the Protestant nature of Irish society, which rankled greatly with him, he was determined to instill in Irish Catholics a sense that it was their "first duty to . . . support the government unless it attacked the Church."[62] The Synod of Thurles in 1850, over which Cullen presided as Papal Legate, railed against those who in Irish society attempted to induce the people "to sympathize with the apostles of socialism and infidelity who in other countries . . . not only undermined the foundations of every government, but artfully assailed the rights of the Apostolic See."[63]

Cullen's attachment to the principle of conformism to established authority in church and state was also linked to skepticism about government treatment of political dissidents. When Gladstone's reform program at the end of the 1860s did not seem to bring peace to Ireland in the manner in which Gladstone hoped, Cullen told the prime minister that the only means of dealing effectively with revolutionary groups was repression.[64] Cullen also shared with Pope Pius IX an astonishment that Britain could support revolution in the Papal States which aimed at depriving the pope of his country and yet see no inconsistency in counteracting such revolutionary tendencies in Ireland.[65] At times his distrust of government could border on paranoia. He wrote to Archbishop Martin Spalding of Baltimore that the British government allowed secret societies such as the Fenian Brotherhood, the Irish Republican Brotherhood (IRB), to flourish in Ireland so that they would cause disaffection between priests and their people, and thus subvert the Catholic faith.[66]

For Cullen the Fenians represented a threat to the church as much as to the state, and therefore he opposed them in every way he could, even forbidding priests to hear the confessions of IRB members. By October 1870 he had declared that members of the Fenian organization were excommunicated. Cullen was convinced that he would have to "encounter the hostility of the multitudes" for his spirited opposition to the revolutionaries but asserted that "nothing will induce me, I trust in God, to go against the dictates of conscience, or to sanction a revolutionary spirit."[67] But he was also aware that physical resistance to one of the most powerful governments in the world was useless. Other bishops took the view that the clergy in general had merely pragmatic antipathy toward Fenianism. Thus, Bishop David Moriarty of Kerry wrote to the prominent Irish politician William Monsell,

> The clergy will preach against the rebellion of account of the evils it will bring on the people, but I am sure that if there was a fair chance of success it would be lawful nay "*dulce et decorum.*"[68]

For their part mid-century governments were convinced that the younger priests were all "rebels at heart."[69]

In the aftermath of the attempt revolution in 1867, many Fenians and their fellow travelers were rounded up and held without trial. This produced, as so often happens in Irish history, a great deal of sympathy for the individuals involved, leading to a movement for amnesty of the political prisoners which by 1869 had attracted the support of up to one million people.[70] By December 1869 the amnesty petition also had the signatures of 1400 out of the 3000 priests in Ireland.[71] For Cullen and the other members of the hierarchy, this was all too much. In one sense for those not inclined to see the nuances in the Irish situation, it rather confirmed the view, as expressed by G. H. Walley MP for Peterborough in the House of Commons on May 23, 1867, that Fenianism was "entirely the result of... the doctrines and discipline of the Roman Catholic hierarchy."[72] On their part the bishops now petitioned Pope Pius IX for a condemnation of the Fenian organization. This the pope delivered in January 1870. Coincidently, the British government also sought such a declaration from the pope. Although the Holy See might regard radical ideas in Ireland as doctrines that were "false, scandalous and pernicious, subversive of ecclesiastical and civil authority, and calculated to excite to sedition and agrarian crime,"[73] there were always dangers in Roman and papal intervention in Irish affairs. Such condemnations did little to restrain those engaged in violence. Further as Archbishop John MacHale pointed out, pronouncements of this kind from Rome appeared to be against Irish interest and to favor the established political order of British rule in Ireland. Papal intervention could therefore serve to undermine the "attachment and submission to the Holy See, both of Clergy and People..."[74]

As all revolutionary groups did, Fenianism in Ireland competed with the church for influence, especially over the minds of the rural and urban poor. This was the class that seemed the most receptive of revolutionary ideas. The Fenians also questioned the right of the church to any say in the political arena.[75] The church for its part was unwilling, despite protestations to the contrary, simply to be confined to the sacristy as its role in Irish society. The religious–social agenda of the church may explain to a large extent its outlook in the Ireland of the mid-nineteenth century. Institutional Catholicism wanted the dismantling of the last vestiges of Protestant ascendancy in Ireland. The Catholic middle classes would fill the void thus created. The church would then have enormous influence over the emergent political elite. The revolutionary IRB posed a definitive challenge to this agenda. But the greatest test for Catholicism was to come in the crucible of nationalist Ireland's twentieth-century struggles.

The Rising and the Church in the Two Irelands

Michael Cronin, one of Ireland's leading moral theologians, wrote in 1917 that rebellion was always a crime and a violation of the natural law as determined by God.[76] At the beginning of the Civil War between the pro- and anti-Treaty forces, the Treaty of 1921 had settled the Anglo-Irish War and established the Irish Free State, the Irish bishops reiterated Cronin's view by declaring that lawful government received its authority from God. They went on to say that everyone was bound in conscience to obey the government:

Regardless of what precise form that government might take . . . . No one is justified in rebelling against legitimate government, wherever it is set up by the nation and acting within its rights.[77]

This statement of unbending principle, aimed at the members of the IRA who refused to accept the treaty, was not one that the bishops adhered to throughout the revolutionary period of 1916–1922. In fact during the Rising in 1916 against the legitimate government in the shape of the British state, the hierarchy as a whole remained noticeably silent. Seven individual bishops had emphatically condemned the attempted revolution,[78] whereas a number of clergy had expressed sympathy for the intentions and circumstances of the rebels, but lamenting their lack of military prowess. Among the latter was Bishop Edward O'Dwyer of Limerick whose stance received thunderous applause from the students at the national seminary, St. Patrick's College, Maynooth, during the bishops' meeting there in June 1916.[79]

There was a clear division of opinion among bishops concerning the circumstances of the Rising. In fact the rebellion was organized by a secret society, the Fenian Brotherhood, which had been condemned by the pope. Furthermore, Catholics in Dublin, to which the rebellion was largely confined, were regularly warned in Lenten regulations that members of the IRB incurred canonical penalties. In addition, the Holy See had telegraphed the Irish bishops during the Rising, saying that the rebels should lay down their arms and make peace.[80]

Only when public opinion swung against the British government owing to the extent of British reprisals, did the hierarchy unite to condemn government brutality, a condemnation that then appeared to British eyes as sympathy for the rebels' enterprise. This was despite the fact that the bishops decided not to have a church-door collection for those who had suffered in the rebellion lest they "incur the imputation of favouring in any way the authors of the unfortunate attempt."[81] The hierarchy's sentiments were summarized on June 22, 1916, by the Archbishop of Armagh Cardinal Michael Logue who declared that the government reaction was "folly," and had the authorities confined themselves to moderately punishing the insurgents "within the laws of humanity," they would have commanded the respect of all Ireland.[82] In view of the growing popularity of Sinn Féin, the political wing of the revolutionaries, tensions within the church mounted. Logue was a resolute opponent of the revolutionary design, an Irish Republic, but by contrast a sizable section of the clerical body had begun to support Sinn Féin.[83]

The bishops were now in a dilemma. Sinn Féin and its military wing had engaged in sinful and unlawful activity so far as Catholic theology was concerned. They were, however, from 1916 on a growing political reality in Ireland with widespread support among both people and priests. How was the church to deal with a political movement that espoused violence and yet had the affections of large sections of Irish public opinion? Until this point many of the bishops had been aligned with the peaceful and constitutional Irish Parliamentary Party, indeed the bishop of Raphoe, Patrick O'Donnell, was its honorary treasurer, but now that party was beginning to look like a spent force. In 1917 the hierarchy did try to stem the tide of revolutionary sympathy by reminding Catholics that all organizations that plotted against either state or church were condemned "under the gravest penalties." The bishops also alluded to the fact that Sinn Fein's desired form of government, a republic, was often associated with "civil tyranny and religious persecution."[84] However, the statement was in general so ambiguously drawn up that, as David

Miller remarks, it was patiently "a comprise between those members of the hierarchy who were terrified of the Sinn Féin movement and those who wished to turn the new movement to the Church's purpose."[85]

The wind in the country was blowing in a revolutionary direction and some bishops trimmed their sails accordingly. In attempting to justify a change of opinion Bishop O'Dwyer recorded in September 1916 that the old moral theology on the inadmissibility of rebellion was "obsolete." Nationality, he continued, was a "comparatively modern idea, and the rights of a nation against another are different from an individual against his sovereign."[86] Such an evolution was also evident in other areas of episcopal thinking. In January 1920 in the course of the War of Independence, the bishops asserted the "right of every civilized nation . . . to choose its own form of government." Moreover, they implicitly rebuked the British government for holding Ireland by force of arms, which was contrary to "the democratic sprit now animating the world."[87] The titular head of the church in Ireland, Cardinal Logue, could rail against the methods of the IRA in the War of Independence in 1919 by saying of them "no object could excuse them, no motive could justify them, no hearts unless hardened and steeled against pity, would tolerate their cruelty." And yet when in 1921 one of the leaders of such cruelty, Michael Collins, was assassinated, Logue could speak without obvious embarrassment of "a young patriot brave and wise."[88]

The previous year the English Catholic weekly *The Tablet* had demanded that Logue be consistent with Catholic principles and set about excommunicating members of Sinn Féin since it was no more than a front organization for the IRB that had been condemned by the church's highest authorities.[89] By now of course priests were deeply involved with every level of Sinn Féin organization and even bishops were on friendly terms with its leaders such as Eamon de Valera. De Valera would make use of his episcopal contacts to solicit support for his views, and he would use bishops as intermediaries with the British government.[90] It is also clear, however, that when a bishop tried to remain faithful to a strict interpretation of church teaching, such as Bishop Daniel Cohalan of Cork who excommunicated members of the IRA, his injunctions were widely ignored by his own clergy.[91] There was then a transformation in the Irish hierarchy from moral guardians of church teaching to, in one sense, fellow travelers with Sinn Féin. This was seen in a most sinister light by John Dillon, leader of the Irish Parliamentary Party. He accused the clergy of

> most dishonestly using S.F. to carry out purposes they have the long nursed—the destruction of our independent party and the recovery of their own . . . power over Irish politics, which the Parnellite [of the 1880 and 1890s] movement had to a very large extent *destroyed*.[92]

For much of the rest of the War of Independence, bishops tended to focus on British atrocities, saying that the policy of repression was parallel only with the Armenian genocide: an egregious exaggeration. Furthermore, the bishops believed the "harsh, oppressive tyrannical regime of [British] militarism" was the cause of the problems besetting Ireland.[93] Insofar as the hierarchy had a scruple about the activities of the IRA, it focused on the somewhat technical point that there had been no declaration of war against Britain. This was a subject addressed by several bishops in pastoral letters in Lent 1921. The lacuna was remedied by de Valera as "President of the Irish Republic" who on March 11 on behalf of the (illegal and fictitious) Irish parliament declared war between Ireland and Britain.[94] If this salved episcopal consciences, it did not nullify the fact that there was no such thing as an Irish state at that time. This reality so impressed the Vatican that the Holy See had prepared a document condemning Irish nationalist violence. The intervention of churchmen and Sinn Féin politicians ensued that the condemnation was never issued.[95]

With the establishment of the Irish Free State in 1922, the ecclesiastical hierarchy had ensured its lasting influence in Irish political life. This was underlined by the fact, as we have seen above, that the bishops rejected the lawfulness of the anti-Treaty war waged by de Valera and his followers in the period 1922–1923. They also refused the sacraments to the anti-Treaty fighters. The techniques of terror and repression used by the Free State government seemed to attract no moral opprobrium from the church. The Republican anti-Treaty forces were not, however, without influence and the Holy See dispatched Monsignor Salvatore Luizo to investigate the circumstances of the Irish Civil War. This caused resentment on the part of bishops and the government. Indeed the Irish foreign minister, Desmond FitzGerald, informed the Holy See at the end of April 1923 that the apparent indifference of the pope to the declaration of the Irish bishops of support for the Free State government in the Civil War was "a source of grave scandal and disedification."[96] Luizo's mission was abruptly terminated.

The church then settled into a cozy relationship with the new state and even managed to reconcile itself to the anti-Treaty republicans when they came to power in the 1930s. This coincided with a resurgence of IRA activity which the bishops were quick to condemn. They warned not only of the moral dangers posed by those who sought to "over throw the state by force of arms" but also of the fact that the would-be revolutionaries were inspired by communism.[97] Support for the IRA was never wide spread after the War of Independence, but it was nevertheless a fact of Irish Catholic life. This gave rise to what J. H. Whyte has described as nationalist Ireland's "ability to profess loyalty to the Church while rejecting its guidance on a particular issue,"[98] support for the IRA.

This problem was especially to the fore in Northern Ireland where Catholic life was dominated by what the prime minister, Sir James Craig, described as "a Protestant parliament and a Protestant State."[99] Such was the sense of grievance of the Catholic community that even high-ranking churchmen kept on intimate terms with individual terrorists. Cardinal Joseph MacRory of Armagh was used as an intermediary by the IRA during World War II in negotiations with de Valera.[100] Members of the Catholic minority supported the IRA wartime campaign and the church lobbied for the reprieve of six IRA men sentenced to death for the murder of a Catholic policeman in 1940. Five were spared.

Insofar as ecclesiastic rulers gave political leadership, it was in emphasizing the injustice of partition that left Catholics in Northern Ireland cut off from their coreligionist in the rest of the island. Indeed MacRory publically stated his hope that the result of World War II would be the abolition of the border.[101] By the time the IRA launched its next campaign against the Northern Ireland state, in the mid-1950s, the bishops were less ambiguous in their repudiation of violence as a means of achieving political objectives. Their forthright stand was even praised by the Northern Ireland prime minister, Lord Brookeborough, who nevertheless regretted that their statement against the IRA "had not been made long before the outrages and bloodshed took place which horrified all right thinking people."[102]

The undulations and moral ambiguities of the Irish hierarchy in regard to revolutionary violence in the period 1916–1923 were, to some extent, a departure from the stance of bishops in the nineteenth century. However, we have seen that even then moral outrage at political violence was conditioned by the facts of Irish political life. In attempting to keep the direction of the Catholic community firmly in their hands, bishops showed themselves to be sensitive political operators. In the fixed conditions of the two states in Ireland, and despite hostility to Catholicism in the face of the social realities of Northern Ireland, bishops in general and consistently reminded Catholics of their obligations as citizens to avoid flirtation with revolutionary groups. But such were the constraints under which Catholics lived in Northern Ireland that political frustration, in the context of the turbulent 1960s, gave way not only to peaceful demands for reform but to violent confrontation with the forces of the Northern Ireland and British state.

The church now faced upheavals on a scale not seen in Ireland since the early 1920s. The problem the bishops faced was, not unlike that of their nineteenth-century predecessors, how to articulate a policy that looked for the amelioration of grievances but in such a way that did seem to justify violence as the only means of forcing concessions from a reluctant government. Ultimately, of course, the aims of redress gave rise to an altogether different motivation for violence: the demand for British withdrawal from Ireland. Church condemnation of the IRA's campaign on that front ought to have been more straightforward. However, a widespread sympathy in the Catholic community for the men of violence, if not necessarily for their methods, and instances of injustice and repression at the hands of the security forces against the Catholic community made the bishop's task altogether more complex.

The Church and the Troubles 1969–1998

Although the IRA would claim in 1972 that some priests in Ireland were taking up arms on behalf of the people,[103] the fact remains that the Catholic Church throughout the years of the recent Troubles consistently condemned the IRA and its methods.[104] But its reasons for doing so and the intensity of its repudiation of violence fluctuated. In the course of the Troubles, the bishops offered unwavering support to the state in rejecting violence as a means of resolving political problems. Thus, the then Bishop Cahal Daly, subsequently cardinal archbishop of Armagh, could write in 1984 that of all the means available to right political wrongs, "violence is demonstrably the only one which cannot succeed and never will succeed."[105] Other bishops could point to the reality of the fact that the chief victims of IRA violence were Catholics, and that the IRA had "a monstrous domination over a whole population" in Catholic areas of Northern Ireland.[106]

When government tried to counteract terrorist violence by means of repressive legislation, differences of opinion opened up in the clerical body. Bishops tended to take the view that even in the situation of state repression political violence was unjustifiable. However, sixty priests signed a statement in January 1972, which declared that "it is not true to say that armed resistance to aggression can never be justified." They also rejected the idea that it was only elected officials who can decide when it is legitimate to resist aggression with force.[107] After the initial years of the Troubles, there was greater homogeneity of outlook on the part of priests and bishops in their response to the violence emanating from the Catholic community. The brutality of the IRA's response to the events of 1971 (interment without trial) and 1972 (Bloody Sunday) caused a reevaluation on the part of clergymen as the campaign of shooting, bombing, and murder intensified.[108]

The church's political power at the outbreak of the Troubles, a phenomenon acknowledged even by the British government,[109] did not always translate into the church's ability to control the political opinions of its adherents. The bishops and clergy acted as a restraint on Catholic violence at the early stages of the Troubles. However, their ability to play that role diminished as time went on.[110] As the reformist intentions of the Northern Ireland Civil Rights Association gave way in the early 1970s to the vicious campaign of IRA violence, a transformation took place in the dynamic of the Catholic community. To the horror of the ecclesiastical authorities, sections of the Catholic community now manifested a "refusal to compromise and [a] willingness to risk (and to inflict) injury and death."[111]

In condemning violence the church did so on the basis of what it judged to be absolute moral principles. It was alleged, however, that too often church authorities were perceived to be less concerned about the consequences of state repression than those of paramilitary violence. This was exploited by the IRA as a means of trying to drive a wedge between the Catholic community and its clerical leaders. The implication was that the church merely reflected the government opinion on the "armed struggle" and was therefore a tool of British imperialism in Ireland. The allegation was not fully justified. Thus, for example, the bishops in Northern Ireland in the face of army brutality in its dealing with the Catholic community declared that "It is a test of civilized people that the methods of its elected government remain civilized even under extreme provocation."[112] Such talk, however, was horrifying to government officials who on other occasions would brand it as "unfortunate and merely playing into the hands of [the IRA]."[113] Another paradoxical consequence for churchmen in condemning the IRA was that they gained a high political profile and "provided yet further evidence for external critics [who] claimed that the church dominated Catholic society and yet did nothing to stop terrorism."[114] Equally it is unclear how much ecclesiastical condemnation had any effect on those perpetrating violence. Even the intervention of Pope John Paul II seemed to have had as little impact on Irish terrorists as that of his nineteenth-century predecessors.[115]

If churchmen were condemned by government, they were also condemned by the terrorists. At the level of rejection of violence, there appeared to a differentiation, so far as the IRA was concerned, between priests who simply confined themselves to condemning violence and those "attacking the legitimizing ideology [of violence], they are to be reckoned as having gone over to the enemy."[116] The Republicans, in the shape of Sinn Féin and the IRA, have interpreted their rise to power and influence in the Catholic community as representing a direct challenge to the authority of institutional Catholicism.[117] For its part the church battled with IRA/Sinn Féin precisely for influence over the Catholic community throughout the whole period of the Troubles. This confrontation took place at every major intersection of the state, political life, and the Catholic people. Beginning with the events of the early Troubles, to the IRA hunger strikes,[118] the talks between the Catholic constitutionalist and the radicals,[119] to the process that led up to the Good Friday Agreement,[120] the representatives of institutional Catholicism were there, and ranged against them were the protagonists from Sinn Féin/IRA. The church presence was in token of the fact that it believed it had a pastoral responsibility in all these situations. But it is also clear that it feared to lose its influence over the Catholic community to the men and women of violence. The fact that Sinn Féin rose to become the biggest political party in the Catholic community in the north of Ireland and the fact that the church, which warned Catholics not to vote for the party and now deals with it in a most friendly manner, is token of the church's adaptability[121] and desire to maintain its influence at every level of public life. Despite all its vicissitudes in the years of the conflict, the Catholic Church in Northern Ireland today still remains "the single most important integrating social force" in the Catholic community and it continues to extend its influence "to all areas of communal life."[122]

Conclusion

Marcus Turner has written of the fact that it was Ireland's religious struggle that forged the political and national identity of the Irish people.[123] That religious struggle against a dominant Protestant culture in a largely Catholic country became enmeshed in the desire for national independence. There grew up a symbiotic relationship between nationalism and Catholicism, which in turn was overlaid, for some, with the ideology of violence as the only means of achieving the political goals that Irish nationalism has set for itself. The church's response in the face of violence was, for the most part, one of an instinctive rejection. Equally, as we have seen, the upholding of distinct moral principles repudiating armed revolutionary struggle was not always either possible or practical for Irish churchmen. The church risked being factored out of the equation as irrelevant if it did not bend its moral position in the face of the force of the peoples' political will. This was especially the case in the revolutionary period 1916–1921. And yet because the church had accommodated itself to the violent tendencies of its member at that period which resulted in partial independence from Britain, the perpetrators of violence in more recent years could not understand why the church did not exhibit the same degree of flexibility in the context of the "armed struggle" of the period 1969–1998.

Churchmen were not slow to draw a distinction between political violence in the recent Troubles and the IRA campaign in the War of Independence. Thus, Cardinal Cahal Daly could write,

> There is no historical continuity whatever between the present, largely faceless leaders of the self-styled "republican movement" and their honourable forebears; there is no moral continuity between their methods and those of the earlier struggle for independence.[124]

Daly would go even further in 2001 at the state funeral and reburial of a number of the "heroes" who had been executed in the War of Independence. Then he would claim that the real successors of the earlier IRA were those who had unequivocally committed themselves to the peace process and the Good Friday Agreement.[125] It is clear that not only terrorist but even the clergy have attempted to rewrite the history of Ireland's violent past for their own purposes.

The role of the church in managing the political machinations of its flock in Ireland has long been a complicated phenomenon. It would at times appear as if the church simultaneously both sided with the political aspirations of its adherents, even in their violent character, and opposed them. This aspect of the matter, as Jim Smyth has pointed out,[126] was given vivid expression by the playwright Sean O'Casey. In *Juno and the Paycock* Act I, O'Casey has Captain Boyle say of the Catholic clergy:

Didn't they prevent the people in '47 from seizin' the corn, an' they stravin'; didn't they down Parnell; didn't they say that hell wasn't hot enough nor eternity long enough to punish the Fenians. We don't forget, we don't forget them things Joxer.[127]

By Act II, and only two days later, the Captain could say, "as far as I know the History o' me country, the priests was always in the van of the fight for Ireland's freedom."[128]

Equally it is perhaps simply naive to think that Irish Catholics would obey their priests and bishops in matters of politics and on issues touching revolutionary violence. Bishops did use the threat of excommunication to try to restrain the more advanced proponents of violence. But when excommunication was used at various points in the nineteenth and twentieth centuries, it proved ineffective. This was because in some instances revolutionaries found sympathetic priests who administered the sacraments to them despite episcopal sanction,[129] or that Catholics engaged in violence no longer looked to the Church for fulfillment in their spiritual lives. By the time of the most recent violent unrest, although bishops did discuss the possibility of excommunication for members of the IRA, they came to the conclusion that it would be ineffective in weaning Catholics from the terrorist mentality and would, therefore, be an empty gesture.[130]

Two issues of great importance were the use of Catholic imagery by revolutionaries and the question of the burial of those involved in violent activity against the state. Already in the nineteenth century Cardinal Cullen had refused to allow one of the minor leaders of the 1848 rebellion, Terrance Bellew MacManus, to receive Catholic burial.[131] That issue also arose in the recent Troubles when the question of the burial of dead terrorists from Catholic churches, with full "military honors," threated to disrupt the whole relationship between the ecclesiastical hierarchy and the members of the church. In the end a compromise was arrived at whereby dead IRA personnel would be give Catholic funerals, provided none of the symbols of paramilitary resistance were displayed.

The manipulation of religious sentiment and imagery was of more and greater importance. The IRA liked to portray its members killed on "active service" as martyrs. This was also the case with those who starved themselves to death on hunger strike in 1981. The idea of death, as a sacrifice for a cause, giving rise to transcendent victory, is a trope with deep resonances for the Catholic imagination. The exploitation of such sentiment has also a long history in violent nationalism. Patrick Pearse had used the occasion of the burial of Jeremiah O'Donovan Rossa in 1915 to give a speech that helped propel the republicans into rebellion the following year. In the course of his speech not only did he say in effect that it was a Christian thing to hate what Britain was doing in Ireland, but he also asserted that one of the miracles of God was to ripen the seeds of revolt sown by the likes of O'Donovan Rossa.[132] More provocatively in a speech at the grave of the 1798 leader Theobald Wolfe Tone on June 22, 1913, he told his auditors, "We have come to the holiest place in Ireland; holier to us even that the place where [St] Patrick sleeps in Down. Patrick brought us life, but this man died for us."[133] It was not until 1972 that Pearse's views would be blasted by a prominent churchman as blasphemy.[134]

Of all the factors that forced the hierarchy of the church to appear to side with the apostles of violence and destruction, none was more prominent than state oppression. Emergency legislation, imprisonment without trial, and the presence of large numbers of military personnel on the streets have been blunt instruments in governments' attempts to grapple with the violence and civil strife that have beset Ireland in the last two hundred years. Too often repression simply fed into a sense of victimhood that in turn fueled further violent resistance. The IRA and its cognate organizations in the nineteenth and twentieth centuries were able to imbue Catholic nationalists with the shibboleth of armed resistance because often governments seemed bereft of any remedial response to Ireland's problems but force. In opposing force and brutality by the agents of the state, churchmen could, at times, appear to be singing from the same hymn sheet as the insurgents. However, the reality is that the Catholic Church struggled to wean the Catholic community away from its disposition to violence. In general, it was unsuccessful in its endeavors.

One factor in the church's relative failure was its inability to be in the vanguard of changing political philosophy. Ideas about the state, participation in political life, the relation of the nation to the state, and the nature of religious and national identity were all subject to change. The problem for the church was that it claimed to act according to principles that processed timeless and transcendental value. Yet it is also patiently clear that the church also amended its views in order to maintain a role in public life. To that extent its claims to universal values were open to question and rendered it a not-always reliable guide for the Irish people in the centuries' long tensions with Britain.

Notes

1. Walter McDonald, *Reminiscences of a Maynooth Professor* (London: Jonathan Cape, 1925), 396–97. See also his *Some Ethical Questions of Peace and War, with Special Reference to Ireland*, reprinted (Dublin: University College Dublin Press, 1998), passim.
2. Quoted in Peter Donnelly, "Political Identity in Northern Ireland: An Issue for Catholic Theology," *Studies: An Irish Quarterly Review* 86, no. 343 (1997): 239.
3. Oliver MacDonagh, "The Politicization of Irish Catholic Bishops, 1800–1850," *Historical Journal* 18, no. 1 (1975): 41.
4. Leahy to Tobias Kirby, quoted in Desmond Bowen, *Paul Cullen and the Shaping of Modern Irish Catholicism* (Dublin: Gill and Macmillan, 1983), 265.
5. Quoted in Richard Kearney, *Postnationalist Ireland: Politics Culture Philosophy* (London and New York: Routledge, 1997), 111.
6. Marianne Elliot, *Watchmen in Sion: The Protestant Idea of Liberty* (Derry: Field Day, 1989), 23. Less convincingly R. V. Comerford has argued that the revolutionary group the Irish Republican Brotherhood (the Fenians) was not intrinsically given to the gun. This does seem strange since the stated purpose of the organization was to bring about change in Irish society by means of revolution. See R. V. Comerford, *The Fenians in Context* (Dublin: Wolfhound Press, 1985), 137.
7. Tom Garvin, "O'Connell and the Making of Irish Political Culture," in *Daniel O'Connell Political Pioneer*, ed. M. O'Connell (Dublin: Institute of Public Administration, 1991), 21. See also R. F. Foster, *Modern Ireland, 1600–1972* (London: Allen Lane, 1989), 317, who says for example of Daniel O'Connell that he was the "Liberator" of Catholics rather than Irishmen.
8. It must be said, however, that the late Cardinal Cahal Daly argued that the War of Independence 1919–1921 was both "just and necessary." See Daly, *Violence in Ireland and Christian Conscience* (Dublin: Veritas, 1973), 31. His fellow bishop William Philbin thought that Daly's views were at times both romantic and dangerous and did not scruple to tell him so. Archives of the Archdiocese of Armagh (AAA) Conway papers 16/3-2 Philbin—Daly, August 30, 1974. Daly sent a copy of the letter to Cardinal William Conway.
9. Bodleian Library Oxford (BLO), Clarendon papers Irish Deposit Box 50, Clarendon—MacHale, December 5, 1847. The date is during the Famine in the course of which the clergy did excoriate the government for its lack of sustained universal relief.
10. Also known as the Irish Republic Brotherhood or the Irish Revolutionary Brotherhood (IRB).
11. See Donal A. Kerr, "The Catholic Church in Ireland in the Age of O'Connell" in *Christianity in Ireland: Revisiting the Story*, ed. Brendan Bradshaw and Dáire Keogh (Dublin: Columba Press, 2002), 170.
12. Alexis de Tocqueville, *Journeys to England and Ireland*, ed. J. P. Mayer (London, 1958), 130.
13. Charles Vane, ed., *Memoirs and Correspondence of Viscount Castlereagh, Second Marquess of Londonderry*, 4 vols. (London: H. Colburn, 1848–1853), vol. III, 97. The warning was repeated again

by Cardinal Leonardo Antonelli on behalf of the pope telling the Irish bishops to expel from the Catholic community "those tarnished with the spirit of republicanism." Dublin Diocesan Archives (DDA) Troy papers AB2/116/6 (64) Antonelli—Irish bishops, February 7, 1795.
14. National Library of Ireland (NLI) Sir John Hippesley papers MS 5027 Moylan—Hippesley, March 1, 1800.
15. Troy's pastoral letter is reproduced in Patrick F. Moran, ed., *Spicilegium Ossoriense*, vol. III (Dublin: Browne and Nolan, 1884), 553.
16. Archives of the Irish College Rome (AICR), Kirby papers Cullen—Kirby, January 2, 1867.
17. Thomas Bartlett, *The Fall and Rise of the Irish Nation: The Catholic Question, 1690–1830*, (Dublin: Gill and Macmillan, 1992), 230.
18. Donal A. Kerr, "Government and Roman Catholicism in Ireland 1850–1940," in *Religion, State and Ethnic Group*, ed. Kerr (Aldershot: Dartmouth Publishing Co., 1992), 285.
19. The whole story has been told more recently and in painstaking detail by Ambrose Macaulay, *The Holy See, British Policy and the Plan of Campaign in Ireland 1885–93* (Dublin: Four Courts Press, 2002).
20. As observed by Cardinal Logue. See AAA Logue papers, February 24, 1911.
21. National Archives of Ireland (NAI) State Papers Office Anderson papers, Fenian police reports Box 4.
22. Quoted in Mathias Buschkühl, *Great Britain and the Holy See 1746–1870* (Dublin: Irish Academic Press, 1982), 84.
23. *Ireland and the Holy See. A Retrospective 1866–1883: Illegal Seditious Movements in Ireland Contrasted with the Principles of the Catholic Church as Shown in the Writings of Cardinal Cullen* (Rome: Propaganda Press, 1883), 3.
24. AICR Kirby papers Moriarty—Kirby, May 1, 1864.
25. AAA Cardinal Patrick O'Donnell Papers II, October 9, 1916.
26. D. W. Miller, *Church, State and Nation in Ireland, 1898–1921* (Dublin: Gill and Macmillan, 1973), 408.
27. Donnelly, "Political Identity," *Studies* (1997): 242.
28. Xavier Carty, ed., *Violence and Protest* (Dublin: Veritas, 1970), 9.
29. *Human Life Is Sacred* (Dublin: Veritas, 1975), 37.
30. E. S. Purcell, *Life and Letters of Ambrose Phillips de Lisle*, 2 vols. (London: Macmillan, 1900), II, 130–31.
31. Charles Townshend draws attention to a statement by Cardinal Cahal Daly published in 1973 to the effect that denunciation of violence will have no effect "so long as the policies which provoke violence are persisted in." Townshend comments, "This pragmatic disclaimer is in fact—if not intention—a complete and elegant justification of political violence." He contrasts it with Pope John Paul II "uncompromising" and "unfashionable" repudiation of violence delivered at Drogheda in September 1979. Townshend is clearly unaware that Daly wrote the speech for the pope on that occasion. See Townshend, *Political Violence in Ireland: Government and Resistance in Ireland since 1848* (Oxford: Clarendon Press, 1983), 394.
32. DDA Troy papers AB2/116/7 (102).
33. Margaret Gibbons, *Glimpses of Catholic Ireland in the Eighteenth Century* (Dublin: Browne and Nolan, 1932), 266. Bishop James Caulfield, of Ferns, told Archbishop Troy that a "shocking number" of priests had taken part in the rebellion. DDA Troy papers Caulfield—Troy, June 9, 1799. See also DDA Troy papers, Troy—Fr. Luke Concanen O. P., October 19, 1799. Concanen was Troy's agent in Rome.
34. Kevin Whelan, "Catholics, Politicisation, and the 1798 Rebellion," in *Irish Church History Today*, ed. Réamonn Ó Muirí (Armagh: Cumann Seanchais Ard Mhacha, 1990), 76.
35. *Faulkner's Dublin Journal*, June 7, 1798.
36. Quoted in A. Cogan, *The Diocese of Meath Ancient and Modern*, 3 vols. (Dublin: J. F. Fowler, 1870), vol. III, 270.
37. Ibid., 271.
38. AAA Reilly Papers, Reilly—Henry Conwell, September 13, 1797.
39. Oliver P. Rafferty, *The Catholic Church and the Protestant State: Nineteenth-Century Irish Realities* (Dublin: Four Courts Press, 2008), 31.
40. John Roche Ardill, *The Closing of the Irish Parliament* (Dublin: Hodge and Figgis & Co., 1907), 54.
41. DDA Troy Papers Troy—Cardinal Stephen Borgia, August 17, 1799.
42. Rafferty, *The Catholic Church*, 35, 39, 44, 48, 57.
43. Bartlett, *The Fall and Rise of the Irish Nation*, 250.
44. Public Record Office of Northern Ireland Redesdale Papers T.3030/11/20/X21 Broderick—Redesdale, September 3, 1803.
45. S. J. Connolly, "The Catholic Question, 1801–12," in *A New History of Ireland Vol. V: Ireland under the Union I 1801–70*, ed. W. E. Vaughan (Oxford: Clarendon Press, 1989), 24.

46. Kerr, "The Catholic Church in Ireland in the Age of O'Connell," 165.
47. Desmond J. Keenan, *The Catholic Church in Nineteenth-Century Ireland: A Sociological Study* (Dublin: Gill and Macmillan, 1983), 180.
48. Ibid., 195.
49. *Irish Catholic Directory* (Dublin: Battersby, 1846), 198.
50. *Morning Chronicle*, May 18, 1824.
51. The manifesto is reproduced in John Healy, *Maynooth College: Its Centenary History* (Dublin: Browne and Nolan, 1895), 361.
52. The best work on this to date is Donal A. Kerr, *"A Nation of Beggars?": Priests, People and the Politics of Famine Ireland 1864–1852* (Oxford: Clarendon Press, 1994).
53. One of the most celebrated cases was that of Major Denis Mahon, an evicting landlord of Strokestown Co. Roscommon shot dead, so it was alleged, after have been denounced by the local parish priest Michael McDermot. Some of the details are given in Rafferty, *The Catholic Church*, 80 ff.
54. Bernard O'Reilly, *John MacHale Archbishop of Tuam: His Life, Times and Correspondence*, 2 vols. (New York: F. Pustet and Co., 1890), vol. II, 114.
55. T. D. McGee, *A Life of Rt Rev. Edward Maginn, Coadjutor Bishop of Derry with Selections from His Correspondence* (New York: P. O'Shea, 1857), 101.
56. James A. Coulter, "The Political Theory of Dr Edward Maginn, Bishop of Derry 1846–9," *Irish Ecclesiastical Record* 98 (1962): 106.
57. AICR Cullen papers Fr. Laurence Forde—Cullen, April 3, 1848.
58. Kerr, *"A Nation of Beggars?"* 161.
59. Michael Doheny, *The Felon Track* (New York, 1849; reprinted Dublin: M. H. Gill, 1951), xxix.
60. *The Tablet*, August 8, 1846.
61. BLO Clarendon papers Irish deposit Box 80 Clarendon—Bedford, July 8, 1848.
62. Cullen—Frederick Lucas M. P. in P. MacSuibhne, ed., *Paul Cullen and His Contemporaries with Their Letters* (Naas: Leinster Press, 1961), 378.
63. *Ireland and the Holy See*, 4.
64. British Library Add MSS 44425 Gladstone Papers Cullen—Gladstone, March 12, 1870, f. 244.
65. Oliver P. Rafferty, *The Church, the State and the Fenian Threat* (London: Macmillan, 1999), 43 and 84.
66. DDA Cullen Papers Letterbook 3 Cullen—Spalding, November 1864.
67. DDA Cullen Papers Letterbook 3 Cullen—Bishop Bernard Ullathorne, November 13, 1861.
68. National Library of Ireland Monsell Papers MS 8319 Moriarty—Monsell, March 2, 1868.
69. Rafferty, *Church, State and Fenianism*, 127.
70. Isaac Butt, *Ireland's Appeal for Amnesty: A Letter to the Right Honourable W. E. Gladstone* (Glasgow and London: Cameron and Ferguson, 1870), 7. This may have been an exaggeration; see Maurice Johnston, "The Amnesty Movement 1868–73," unpublished M.A. thesis (St. Patrick's College Maynooth, 1982), 275, which suggests a figure of 600,000.
71. *Freeman's Journal*, December 24, 1869.
72. Quoted in E. R. Norman, *The Catholic Church and Ireland in the Age of Rebellion* (London: Longmans, 1965), 106.
73. Archives of Propaganda Fide (Rome), SC Irlanda 35 (1865–1867): 107.
74. As reported to Lord Lyons. See The National Archives London (TNA) FO 43/58, October 25, 1856.
75. See the Fenian newspaper *The Irish People*, September 27, 1864.
76. Michael Cronin, *The Science of Ethics*, 2 vols. (Dublin: H. M. Gill, 1917), vol. II, 96.
77. *Irish Catholic Directory* (Dublin, 1923), 523.
78. J. H. Whyte, "1916—Revolution and Religion," in *Leaders and Men of the Easter Rising: Dublin 1916*, ed. F. X. Martin (London: Methuen, 1967), 221.
79. Thomas J. Morrissey, *Bishop Edward Thomas O'Dwyer of Limerick 1842–1917* (Dublin: Four Courts Press, 2003), 381.
80. TNA F.O. 380/8/53, May 3, 1916.
81. AAA Logue paper File II, June 1916.
82. *Irish Catholic Directory* (Dublin, 1917), 518.
83. Oliver P. Rafferty, *Catholicism in Ulster 1603–1983: An Interpretative History* (Dublin: Gill and Macmillan, 1994), 200.
84. *The Irish Catholic*, July 7, 1917.
85. Miller, *Church, State and Nation*, 392.
86. Morrissey, *O'Dwyer*, 383.
87. *Irish Catholic Directory* (Dublin, 1921), 532.

88. Quoted in Peter Donnelly, "Violence and Catholic Theology: A Response to Oliver Rafferty," *Studies: An Irish Quarterly Review* 83, no. 331 (1994): 331.
89. *The Tablet*, December 4, 1920.
90. See de Valera to Bishop Joseph MacRory (a future cardinal) AAA MacRory Papers de Valera—MacRory, January 17, 1921.
91. Miller, *Church, State and Nation*, 476.
92. Trinity College Dublin, Dillon papers Dillon—T. P. O'Connor, December 25, 1918.
93. From a statement issued by the bishops on October 19, 1920. See *Irish Catholic Directory* (1921): 556.
94. *Freeman's Journal*, March 12, 1921.
95. Dermot Keogh, *The Vatican, the Bishops and Irish Politics 1919–39* (Cambridge: Cambridge University Press, 1986), 41.
96. Patrick Murray, *Oracles of God: The Roman Catholic Church and Irish Politics 1922–37* (Dublin: University College Dublin Press, 2000), 193.
97. *Irish Catholic Directory* (1932), 622.
98. J. H. Whyte, *Church and State in Modern Ireland 1923–70* (Dublin: Gill and Macmillan, 1971), 11.
99. *Parliamentary Debates Northern Ireland*, vol. 16, 1095.
100. AAA MacRory papers October 1940, a brief document in MacRory's hand that outlines the points the IRA wished him to make to de Valera.
101. *Irish Catholic Directory* (1941): 656–57.
102. *The Irish News*, January 21, 1956.
103. Hence the IRA newspaper *An Phoblacht*, March 1, 1972.
104. This is the conclusion of Gerald McElroy in *The Catholic and the Northern Ireland Crisis 1968–86* (Dublin: Gill and Macmillan, 1991), 159.
105. Cahal Daly, *Renewed Heart for Peace: Address for World day of Peace*, January 1, 1984.
106. Bishop William Philbin, *Ireland's Problem* (Dublin: Veritas, 1974), 4 and 7.
107. Joseph McVeigh, *A Wounded Church: Politics and Justice in Ireland* (Cork and Dublin: Mercier Press, 1989), 79.
108. Oliver P. Rafferty, "The Catholic Church and the Nationalist Community in Northern Ireland since 1960," *Eire-Ireland* 43, nos. 1 and 2 (2008): 113.
109. James Callaghan, the British Home Secretary at the outbreak of the Troubles, said that Cardinal William Conway of Armagh was the most substantial political figure in the Catholic community. See Callaghan, *A House Divided: The Dilemma of Northern Ireland* (London: Collins, 1973), 97.
110. John McGarry and Brendan O'Leary, *Explaining Northern Ireland* (Oxford: Wiley-Blackwell, 1995), 111.
111. Joseph Ruane and Jennifer Todd, "Irish National and the Conflict in Northern Ireland," in *Rethinking Northern Ireland: Culture, Ideology and Colonialism*, ed. David W. Miller (London: Longman, 1998), 63.
112. *Justice, Love and Peace: Pastoral Letters of the Irish Bishops 1969–79* (Dublin: Veritas, 1979), 41–42.
113. TNA CJ4/1544 W. R. Haydon to Second Secretary Foreign Office London, January 6, 1976.
114. Duncan Murrow, "Church and Religion in the Ulster Crisis," in *Facets of the Conflict in Northern Ireland*, ed. Seamus Dunn (Basingstoke: Macmillan, 1995), 160.
115. See *The Pope in Ireland: Addresses and Homilies* (Dublin: Veritas, 1979), 21 and 56.
116. Seamus Murphy, "I Don't Support the IRA but . . .," *Studies: An Irish Quarterly Review* 82, no. 327 (1993): 283.
117. As Gerry Adams, the president of Sinn Féin, told a prominent Irish journalist. See Finnuola O'Connor, *In Search of a State: Catholics in Northern Ireland* (Belfast: Blackstaff Press, 1993), 295.
118. *The Irish Times*, November 12, 1980.
119. David McKittrick and David McVea, *Making Sense of the Troubles* (Belfast: Blackstaff, 2000), 232.
120. Gerry Adams, *A Farther Shore: Ireland's Long Road to Peace* (New York: Random House, 2004), 146. See also Paul Bew and Gordon Gillispie, *The Northern Ireland Peace Process 1993–1996: A Chronology* (London: Serif, 1996), 151.
121. Much as in the same way the church accommodated itself to de Valera's rise to power in the Irish Free State despite having excommunicated his followers in the Irish Civil War. See Catharine O'Donnell, *Fianna Fáil, Irish Republicanism and the Northern Ireland Troubles, 1968–2005* (Dublin, 2007), 8–11.
122. Joseph Ruane and Jennifer Todd, *The Dynamics of Conflict in Northern Ireland: Power, Conflict and Emancipation* (Cambridge: Cambridge University Press, 1996), 74.
123. Marcus Turner, *Ireland Holy War: The Struggle for a Nation's Soul 1500–2000* (New Haven and London: Yale University Press, 2000), 14.

124. Cahal Daly, *Peace the Work of Justice: Addresses on the Northern Tragedy 1973–1979* (Dublin: Veritas, 1980), 85.
125. *The Guardian*, October 14, 2001.
126. Jim Smyth, "Review of the Catholic Church and the Protestant State Nineteenth Century Irish Realities," *English Historical Review* 124, no. 508 (2009): 721–23.
127. Ronald Ayling, ed., *Seven Plays by Sean O'Casey* (New York: St. Martin's Press, 1985), 61.
128. Ibid., 69.
129. Mark Ryan, *Fenian Memoirs* (Dublin: M. H. Gill, 1946), xxiv.
130. AAA Conway papers 16/1, January 23, 1974.
131. The details can be followed in Rafferty, *The Catholic Church*, 142–58.
132. Patrick Pearse, *The Coming Revolution: The Political Writings and Speeches of Patrick Pearse* (Cork: Mercier Press, 2012), 111–12.
133. Ibid., 51.
134. Francis Shaw S. J., "The Canon of Irish History: A Challenge," *Studies: An Irish Quarterly Review* 61, no. 242 (1972): 113–53.

5

Responsibility and Limitation: The Early Christian Church and War

Darrell Cole

Why would the Christian church ever say yes to war? After all, the founder of the church famously ordered his disciples to "turn the other cheek" and to never seek revenge (Matt. 5:39). The Apostle Paul reinforced these injunctions when he advised his Roman audience never to seek revenge but to live at peace with everyone (Rom. 12:17–20). Nevertheless, we find Christians participating in the military almost from the beginning. Two dominant themes emerge as we investigate how this came about: First, there is a recognized need to act responsibly toward the earthly city. Second, responsible action may mean taking part in acts of force for the common good, but those acts of force must be consonant with achieving justice, peace, and order, and they must be carried out with justice. Thus, the responsible use of force means limitations on that use.

The popular notion of Christian attitudes toward war can be summarized as follows: the neat historical trajectory of pacifism, then just war, and, finally, holy war. Roland Bainton provides an admirably clear example of this kind of thinking:

> The three Christian positions with regard to war . . . matured in chronological sequence, moving from pacifism to the just war to the crusade. The age of persecution down to the time of Constantine was the age of pacifism to the degree that during this period no Christian author to our knowledge approved of Christian participation in battle.[1]

Exactly when and how pacifism ceded to just war is a matter of some dispute but two points remain a constant in the popular view. First, that the early Church was uniformly passive and that Origen is an exemplar of this sort of pristine Christianity. Second, that the post-Constantinian Church was ready to do battle and that Augustine is the one who initiates the full-blown just war tradition. Alan Watt has accurately summarized the popular scholarly opinion as one in which "Augustine was the first mature Christian to struggle in public and intellectual manner with the justification, goals and means of armed conflict."[2]

Figures such as Origen are used by some contemporary pacifist theologians as examples of true, untainted, Christian belief. John Howard Yoder went so far as to argue that the evidence is so strong for a dominant early pacifist church that Christians cannot be faithful to the early church unless they are pacifists.³ According to this line of thought, the kind of Christianity we see in the early church, the one exemplified by the likes of Origen, is one that rejects the Caesar system as inherently evil. Those soldiers who became Christians and remained in the military were mainly bureaucrats who did not employ violence in their duties. The swords they carried were merely a symbol of their administrative status. Such Christians were never fully approved of in the Christian community but they were not excommunicated.

This popular position on the early Christian attitude toward war is very debatable. There is little evidence of a homogeneous Christian attitude toward war during any period in history, including the pre-Constantinian period. In fact, there is little evidence that Church Fathers such as Origen held a unified, unambiguous view of war. Looking at the Origenist tradition, represented by Clement of Alexandria (ca. 150–215), Origen (ca. 185–254), Eusebius of Caesarea (ca. 260–339), and Ambrose of Milan (ca. 339–397), along with Augustine (ca. 354–430), is a fruitful pursuit when considering the questions of why and how Christians began to think about the just use of force.⁴ For it is from this group of theologians that we can see how Christian philosophers first began to think about how Christians ought to engage more positively with the larger, secular communities they find themselves.

The message of the Origenist tradition is simple. The world as a Satanic world order must always be rejected but there is a responsibility for one's neighbors that must be recognized. Moreover, there is a responsibility for order, justice, and peace that must be recognized if human life is to be achieved above the level of mere subsistence. We include Clement of Alexandria, even though he flourished before the time of Origen, because of his influence on the teaching of Origen and his followers. Eusebius is an inheritor of Origen's theology. Ambrose is included because he takes the Origenist strands of thinking available to him concerning Christian attitudes toward the state and war, and weaves them in such a way as to prepare the theological way for Augustine's approach to the state and war. Thus, Ambrose provides a kind of theological relay station between the Eastern, Origenist tradition and Augustine.

My argument is that we can find Christians accepting a modified, controlled, and limited use of force by the second century and that the themes so dominant in Augustine are already in place for him to use. Thus Augustine did not create the Christian just war tradition out of whole cloth but used what came before him. In other words, Augustine is a builder upon the foundation laid for him by previous contributors to the problems of Christian involvement with earthly politics.

Clement of Alexandria

Clement's views of military service appear to be at odds with one another. We see this apparent inconsistency in his treatise *The Teacher*, in which he posits Christ as the teacher of Christian morality. On the one hand we find Christ teaching that Christians should be trained in peace and not in war: "We do not train women like Amazons to be manly in war, since we wish even the men to be peaceable" (*The Teacher* 1.12.98; see also *Stromata* IV 8.61). On the other hand, we find Christ teaching through John the Baptist that soldiers ought not to quit soldiering but to "be content with their wages only" (Clement is quoting from Luke 3:14 at this point). Moreover, Clement draws a portrait of Moses as an exemplary and praiseworthy military leader. In particular, he has this to say about Moses leading the Hebrews out of the land of Egypt only after despoiling their previous taskmasters:

> Whether, then, as may be alleged is done in war, they thought it proper, in the exercise of the rights of conquerors, to take away the property of their enemies, as those who have gained the day from those who are worsted . . . or as in peace, took the spoil as wages against the will of those who for a long period had given them to recompense, but rather had robbed them, it is all one. (*Stromata* I 24)

Thus, it is morally indifferent whether Moses led the Hebrews to despoil the Egyptians as an act of war or of peace. The act of war was in this case just rather than unjust because the Hebrews had good reasons for waging war on the Egyptians who treated them unjustly. Thus Clement recognizes a distinction between just and unjust wars and praises the actions of the leader of this just war. He even goes on to praise the various tactics Moses used as a military commander.

Clement's disparate views on military service can be accounted for when we consider his overall view of the Christian life as one of various stages of moral development. For Clement, the Christian life is seen as a kind of journey—a moral journey—in which those on the lower level share many of the characteristics of the pagan.[5] As Christians progress, they obtain a higher form of knowledge of God and this knowledge transforms them into morally and spiritually higher beings. Gaining knowledge of God takes time and effort. Those Christians who remain in secular jobs cannot hope to have the time to progress, which is not to say that such Christians can make no moral progress. Thus Clement argues,

> It is a man's very nature to be on intimate terms with God. We . . . direct each animal to the kind of work most natural to it; in the same way we call upon man, who is truly a heavenly creature and who has been made for the vision of the heavens, to come to a knowledge of God. Laying hold of what is intimately and peculiarly his own as distinct from other living things, we advise him to outfit himself with godliness as an adequate preparation for his eternal journey. If you are a farmer, we say, till the earth, but acknowledge the God of farmers; if you love seafaring, sail on, but remember to call upon the celestial Helmsman. If you were in the army when you were seized by the knowledge of God, obey the Commander who gives just commands. (*Exhortation to the Greeks* X.100.2)

So farmers, sailors, and soldiers can all progress toward God to some degree, though such pursuits would have to be abandoned if one wished to make the fullest progression possible. The key for each secular job is to do the job well and to acknowledge God in the job, which, for soldiers, means obeying just commands. Here we see the first glimmer of the idea that will soon become dominant in most Christian thinking on war: soldiering can be good but it must be limited to just uses of force.

Origen

Origen is a veritable hero among modern pacifists. Only Tertullian ranks with him as a sterling example of the primitive church's alleged absolute commitment to peace. Even Louis Swift, who is quick to recognize the problems with pacifist interpretations of pre-Constantinian Church Fathers, refers to Origen as an unambiguous pacifist.[6] Certainly Origen is opposed to Christian participation in war but it is probably wrong to refer to him as a pacifist in the way the term is usually used: as someone who believes that all use of force is immoral.

Origen did not write much about Christian participation in the military. Largely concerned with scriptural exegesis, Origen used allegory as a tool to formulate a multilevel system of Christianity similar to Clement's, with a spiritual elite on top and the simpler, ordinary Christians below. But Origen's system of moral and spiritual formation is not as straightforward as Clement's, because he has little to say about the stages that occur in the maturation process. Origen elaborates in great detail the duties of the elite but says almost nothing about the duties of the ordinary Christian. The elite according to Origen are those who have renounced things fleshy and earthly. Those who wish to progress in their spiritual formation must completely renounce creation in order to understand that one has been transformed into a new being in Christ (*Treatise on the Passover* 6.11–12).

Origen shares with Clement the idea that all Christians possess the ability to reach the upper hierarchy of spirituality but only those who devote themselves to the study of Scripture and who renounce all worldly things actually reach maturation. Those who cannot devote themselves to study and who remain in secular jobs must remain at a lower level. Origen was no idealist. He realized that the majority of Christians would remain at a lower level and how this realism informs his thinking about warfare and military service is not as pacific as one might believe.

The only work in which Origen is concerned with Christians participating in the military is the polemical *Contra Celsum*, written against the Roman conservative Celsus who charged Christians with spiritual, moral, social, and political crimes.[7] Origen insists that there are two ways of Christian living, with the more excellent way for persons of "superior attainments in wisdom and truth" (*Contra Celsum* V 33). In an argument that would appeal to someone like Celsus, a conservative steeped in Greco-Roman philosophical ideas of human perfection, Origen makes the case that Christian perfection is the highest possibility for human life. For our purposes, the key passage occurs where Origen answers the charge that Christians are unpatriotic because they do not participate in public and civil life. Such people refuse to take a responsible role in the community in which they live (*Contra Celsum* VIII 63–75). Celsus is worried about what Robert Wilken has called an undermining "counterculture" that could threaten the security of the empire.[8] Origen's first reply is to argue that, if everyone were Christian, there would be no need to see to the security of the empire for there would be no threats to that security (*Contra Celsum* VIII 68). Origen then makes an extraordinary move. He equates all Christians with the pagan priesthood, which was not required to participate in the Roman military, but instead was required to pray for the emperor and soldiers to triumph in battle:

> And, of course, in war time you do not enlist your priests. If this is a reasonable procedure, how much more so is it for Christians to fight as priests and worshippers of God while others fight as soldiers. Though they keep their right hands clean, the Christians fight through their prayers to God on behalf of those doing battle in a just cause and on behalf of an emperor who is ruling justly in order that all opposition and hostility toward those who are acting rightly may be eliminated. (*Contra Celsum* VIII 73)

Moreover, Christians provide the emperor with an irreplaceable aid: they overcome with prayer the very demons that cause wars. In so doing, Christians do more good for the security of the community and act more responsibly for the community than soldiers. Thus, Christians do not go on campaign with the emperor but they do go to battle for the empire "by raising a special army of piety through our petition to God" (*Contra Celsum* VIII 73).

The attitude toward the emperor and war in this passage is remarkable because it seems so unlike the Origen that comes down to us via the pacifist interpretation which roots Christian opposition to war during this pristine era in a general renunciation of Roman government and military as inherently evil. We can readily see the problem with this interpretation of Origen. We only have to imagine Origen making similar arguments for other inherently evil institutions and practices, such as prostitution, to show the misconception of the pacifist interpretation. Thus, if we follow the pacifist interpretation of Origen, we could also imagine him arguing that Christians ought to pray for the success of a well-ordered brothel. In his positive attitude toward Roman government, Origen goes so far as to argue that the emperor Augustus was providential for Christianity because the Pax Romana, established and maintained through the use of military force, provided a unity to the land that enabled Christianity to spread (*Contra Celsum* II 30). Origen, then, does not judge the Roman government and its use of force as something inherently evil but rather as a providential good.

Origen does, however, place a limit on what can count as a good from the Roman government. When the government fights justly in a just cause, it is to be supported. Christians support just rule from the emperor, which includes fighting wars against hostile enemies. On this point, Origen draws an analogy from the life of bees. He points to the well-ordered activity of bees, argues that such a life is a fitting lesson for human beings, and declares that "if wars are ever necessary, they ought to be just and ordered" (*Contra Celsum* IV 82). When the state fights just and ordered wars, Christians should support the state with prayers. For Origen, this kind of spiritual activity is the highest form of human activity.

Origen has argued that Christians ought to support the state's function of using force for the common good, albeit only spiritually (which, we say again for emphasis' sake, in Origen's Christian Platonism is more real and does more good than the soldiers wielding earthly, material weapons), but he must still deal with the question of how this positive view of the state's function of using force squares with the spirit of love demanded of all Christians, regardless of where they are in their spiritual formation. In his treatise *On Prayer*, Origen expounds on the spirit of love that should be seen in the Christian duty of forgiving the debts of others as they discharge their own debts. Origin links this section of the Lord's Prayer to Paul's command to the Romans that all Christians should render what is due to others, including the tribute, fear, and honor due to the governing authorities (*On Prayer* 28.1–2). Thus, for Origen, the spirit of love of neighbor is found in taking responsibility for the common good by praying for the success of the state to bring order, justice, and peace for everyone against evildoers. Such duties of responsibility are duties of love, and the debt must be paid.

In sum, Origen opposes military service for Christians, but he does not oppose all war, nor does he consider the state an inherently evil institution. When the state responds to evil with a just use of force, this is a positive good and ought to be supported by Christian prayer. God will respond to prayers in a just cause so that the unjust may be destroyed. Origen, therefore, does not reject the use of force as something inherently evil. True, Christians are not to employ force themselves because that is not their job. The job of the Christian is to show responsible love toward their neighbors by praying for the success of a just use of force. Thus, we again find an acceptance of the use of force but limitations on what can count as a morally praiseworthy use of force.

Origen is clear in his arguments against Celsus that Christians should be thought of as in the same political class as pagan priests: people with the job of praying for victory in a just cause rather than wielding swords and spears to attain that victory. Presumably, then, Origen would be against Christians joining the military. However, there are times when Origen's ambiguity about the obligations and duties of the simple, ordinary Christian makes it possible to read him as a cautious advocate for Christian participation in war. When Origen discusses the material blessings accorded to the people of Israel, he likens the Jews to ordinary Christians who receive Scripture carnally, and, so, receive carnal blessings (*Homilies on Leviticus* 16.3). One could argue that the logic of this position leads to the claim that ordinary Christians can participate in wars as the children of Israel do. Origen never makes this claim but one of his followers will follow the logic of Origen's argument in just this way and defend military service as an option for ordinary Christians.

Eusebius of Caesarea

Eusebius preserved the multilevel system of Christianity found in Clement and Origen, and pressed it to its logical conclusion by differentiating more sharply the duties and obligations accorded to each level. For Eusebius, there are two levels of Christianity and each level is justified on its own terms, with its own kind of heroes, and one is not required to be in the upper level to be thought of as a true Christian. In the sixth book of his *Ecclesiastical History*, Eusebius presents Origen as the supreme example of the upper level Christian, the level of the pure spiritual life. But the lower level has its Christian heroes too, and Constantine is that hero. Eusebius manages this change of attitude toward secular politics and soldiering by spiritualizing history as well as Scripture.

Eusebius followed Clement and Origen in holding that the Pax Romana instituted by the emperor Augustus was providential for Christianity (*Demonstration of the Gospel* 3.7.140). Eusebius takes the idea a step forward: the monarchy as it came to rest on Constantine and the spread of the Gospel are two blessings from God and together they fulfill Old Testament prophecies concerning universal peace and harmony (*In Praise of Constantine* 16.3–7). Eusebius goes so far as to crown Constantine as a type of Christ who consummates a marriage of Church and Empire. The result of this marriage is that the mundane is now part of the spiritual. The ordinary Christian should and must fight for the emperor. The more spiritual sort of Christian will follow Origen's advice and remain separated from the world, but not so far that they would fail in Christian love and concern for the common good; hence they would pray for the emperor and for success in using force against those who would threaten the common good. The key passage occurs in the *Demonstration of the Gospel*:

> As a result, two life styles have been established in the Christian Church. The first, which goes beyond nature and the usual manner of life, is not involved at all with [earthly matters]. Out of an extraordinary love for things heavenly it departs from the common and customary patter and is devoted wholly to the worship of God.... The other is subordinated and more concerned with human affairs.... It lays down the practical rules for those fighting in a just war.... For such individuals there is a secondary state of perfection which is suitable in its own way for their kind of life. Thus, no one is excluded from sharing in the Savior's coming. (I 8)

Like Clement, Eusebius sees the ordinary Christian as one who has the ability to achieve a kind of spiritual perfection while remaining in an earthly job, including the military. Such perfection is inferior to what may be achieved by the spiritual elite but it is a real perfection. The spiritual elite too have a role to play in the state but not one of military participation. They must pray for the good of the state. There is even evidence that Eusebius was the first to propose a kind of military chaplaincy (*Life of Constantine* 4.65.2–3). The logical consequence of this position is not what we have come to think of as the just war tradition but the holy war position. According to Eusebius, Constantine's battles are not merely just, though they are certainly that, but actually holy. Constantine is achieving real spiritual good in his military battles and, so, it is unthinkable for Christians not to support him with prayers and able-bodied men for the military.

The answers to the questions of why Christians would ever become involved with the use of force and what should the result look like if Christians do become involved are evident again in Eusebius. Christians have a responsibility for the empire but they exercise this responsibility in ways that place limits on the use of force. For Eusebius, all Christians have a responsibility for the state. Ordinary Christians fulfill their duties by taking part in the use of force, whereas the spiritual elite fulfill their duties by praying for the success of those uses of force. But that force must be just in order for it to be the kind of action that leads to spiritual perfection. The Christian soldier cannot achieve spiritual perfection by ignoring the rules of fighting just wars and the spiritual elite cannot achieve spiritual perfection by praying for rulers who fight unjust wars or for soldiers who fight unjustly. Thus Eusebius has built into his theological politics theological reasons for limiting the use of force even in holy wars and those limitations are spelled out in the just war tradition.

Ambrose of Milan

Ambrose, the governor of the province of Aemilia–Liguria before he became Bishop of Milan in 374, is the key figure in Christian thinking on the use of force that links early Eastern Fathers with the most important figure in the early Western tradition: Augustine. He shares with Eusebius the belief that the advent of Constantine means the potential of spiritual goods achieved in military battle. Like his Greek predecessors, Ambrose was troubled by the problem of how to maintain principles of Christianity when responsible citizenship demanded participation in the use of force. With Origen in particular he shared a concern for how a spirit of love is to be reconciled with the use of force. He solves the problem by tying love to the use of force in a way that makes acts of force acts of love.[9]

Do Christians have the same duty as their Old Testament forbears to aid others in trying to establish peace here and now? Ambrose answers this question by taking a distinctly Eusebian approach that also looks forward to Augustine. Ambrose considered the Bible as the supreme authority for guidance in action. He culls guidance from scripture to shape the moral life. In a revealing passage from his *On the Duties of the Clergy* (modeled on Cicero's *On Duties*), he concludes the work by pointing out that they (the three books) "offer you a large number of examples, for almost all the examples drawn from our forefathers, and also many words of theirs, are included within these three books; so that ... a succession of old-time examples set down in such a small compass may offer much instruction" (III 138). Thus the lives of the Old Testament Fathers are models of action for Christians. One characteristic common among many of the Old Testament Fathers is the virtue of courage displayed in just wars. Ambrose praises Moses, Joshua, David, and Judas Maccabaeus as fitting models of courage for Christians in just battles.

For Ambrose, the virtue of love justifies Christian participation in the military. The virtue of love, on the one hand, does not allow for acts of force for self-preservation. We see this in the way he answers the question about whether or not Christians can follow Cicero in holding that a better man is morally in the right when he chooses to save his own life over that of a lesser man:

> Although it seems better for the common good that a wise man rather than a fool should escape from shipwreck, yet I do not think that a Christian, a just and a wise man, ought to save his own life by the death of another; just as when he meets with an armed robber he cannot return his blows, lest in defending his life he should stain this love toward his neighbor. (*On Duties* 3.4.27)

Thus, the virtue of love is destroyed when Christians resort to self-defense. On the other hand, he has this to say about John the Baptist's advice to soldiers:

> The Baptist gave a fitting response to each kind of people, one for all; thus, to the tax collectors, that they should not exact payment beyond what was appointed; to the soldiers, that they should falsely accuse no one, not require loot, teaching, therefore, that the pay of the soldiery is fixed, lest when extravagance is sought, plunder is rife. But these and other precepts are appropriate for all occupations, and the practice of compassion is shared . . . for compassion is the fullness of the virtues, and, therefore, the form of the perfect virtue is laced before all. (*Exposition of the Holy Gospel according to Saint Luke* II:77)

Here the virtue of compassion (or love) compels soldiers to do their jobs justly. With this thought in mind, let's look at what Ambrose has to say about courage in connection with love as seen in the actions of Moses:

> The glory of fortitude, therefore, does not rest only on the strength of one's body or of one's arms, but rather on the courage of the mind. Nor is the law of courage exercised in causing, but in driving away all harm. He who does not keep harm off a friend, if he can, is as much in fault as he who causes it. Wherefore holy Moses gave this as a first proof of his fortitude in war. For when he saw an Hebrew receiving hard treatment at the hand of an Egyptian, he defended him, and laid low the Egyptian and hid him in the sand. (*On Duties* 1.36.179)

Thus the virtues of love and courage are destroyed when Christians refuse to use force to protect their neighbors. So love and courage move Christians to use force in the protection of others but not for themselves. As one notable biographer of Ambrose has put it, justice has become "integrated with charity."[10]

The whole purpose of war, according to Ambrose, is to establish peace (*Discourse on Psalm* 118 21.17). He follows Eusebius in basing his entire approach to Christian participation in the military in the rights and responsibilities of earthly rulers. The hand of God works in both the temporal and spiritual levels. Thus it should come as no surprise that the Pax Romana should be a part of God's plan (*Discourse on Psalm* 45 21). God works through earthly rulers and their armies for his purposes, so that Ambrose can assure the emperor Gratian that not only does he do no moral wrong when he fights against the barbarians for the sake of the empire, but that he should "go forth, sheltered, indeed, under the shield of faith, and girt with them sword of the Spirit; go forth to the victory, promised of old time, and foretold in the oracles given by God" (*On the Faith* 2.16.136). Gratian, then, fights not a mere just war when he defends the empire, but a holy one.

Ambrose does not believe that all Christians ought to use force in order to protect their neighbors. Following a now well-established tradition, he argues that "the Church does not overcome the powers of the enemy with the weapons of this world, but with spiritual arms . . . . The weapons of the Church are faith, the weapons of the Church are prayer, which overcomes the enemy" (*On Widows* 8.49). Ambrose begins the discussion on courage in *On Duties* by distinguishing the acts of courage proper to the clergy from the acts of courage proper to the layman. He begins by arguing that courage is divided into two parts, matters of war and matters at home,

> but the thought of warlike matters seems foreign to the duty of our office [as clergy], for we have our thoughts fixed more on the duty of the soul than on that of the body; nor is it our business to look to arms, but rather to the affairs of peace. Our fathers, however, as Joshua, the son of Nun, Jerubbaal, Samson, and David gained great glory also in war. (*On Duties* 1.35.175)

The clergy and the soldiers have the same duty to fight evil so that order, justice, and peace may be secured. But they carry out that duty in different ways: the clergy with prayer and the soldiers with acts of force.

Ambrose encouraged the use of force for the protection of others but he did not give carte blanche to how Christians can carry out that duty. He places limitations on the force that can be used in a just cause. Ambrose points out that the Old Testament hero David "never waged war unless he was driven to it. Thus prudence was combined in him with fortitude in the battle" (*On Duties* 1.35.176–77). Thus just wars are always wars of necessity. This is no small point. The state may be the ordained provider of order through force but not every act of force by the state is just.

What counts as a necessary and just war for Ambrose? We can glean from the above quoted passages on the connections between courage and the other virtues that wars to defend the state from unjust aggression are necessary and just (*On Duties* 1.35.176–77; 1.27.129). When we look at his comments of the story of the crime of Gibeah against the wife of a Levite (as related in Judg. 19), Ambrose points out that

> What regard for virtue our forefathers had to avenge by a war the wrongs of one woman which had been brought on her by violation at the hands of profligate men . . . . What great regard our forefathers had for virtue is shown by the fact that forty thousand men drew the sword against their brethren of the tribe of Benjamin in their desire to avenge the wrong done to modesty, for they would not endure the violation of chastity. (*On Duties* 3.19.110 and 116)

Thus we can glean from this passage that wars to punish wrongdoing are necessary and just.

Ambrose also distinguishes between just and unjust tactics within war. In his discussion of justice in *On Duties*, Ambrose argues,

> It [justice] must even be preserved in all dealings with enemies. For instance, if the day of the spot for a battle has been agreed upon with them, it would be considered an act against justice to occupy the spot beforehand, or to anticipate the time. (1.29.139)

Moses, Joshua, and Elisha are used as figures to illustrate what it means to show justice to enemies. So justice demands that no unfair advantage of the enemy should be taken. Here Ambrose is concerned chiefly with unfair advantages taken by breaking agreements.

Ambrose also emphasizes that mercy should be shown to a defeated enemy. In a passage where he distinguishes the useful from the virtuous, he uses David's treatment of his enemies as an example for Christians to follow:

> He also thought that justice should be shown to those who had borne arms against himself the same as to his own men. Again, he admired Abner, the bravest champion of the opposing side, whilst he was their leader and was yet waging war. Nor did he dispose him when suing for peace, but honored him by a banquet. When killed by treachery, he mourned and wept for him. He followed him and honored his obsequies, and evinced his good faith in desiring vengeance for the murder; for he handed on that duty to his son in the charge that he gave him, being anxious rather that the death of an innocent man should not be left unavenged, than that anyone should mourn for his own. (*On Duties* 2.7.33)

Finally, Ambrose uses the story of Elisha's mercy to the Syrian army (recounted in 2 Kings 6) to argue that justice demands that defeated enemies be shown mercy (*On Duties* 3.14.87; see also *Exposition of Luke* 5.76).

The elements of Ambrose's just war position are clear. The only morally good purpose of war is to establish a just peace and this is accomplished by defending the common good from attack or by punishing wrongdoing. When the political ruler is a Christian, like Gratian, the just wars he wages on behalf of the common good are not simply just but holy as well, since they issue in spiritual goods as well as material ones. All Christians, compelled by the virtue of love, have a responsibility to aid in the fighting of just wars that protect the common good, either by prayer or by participation. Finally, just as there are limits on what can count as a just war, so there are limits on what can count as just fighting in war. Mercy should be accorded to a defeated enemy and there should be no treachery.

Augustine

The themes we have been exploring are responsibility and limitation: responsibility for the order and peace of the earthly city and limitation on the use of force in a just cause. These themes come to a head in Augustine whose thinking on Christian participation in war represents what would become foundational for the Christian West. For Augustine, human beings are the sort of creatures who need coercive government to provide for the peace, order, and justice for all. Christians, therefore, have a responsibility to support the governing structures that use force for protection of the common good but there are limitations on what can count as a justified use of that force.

Augustine held that the sin of the first human beings tainted the entire human race. He argues that it is difficult to imagine the magnitude of that first sin because Adam, by sinning, "merited eternal evil, in that he destroyed in himself a good that might have been eternal. In consequence, the whole of mankind is a condemned lump" (*City of God* 21.12). So all of humankind is inherently at odds with God and deserving condemnation. Those who receive God's undeserved grace are to seek their proper place in God's order. As Peter Brown puts it, following God's harmony "is the sum total of Christian behavior."[11] Because the human condition is one of inherent disobedience to God, Augustine argues that human beings will remain essentially the same in nature. Thus Eugene TeSelle rightly argues that Augustine does not hold out any hope for human to improve from the moral standpoint.[12]

Augustine's mature view of the governing authorities is that they are the earthly power that holds human sin in check.[13] He argues that

> Surely it is not in vain that we have such institutions as the power of the king, the death penalty of the judge, the hooks of the executioner, the weapons of the soldier, the stringency of the overlord and even the

strictness of a good father. All these things have their own method, reason, motive and benefit. When they are feared, evil men are held in check, and the good enjoy greater peace among the wicked. (*Letter* 153.6)

Human nature is so constituted that the use of force by the governing authorities, or at least the threat of the use of force, is what makes good order possible in the earthly city. All citizens, including Christians, benefit from the peace and order provided by the governing authorities. Christians, therefore, should value the "peace of Babylon" (*City of God* 19.26).

Augustine does not think that every Christian has a responsibility participate in the governing authorities' use of force. In a letter to the Roman General Boniface, Augustine exhorts him to continue in the military profession in order that he may play a role in protecting the common good. Augustine comforts him with those passages in Scripture in which John the Baptist, Jesus, or some Apostle encounters a Roman military figure and never hints at the moral unacceptability of their profession. However, Augustine still holds that

Those who serve God with the highest self-discipline of chastity, by renouncing all these worldly activities, have a more prominent place before Him: "But everyone hath his proper gift from God, one after this manner and another after that" [quoting 1 Cor. 7:7]. Thus, some fight for you against invisible enemies by prayer, while you strive for them against visible barbarians by fighting. (*Letter* 189)

So we find Augustine remaining true to the older, Eastern tradition of considering Christians remaining in the world as lower status Christians, for those who have removed themselves from earthly jobs have a more prominent place before God. But notice that even these non-worldly Christians have an obligation to pray for the earthly success of earthly rulers.[14]

What makes a man like Boniface an appropriate agent of the use of force? One important virtue shared by all Christians is love—*caritas*, the Latin rendering of the Greek *agape*. *Caritas* describes the love that God has for human beings, a love that serves as a model for the love that Christians are to have for each other. Augustine follows Ambrose in holding that there is no inherent contradiction in love and using force on others. In fact, using force on others may, indeed, be an apt expression of love. To go one step further, the virtue of love and how it informs the decision making of the Christian in a political arena that demands the use of force for the common good, and the decision making of the Christian actually given the job of using force, is what distinguishes the Christian politician and soldier from the pagan. When Augustine treats the problem of who can be fit for using force, he argues that "no one is fit for the task of inflicting punishment unless—by the greatness of his love—he has overcome the hate by which those who seek to avenge themselves are usually enraged" (*Sermon on the Mount* 20.63). So the just user of force is marked by love in distinction to the hate that marks the one who seeks revenge.

We should point out that there is some scholarly disagreement over the importance of charity in Augustine's views on war. On one end of the scale, Paul Ramsey would make it the centerpiece of Augustine's just war teaching.[15] On the other end of the scale, James Turner Johnson finds little in Augustine's just war teaching based on charity.[16] Johnson argues that Ramsey concentrated on Augustine's complaints against using for purposes of self-defense in *On Free Will*, and how charity fits into that complaint, instead of the more directly relevant texts on just war found places such as *City of God* and *Reply to*

Faustus. Johnson is probably right that Ramsey placed too much emphasis on charity in Augustine's just war teaching but, as I hope to show, Augustine is surely as concerned as Ambrose and the Greek Fathers about how the greatest of Christian virtues can be made to harmonize with doing physical harm to others.

Augustine distinguishes the kinds of love that inform the users of force in a celebrated passage of dialogue from *On Free Will* in which he is concerned about how acts of killing in self-defense may betray a disordered desire, one out of harmony with God's order. Augustine distinguishes between the private person who kills out of a disordered desire to protect self and the self's material goods and the soldier who kills dispassionately for the common good:

> For that he be slain who lays plans to take the life of another is less hard [to bear] than the death of him who is demanding his own life [against the plotter] . . . . The soldier in slaying the enemy is the agent of the law, wherefore he does his duty easily with no wrong aim or purpose . . . . That law, therefore, which is for the protection of the citizens . . . can be obeyed without wrong desire . . . but I cannot see how these men [who defend themselves privately], while not held guilty by the law, can be without fault; for the law does not force them to kill, but leaves it in their power. (*On Free Will* I 5)

The point of the passage is Augustine's concern about the wrong kind of desire informing the Christian. It is not wrong to desire to save your own life when attacked by an unjust person, but it is wrong to desire it so much that you are willing to kill the unjust person to save yourself.[17] The soldier, however, does not kill out of the wrong kind of desire. The soldier's aim and purpose are both just: they are given jobs to protect others and not themselves. The private person does not have the soldier's responsibility to use force for the common good. That responsibility is what separates the private person from the soldier. We see the point repeated when Augustine uses John the Baptist's words of advice to soldiers as proof against the Manichaeans who deny the use of force to Christians:

> Otherwise John, when the soldiers who came to be baptized asked, What shall we do? would have replied, Throw away your arms; give up the service, never strike, or would, or disable anyone. But knowing that such actions in battle were not murderous, but authorized by law, and that the solders did not thus avenge themselves, but defend the public safety, he replied, do violence to no man, accuse no man falsely, and be content with your wages. (*Reply to Faustus the Manichaean* 22.74)

Thus soldiers act out of a sense of military duty and not out of personal revenge: that is precisely what makes their acts possibly just (other criteria will have to be met).

The distinction between a private person and a soldier is key for Augustine. Private persons cannot defend their persons or their property without violating charity. Soldiers may do so in the line of duty without violating charity. Keeping this distinction in mind may help us avoid some of the pitfalls we encounter when we try to appropriate Augustine for contemporary problems in war. J. Warren Smith, for example, interprets the famous passage in *On Free Will* to mean that Augustine would allow for what is known as preemptive war (striking an enemy first when that enemy clearly intends to launch an imminent attack) but not a preventive war (striking an enemy that may one day plan an attack) even though both sorts of attack are self-defensive in nature.[18] Smith is able to make such an argument because Augustine allows for a law that makes it permissible for a private person to strike first against a highway robber or an would-be rapist. This imputes to Augustine a lesser evil position normally associated with modern moral realism and not with the theologian who maintained that certain acts such as lying and nonspousal sex were absolutely forbidden.[19] However, we must keep in mind that, for Augustine, it is human law that allows a lesser evil (preemptive acts of force by private persons for the sake of earthly goods) in order to avoid a greater one (thieves and rapists achieving their unjust goals). This does not mean that what the law allows is permissible for Christians who desire to remain within the bounds of charitable action. Christians as private persons may not use preemptive force for any reason without staining their love toward their neighbors. Christians as soldiers may not fail to use such force without staining their love toward their neighbors. Thus, it is not a lesser evil when soldiers use force to protect earthly goods—that is their God-ordained job. For Augustine, to think otherwise is to think that God ordered lesser evils that greater good may result. This sort of thinking can lead to unconvincing readings of Augustine on the resort to war. Once one begins with the claim that Augustine believes that "fighting to defend perishable property is a form of culpable cupidity," it leads to claims such as "it is hard to see how he could view defense of territorial integrity and the right of self-government to be a just war aim."[20] Smith tries to avoid the apparent contradiction in Augustine by arguing that such wars are not really being fought to defend transitory goods but to "prevent an injustice being inflicted upon the state and the people about to be attacked." Of course, this ignores the fact that the injustice being prevented is one of having territorial integrity violated. No such arguments are needed if one keeps in mind Augustine's moral distinction between public and private person. There is no contradiction in Augustine because he holds that acts of protecting earthly goods are a form of culpable cupidity only when a private person commits them. There is no culpable cupidity present when the state carries out its God-ordained function of protecting citizens, including their lives and their property.

Christians have a responsibility to support the governing authorities in their uses of force but responsibility brings limitations. Not every use of force contemplated by the governing authorities should be supported. Wars can be fought for many reasons, some of them immoral and not worthy of Christian support. Augustine goes to the heart of the issue when he argues that

> There is no man who does not wish for peace. Indeed, even when men choose war, their only wish is for victory; which shows that their desire in fighting is for peace with glory.... Even wars, then, are waged with peace as their object, even when they are waged by those who are concerned to exercise warlike prowess, either in command or in the actual fighting. Hence it is an established fact that peace is the desired end of war. For every man is in the quest of peace, even in waging war, whereas no one is in the quest of war when making peace. In fact, even when men wish a present state of peace to be disturbed they do so not because they hate peace, but because they desire the present peace to be exchanged for one that suits their wishes. (*City of God* 19.12)

Human beings are the sort of creatures who will always desire peace, or to be more precise, a certain peaceful state of affairs. Thus all wars are fought to achieve a certain peaceful state of affairs. But not all wars are just; not all attempts to achieve a different peaceful state of affairs are just acts. To use an obvious example, even Adolph Hitler did not desire war for the sake of war. He desired a certain peaceful state of affairs for Germany, one that did not exist before he used force. So what would make his acts of force unjust in the eyes of someone like Augustine? We can answer that question first by looking at Augustine's argument against the Manicheans concerning the wars ordered by God in the Old Testament. Augustine argues that whatever God orders must be just. So if he commands the Israelites to fight, then such fighting is just. God, who can order such wars, acts "not in cruelty but in righteous retribution, giving to all what they deserved, and warning those who needed warning" (*Reply to Faustus* 22.74). Thus God gives justice to the enemies of Israel when Israel makes war against them. The message is clear: the acts of war by Israel are not just simply because God commands them, but God commands them because Israel's enemies deserved to be attacked. So justice in war is like justice in every other matter; it is giving others their due. In a just war, the enemy deserves to be attacked.

Knowing when an enemy deserves to be attacked can be a problem when God does not give direct revelation about the matter. The Israelites knew they were acting justly, knew their enemies deserved to be attacked, because God confirmed it. Augustine, along with every other important figure in the early Church, holds that God no longer gives that sort of direct revelation. Thus the question becomes how do Christians know whether or not their governing authorities are giving their enemies their due when they attack them? Augustine answers this question when he queries the evil in war:

> The real evils in war are love of violence, revengeful cruelty, fierce and implacable enmity, wild resistance, and the lust of power, and such like; and it is generally to punish these things, when force is required to inflict the punishment, that, in obedience to God or some lawful authority, good mean undertake wars, when they find themselves in such a position as regards the conduct of human affairs, that right conduct requires them to act, or to make others act in this way. (*Reply to Faustus* 22.74)

Here we have a clear demarcation of good and bad uses of force. Evil uses include fighting for love of violence, revenge, lust of power, and so forth. When Augustine argues that Roman virtue is responsible for Roman success in war, he points out that even in the case of pagan history, we can discern good from bad desire for glory by discerning good from bad uses of force. He uses the legendary stories of the Assyrian King Ninus to make his point: "Now, to attack one's neighbors, to pass on to crush and subdue more remote peoples without provocation and solely from the thirst for dominion—what is one to call this but brigandage on the grand scale?" (*City of God* 4.7). The wars of Assyria under Ninus, which look very much like the wars waged by Hitler and all his kind, were unjust because he simply wanted to conquer others and extend his empire. Good uses that should be supported by Christians are those that counter the evil uses by people such as Ninus and Hitler.

We should not take from the example of Ninus that all acts of territorial expansion are unjust. When Augustine comes to the wars that led to the expansion of the Roman Empire, he argues that some of those wars were just:

> Now obviously the Romans had a just excuse for undertaking and carrying on those great wars. When they were subjected to unprovoked attacks by their enemies, they were forced to resist not by lust for glory in men's eyes but by the necessity to defend their life and liberty. (*City of God* 3.10)

The key difference between Ninus's and Rome's unjust wars of expansion is their causes and intentions. The cause for Ninus was the desire to expand and to achieve military glory. The cause for Rome was defense of the empire.

Ninus is an example of a bad ruler exercising his authority to make unjust wars. Good political leaders are those who wage just wars. Augustine argues that

> A great deal depends on the causes for which men undertake wars, and on the authority they have for doing so; for the natural order which seeks the peace of mankind, ordains that the monarch should have the power of undertaking war if he thinks it is advisable, and that the soldiers should perform their military duties in behalf of the peace and safety of the community. (*Reply to Faustus* 22.75)

Here we see even more limits set for Christians. Only the governing authorities can make the decision to use force. No private person is allowed to do so. Also, what counts as a just war is now made clearer: those wars fought for the peace and safety of the community.

Augustine's arguments about war certainly make it clear that all wars of self-defense are just wars (unless, of course, the state has done something that makes them deserving of attack), but that is not the only sort of just war. He argues that

> As a rule just wars are defined as those which avenge injuries, if some nation or state against whom one is waging war has neglected to punish a wrong committed by its citizens, or to return something that was wrongfully taken. (*Questions on the Heptateuch* 6.10)

Here Augustine relies upon a Ciceronian tradition that punitive wars are just. John Langan has gone so far as to argue that all just wars in the eyes of Augustine are punitive wars.[21] Three things must be said about this argument. First, Augustine never actually collapses all just wars under the punitive heading. Second, one would be hard pressed to see how Augustine could possibly do this considering his discussion of the just defensive wars carried out by the Romans (*City of God* 3.10), where the punitive measures appear far from his mind. Third, Augustine's theory of equating divine authorization with praiseworthy action (seen in *Reply to Faustus* 22.74) leaves the door open for any kind of just use of force, punitive or otherwise. In other words, the justice of a war cannot be constrained by punitive concerns. One might, however, be even more tempted to argue that all just wars in the eyes of Augustine are self-defensive in nature, insofar as all are undertaken as a response to injustice and, so, may be seen as acts of force to restore the justice, peace, and order of some community.

Christians who have the responsibility to pray for the success of men such as Boniface do so because they, too, benefit from the peace of Babylon. Some wars can bring justice, order, and peace of an earthly kind. But Augustine cautions that

> Now when victory goes to those who were fighting for the juster cause, can anyone doubt that the victory is a matter for rejoicing and the resulting peace is something to be desired? The things are goods and undoubtedly they are gifts of God. But if the higher goods are neglected, which belong to the City on high . . . . If these good are neglected and those other goods are desired as to be considered the only goods, or are loved more than the goods which are believed to be higher, the inevitable consequence is fresh misery, and an increase of the wretchedness already there. (*City of God* 15.5)

Victories that bring about justice, order, and peace are to be desired. But when we look to an advantage from such goods that they cannot give us—namely, the higher goods of the heavenly city, which give us true justice, order, and peace—we will be miserable. For earthly wars can never bring everlasting justice, order, and peace. This also means that wars instigated for higher goods are unjust because they have no chance of succeeding. Augustine is adamant that earthly wars, even just ones, have no spiritual significance.

Thus, Markus is right to insist that, far from checking early Christian pacifist thought, which he had no need to check since this had been ably done by Eusebius and Ambrose, Augustine checked the tendency toward holy war fighting found in Eusebius and Ambrose.[22]

Just wars are sometimes necessary but those who wage them must act justly in the waging of the war. To have justice on your side does not give you the freedom to do whatever you like to the enemy. Augustine urges Boniface that "When you word is pledged, it must be kept even with the enemy against whom you wage war" (*Letter* 189). Thus he follows Ambrose in holding that all agreements with the enemy must be kept even if they prove to be disadvantageous. Augustine goes on to advise Boniface that "mercy is due him who is defeated or captured, especially where no disturbance of peace is to be feared." Thus mercy is accorded all defeated enemies but especially when there is nothing more to fear from them. Augustine is probably thinking about the common practice of putting to death one's enemies as a safeguard against future injustices. Augustine also has this to say about the sack of Rome:

> All the devastation, the butchery, the plundering, the conflagrations, and all the anguish which accompanied the recent disaster at Rome were in accordance with the general practice of warfare. But there was something that established a new custom, something which changed the whole aspect of the scene. (*City of God* 1.7)

The difference in the sack of Rome was that the barbarians actually spared the people who sought sanctuary in the largest basilicas. Augustine attributes this new mercy in war to "the name of Christ and the influence of Christianity." Thus mercy extends not only to enemies in defeat but also to those innocent people who do not take up arms in war. They do not deserve to be killed.

Augustine is adamant that Christians have a responsibility to protect the earthly common good and that this responsibility extends to participating in the military. He is just as adamant that Christians fulfill this responsibility in a just way. In maintaining this position of responsibility limited by justice, Augustine builds upon a tradition already begun by the likes of Clement, Origen, Eusebius, and Ambrose. Augustine agrees with his forbears that clergy should be exempt from military duty but not exempt from praying for the success of the right uses of force. Augustine disagrees with Eusebius and Ambrose over the issue of holy war. For Augustine, war does not serve a spiritual purpose, cannot achieve spiritual goods. Therefore, all holy wars are unjust because they cannot hope to achieve what they are supposed to achieve. Finally, Augustine shares with his forbears a concern with what is known as the *jus ad bellum* part of the just war tradition, which attempts to establish criteria that help us decide if a given war ought to be waged. Beyond agreeing with Ambrose about keeping agreements and showing mercy, and exhibiting a marked distaste for indiscriminate killing, Augustine has little to say about just tactics, the *jus in bello*.[23]

Notes

1. Roland Bainton, *Christian Attitudes toward War and Peace* (New York: Abingdon Press, 1960), 66.
2. Alan J. Watt, "Which Approach? Late Twentieth-Century Interpretations of Augustine's Views on War," *Journal of Church and State* 46, no. 1 (Winter 2004), 99. Even the American Roman Catholic bishops, officially committed to the just war tradition, champion Origen as a figure representative of

the alternative commitment to pacifism. See National Conference of Catholic Bishops, *The Challenge of Peace: God's Promise and Our Response*, par. 111–15.

3. John Howard Yoder, *Christian Attitudes to War, Peace, and Revolution: A Companion to Bainton* (Elkhard, IN: Goshen Biblical Seminary, 1983), 27–34.
4. Any complete list of theologians who constitute the Origenist tradition would include Basil and Gregory of Nyssa. I have omitted them for the sake of space. However, in so doing, I am not attempting to hide views from the reader that may count against my thesis. Much of what we find in Clement and Origen can be found in Basil and Gregory.
5. Salvatore R. C. Lilla gives a full account of these stages in *Clement of Alexandria: A Stud in Christian Platonism and Gnosticism* (New York: Oxford University Press, 1971), 60–117.
6. Louis J. Swift, *The Early Fathers on War and Military Service* (Wilmington, NC: Michael Glazier, 1983), 52.
7. Robert L. Wilken provides a convincing portrait of Celsus as the consummate Roman conservative. See Wilken's *The Christians as the Romans Saw Them* (New Haven, CT: Yale University Press, 1984), 94–125.
8. Wilken 120.
9. Francois Heim has argued that Ambrose possessed a horror of bloodshed, which is expressed in the Ambrose's letter to Studius (*Letter* 25). However, the argument is misleading. In the letter Ambrose expresses his dissatisfaction with capital punishment in general and with clergy participation in particular. There is obviously a great deal of difference between using force to deal with captured criminals and using force to deal with free enemies. See Heim's "Le Theme de la Victoire Sans Combat Chez Ambroise," in *Ambroise de Milan: Dix etudes*, ed. Y. M. Duval (Paris, 1974), 267–81.
10. Angelo Paredi, *Saint Ambrose: His Life and Times*, trans. M. Joseph Costelloe (Notre Dame: University of Notre Dame Press, 1964), 318.
11. Peter Brown, "Political Society," in *Augustine: A Collection of Critical Essays*, ed. R. A. Markus (New York: Anchor Books, 1972), 317.
12. Eugene TeSelle, "Toward an Augustinian Politics," in *The Ethics of St. Augustine*, ed. William S. Babcock (Atlanta: Scholars Press, 1991), 153.
13. While Markus is right to point out that the basic core of Augustine's views on war never changed, his views on the role of governing authorities did undergo a change, as the older Augustine's reading of the epistles of Paul led him to move away from the kind of Christian Platonism found in Clement and Origen, which viewed the role of the governing authorities in a more positive light. See R. A. Markus, "Saint Augustine's Views on the Just War," in *The Church and War*, ed. W. J. Sheils (UK: Basil Blackwell, 1983), 1–14.
14. The failure to recognize that Augustine is still thinking within the Eastern Christian terms of levels of Christianity can lead to confusion about the scope of application for just users of force, particularly when one fails to recognize the lack of a consistent pacifism even in the early Greek Fathers. To claim that some Christians should not use force is not to claim that no Christian should use force. One attempt to argue otherwise for Augustine in order to make him a more consistent pacifist can be found in David A. Lenihan's "The Just War Theory in the Work of Saint Augustine," *Augustinian Studies* 19 (1988): 37–70. More convincing is Robert L. Holmes's position that Augustine held to a kind of personal pacifism. See Holmes's "St. Augustine and the Just War Theory," in *The Augustinian Tradition*, ed. Gareth B. Matthews (Berkeley, CA: University of California Press, 1999), 323–44.
15. See, especially, Paul Ramsey, *War and the Christian Conscience: How Shall Modern War Be Conducted Justly?* (Durham, NC: Duke University Press, 1961).
16. James Turner Johnson, "Morality and Force in Statecraft: Paul Ramsey and the Just War Tradition," in *Love and Society: Essays in the Ethics of Paul Ramsey*, ed. James T. Johnson and David H. Smith (Missoula, MT: Scholars Press, 1974), 93–114.
17. Stress should be put on the word "killing," for Augustine does not argue that any use of force against an unjust assailant would be wrong. Evodius is concerned about why someone should be thought just who took the life of another human being in order to protect transient goods. The idea is that killing to protect temporal goods betrays a disordered desire. Augustine does not say, nor does he put it in the mouth of Evodius, that nothing can be done to protect worldly goods against a robber. Augustine repeats his disapproval of killing in self-defense in *Letter* 47, but again, he specifically mentions killing and not all acts of force. Thus, I disagree with Langan's argument that Evodius has force in mind and not mere killing. See John Langan, "The Elements of St. Augustine's Just War Theory," in *The Ethics of Saint Augustine*, ed. William S. Babcock (Atlanta, GA: Scholars Press, 1991), 177.
18. J. Warren Smith, "Augustine and the Limits of Preemptive and Preventive War," *Journal of Religious Ethics* 35, no. 1 (2007): 141–62.

19. See, for example, the arguments found in Augustine's *On Lying* and *On the Good of Marriage*.
20. Smith, 158.
21. John Langan, 174.
22. Markus, 11–12.
23. This has not precluded modern theologians from attempting to cull a full-blown *jus in bello* from Augustine, as we see in Paul Ramsey (see Note 15).

6

The Medieval Papacy and Holy War: General Crusading Letters and Papal Authority, 1145–1213

Rebecca Rist

Throughout the High Middle Ages, the papacy was the principal instigator of crusading. One crucial way in which twelfth-century popes asserted their authority to promulgate crusades and simultaneously enforce their authority more generally was by means of their correspondence—both general crusading letters and letters to individuals that were dispatched to the Christian faithful throughout Europe.[1] Yet although the role of the papacy in disseminating the idea of crusade constitutes a central topic of crusading history, such letters have not been the subject of as much detailed scholarship as might be supposed. Indeed the subject of papal authority over crusading has been more thoroughly investigated in relation to popes of the thirteenth century because the increasing formulization of the idea of crusade in canon law makes drawing conclusions about the theological and legal background against which popes issued appeals much easier. For the twelfth century, certain features of general crusading letters, such as the granting of papal indulgences, or the special privileges granted for the protection of persons and property under the Holy See for the duration of a crusade, have also been thoroughly investigated.[2] However, there has been surprisingly little recent analysis of their language and ideas that reveal the methods popes used to fix the initiative for crusading on themselves and keep it there, despite at times temporary loss of control. The degree to which a pope believed he should assert his authority over a particular crusade depended on his personal interest in each campaign and the political circumstances at the time he issued the appeal. Yet a detailed analysis of their language reveals the methods used by popes to initiate crusades and maintain their momentum.

Twelfth-century popes felt the frequent need to reassert their magisterium and saw it as their right and even duty to call for crusades in virtue of their role as pontiffs and successors of St. Peter. When popes addressed the Christian faithful as "sons" (*filii*) in their correspondence, they deliberately emphasized their paternal role.[3] They also employed such language when addressing the clergy as *filii*, although—since bishops were descendants of the apostles—they addressed these as brothers (*fratres nostri*) rather than sons.[4] The authority popes asserted was threefold. First they believed that their status as pontiffs meant that they wielded the appropriate authority to promulgate crusades. Second, they claimed the authority to promulgate crusading as successors of previous popes who had also authorized crusades, in particular Urban II (1088–1099), the founder of the crusading movement.[5] Third, even more fundamentally, they asserted simple papal authority not just as individual popes who happened to be promoters of crusades, but qua popes. The language popes employed reveals the emphasis they placed on deriving this authority from St. Peter. For it was as successors of St. Peter that they had inherited his powers of binding and loosing as well as the power to grant indulgence for sins.[6]

In 1145 Eugenius III (1145–1153) issued the crusade encyclical *Quantum praedecessores*. Does the fact that no general crusading letters to the faithful calling for aid to the Holy Land existed before Eugenius mean that popes of the second half of the twelfth century felt a greater need to assert their authority over crusading than their predecessors? Eugenius's issue of the general crusading letter *Quantum praedecessores* was a startling action. Although the fall of Edessa constituted an excellent reason for such a letter, Urban II had not issued one in 1095 in a time of great, if not comparable emergency when the Byzantine emperor Alexius I Comnenus had sent an embassy to the pope to encourage the West to help defend the Eastern Church against the Seljuk Turks.[7] Yet many factors influenced Eugenius to think that there was a need to make a general appeal to the faithful in 1145—a need not present in 1095. Concern that a crusade might be launched by Louis VII of France without papal authorization may have been one. The unsuccessful crusading campaign of Bohemond in 1107 over which Paschal II (1099–1118) seems to have lost control, becoming perhaps unwittingly involved in Bohemond's plans for a conquest of the Byzantine Empire, may have also acted as a warning to Eugenius, faced with the urgent crisis of Edessa and a French king who had simultaneously received the news of its fall from an envoy of Frankish princes.[8] He may have guessed that the king would be eager to lead a crusade.

If so, he was not the first twelfth-century pope to worry about loss of control over a papally authorized crusade. The confirmation of the order of Templars by Honorius II (1124–1130), in whose pontificate a crusade had been launched without papal authorization,[9] and their licensing in the founding charter of Innocent II (1130–1143), *Omne datum optimum*, confirms that the twelfth-century papacy was keen to constitute "a permanent source of papally-controlled a-political soldiery," or in the words of Bernard of Clairvaux, its own "militia" to combat "malitia."[10] Here was another way of asserting papal authority: popes could rely on such a force where they could not rely on the secular army since: however favorable to the papal cause, the latter would always have mixed allegiances.

Quantum praedecessores was not entirely without precedent. We possess evidence for a letter of Calixtus II which promulgated a crusade to the Holy Land—he referred to it in a letter to Tarragona in which he extended to those who had traveled to help Christians in Spain the same remission of sins as those who had traveled to the Near East.[11] Eugenius III's appeal should therefore be seen as part of a continuous effort by popes to maintain papal authority. It seems that there might also be some sort of precedent to *Quantum praedecessores* at an even earlier date. Prior to the Hildebrandine period of Church reform and the call of Gregory VII (1073–1085) for aid for the Eastern Church in 1078, we have evidence for two appeals for help for the Holy Land: a letter from Guilbert of Aurillac—later Sylvester II (999–1003)—and a letter of Sergius IV (1009–1012). Neither letter, however, provides much understanding for *Quantum praedecessores*. That of Sergius IV was a forgery, composed after the council of Clermont of 1095, while that of Guilbert, though a call for help for the Church of Jerusalem and thus to some extent comparable, is principally concerned with raising alms; military intervention was mentioned but dismissed.[12]

Following the example of Eugenius III, during the twelfth century Alexander III (1159–1181), Lucius III (1181–1185), Gregory VIII (1187), Clement III (1187–1191), Celestine III (1191–1198), and Innocent III (1198–1216) all sent out appeals to ecclesiastical authorities and/or temporal powers, both individually and collectively, to procure aid for the Holy Land in the form of men to fight crusades and money to assist them. Eugenius issued two general crusading letters concerned with crusading in the Near East: the afore-mentioned *Quantum praedecessores* of December 1, 1145, which was reissued on March 1, 1146, and *Divina dispensatione* of October 5, 1146—not to be confused with another of the same name, *Divina dispensatione* (April 11, 1147), which was concerned with a military venture against the Wends contemporaneous with and connected to the Second Crusade but not about the Second Crusade itself.[13] Alexander III issued four crusading letters: *Quantum praedecessores* (July 14, 1165), which bore the same name as that of Eugenius but contained new material, *In quantis pressuris* (June 29, 1166), *Inter omnia quae* (July 29, 1169), and *Cor nostrum et* (January 16, 1181).[14] Lucius III reissued *Cor nostrum et* (November 6, 1184/1185).[15] Those of Gregory VIII included *Audita tremendi* (October 29, 1187), reissued on November 3, 1187, and *Quam divina patientia* (November 29, 1187).[16] Clement III issued *Quam gravis et* (February 10, 1188) and reissued it to certain specific clergy on May 27, 1188.[17] Celestine III issued *Divitiae summae* (August 1, 1195).[18]

Some of these appeals were merely reissues of previous letters—sometimes addressed to different recipients[19]; some were "new" letters but contained more sections that were lifted from previous letters than original material; others were overridingly fresh creations. The majority were a mixture of both new and repeated language in varying quantities, but a minority, for example, the first issue of *Audita tremendi* or *Quam divina patientia* of Gregory VIII, contained few or no repeated phrases. Crusading was an important part of the papal agenda: Anastasius IV (1153–1154), Adrian IV (1154–1159), Alexander III (1159–1181), Lucius III (1181–1185), and Urban III (1185–1187) were the only popes of the second half of the twelfth century who issued no such general crusading letters.

Yet even after Eugenius III had set the precedent and the practice of sending such letters to the faithful about the state of the Holy Land was fully established, both in response to particular crises such as Hattin in 1187 and at other times simply to maintain interest, it was still very difficult enough for popes to maintain their authority over crusading. In 1145 Eugenius's first issue of *Quantum praedecessores* fell flat and his call was only revived when reissued in conjunction with the dynamic preaching of St. Bernard of Clairvaux at Vézelay,[20] and Bernard's own letter to the universal Christian faithful, *Sermo mihi ad vos*.[21] Arguably Eugenius's final approval of Bernard's preaching campaign in Germany led to a loss of control that allowed for the promulgation of a venture against the Wends, ensuring that the nature of the original crusade changed considerably.[22] None of Alexander III's letters, including *Quantum praedecessores* (1165), which conveyed the news that Muslim forces had reached the gates of Antioch, *In quantis pressuris* (1166), a more general appeal for help to the Holy Land, *Inter omnia quae* (1169), which expressed concern about the diminishing population of the Holy Land, and *Cor nostrum et* (1181), which described sinister rumours that have reached the pope from the regions of Jerusalem, seem to have inspired the faithful to crusade in the numbers that Alexander hoped. Even Innocent III, despite all his planning and forethought, was unable to prevent the diversion of the Fourth Crusade to Constantinople.

Letters of Innocent III concerned with the Fourth Crusade include *Post miserabile* (August 15, 1198), *Nisi nobis dictum* (January 4, 1199), and *Graves orientalis terrae* (December 31, 1199); three general letters issued in 1208 including *Tetendisse Dominus arcum* (May 29), *Utinam Dominus et* (December 10), and a second *Utinam Dominus* (December 10); and with the Fifth Crusade *Quia major* (April 19–29, 1213).[23] Although only the first years of Innocent's pontificate belong to the twelfth century, not just his general letters for the Fourth Crusade of 1198, but also these later early-thirteenth-century letters are important for understanding papal authority over crusading and more widely.[24] With their show of biblical learning and at the same time precise attention to practical detail, they provided a yardstick for determining to what extent papal policy regarding the promulgation and organization of crusading changed or remained static. From the point of view of style alone, it is worthwhile to compare Innocent's originality of language and slick presentation with those of his twelfth-century predecessors.

Yet despite the influence to a greater or lesser extent of Eugenius III's *Quantum praedecessores* on all general crusading letters of his successors in terms of language and ideas, and the fact that large amounts of text were often repeated from earlier letters, these letters nevertheless varied in tone, style, length, and quality of expression. Such variations can be very clearly seen, for example, in Gregory VIII's striking and original *Audita tremendi* (1187) which was very different from Alexander III's *Cor nostrum* (1181) which appears much more derivative of Eugenius's *Quantum praedecessores*.

Nevertheless, despite such variation in tone, and with the exception of the very brief *Quam divina patientia* of Gregory VIII and the second *Utinam Dominus* of Innocent III, there was a definite pattern to the format of these letters that followed the order laid out in Eugenius III's *Quantum praedecessores*. This began with a greeting designed to include all the faithful, although particular ecclesiastics or kings might be specified. There followed a mini-history of the endeavors of crusaders in the Holy Land; next the pope gave the reason why he was making his particular appeal, and then came the call for aid itself. Here an *exemplum/exempla* might be given by way of encouragement, often taken from a passage or passages of Scripture. A formulaic recitation followed which detailed the various privileges that would accrue to crusaders, including the indulgence, the different types of protection they were granted, and how they were to deport themselves while travelling. All this might be followed by further promises of protection for fighters and their possessions. Indeed the letters often ended in a "double whammy"—a repetition of the indulgence and an assurance of the promised heavenly reward for those who took part.[25] Not all letters necessarily contained all these elements, and some emphasized or excluded certain of them. Nevertheless, most are to be found in the majority of letters.

Thus the language of Eugenius III's *Quantum praedecessores* remained the model or blueprint for that used by subsequent popes whose language and ideas about crusading changed little from leter to letter. *Quantum praedecessores* emphasized Christ's passion and referred to the Muslim foe as "the enemies of the cross" (*inimici crucis Christi*). It stressed that fighting in a crusade was a defensive, liberating operation and used emotive words and phrases to rouse the faithful to action.[26] It also referred to the crusade in euphemistic terms as a "holy work" or "holy journey" (*sanctum opus/sanctum iter*).[27] Hence crusaders were those who had taken up the cross in order to fight for the Lord.[28]

Such words and phrases helped to define what Eugenius believed a crusade to be and are to be found in the general crusading letters of all subsequent popes.[29] This was partly because many general crusading letters were reissues or part reissues of previous letters that took *Quantum praedecessores* as their model. Yet this was only one factor since subsequent popes could have changed that model had they wished. Rather, the similarities reflected that the idea of what constituted a crusade, or at least what a crusade should be, changed little during the second half of the twelfth century. Indeed we see only minor variants in the way crusading is described from one letter to the next. He indicated his desire to emphasize the link between crusading and pilgrimage—just as his predecessor Urban II had done. Innocent III shows a widened concept of crusade in his regulations with regard to the commutation of crusader vows, because he was the first pope to *encourage anyone* to take the cross.[30] It is striking that the idea of a crusade as a defensive war to protect the Holy Places (particularly Christ's tomb) and to liberate the Eastern Church is presented as one of the goals of all general crusading letters—and in none of them is there either a direct use of the term "Holy War" or any idea of the conversion of the infidel.[31]

So in considering how the popes *intended* the general crusading letters to be perceived, it is important to bear in mind how they were actually *received* and *used*. Certainly the authenticity of general crusading letters is undoubted. Yet this does not mean that, for example, *Quantum praedecessores* should only be analyzed in its own right because it was a general letter of Eugenius III. It should also be read in the context in which it appears—as a source for the politics of the twelfth-century papacy that was used by the contemporary chronicler Otto of Freising in his history of the deeds of the emperor Frederick Barbarossa.

In analyzing the issue of papal authority in the general crusading letters, we need to remember three things. First, we are dealing with a formal writing style deliberately employed to give that seriousness of tone deemed necessary by the curia for general appeals to the faithful. Second, the language of the letters suggests that the curia had a set of stock formulas and phrases to draw on, not only for general crusading letters concerned with the Near East, but also for general letters concerned with other ventures against non-Christians. It seems likely that, as well as using their own learning, such writers drew on these formulas as they would have drawn on the *Sententiae* of Peter Lombard—composed between 1148 and 1151 and in circulation—in order to make detailed reference to Scripture. Third, it is impossible to determine how much these letters were the personal production of a particular pope and how much crafted by notaries under only nominal papal direction. The emotive quality and variety of expression of a letter such as Gregory VIII's *Audita tremendi* or the letters of Innocent III make it appear likely that popes sometimes, if not frequently, had a direct personal input.

Nevertheless, the meager evidence on the papal curia of this period makes such a claim impossible to prove. What can be surmised is that it is highly likely that, as with the letters of Bernard of Clairvaux concerned with the Second Crusade and the venture against the Wends that echo language used in Eugenius III's correspondence, the respective degree of input of master and notary varied considerably.[32] Some of Bernard's letters, written up by his notary Nicholas of Clairvaux, are under his name, some are his own production, while others were written in a style which Nicholas felt fitting for Bernard's name and place in society.[33]

Popes emphasized their authority over crusading at the beginning of these general crusading letters and continued to reiterate it throughout, particularly in sections dealing with the granting of remission of sins for those taking part—either by fighting themselves or by sending men or money—in a crusading enterprise, with the organization of the crusade—for example, the establishment of a papal tax on ecclesiastical revenue in letters of Innocent III—and the detailing of privileges for crusaders. It was also emphasized in the exhortative sections for the defense of the Holy Land and liberation of the Eastern Church. Repeatedly we find phrases that emphasized the *auctoritas* of the pope.[34] These reminded not only the reader or listener of the apostolic succession of the popes but also that the pope's powers were those of St. Peter himself.[35] There were also more direct references to the power of the papacy over the Church,[36] and even references to the pope's personal authority.[37] Many of these phrases had a long history of usage by the papacy, were standard when addressing the faithful, and were not unique to the general crusading letters. Nevertheless, their prominence and frequency suggested that they were not merely formulaic but for a definite purpose. In particular their emphasis on the pastoral duty inherent in the papal office was tied to claims to authority.[38]

Sometimes a pope used a particularly striking phrase not found in previous general crusading letters to assert that authority. So in the general letter of Clement III *Quam gravis et* his use of the phrase *res publica Christiana* ("the Christian state") not only emphasized that Clement saw himself as responsible for the concerns of Christendom, but was a loaded political statement.[39] The term *res publica Christiana* continued a tradition dating back to Augustine of Hippo and beyond: earthly states were not important in comparison with the universal Christian state whose founder and monarch was Christ and of which the pope through St. Peter was Christ's vicar.[40] It is therefore no surprise that in Innocent III's correspondence we frequently find the phrase:

> . . . and so that we should not seem to be laying on others heavy and insupportable burdens which we are not willing to move with a finger of our own, speaking but doing either nothing or very little . . .[41]

This emphasized that the pope had power to impose his wishes on the faithful and recognized the responsibilities that went with this authority. By means of this phrase he prefaced his declaration that the curia would itself provide money for crusading and not rely solely on the taxation of others.

Emphasis on papal authority was conveyed not only by the use of such magisterial language but also by constant quotations from and references to the Old and New Testament. Here the books of *Maccabees*, which contained texts particularly relevant to the loss of Jerusalem, and the Psalms were popular Old Testament choices.[42] Quotations from the New Testament were particularly numerous in the letters of Innocent III. References were often piled up consecutively and such clever manipulation of quotations in itself emphasized the writer's authority, a technique also frequently employed in the sermons of crusade preachers.

Indeed the emotional and emotive nature of many parts of their letters shows that popes intended them to be used to preach as well as to authorize crusades. Mundanely formulaic and practical passages were juxtaposed with emotive appeals, confirming that these letters were intended to be much more than propaganda tools—although infact such juxtaposition provided a frame for the emotive passages that made them all the more striking. Crusading letters both preached directly to the faithful and acted as models and guides for preachers. They were influential on crusade sermons not only in terms of ideas but also in phraseology and the use of Scripture. Yet besides working on the emotions, another purpose of at least some of these letters was to instruct the faithful and give spiritual and theological guidance. Nevertheless, information on the Holy Land itself and strictly theological questions was limited. The primary goal of the letters was always to stir up emotion and instill enthusiasm to partake on crusade, not to give instruction on the politics or theology of crusading.

Such letters reveal that the *idea* of crusade was not significantly developed or changed by the papacy during the twelfth century. That there is little difference from letter to letter in the description of crusading strongly indicates that popes had no intention of changing either the way they authorized crusades or their concept of what constituted a crusade. The aims of crusading—the liberation and defense of the Holy Land—and the ideas that underpinned it—a desire to help the eastern Church, pity for the distress of Christians in the Near East, sadness that the places of Christ's birth life and passion were threatened by, or in the hands of, the Muslims, and the grant of the indulgence for those who went on crusade—were as important in Eugenius II's issue of *Quantum praedecessores* in 1145 as in Innocent III's reissue of *Quia major* in 1213. Even the letters of Innocent III with their renewed vigor and enthusiasm for crusading, their particular concentration on the details of administration, and their employment of a more sophisticated and embellished language contained the same fundamental aims as those preceding them. Similarly there was little development in the *language* used to describe crusading during the twelfth century. With a few exceptions such as Gregory VIII's *Audita tremendi* in 1187 which used rather different language from the norm, we find the same euphemistic phrases and emotive devices constantly employed throughout such papal correspondence. Only with the letters of Innocent III, with their more frequent appeal to Scripture and elaborate and colorful metaphors and similes, do we see significant linguistic development.

There was another, further, important difference between Innocent III's letters and those of his predecessors. In the case of Innocent, we see a change not in the papal *idea* of crusading but in papal *attitudes* toward it. With Innocent crusading was planned and organized as never before—which is why historians have so often referred to crusading being "institutionalized" during his pontificate. Even Alexander III's correspondence, perhaps most comparable to Innocent in that he too enjoyed a long pontificate and issued a number of crusading appeals, and which showed acute concern about the worsening situation in the Holy Land, displayed no comparable interest in the administration and practical details of crusading.

Innocent's letters had two aims: to administer crusades in a new and orderly fashion, and to reinvigorate the idea of crusading itself. Hence it is not so much that he changed the idea of crusading as that he relaunched it. Indeed some letters were almost as concerned with the organization of crusades, their financing, administration, and how they were to be preached, as they were with exhorting the faithful to fight. For Innocent the crusades were not so much a way of expressing and channeling religious piety—an idea successfully employed by Urban II for the First Crusade and which Eugenius III hoped to revive in *Quantum praedeccessores*—as one facet of a much wider papal plan of Christian action against all unbelievers which was profoundly to influence the nature of later crusading.

Nevertheless, papal authority needed to be established not only in the initial call for a crusade but throughout the venture. At a practical level there was the necessity of keeping the initiative for crusading on the papacy once it had been initially fixed there, and when necessary to practise damage limitation to deal with apparent losses of control. This was most obvious in the case of the Fourth Crusade, in which Innocent III seems to have been unable, or at any rate hesitant, to prevent diversions to Zara and Constantinople. Problems of distance and lack of easy communications between Rome and the Holy Land meant that it was difficult for popes to maintain a grip on ventures which they could only direct from afar and where the risk of disorder—due to the nature of a crusade as a collective act of pious violence—was already immense. Elaborate details found in some of the general crusading letters, about how crusaders should comport themselves while on crusade, indicated not only that crusading was viewed as a form of pilgrimage, but also papal concern to influence from the outset the tone in which a crusade was to be fought.[43]

We are of course dealing with a period of over fifty years in which the need by popes to assert their authority differed with fluctuating circumstances, and papal actions with regard to crusading varied depending on their political position at the curia in Rome at any given time. The concerns of Innocent III's papacy of eighteen years—including major struggles with the German emperor—were quite different from those of Gregory VIII who only held office for a few months. Crusades were only one of many papal interests in the second half of the twelfth century, and maintaining authority over them was but one of the many ways—more dear to the hearts of some popes, particularly Innocent III, than others—of asserting that authority.

Yet why should twelfth-century popes have felt the need to assert their authority not only over the crusades but more generally? To answer this question we need to understand the ecclesiastical and secular politics of the second half of the twelfth century. Strained relations between Rome and the eastern Church—which had existed for centuries and were exacerbated by the First Crusade—continued with the Council of Constantinople of 1169 at which the increasing bitterness of Greek feeling against the Latin bishops of Alexander III became openly apparent when Michael III Anchialus, patriarch of Constantinople, declared that the pope had forfeited the chief priesthood because of the heresy of the Latins.[44] Popes were no less aware than their predecessors of the importance of the papacy in maintaining its claim to be head of the universal Christian Church and were eager to assert their authority in support of the new Latin patriarchates of Antioch and Jerusalem—set up after the First Crusade—by the establishment of a Latin hierarchy.[45] Furthermore, upheavals at the curia and the particular problem of the threat of anti-popes elected by secular powers or rival ecclesiastical factions—no less than four were elected during the pontificate of Alexander III—made the need to assert authority a continuing priority, especially with the "post-Hildebrandine mentality" of asserting and maintaining papal independence from the German emperor, and expanding and strengthening papal government in Rome: aims that tended to lead to a direct equating of the papal cause with the cause of the Church.[46]

The complexities of exerting this papal authority in practice can be clearly seen in the relationship between Eugenius III and his one-time teacher Bernard of Clairvaux. Bernard was not prepared to accept the plans of Louis VII and preach a crusade until he had expressed orders from Rome.[47] Once sure of the pope's support, however, he took up the cause with great enthusiasm, as he revealed in his letter *Sermo mihi ad vos* to Eugenius recounting the success of his preaching, but expressing concern that it be carried through in an orderly fashion.[48] His encouragement of a venture against the Wends, described in another letter *Est sermo mihi ad vos*, was his own particular contribution and one which Eugenius III only endorsed after persuasion.[49] Indeed Bernard seems to have seen it as an extension of the Second Crusade. In both letters he described crusading as an opportunity to take up the *signum crucis* and to defend the name of Christ with zeal in the hope of eternal salvation.[50] Yet despite this, in his seminal work *De Consideratione* he showed that he regarded the crusade as the ultimate responsibility of the pope alone[51] and took the opportunity to recall the pope to a heritage from which he must not be diverted.[52] For the same reason he failed to appreciate Eugenius's later reluctance to call for further crusading.[53]

As the example of Bernard and Eugenius's relationship reveals, there was always a problem for popes about what authority they might have for crusades and how that authority played out in practice. The fact that the call for the Second Crusade would not have been a success without Bernard's preaching reveals the relative powerlessness of a pope to promulgate crusades without influential helpers to do the grassroots preaching. Due to Bernard and Eugenius's frequent correspondence, linked as they were by the bond of Cistercianism, we know more about this pope–preacher relationship than any other. Yet the importance of a preaching campaign in establishing the authority of a pope wishing to call a crusade was enormous, not least because crusading propaganda was "in one sense a dramatic expression of the international standing of the papacy."[54]

Twelfth-century popes therefore saw in the crusades a welcome opportunity to assert papal authority and penned the general letters to the Holy Land as much with this wider aim as for their undoubted wish to both take and keep control over specific crusades and to preserve the Holy Land in Christian hands—which was also crucial for maintaining their claim to authority over the *res publica Christiana*. Furthermore, by promulgating and encouraging crusading they were not only asserting their belief that the papacy alone could direct crusades, but confirming the opinion of the pontiff's role that was held by all clergy of the Western Church. Bernard of Clairvaux, the great political wheeler and dealer of his day, was not only unwilling to give counsel on, or preach, the Second Crusade until it had been authorized by Eugenius III, but also expressed in the *De Consideratione*, the belief that a crusade is a holy war that must be initiated by the pope alone, thereby by implication demeaning any venture against non-Christians led by secular leaders.[55] Indeed in one letter to Eugenius he reproached him for his lack of enthusiasm for a new crusade.[56]

That such beliefs were not held by Bernard alone is shown by their later formalization by canonists. For twelfth-century canon lawyers a crusade was initiated by God through the pope[57]: a theory that in addition to advantages had serious drawbacks as well for the papacy when left to deal with the enormous disappointment resulting from successive crusades, in particular from the Second Crusade, for which Bernard of Clairvaux himself felt obliged to justify his role in the *De Consideratione*, and from the Fourth, if not at the popular level, at least in terms of the achievement of the original goals of Innocent III.[58]

Yet despite the influence of Bernard on the idea that a crusade must be *initiated* by the pope, during the twelfth century the idea that a secular leader could *lead* it remained by no means alien, as the (unsuccessful) crusade of Henry VI in 1197 revealed. Nevertheless, this particular venture of the emperor may help to explain Innocent III's particular wish not only to *initiate* but to *control* the Fourth and Fifth Crusades, as was shown by the almost obsessive instructions for the details of the conducting of crusading, in particular regarding the collecting of the ecclesiastical taxation of a fortieth over one year for the Fourth Crusade and the subsequent collection of a twentieth over three years for the Fifth.[59]

Certainly popes of the second half of the twelfth century were influenced by canon law as well as by the possibilities of preaching. Canon law gave authority to their calls for crusades and helped to define crusading itself. Yet Gratian's *Concordia discordantium canonum*, written ca. 1140, and well known to the later twelfth-century popes, and the works of decretists—those who commented on or glossed the *Decretum* such as Paucapalea, Rolandus Bandinelli, Huggucio (the latter supplied justifications of the Church's right to wage war), and Rufinus—provided no formalization of crusading in canon law.[60] For the formulization of the specifically crusading vow we have to wait for the thirteenth-century decretalists—those who commented on *papal* decretals, and in particular Hostiensis' *Summa aurea*.[61]

Nevertheless, the twelfth-century canonists paved the way for later formalization since there was much written by Gratian and others on the vow of which the crusading vow is a later subset.[62] Furthermore, Gratian's *Causa 23* of the *Concordia discordantium canonum*, which examined the whole problem of violence and the Christian life, dealt with the hypothetical situation of bishops who had fallen into heresy and were trying to force neighboring Catholics into heresy also, using this example to tackle the question of what constitutes a just war.[63] So this text tells us much about twelfth-century legal debates on the topos of Christian violence, albeit against the heretic—also the subject of Augustine's concerns in his discussion of the just war on which Gratian drew heavily—not the infidel.[64]

Thus, although theories of just war at this period are developing but not yet formally defined, it is important to analyze what contemporary canonists such as Gratian and the decretists wrote about the problem of reconciling violence and the Christian life because they give us some insight into the background of popes who were attempting to harness the idea of a holy war, a type of just war, to crusading, and therefore a better understanding of their correspondence.[65] Some popes, such as Alexander III and Innocent III, had been trained in the law and would have been particularly well versed in canon law. It is likely that they would have seen crusading in a legal as well as a spiritual and political context, and have felt the need to harness the idea of a holy war to crusading to give it legitimacy as a form of piety.

Hence in using their authority to promulgate crusades, and gaining authority for the papacy by so doing, popes gave support to a legitimate outlet for violence, harnessing it to the papal cause. Those who did not respect the popes' authority to promulgate crusades and chose to ignore or contravene the instructions of the general letters could be excommunicated in accordance with the theory of the two swords wielded by the Church: that of spiritual coercion—interdict, excommunication, and other spiritual penalties that might be employed against an offender—and material coercion (physical force and violence), since Gratian claimed in the *Decretum* that the Church had the right to use the former and authorize the use of the latter when necessary to secure obedience to legitimate commands.[66] So in *Quia major* Innocent III used the sword of spiritual coercion by threatening excommunication against those who impeded the crusade or aided Muslims and so hindered crusading efforts.[67]

That seeking to justify crusades through canon law became a preoccupation of popes during the second half of the twelfth century is revealed in the legislation of contemporary councils. Such councils had been used by previous popes to promulgate ventures against non-Christians: the Council of Clermont (1095), at which the First Crusade was preached, the Council of Toulouse (1118), at which Gelasius II decided in favor of a venture against Muslims in Spain and exhorted Spanish Christians to give help, and the Council of Pisa (1135), at which Innocent II granted to those fighting against the anti-pope Anacletus II the same indulgence as Urban II had given at Clermont.[68] Councils, both provincial and general, were also used to tackle the related problem of heresy, regarded as an error of thinking that manifested itself in different forms.[69] The Synod of Rheims (1148) showed an awareness of the increasing problem of heretics in Gascony and Provence (Canons 1 and 18).[70] At the Third and Fourth Lateran Councils (1179 and 1215, respectively), following on from Lateran I of 1122—which confirmed the grant of the indulgence for crusades in the Near East[71]—and Lateran II of 1139, important new initiatives were proposed. First, steps were taken toward defining and laying down guidelines on the treatment of non-Christians: relevant canons of both councils bear the title *De Iudaeis et Sarracenis* ("Concerning Jews and Saracens").[72] Second, action was taken against heretics: Canon 27 of Lateran III decreed the confiscation of goods of those condemned for heresy and gave to fighters against heresy the same indulgence and other privileges enjoyed by crusaders in the Near East, assimilating them with those who fought against the infidel in the Holy Land.[73] Canon 3 of Lateran IV dealt more widely with the repression of heresy and the liberation of the Holy Land.[74]

Indeed the importance of the Third Lateran Council makes it surprising that it is not invoked in *Cor nostrum et* of Alexander III, in the four general crusading letters of Innocent III for the Fourth Crusade or the three he issued in 1208. It was, however, mentioned in Innocent's *Quia major* of Innocent III that decreed a sentence of excommunication for those who aided Muslims by bringing weapons, iron, or wood for Muslim ships or are employed as steersmen for them, in accordance with Lateran III.[75] Furthermore, Innocent III's great constitution, *Ad Liberandam*, and which forbade Christians to aid Muslims or enter into commerce with them, was promulgated at the Fourth Lateran Council and acted as a blueprint for the Fifth Crusade.[76]

It is therefore perhaps surprising that the decrees of the Lateran Councils are not mentioned more frequently in the general crusading letters. Even the provincial Council of Clermont, seminal for crusading, was not mentioned specifically by Eugenius III in *Quantum praedecessores* despite the emphasis that Urban II had acted as a *tuba caelestis* ("heavenly trumpet") in sounding the call for the deliverance of the Holy Roman Church.[77] However, important particular crusades were for particular popes, who did not regard their letters concerning the Holy Land as so important for establishing their authority for crusading that they needed to detail conciliar legislation which had a bearing on the crusades they promulgated. This strongly suggests that the letters were not penned by popes and their notaries with a primarily didactic purpose in mind.

Nevertheless, although the general crusading letters never refer specifically to the legislation of church councils, they do give some indication of the appointment of papal legates for particular crusades. For the First Crusade Urban II had elected Adhémar bishop of Le Puy, to represent him—a prudent move from other points of view besides the assertion of papal authority since Adhémar helped maintain a degree of cohesion among the crusade leaders, although his position as a cleric whose jurisdiction was the spiritual guidance of the crusade rather than the actual fighting, limited his authority and led to tensions with Raymond of St. Giles, the other leader of the contingent in which he traveled.[78] The use of "crusading" legates by subsequent popes, as so much else about the crusades, was based on the example set by Urban II.

References to legates in some general crusading letters were to those sent out by popes with the specific job of *preaching* crusades. By their preaching and administration these acted as enforcers of the letters, a necessary role for the maintenance of papal authority since popes could not usually be present in person to help the faithful prepare for a crusade. Even Innocent III, who personally took on some of the preaching of the Fifth Crusade, established an elaborate machinery for its preparation.[79] Many papal general letters referred to the use of such "preaching" legates. Calixtus II mentioned in a general letter concerned with Spain that he was appointing the archbishop of Tarragona as his legate for ventures against Muslims.[80] Or later in *Divina dispensatione* of April 11, 1147, Eugenius III informed the faithful in his general letter authorizing a venture against the Slavs that he was sending them his legate Anselm of Havelberg to maintain peace and unity.[81] In *Divitiae summae* Celestine III urged the faithful to care for the cardinals he was sending to preach the crusade[82]; while in a further letter *Misericors et miserator* he exhorted the archbishop of Canterbury, commissioned with the care of the papal legation, to urge the king of England and the English nation to help.[83] Innocent III stated in *Post miserabile* that he was sending two cardinals, Sofredo and Peter Capuano, as legates to organize the preaching and collection of tax for the Fourth Crusade.[84] It is therefore surprising that Archbishop Ubaldo, whom Gregory VIII appointed as legate for the Third Crusade—he subsequently led the Pisans on this crusade in 1189—was not mentioned in either *Audita tremendi* or *Quam divina patientia*.[85]

So the promulgation of general crusading letters with regard to the Holy Land was one major device by which popes of the second half of the twelfth century asserted their authority for crusades. However, the importance of any individual letter in the eyes of the pope who issued it depended on a variety of factors: the particular circumstance for which a crusade was called—whether it was an appeal in response to an imminent or actual disaster or less immediately pressing—the personal interest in crusading of the particular pope who made the call, and the different political circumstances in which the pope found himself. Yet there were other ways besides the issuing of general crusading letters by which a pope could make his authority for crusading feel: by his employment of legates and prelates, by the use of the military orders, and by the establishment of a strict hierarchy in the Latin patriarchates, ways that the letters did not particularly dwell on.

That, with the exception of *Audita tremendi* of October 29 and November 3, 1187, the language and ideas used in the general crusading letters did not substantially differ from letter to letter, that some popes chose to reissue fully or in part letters of their predecessors and that we do not see a great development in the nature of the general crusading letters—for example, the privileges granted in *Quantum praedecessores* of Alexander III are the same as *Quantum praedecessores* of December 1, 1145, and March 1, 1146, of Eugenius III[86]—shows that successive popes had no desire to change the crusading ideal radically, with the important exception of the theology of the indulgence that was only fully developed during the pontificate of Innocent III.[87] It is only in Innocent III's general crusading letters, with their idiosyncratic formats and expressions, that we see a renewed seriousness of purpose and an attempt to change the style. That very similar language is also used in the general letters concerned with Spain and the Baltic puts the general crusading letters concerned with the Holy Land in context: they were there to assert papal authority, but perhaps no more than other papal letters to the faithful.

Notes

1. I have used the phrase "general crusading letters" when referring to papal appeals, rather than referring to them as "crusading bulls" or "crusading encyclicals," because the latter terms suggest a degree of formal organization associated with modern papal documents that are inaccurate and anachronistic. However, merely describing them as "letters" does not encapsulate their purpose of a wide appeal to the Christian faithful. For the first see Eugenius III, "Quantum Praedecessores" (December 1, 1145), in *Ottonis et Rahewina Gesta Friderici I Imperatoris*, ed. Bernhard von Simson, Bk 1 (Hannover, Leipzig: Impensis biblopolii Hahniani, 1912), 55–57. For another example see Gregory VIII, "Audita tremendi severitate" (October 29, 1187), in *Chronicle of the Reign of Henry II and Richard I*, vol. 2, *Chronicles and Memorials*, ed. William Stubbs (London: Longman, Green, Reader, and Dyer, 1867), no. 49, 15–19.
2. Nikolaus Paulus, *Geschichte des Ablasses im Mittelalter* (Paderborn: Schöningh, 1922), vol. 1, 120–21; Jonathan S. C. Riley-Smith, *What Were the Crusades?* (London: Palgrave Macmillan, 1977), 57–62; Riley-Smith, *What Were the Crusades?*, 55–57; James Brundage, *Medieval Canon Law and the Crusader* (Madison, London: University of Wisconsin Press, 1969), 159–90.
3. For example, Eugenius III, *Quantum Praedecessores* (December 1, 1145), 55.
4. For example, Innocent III, "Post Miserabile Hierosolymitanae" (August 15, 1198), in *Die Register Innocenz' III*, vol. 1: *Pontifikatzjahr 1198/9*, ed. Othmar Hageneder and Anton Haidacher (Rome, Graz, Vienna, and Cologne: Verlag der Österreichsichen Akademie der Wissenschaften, 1968), 501; for example, Gregory VIII, "Audita Tremendi" (November 3, 1187), in *Historia de Expeditione Friderici Imperatoris*, ed. Anton Chroust, Monumenta Germaniae Historica, Scriptores Rerum Germanorum N. S. 5 (Berlin: Weidmannsche Buchhandlung, 1928), 6.
5. For example, Alexander III, "Quantum Praedecessores" (July 14, 1165), "Epistolae et Privilegia," *Opera Omnia, Patrologia Cursus Completus*, Series Latina, comp. Jacques P. Migne (Paris, 1841–1864), (henceforward *PL*) 200, col. 384; for example, Eugenius III, "Quantum Praedecessores" (December 1, 1145), 55; Alexander III, "Quantum Praedecessores," col. 384.
6. For example, Innocent III, "Quia Major Nunc" (April 19–29, 1213), in *Studien zum Register Innocenz' III*, ed. Georgine Tangl (Weimar: H. Böhlau, 1929), 91.
7. Riley-Smith, *What Were the Crusades?*, 21.

8. John G. Rowe, "Paschal II, Bohemond of Antioch and the Byzantine Empire," *Bulletin of the John Rylands Library* 49 (1966): 200; Jean B. Richard, *Histoire des Croisades* (Paris: Fayard, 1996), trans. Jean Birrell, *The Crusades, c. 1071–1291* (Cambridge: Cambridge University Press, 1999), 156.
9. Jonathan S. C. Riley-Smith, *The First Crusaders, 1095–1131* (Cambridge: Cambridge Unversity Press, 1997), 10, 185.
10. Maureen Purcell, *Papal Crusading Policy 1244–1291* (Leiden: Brill, 1975), 12; Bernard of Clairvaux, "De Laude Novae Militiae," in *Opera Sancti Bernardi Opera*, ed. Jean Leclercq, Charles H. Talbot, and Henri M. Rochais, 8 vols. (Rome: Editiones Cistercienses, 1957–1978), vol. 3, 216.
11. Calixtus II, "Pastoralis Officii" (April 2, 1121–1124), "Epistolae et Privilegia," col. 1305; Richard, *Histoire des Croisades*, trans. Birrell, *The Crusades, c. 1071–1291*, 145; Jonathan S. C. Riley-Smith, "The Venetian Crusade of 1122–1124," in *I Comuni Italiani nel Regno Crociato di Gerusalemme*, ed. Gabriella Airaldi and Benjamin Z. Kedar (Genoa: Università di Genova, Istituto di Medievistica, 1986), 339–50; Riley-Smith, *The First Crusaders, 1095–1131*, 9, 11, 78.
12. Hans E. Mayer, *The Crusades* (Oxford: Oxford University Press, 1972), 17; although Hans Martin Schaller argues that the letter of Sergius IV may be genuine in "Zur Kreuzzugsensyklika Papst Sergius IV," in *Papstum, Kirche und Recht im Mittelalter. Festschrift für Horst Fuhrmann*, ed. Hubert Mordek (Tübingen, Germany: Max Niemeyer, 1991), 150–53.
13. Eugenius II, *Quantum Praedecessores* (December 1, 1145), 55–57; Eugenius III, "Divina Dispensatione" (October 5, 1146), in *Papsturkunden in Malta*, ed. Paul A. F. Kehr (Nachrichten der Gessellschaft der Wissenschaften zu Göttingen, 1972), 389–90; Eugenius III, "Divina Dispensation" (April 11, 1147), "Epistolae et Privilegia," *PL* 180, cols. 1203–4. Adrian IV issued another important letter, "Quantum Strenui," to the archbishop of Rheims and his suffragans ordering him to encourage people to go to the support of the Knights Templar. It was not, however, a "general crusading letter." See Adrian IV, "Quantum strenui" (November 13, 1157), "Epistolae et Privilegia," *PL* 188, cols. 1537–38.
14. Alexander III, *Quantum Praedecessores*, cols. 384–85.
15. Lucius III, "Cor Nostrum et" (November 6, 1184/1185), in *Papsturkunden in Sizilien*, ed. Peter A. F. Kehr (Berlin: Nachrichten der Gesellschaft der Wissenschaften zu Göttingen, 1899), 329–30.
16. Gregory VIII, *Audita Tremendi Severitate* (October 29, 1187), 15–19; Gregory VIII, *Audita Tremendi* (November 3, 1187), 6–10; Gregory VIII, "Quam Divina Patientia" (November 29, 1187), in *Scriptores Rerum Danicarum Medii Aevi*, ed. Jacob Langebek, 7 vols. (Hafniæ, 1772–1792), 345–46.
17. For example, Clement III, "Quam Gravis et" (February 10, 1188), in *Giraldus Cambrensis, Opera*, ed. John S. Brewer, James F. Dimock, and George F. Warner, *Giraldus Cambrensis, Opera*, vol. 8 (London: Longman, Green, Longman, and Roberts, 1891), (Kraus Reprint Ltd., 1964), 236–39; Clement III, "Quam Gravis et" (May 27, 1188), in *Acta Pontificum Romanorum Inedita*, vol. 3: *Urkunden der Päpste vom Jahre c. 590 bis zum Jahre 1197*, ed. Julius von Pflugk-Harttung (Stuttgart: Kohlhammer, 1886), 363–64.
18. Celestine II, "Divitiae Summae Divinitatis" (August 1, 1195), in *Urkundenbuch des Hoschstifts Hildesheim und Seiner Bischöfe*, ed. Karl Janicke, vol. 1 (Leipzig: S. Hirzel, 1896), 483–85. See also Celestine III, "Misericors et Miserator" (July 25, 1195), in *Ralph of Diceto, Opera Historica*, ed. William Stubbs, vol. 2 (London: Longman, 1876), 132–35, which was not a "general crusading letter" but was addressed to Hubert archbishop of Canterbury, legate of the Apostolic See and his suffragans.
19. For example, Clement III, *Quam Gravis et* (February 10, 1188), 236–39; Clement III, *Quam Gravis et* (May 27, 1188), 363–64.
20. Richard, *The Crusades, c. 1071–1291, The Crusades, c. 1071–1291*, 157.
21. Bernard of Clairvaux, "Sermo Mihi ad vos," ed. Jean Leclercq, "L'Encyclique de saint Bernard en faveur de la croisade," *Revue Bénédictine* 81 (1971): 295–300.
22. Eugenius III *Divina Dispensatione* (April 11, 1147), cols. 1203–4.
23. Innocent III, "Post Miserabile Hierosolymitanae," 499–505; Innocent III, "Nisi Nobis Dictum" (January 4, 1199), *Opera Omnia, PL* 214, cols. 832–35; Innocent III, "Graves Orientalis Terrae" (31 December 1199) *Die Register Innocenz'III*, Publikationen des Österreichischen Kulturinstituts in Rom, 2 Abteilung, 1 (Graz-Wien-Köln: Böhlau, 1964–1997), vol. 2: *Pontifikatzjahr 1199/2000*, ed. Othmar Hageneder, Werner Maleczek, and Alfred A. Strnad, 491–97; Innocent III, "Tetendisse Dominus Arcum" (May 29, 1208), *Opera Omnia, PL* 214, cols. 832–35; "Innocent III, 'Utinam Dominus et'" (December 10, 1208), *Opera Omnia, PL* 215, cols. 1500–503; Innocent III, "Utinam Dominus" (December 10, 1208), *Opera Omnia*, col. 1503; Innocent III, "Quia Major Nunc," 88–97. Innocent III also issued "Plorans Ploravit Ecclesia" to the Syracusan bishop (of Luca) and the abbot of Sambuca. See Innocent III, "Plorans Ploravit Ecclesia" (June 1198), in *Die Register Innocenz'III*, ed. Othmar Hageneder and Anton Haidacher,

Publikationen des Österreichischen Kulturinstituts in Rom, 2 Abteilung, 1 (Graz-Wien-Köln: Böhlau, 1964–1997), vol. 1: *Pontifikatzjahr 1198/9*, 430–33.
24. Innocent III also issued a general crusading letter in 1205 but this has not been found; see Helmut Roscher, *Papst Innocenz III und die Kreuzzuge*, Forschungen zur Kirschen-und Dogmengeschichte, vol. 21 (Göttingen: Vandenhoeck u. Ruprecht, 1969), 125.
25. Eugenius III, *Quantum Praedecessores* (December 1, 1145), 55–57.
26. For example, Eugenius III, *Quantum Praedecessores* (December 1, 1145), 55–57, passim. Latin phrases include *sanguinis effusione, sine magno dolore et gemitu, a paganorum spurcitia,* and *in infidelium concalcationem datae sunt et dispersae.*
27. Such phrases might be expanded upon, for example, *tam sanctum tamque pernecessarium opus et laborem devotionis,* in Eugenius III, *Quantum Praedecessores* (December 1, 1145), 55–57.
28. Eugenius III, *Quantum Praedecessores* (December 1, 1145), 55–57, passim. Latin phrases include *crucem acceperint* and *qui Domino militant.* The same phrases are found in Eugenius III, "Quantum Praedecessores" (March 1, 1146), ed. Peter Rassow, *Neues Archiv der Gessellschaft für ältere Deutsche Geschichtskunde* 45, 302–305.
29. For example, Alexander III, *In Quantis Pressuris*, 253.
30. Alexander III, *Cor Nostrum et*, col. 1295; the Latin phrase includes *laborem Huius Peregrinationis*; Innocent III, *Quia Major Nunc*, 94.
31. Muslim conversion was not a goal of crusades to the Holy Land. Benjamin Z. Kedar, *Crusade and Mission* (Princeton, NJ: Princeton University Press, 1964), 60–61.
32. Bernard of Clairvaux, *Sermo Mihi Ad Vos*, 295–300; Bernard of Clairvaux, "Est sermo mihi ad vos," ed. Jean Leclercq, "L'Encyclique de Saint Bernard en Faveur de la Croisade," *Revue Bénédictine* 81 (1971): 286–88.
33. Leclercq, *L'Encyclique de Saint Bernard en Faveur de la Croisade*, 306–7.
34. For example, Eugenius III, *Quantum Praedecessores* (December 1, 1145), 57.
35. Walter Ullmann, *The Growth of Papal Government in the Middle Ages* (London: Methuen, 1955), 19. For example, Clement III, *Quam Gravis et* (February 10, 1188), 239; for example, Celestine III, *Divitiae Summae Divinitatis*, 485. See also Clement III, *Quam Gravis et* (February 10, 1188), 237.
36. For example, Gregory VIII, *Audita Tremendi Severitate* (October 29, 1187), 18–19.
37. Adrian IV, *Quantum Strenui*, col. 1538.
38. Christopher R. Cheney, *Pope Innocent III and England* (Stuttgart: Hiersemann, 1976), 3–4.
39. Clement III, *Quam Gravis et* (February 10, 1188), 236; Clement III, *Quam gravis et* (May 27, 1188), 363; Raoul Manzelli, "La res Publica Christiana e l'Islam," *Settimane di Studio del Centro Italiano di Studi sull'Alto Medioevo*, vol. 12, Spoleto, 1965, 115–47.
40. Ullmann, *The Growth of Papal Government in the Middle Ages*, 8–9.
41. "... verum ne nos aliis onera gravia et importabilia imponere videamus, digite autem nostro ea movere nolumus, dicentes tantum et aut nihil aut minimum facientes ..." For this expression (and variants on it) see Innocent III, *Plorans Ploravit Ecclesia*, 432; Innocent III, *Post Miserabile Hierosolymitanae*, 502; Innocent III, *Nisi Nobis Dictum*, col. 834; Innocent III, *Graves Orientalis Terrae*, 493; Innocent III, *Quia Major Nunc*, 93.
42. For example, Eugenius III, *Quantum Praedecessores* (December 1, 1145), 56; Gregory VIII, *Audita Tremendi* (November 3, 1187), 6.
43. For example, Eugenius III, *Quantum Praedecessores* (March 1, 1146), 304; Brundage, *Medieval Canon Law and the Crusader*, 10–18.
44. Horace K. Mann, *Nicholas Breakspear—Hadrian IV—A.D. 1154–1159, The Only English Pope* (London: Kegan Paul, Trench, Trubner, 1914), 87–88.
45. Jean B. Richard, *Les Relations Entre l'Orient et Occident au Moyen Age: Études et Documents* (London: Variorum Reprint, 1977), 228–29.
46. Purcell, *Papal Crusading Policy 1244–1291*, 19.
47. Vacandard, *Saint Bernard et la Seconde Croisade*, 404.
48. Bernard of Clairvaux, "Parcat vobis Deus," *Sancti Bernardi Opera*, vol. 8, ep. 247, 141; Bernard of Clairvaux, *Sermo Mihi ad vos*, 299–300.
49. Eugenius III, *Divina Dispensatione* April 11, 1147, cols. 1203–4.
50. Bernard of Clairvaux, *Est Mihi Sermo ad vos*, 286–88; Bernard of Clairvaux, *Sermo Mihi ad vos*, 295–300.
51. Bernard of Clairvaux, "De Consideratione," *Five Books on Consideration: Advice to a Pope (De Consideratione)*, trans. John D. Anderson and Elizabeth T. Kennan (Kalamazoo, MI: Cistercian Publications, 1976), Book II, 413.

52. Bernard of Clairvaux, *De Consideratione*, Book III, 431–32.
53. Bernard of Clairvaux, "Non est leve Verbum," *Sancti Bernardi Opera*, vol. 8, ep. 256, 164.
54. Colin Morris, "Propaganda for War: The Dissemination of the Crusading Ideal in the Twelfth Century," in *The Church and War*, ed. William J. Sheils, *Studies in Church History* 20 (Oxford, 1983), 100–101.
55. Elphège Vacandard, "Saint Bernard et la Seconde Croisade," *Revue des Questions Historiques* 38 (1885): 404.
56. Bernard of Clairvaux, *Non est leve Verbum*, ep. 256, 164.
57. Bernard Flood, "St. Bernard's View of Crusade," *Cistercian Studies* 9 (1974): 26.
58. Jane E. Sayer, *Innocent III: Leader of Europe, 1198–1216* (London: Longman, 1994), 175.
59. Innocent III, *Nisi Nobis Dictum*, col. 834; Innocent III, *Graves Orientalis Terrae*, 493–95; Innocent III, *Quia Major Nunc*, 93, 96; see Cheney, *Pope Innocent III and England*, 267–68.
60. Frederick H. Russell, *The Just War in the Middle Ages* (Cambridge Studies in Medieval Life and Thought, Third Series, vol. 8 (Cambridge: Cambridge University Press, 1957), 112–19; Russell, *The Just War in the Middle Ages*, 118; James Brundage, "Holy War and the Medieval Lawyers," in *The Holy War*, ed. Thomas P. Murphy (Columbus, OH: Ohio State University Press, 1976), 110–11.
61. Russell, *The Just War in the Middle Ages*, 195–212; Brundage, *Medieval Canon Law and the Crusader*, 99; Hostiensis also discussed various species of war including the "Roman War," a type of Holy War, thus helping the formalization of the idea of crusade to develop—Brundage, *Holy War and the Medieval Lawyers*, 118.
62. Brundage, *Medieval Canon Law and the Crusader*, 39–40.
63. Brundage, *Holy War and the Medieval Lawyers*, 106; Gratian, "Causa 23," in *Corpus Iuris Canonici*, ed. Aemilius E. Friedberg, vol. 1: *Decretum Magistri Gratiani* (Leipzig: ex officina Bernhardi Tauchnitz, 1879), cols. 889–965.
64. Ernest-Dieter Hëhl, *Kirche und Krieg im zwölft Jahrhundert: Studien zu Kanonischen Recht und Politischer Wirklichkeit* (Stuttgart: Hiersemann, 1980), 46–48.
65. Brundage, *Holy War and the Medieval Lawyers*, 116–17.
66. John of Mantua also justified the right of a pope to authorize the use of force. Brundage, *Holy War and the Medieval Lawyers*, 106; Riley-Smith, *The First Crusaders, 1095–1131*, 51.
67. Innocent III, *Quia Major Nunc*, 94–95.
68. Charles J. Hefele, *Histoire des Conciles d'après les Documents Originaux*, trans. Henri Leclercq (Paris: Letouzeyet Ané, 1907–21), vol. 5.1, 388–89; Hefele, *Histoire des Conciles d'après les Documents Originaux*, vol. 5.1, 567; Ernest-Dieter Hëhl, "Was ist Eigentlich ein Kreuzzug?" *Historische Zeitschrift* 259 (1994): 321, Note 65.
69. Othmar Hageneder, "Der Häresiebegriff bei den Juristen des 12. und 13. Jahrhunderts," *The Concept of Heresy in the Middle Ages (11–13 Centuries), Proceedings of the International Conference Louvain May 13–16, 1973*, Mediaevalia Lovaniensa, Series I Studia IV (The Hague: Leuven University Press; Martinus Nijhoff, 1976), 50–51.
70. Hefele, *Histoire des Conciles d'après les Documents Originaux*, vol. 5.1, 824–26.
71. Richard, *The Crusades, c. 1071–1291*, trans. Birrell, *The Crusades, c. 1071–1291*, 145.
72. Peter Herde, "Christians and Saracens at the Time of the Crusades: Some Comments of Contemporary Medieval Canonists," *Studia Gratiana* 12 (1967): 363.
73. Brundage, *Holy War and the Medieval Lawyers*, 123.
74. Robert Foreville, "Procédure et Débats Dans les Conciles Médiévaux du Lateran 1123–1215," *Rivista di Storia della Chiesa in Italia* 9 (1965): 34.
75. Innocent III, *Quia Major Nunc*, 95.
76. Russell, *The Just War in the Middle Ages*, 196; "Ad Liberandam," in Richard, *The Crusades, c. 1071–1291*, trans. Birrell, *The Crusades, c. 1071–1291*, 279.
77. Eugenius III, *Quantum Praedecessores* (December 1, 1145), 55.
78. Richard, *Orient et Occident au Moyen Age: Contacts et Relations XII–XV Siècles*, 58.
79. Michele Macarrone, "Studi zu Innocenzo III. Orvieto e la Predicazione Della Crociata," *Italia Sacra* 17 (1972): 3–163.
80. Calixtus II, "Pastoralis officii" (April 2, 1121–1124), *Epistolae et Privilegia*, PL 163, col. 1305; Richard, *Orient et Occident au Moyen Age*, 56; Riley-Smith, *What Were the Crusades?*, 13.
81. Eugenius III, *Divina Dispensatione* April 11, 1147, col. 1203.
82. Celestine III, *Divitiae Summae Divinitatis*, 484–85.
83. Celestine III, *Misericors et Miserator*, 135.
84. Innocent III, *Post Miserabile Hierosolymitanae*, 502; Richard, *The Crusades, c. 1071–1291*, trans. Birrell, *The Crusades, c. 1071–1291*, 243.

85. Richard, *The Crusades, c. 1071–1291*, trans. Birrell, *The Crusades, c. 1071–1291*, 218; Gregory VIII, *Audita Tremendi Severitate* (October 29, 1187), 15–19; Gregory VIII, *Audita Tremendi* (November 3, 1187), 6–10; Gregory VIII, *Quam Divina Patientia*, 345–46.
86. Eugenius III, *Quantum Praedecessores* (December 1, 1145), 56–57; Eugenius III, *Quantum Praedecessores* (March 1, 1146), 303–5; Alexander III, *Quantum Praedecessores*, cols. 385–86.
87. Riley-Smith, *What Were the Crusades?*, 57–62.

7

"Generosity . . . in the Slavery of This Brave Cavalier": Sanctity Honor and Religious Violence in the French Mediterranean

Brian Sandberg[1]

A 1608 book celebrates the religiosity and perseverance of François Vintimille, a French nobleman who had recently suffered the humiliation of enslavement in the Barbary Coast, describing the "generosity . . . in the slavery of this brave cavalier."[2] French nobles participated readily in religious warfare in the early modern Mediterranean. During the sixteenth and early seventeenth centuries, many French nobles joined the Knights of Malta, the Cavalieri di Santo Stefano, and other armed organizations in order to participate in anti-Muslim military expeditions and naval raiding campaigns across the Mediterranean. Many of these noble combatants were captured and enslaved in North Africa and the Ottoman Empire during this period, creating anomalous positions for these military and social elites, who often experienced prolonged captivities and miserable conditions while waiting for ransom negotiations to win their release. Yet, this early seventeenth-century noble slave narrative situates honor and "generosity" precisely in the humiliating experience of slavery.

This chapter examines the conceptions of honor employed by the bellicose nobles who participated in Mediterranean warfare and religious conflict in the early modern period. Using manuscript correspondence, printed pamphlets, and published treatises, I will examine how the dynamics of interfaith conflict, religious violence, galley warfare, enslavement of prisoners, and cross-cultural ransoming all challenged French nobles' conceptions of honor, especially in the realm of sanctity honor. I argue that early modern French nobles' conceptions and practices of honor seriously question the model of a pan-Mediterranean honor/shame dichotomy and reveal dimensions of religious violence in the early modern Mediterranean world.

Questioning Honor and Shame

Current anthropological and historical interest in honor is largely an outgrowth of the pioneering work of the structuralists Julian Pitt-Rivers and J. G. Peristiany in the 1960s, which proposed the idea of a particular Mediterranean conception of honor, frequently referred to as the *honor/shame model*.[3] The honor/shame model argues that Mediterranean societies from Greece to Morocco share a common conception of male honor juxtaposed against female shame. Honor and shame are reciprocal values won and lost in a zero-sum game that is quintessentially male, but that may be enacted through females. Honor, according to this formulation, operates through both *external* and *internal* channels, two aspects that approximate the concepts of "reputation" and "character." In a generalized form, this two-aspect conception of honor has been referred to as the *bipartite theory* of honor. Pitt-Rivers refers to the internal facet of honor as "honor = virtue" and the external facet as "honor = precedence."[4] Although many studies on non-Mediterranean forms of honor have also employed a bipartite theory, Mediterraneanists have to a certain extent appropriated bipartite theory, claiming to find both a particular two-aspect form of honor and a special relationship between honor and shame in Mediterranean societies.[5] The Mediterranean honor/shame model has become widely influential and probably the most utilized analytic concept in studies of honor.

However, the Mediterranean honor/shame model is vulnerable to a number of criticisms. The theory's overly wide application and simplifications do not account well for subcultural variations of honor conceptions or behavior within specific societies. The idea of a distinct Mediterranean culture with a code of honor that separates it from all other cultures is partly an outgrowth of the entrenched idea of a fundamental split between northern and southern European societies. Michael Herzfeld and other anthropologists have studied the formation of stereotypes about "Mediterranean" societies and have questioned the very notion of a unified "Mediterranean" culture. Herzfeld uses semiotic analysis to argue that considering the Mediterranean as a distinct unit is nothing but a convenient construction that anthropologists use.[6] Critics of Mediterraneanness, including Herzfeld, have specifically challenged the idea of a pan-Mediterranean notion of honor and shame.[7] Frank Henderson Stewart argues that "in the discussion of honor it is never appropriate to treat the peoples who border the Mediterranean as a discrete unit."[8] He also rightly points out that a distinction between the ideas of honor in northern versus southern Europe has not been clearly established. Greek, Spanish, Portuguese, Italian, and Maghrebian notions of honor no longer seem as similar as Peristiany and Pitt-Rivers originally proposed.[9]

Conversely, the honor/shame model has been applied to examinations of honor in Western and non-Western societies well outside the Mediterranean region, suggesting that it does not describe specifically Mediterranean culture. Indeed, the model's ability to consider a wide geographic space and a pluralistic cultural area—the Mediterranean—as an analytic unit provides a strong comparative basis for the theory, at least among societies ringing the Mediterranean. The model's notion of honor is sufficiently broad to be relevant in many disparate cases, facilitating its comparative usefulness. Many anthropologists have both compared and contrasted European honor culture with conceptions of honor in non-Western societies.[10] Scholars have applied or adapted the Mediterranean honor/shame model to studies of honor in various cultures in different historical periods.[11] Historians have employed the honor/shame model in investigations of early modern French notions of honor among nobles, artisans, peasants, and women.[12]

The honor/shame model's notion of honor and shame as opposites operating in a zero-sum game is highly problematic. A division of the Mediterranean moral system into male honor and female shame creates a suspect and unnuanced view of gender relations in the theory.[13] The model completely ignores religious beliefs and practices, considering honor and shame as essentially secular social constructs. Finally, Peristiany and Pitt-Rivers seriously hampered their model by adopting an ahistorical perspective that allowed for little examination of developments and transformations of the idea of honor over time.[14]

The Mediterranean honor/shame model has arguably reached the limits of its usefulness and must be seriously modified or completely rejected as an analytical tool for studying honor.[15] Realizing the flaws of bipartite models, some researchers have explored analyzing honor as a unitary concept. Single-concept theories could envision honor simply as respect, or moral worth, or self-importance. Frank Henderson Stewart, for example, uses a unitary model of honor, seeing personal honor as a "right" embodied in the institution of the "pledge of honor." Considering honor as a unitary concept is very vague and limiting, however, because it forces diverse and conflicting notions and actions into one nuanced category.[16] Recent historical studies of honor in the early modern Mediterranean focus on the dimensions of credit, service, and masculinity in honor conceptions and relationships.[17] These new approaches suggest ways of reconceptualizing honor in early modern France and the French Mediterranean.

Honor and Violence in Early Modern French Noble Culture

Early modern French honor culture has long fascinated us with its color, pageantry, and dramatic rituals. The nobility's coats of arms, honorific titles, tournaments, swords, and duels easily evoke honor ideals even today. The rich imagery of honor has inspired literature, drama, and visual art from contemporaries to nineteenth-century Romantics to twentieth-century novelists and filmmakers—so much so that literary expressions of honor codes are often taken to be the dominant forms of honor within a society.

Renaissance French art often centers around honor themes, both because nobles patronized the arts and because many artists were themselves noble. Sixteenth- and seventeenth-century writers Michel de Montaigne, Agrippa d'Aubigné, Pierre Corneille, and Cyrano de Bergerac all discussed honor explicitly. Seventeenth- and eighteenth-century critics of early modern honor culture such as Molière and Voltaire did little to suppress interest in it. Among the best-known nineteenth-century Romantic works concerning early modern honor culture are the novels of Alexandre Dumas. Paintings by Romantic artists such as Eugene Delacroix and Paul Delaroche also focused on nobles and royalty in the French religious wars. Late nineteenth-century artists such as Henri Motte continued to reference early modern noble honor. Edmond Rostand's *Cyrano de Bergerac*, first produced in 1897, drew heavily on early modern expressions of honor. Film adaptations of *Les trois mousquetaires*, *La Reine Margot*, and numerous swashbuckling epics in French, English, and other languages have helped keep early modern honor imagery alive in the twentieth and twenty-first centuries.[18]

Poets, playwrights, moralists, and jurists certainly did discuss honor intensely in the sixteenth and early seventeenth centuries, and literary constructions offer some insights into the early modern world of honor. The most famous literary discussion of early seventeenth-century noble conceptions of honor is probably Pierre Corneille's tragicomedy *Le Cid*. In this play Corneille's hero Don Rodrigue, caught between the dictates of honor and his feelings of love, struggles to understand the meanings and duties of honor. Don

Rodrigue's famous soliloquy reveals the depth of his inner emotional conflict, as well as the complexity of his society's understanding of honor. Corneille's blending of the concerns of family honor, personal honor, justice, and duty reflect rather well his noble contemporaries' conceptions. The images of blood, vengeance, glory, and death so vivid in Corneille's lines were commonly evoked by noblemen who never attempted a poem or a play.[19]

Literary discussions of honor such as Corneille's only reflect certain aspects of honor culture however. Contemporary letters, journals, and memoirs provide a better means of accessing nobles's honor discourse and their honor acts. Warrior nobles actually discussed honor regularly in their own writings, in both abstract and practical terms. Honor vocabulary was so diverse and pervasive in early modern French society that a contemporary dictionary lists more than ninety usages of the word *honneur* in its different forms.[20] Warrior nobles employed both routine and tactical honor discourses in a wide array of documents, from personal letters and memoirs to published pamphlets and literature—all of which were produced with distinct aims in diverse contexts. How then do we interpret these sources?

French literary scholars have examined the concept of *honnêteté* in poetry, prose, and theatrical works.[21] Historians have developed other interpretations of *honnêteté* and its practices, often employing Norbert Elias's model of a "civilizing process" that allegedly shaped Bourbon court culture and then progressively transformed early modern French society.[22] Other historians have concentrated on analyses of dueling as an expression of noble honor and masculinity.[23] Arlette Jouanna's interpretation of sixteenth-century noble honor conceptions revolves around a binary model that is built on the ideas of virtue and reputation, but that is more flexible than the honor/shame model.[24]

In my recently published book, *Warrior Pursuits: Noble Culture and Civil Conflict in Early Modern France*, I argue that early modern French nobles constructed complex notions of honor that involved distinct dimensions of sanctity, dignity, reputation, and precedence. My research on noble culture in Languedoc, a Mediterranean province of France, reveals that the nobles there do not seem to have had a completely different conception of honor than the nobles of Guyenne or France in general. See Table 1 for details on this specific honor culture.

I would like to consider how these conceptions of honor were deployed as French nobles engaged in religious violence and social interactions across the Mediterranean world.

Sanctity Honor and Mediterranean Conflict

I will now focus on one dimension of early modern French conceptions of honor—namely, sanctity honor—through a particular text, Henry du Lisdam's *L'Esclavage du brave chevalier de Vintimille* published in 1608. This curious text offers a slave narrative of a southern French noble who was captured while serving in the Knights of Malta in the Mediterranean and subsequently enslaved in North Africa. Sanctity honor is present throughout the text, as the chevalier de Vintimille faces a series of challenges to his faith and his honor. My analysis of sanctity honor applies John A. Lynn's theory of motivational systems in armies. Lynn argues that armies use initial, sustaining, and combat motivation to recruit, train, and deploy soldiers and officers effectively.[25] My analysis of

Table 1
Model of Honor Culture Used by French Nobility

	Honor as Sanctity	Honor as Quality	Honor as Reputation	Honor as Precedence
Definition	Holiness and character	Noble status and degree	Virtue and courage	Prerogative and privilege
Source	Natural and divine	Birth inheritance promotion	Royal service exercise of office	Office rank
Expression	Piety	Dignity	Pride	Superiority
Personal performances	Religiosity defense of faith reverence	Homage marriage	Combat	Dueling favors
Communal performances	Veneration	Adoration	Accolade	Deference
Regulator	Religious authority	Legal authority	Peer opinion	Honor code
Masculinity	Fraternal masculinity	Paternalistic masculinity	Exemplary masculinity	Aggressive masculinity

Note: An earlier version of this model appeared in my dissertation: Brian Sandberg, "Bonds of Nobility and the Culture of Revolt: Provincial Nobles and Civil Conflict in Early Modern France, 1610–1635" (University of Illinois at Urbana-Champaign, 2001)

L'Esclavage du brave chevalier de Vintimille expands Lynn's theory to consider religious aspects of initial, sustaining, and combat motivations in the chevalier de Vintimille's experiences.

In Lisdam's text, Malta, "this eye of Europe, the front and the key of Christianity, the right arm of the Church, the heart of religion, the most animated daughter of the successor to Saint Peter," attracts the chevalier de Vintimille, who wishes to serve "in combats against the Turk."[26] Religiosity and sanctity honor indeed provided the initial motivation for many Catholic nobles to engage in warfare against Muslim enemies in the Mediterranean. Catholic pamphlets and treatises promoted a crusading culture against heretics and infidels in the late sixteenth and early seventeenth centuries, which Robert Sauzet has described as "nostalgia for crusade."[27] *L'Esclavage du brave chevalier de Vintimille* fits within this genre, envisioning the Knights of Malta as crusading warriors doing the work of God: "What glory! These flying buttresses of the Gospel persevere under the foresight of a Grand Master who has the honor of the Church of God; ... Guard the rank of his grandeur, animating the courage of these knights through his majesty."[28]

Sanctity honor was intertwined with nobles' preparations for warfare, expressed through personal and collective piety. Prior to departing on his naval voyage, the chevalier spends time in devotions, "where this Saint Penitent [Mary] Magdalene taught the sinners lessons in repentance."[29] Such devotional activity by a warrior noble seems to have helped sustain his morale and prepare him for future combat. Conceptions of sanctity undergirded Catholic nobles' participation in military and naval campaigns in the Mediterranean, providing sustaining motivations for would-be crusaders. Thus, *L'Esclavage du brave chevalier de Vintimille* emphasizes that the chevalier "all filled with valor and courage, proved himself through his patience against all the shocks that test those whom fortune has left at the mercy of calamities."[30]

Sanctity honor also plays a role in the combat motivation of French nobles engaging in Mediterranean warfare. The narrative encourages the idea of combating for a holy religious cause, at one point indicating that "it is the cause that honors the effects."[31] The source of honor, then, is the divinely sanctioned cause of fighting in the name of God: "Nothing is impossible for those who combat for God's quarrel, without searching for their own profit. The sun is ready to stop and all things favor the honor of their Creator, for those who answer the alarms to sustain the Church."[32] The narrative promotes a controlled form of honor that is divinely granted, but defined by personal character and holiness. The author insists that "a manly courage always lets itself be governed by reason."[33] Here, Catholic religiosity embraces a Neostoic celebration of the power of mental and bodily self-discipline.[34]

French nobles displayed sanctity honor through their behavior in the seemingly dishonorable experiences of captivity in North Africa and the Ottoman Empire. Captivity narratives, such as *L'Esclavage du brave chevalier de Vintimille*, stress the holiness of suffering through slavery at the hands of Muslim masters. The potentially shameful condition of slavery is transformed into a test of faith that can confirm and enhance sanctity honor. These texts portray sanctity honor in fascinating ways that reveal serious limitations of the conventional Mediterranean honor/shame paradigm.

The suffering of the chevalier in slavery highlights a number of contradictions in French noble honor culture. Although *L'Esclavage du brave chevalier de Vintimille* is a strongly Catholic text, the author indicates that "we see the Heretics going more constantly to martyrdom than the Christians. How thus can we know the truth from lies?"[35] True sanctity honor thus seems to be incredibly rare—since heretics are denied sanctity honor despite their brave deaths, while many "Christians" (here referring exclusively to Catholics) apparently fail to exhibit sanctity honor when confronted by trials of faith.

L'Esclavage du brave chevalier de Vintimille offers a testimonial to a rare display of true sanctity honor in desperate circumstances. The chevalier was stripped and humiliated, suffering cold, nakedness, pain, and malnutrition in solitary confinement for a period. Yet the narrative stresses that "It is a great satisfaction to endure something for the love of God."[36] The French noble is then beaten and forced to march and labor in chains. Throughout the text, he is repeatedly mocked and enticed to convert to Islam. The narrative promises the reader that God protects the faithful in slavery: "your life is in the hands of God: make him a present of your conscience."[37]

A renegade leader mocks the captured chevalier by alluding to the Knights of Malta's reputation for charity and brotherhood, saying that "the greatest part of their glory consists in loving the fortune of their companions more than their own advancement."[38] To promote "this great charity," the renegade orders the heads of executed chevaliers to be placed together on the walls of his castle. This passage focuses on the cruelty of the renegade's actions and the sadness of the captured chevalier, yet the text simultaneously reinforces the Knights of Malta's claims to fraternal masculinity and sanctity honor by distancing the chevalier from the cruelty of this ex-Christian convert to Islam.

The text repeatedly insists on the power of God's providential hand, as in describing the circumstances of the chevalier's capture. In the midst of combat, the chevalier was surrounded and in a desperate situation, when a French renegade among the Moors recognized him as French and beckoned to the chevalier to surrender, and this was "as if God suddenly reached out a hand from heaven."[39] The text calls on readers to "recognize that you are not capable of combating the assaults of Satan. Being alone, always call on our Lord to aid you."[40] The chevalier de Vintimille seeks the protection of the Virgin Mary, who responds to his prayers by sustaining him during his captivity through visionary contact and intercession. The text offers various proofs of the Virgin's intercessory powers, detailing that the chevalier is eventually liberated from slavery on Pentecost, arrives in Christian territories on the feast of Saint John, and then finally returns to Marseille on the feast of the Virgin Mary. The chevalier's experiences thus offer an exemplary demonstration of reformed Catholic piety to readers, demonstrating the effectiveness of reliance on prayer, saintly intercession, and divine Providence.

Conclusion

L'Esclavage du brave chevalier de Vintimille provides a window into Catholic identities and noble culture in early modern France and the Mediterranean. The text was published under the patronage Henri de Bourbon, duc de Montpensier, the provincial governor of Normandie and a royalist military commander for Henri IV during the religious wars of the 1580s and 1590s. Its message of piety, devotion, suffering, and endurance fit well with contemporary Catholic reform ideals of religiosity in France.

The chevalier's performances of sanctity honor, which are described in his slave narrative, suggest new ways of conceptualizing honor in the early modern Mediterranean by foregrounding the importance of piety and religious conflict in shaping noble culture. Binary notions of honor or shame offer little insight into the complex world of crusading warfare, elite slavery, and ransom negotiating that were central to the lives of militant Catholic nobles or their Ottoman, North African, and renegade enemies.

Notes

1. Research for this essay was made possible by generous research support from Northern Illinois University, the University of Wisconsin at Madison, the Medici Archive Project, and the National Endowment for the Humanities. Any views, findings, conclusions, or recommendations expressed in this publication do not necessarily represent those of the National Endowment for the Humanities.
2. Henry du Lisdam, *L'Esclavage du Brave Chevalier François Vintimille, des Comtes de Marseille, & Olieule, à Present Commandeur du Planté & Cadillan. Où l'on Peut Voir Plusieurs Rencontres de Guerre Dignes de Remarque* (Lyon: Claude Morillon, 1608), 12.
3. The seminal work on honor/shame is J. G. Peristiany, ed., *Honour and Shame: Values of Mediterranean Society* (Chicago: University of Chicago Press, 1966). For a brief assessment of the honor/shame model, see Frank Henderson Stewart, *Honor* (Chicago: Chicago University Press, 1994), ix, 75–78.
4. See Julian Pitt-Rivers, "Honour and Social Status," in *Honour and Shame: The Values of Mediterranean Society*, ed. J. G. Peristiany (Chicago: University of Chicago Press, 1966), 19–78. The designation *bipartite theory* appears in Stewart, *Honor*, 11–13, 19.
5. For a summary of the honor/shame model and anthropological literature relating to it, see David D. Gilmore, "Introduction," in *Honor and Shame and the Unity of the Mediterranean*, ed. David D. Gilmore, Special Publication of the American Anthropological Association, 22 (Washington, DC: American Anthropoligical Association, 1987), 2–21.
6. Michael Herzfeld, "Honour and Shame: Problems in the Comparative Analysis of Moral Systems," *Man*, New Series, 15 (June 1980): 339–51; Michael Herzfeld, "'As in Your Own House': Hospitality,

Ethnography, and the Stereotype of Mediterranean Society," in *Honor and Shame and the Unity of the Mediterranean*, ed. David D. Gilmore, Special Publication of the American Anthropological Association, 22 (Washington, DC: American Anthropological Association, 1987), 75–89; Michael Herzfeld, "Practical Mediterraneanism: Excuses for Everything, from Epistemology to Eating," in *Rethinking the Mediterranean*, ed. W. V. Harris (Oxford: Oxford University Press, 2005), 45–63.
7. Michael Herzfeld, *Anthropology through the Looking-Glass: Critical Ethnography in the Margins of Europe* (Cambridge: Cambridge University Press, 1987), 7–12.
8. Stewart, *Honor*, 76–8.
9. Scott Taylor, "Credit, Debt, and Honor in Castile, 1600–1650," *Journal of Early Modern History* 7 (2003): 8–27; Matthew T. Racine, "Service and Honor in Sixteenth-Century Portuguese North Africa: Yahya-u-Tacfuft and Portuguese Noble Culture," *Sixteenth Century Journal* 32 (Spring 2001): 67–90; Elizabeth S. Cohen, "Honor and Gender in the Streets of Early Modern Rome," *Journal of Interdisciplinary History* 22 (Spring 1992): 597–625.
10. See Stewart, *Honor*, for a comparison of Bedouin 'ird and European "honor." He also surveys anthropological literature on non-Western honor. For articles comparing honor in North Africa and southern Europe, see *Honor and Shame and the Unity of the Mediterranean*, ed. David D. Glimore. For studies of honor in colonial Latin America, see *Faces of Honor: Sex, Shame, and Violence in Colonial Latin America*, ed. Lyman L. Johnson and Sonya Lipsett-Rivera (Albuquerque: University of New Mexico Press, 1998).
11. William M. Reddy, *The Invisible Code: Honor and Sentiment in Postrevolutionary France, 1814–1848* (Berkeley, CA: University of California Press, 1997); William Ian Miller, *Humiliation: And Other Essays on Honor, Social Discomfort, and Violence* (Ithaca: Cornell University Press, 1993); Shearer Davis Bowman, *Masters and Lords: Mid-19th-Century U.S. Planters and Prussian Junkers* (New York: Oxford University Press, 1993); Richard E. Nisbett and Dov Cohen, *Culture of Honor: The Psychology of Violence in the South* (Boulder, CO: Westview Press, 1996); Bertram Wyatt-Brown, *Honor and Violence in the Old South* (New York: Oxford University Press, 1986), which is an abridgement of *Southern Honor: Ethics and Behavior in the Old South* (New York: Oxford University Press, 1982); Grady McWhiney and Perry D. Jamieson, *Attack and Die: Civil War Military Tactics and the Southern Heritage* (Tuscaloosa, AL: University of Alabama Press, 1982).
12. Malcolm Greenshields, *An Economy of Violence in Early Modern France: Crime and Justice in the Haute Auvergne, 1587–1664* (University Park, PA: Pennslyvania State University Press, 1994).
13. For gender histories employing nuanced conceptions of feminine honor, see Elizabeth S. Cohen, "Honor and Gender in the Streets of Early Modern Rome," *Journal of Interdisciplinary History* 22 (Spring 1992): 597–625; Natalie Zemon Davis, *The Return of Martin Guerre* (Cambridge, MA: Harvard University Press, 1983).
14. David D. Gilmore, "Introduction: The Shame of Dishonor," in *Honor and Shame and the Unity of the Mediterranean*, ed. David D. Gilmore, Special Publication of the American Anthropological Association, 22 (Washington, DC: American Anthropological Association, 1987), 2–21; David D. Gilmore, "Honor, Honesty, Shame: Male Status in Contemporary Andalusia," in *Honor and Shame and the Unity of the Mediterranean*, ed. David D. Gilmore, Special Publication of the American Anthropological Association, 22 (Washington, DC: American Anthropological Association, 1987), 90–103; Stanley Brandes, "Reflections on Honor and Shame in the Mediterranean," in *Honor and Shame and the Unity of the Mediterranean*, ed. David D. Gilmore, Special Publication of the American Anthropological Association, 22 (Washington, DC: American Anthropological Association, 1987), 121–34.
15. For a critique of the honor/shame model, see Amanda Weidman, "Beyond Honor and Shame: Performing Gender in the Mediterranean," *Anthropological Quarterly* 76 (Summer 2003): 1534–18.
16. Stewart, *Honor*, 12–13. Interestingly, Pitt-Rivers suggested the idea of honor as a "right," but did not fully develop the idea: "Honour is the value of a person in his own eyes, but also in the eyes of his society. It is his estimation of his own worth, his *claim* to pride, but it is also the acknowledgement of that claim, his excellence recognized by society, his *right* to pride." Julian Pitt-Rivers, "Honour and Social Status," in *Honour and Shame: The Values of Mediterranean Society*, ed. J. G. Peristiany (Chicago: University of Chicago Press, 1966), 21. Robert Nye also seems to consider the idea of honor as a right. Nye, *Masculinity and Male Codes of Honor in Modern France*, 216–17.
17. Scott Taylor, "Credit, Debt, and Honor in Castile, 1600–1650," *Journal of Early Modern History* 7 (2003): 8–27; Matthew T. Racine, "Service and Honor in Sixteenth-Century Portuguese North Africa: Yahya-u-Tacfuft and Portuguese Noble Culture," *Sixteenth Century Journal* 32 (Spring 2001): 67–90.
18. Notable films focused on early modern noble honor include *The Three Musketeers* (1921), *Captain Blood* (1935), *Mary of Scotland* (1936), *The Sea Hawk* (1940), *The Spanish Main* (1945), *The Three*

Musketeers (1948), *Cyrano de Bergerac* (1950), *Le Bossu* (1959), *Les Trois Mousquetaires* (1961), *The Three Musketeers* (1973), *La Reine Margot* (1994), *Henri IV* (2010), *La Princesse de Montpensier* (2010), and *The Three Musketeers* (2011).
19. Pierre Corneille, *Le Cid*, act 1, sc. 1, lines 291–350.
20. Jean Nicot, *Thresor de la Langue Francoise, Tant Ancienne que Moderne* (Paris: David Douceur, 1621), 338–39. A host of closely related words, such as *reputation* and *vertu*, further expanded the honor vocabulary.
21. On *honnêteté*, see works by Michael Moriarty, Emmanual Bury, Jorge Arditi, Jean Mesnard, Noémi Hepp, and Lewis C. Seifert. For a brief introduction to the concept, see Lewis C. Seifert, *Manning the Margins: Masculinity and Writing in Seventeenth-Century France* (Ann Arbor, MI: University of Michigan Press, 2009), 21–28, 258n2, 259n3.
22. Ellery Schalk, *From Valor to Pedigree: Ideas of Nobility in France in the Sixteenth and Seventeenth Centuries* (Princeton, NJ: Princeton University Press, 1986); Norbert Elias, *The Court Society*, trans. Edmund Jephcott (New York: Pantheon Books, 1983); Norbert Elias, *The Civilizing Process: The History of Manners and State Formation and Civilization*, trans. Edmund Jephcott (Oxford: Blackwell, 1982).
23. Stuart Caroll, *Blood and Violence in Early Modern France* (Oxford: Oxford University Press, 2006); Pascal Brioist, Hervé Drévillon, and Pierre Serna, *Croiser le fer. Violence et Culture de l'épée dans la France Moderne (XVIe–XVIIIe siècle)* (Seyssel: Champ Vallon, 2002); François Billacois, *Le duel dans la Société Française des XVIe-XVIIe Siècles. Essai de Psychosociologie Historique* (Paris: Éditions de l'École des Hautes Études en Sciences Sociales, 1986).
24. Arlette Jouanna succinctly summarizes her explanation of noble honor in Arlette Jouanna, Jacqueline Boucher, Dominique Biloghi, and Guy Le Thiec, *Histoire et Dictionnaire des Guerres de Religion* (Paris: Robert Laffront, 1998), 976–79. For another example, see William M. Reddy, *The Invisible Code: Honor and Sentiment in Postrevolutionary France, 1814–1848* (Berkeley, CA: University of California Press, 1997), 20–2.
25. John A. Lynn, *The Bayonets of the Republic: Motivation and Tactics in the Army of Revolutionary France, 1791–94* (Urbana, IL: University of Illinois Press, 1984), 21–40.
26. Lisdam, *L'Esclavage du Brave Chevalier François Vintimille*, 7, 9.
27. Robert Sauzet, *Au Grand Siècle des Âmes. Guerre Sainte et Paix Chrétienne en France au XVIIe Siècle* (Paris: Perrin, 2007), 13–27.
28. The original reads "quelle gloire! ces arcs-boutās de l'evangile perseverent sous la prevoyance d'un grand maistre, qui a l'honneur de l'eglise de dieu; & pour arrrester les courses d'une confusion qui se glisse par toute chose, garde le rang de sa grandeur, animant par cette majesté le courage de ces cavaliers." Lisdam, *L'Esclavage du Brave Chevalier François Vintimille*, 10.
29. The original reads "où cette saincte Penitente la Magdalene, a Apris aux Pecheurs les Leçons du Repentir." Lisdam, *L'Esclavage du Brave Chevalier François Vintimille*, 14.
30. The original reads "tout chargé de valeur, tout courage, a espreuvé sous les forces de sa patience, tous les branslemens qu'espreuvent ceux que la fortune laisse à la mercy des malheurs." Lisdam, *L'Esclavage du Brave Chevalier François Vintimille*, 12–13.
31. The original reads "C'est la cause qui honore les effets." Lisdam, *L'Esclavage du Brave Chevalier François Vintimille*, 45.
32. The original reads "Il n'y a rien d'impossible à celuy qui combat pour la querelle de Dieu, sans chercher son profit particulier. Le Soleil est prest de s'arrester, & toutes choses favorisent à l'honneur de leur Createur, celuy qui va aux alarmes pour soustenir l'Eglise." Lisdam, *L'Esclavage du Brave Chevalier François Vintimille*, 43.
33. The original reads "un courage masle se laisse tousiours gouverner à la raison." Lisdam, *L'Esclavage du Brave Chevalier François Vintimille*, 28.
34. On late sixteenth- and early seventeenth-century Neostoicism, see Denis Crouzet, *Les Guerriers de Dieu. La Violence au Temps des Troubles de Religion (vers 1525–vers 1610)*, 2 vols. (Seyssel: Champ Vallon, 1990).
35. The original reads "Mesme nous voyons les Heretiques aller plus constamment au martyre, que les Chrestiens. A quoy donc cognoistre la verité du mensonge?" Lisdam, *L'Esclavage du Brave Chevalier François Vintimille*, 44–45.
36. The original reads "C'est un grand contentement d'endurer quelque chose pour l'amour de Dieu." Lisdam, *L'Esclavage du Brave Chevalier François Vintimille*, 49.
37. The original reads "ta vie est en la main de Dieu: fais luy un present de ta conscience." Lisdam, *L'Esclavage du Brave Chevalier François Vintimille*, 67.

38. The original reads "la principale partie de leur gloire consistoit à aymer plus la fortune de leurs compagnons, que leur propre advancement." Lisdam, *L'Esclavage du Brave Chevalier François Vintimille*, 78–79.
39. Lisdam, *L'Esclavage du Brave Chevalier François Vintimille*, 38.
40. The original reads "estime que tu n'es pas capable de combatre les assauts de Satan. Estant seul, appelle tousiours nostre Seigneur pour t'aider . . . ." Lisdam, *L'Esclavage du Brave Chevalier François Vintimille*, 69–70.

8

Deferral of War: The Religious Sign System of Ritual Violence

Christopher S. Morrissey

It seems that religion performs an essential function by deferring war and violence for a time.[1] It may accomplish this through the use of ritual systems that enact violence in highly controlled and culturally beneficial ways instead; for example, in an animal sacrifice and the ensuing communal meal. Such rituals could then also serve in turn as admonitions for the cultural community, but in an indirect way, that is, by the richly layered significations of meaning that they generate; for example, the sacrificial animal dies in our place, saving us from violence that could otherwise be visited on us. This semiotic significance of religion, as a deferral of war, is an idea that is perhaps best elucidated by contrasting the work of three thinkers who offer three approaches to the idea: René Girard, Eric Gans, and Thomas Sebeok.

Three Approaches to Understanding Religion's Deferral of War

The obscure theory known as "generative anthropology" (GA) was invented by UCLA French professor Eric Gans as an attempt to explain the origin of language.[2] Gans imagines a scenario where language is discovered as a tool for the deferral of violence. When hominids, aiming at an object of desire, abort their gestures of appropriation, aborting them out of fear of an imminent escalation of violence, the first ostensive sign is born. The gesture that points to the object of desire is now an aborted gesture of appropriation that functions as a sign signifying that object or that desire. Language, in this model, then confers an adaptive advantage on the species, as the species slowly comes to learn how language can beneficially defer violent situations. Religious rituals can then grow out of this foundational discovery of language that makes possible for the human race the beneficial power of salutary deferral.

Gans's interesting thought experiment, however, may be seen to suffer from a fatal flaw. His work may indeed be academically obscure, but it does very much share something in common with the much more well-known approaches to language of twentieth-century semiology. Just like the semiological approaches to language, GA similarly gives an account of the origin of language that severs the human animal from its animality. For GA, this severance happens because GA mistakenly makes "the sign" something distinctive only of the human.

It seems that a better alternative to GA's account of human evolution is provided by Thomas Sebeok's hypothesis, which also adequately distinguishes adaptation (determined via genetic mutation and natural selection) from exaptation (e.g., the biologically underdetermined development of language). But Sebeok's hypothesis that language in the root sense is part of a "primary modeling system" (the biologically underdetermined part) avoids the error characteristic of GA and similar semiological approaches that share a similar assumption when treating semiosis (the action of signs) from which Sebeok dissents. These semiological approaches arguably adopt a reductive hypothesis of language, reducing it to what is in fact only "the secondary modeling system" of linguistic communication, which system in turn makes possible cultural experience, "the tertiary modeling system." Moreover, in a way that better fits with Sebeok's distinction between the three modeling systems, René Girard's hypothesis can be seen to account for the evolution of these modeling systems from rituals of violence.

René Girard's mimetic theory has articulated what he has described in his own words as "a general theory of culture and its origins."[3] Girard's mimetic theory, which observes "the need for a purely generative anthropology,"[4] in which religion and all culture have violent origins, answers the question of the origin of the first symbolic sign in human history. Girard sees that origin as a reenactment of a violent scapegoating murder, namely, a surrogate victim *stands for something else* as a ritual sign. He thus offers the scapegoat as the foundation for the phenomenon of substitution in ritual violence.

Girard focuses on "the unstable structure of human relations in a world still ruled by violence and scapegoating," that is, ruled by "the god or gods" of archaic religion, which he defines as characterized by the violent rituals of substitution.[5] Concerning the historical order of the evolution of this violent sacred, Girard insists on "the necessity of pre-linguistic solutions against violence,"[6] meaning that the very first scapegoating murder must have occurred temporally before the origin of the first symbolic sign of religious ritual.

I would like to highlight the significance of Girard's reason for insisting on this. Namely, Girard emphasizes the fact that there are "biological aspects which have to be taken into account" in understanding the origin of language.[7] The significance of Girard's approach is that his evolutionary hypothesis is consonant with the hypothesis of Thomas Sebeok about the place of language in defining the human species.[8] For Sebeok, the modeling device of *language* (primary modeling system), understood as species-specific to humans and distinct from *speech* and *communication* (secondary modeling system), is what properly enables humans to construct the sort of cultural models (tertiary modeling system) unique to the human species.[9] In light of Sebeok's theory, I would like to suggest in this chapter how Girard's hypothesis can account for the origin of violent religious ritual at precisely the moment of the origin of the human species, understood in Sebeok's terms.

In order to show how promising Girard's theory is with respect to explaining the origins of what Sebeok describes, the species-specific modeling system in humans, I would first like to contrast Girard's mimetic theory with the attempted modification of mimetic theory by Eric Gans, who has developed that variation on it known as Generative Anthropology (GA). Gans and Girard have a fundamental, irreconcilable difference concerning the origin of language. I argue that the work of Sebeok shows the distinct advantage that Girard's theory has in its attempt to describe the origin of the human modeling system, known to Sebeok as "language." First, I will highlight the controversy between Gans and Girard; second, I will argue for the limits of Gans's approach in light of Sebeok's hypothesis; finally, I will suggest how Girard's insights can be read as consonant with those of Sebeok.

The Controversy Over René Girard's "Mimetic Theory"

Gans's hypothesis is that a gesture becomes the first sign when it is mimicked by the entire animal group so that it now prevents them all from engaging in a vicious contest of violent reciprocity. Girard notes that this seems to be an unrealistic solution, one incapable of defusing any escalating contagion of mimetic violence:

> How can a simple gesture, regardless of how ostensible it may be, prevent the mimetic doubles from killing each other? As if violence did not exist! It is another way of denying violence. I think this is, again, a rhetorical manoeuvre to negate the primacy of religion in human culture. If one accepts Gans' hypothesis, then all other forms of social contract have also to be accepted. In order to have language, an embryonic form of culture is needed, some kind of cultural sheltering from violence. There must already be a non-linguistic solution to the problem of violence, which inevitably is a religious solution, and that is the result of the scapegoat mechanism, of the spontaneous grouping against an arbitrary common victim. For me, all insight into human origins must be anthropological. Every observation suggests that, in human culture, sacrificial rites and the immolation of the victim come first and this is the origin of everything else, starting with language.[10]

Girard concedes that "Eric is a great observer and his analyses of modern society are admirable, but . . ."[11]:

> . . . in limiting the role of the emissary victim, [Gans] impoverishes mimetic theory and lets fall away whole areas of archaic anthropology, depriving us of a whole mass of significant and revealing [lit: tasty] correspondences that are fully illuminated by that theory. Nothing seems to me to justify his attitude other than that modern allergy to the religious described by Cesareo Bandera.[12]

Girard's objection hinges on his observation that language is incapable of preventing any crisis of contagious, violent undifferentiation. Instead, there must first be a violent scapegoat before any language can emerge in the peaceful aftermath the scapegoat brings:

> We cannot do away with the actual killing of a victim. This is the moment of supreme crisis. The moment when the group should be most willing to give up violence—the moment of maximum undifferentiation, when pure revenge is working at all levels—is also the moment when they can least give up violence, because they are angry, and their fury gets the better of them. At this stage—at the moment of supreme rage, supreme excitement, when you are out of your mind, ecstatic in the way of violence—there is no scope, no possibility, for social contracts. This is the problem with Gans: he minimizes violence, for he suggests an entirely linguistic form of dealing with violence. Indeed, he simply suppresses violence, and he envisages an embryonic social contract. Rather, I posit it at the very centre as far as the beginning of culture is concerned.[13]

In other words, proper attention must be paid to the prelinguistic, which lays the foundation for the linguistic phenomena that later make possible properly human culture, that is, culture founded on religion and its ritual prohibitions and highly controlled acts of violence. Girard insists on human culture that

> the scapegoat system makes it possible at a pre-linguistic level. At some stage of the evolutionary path—which turns primates into humans—a sort of prohibition of a religious nature or some sort of fear of an immense invisible power at the most basic level triggered prohibitions against violence.[14]

In the beginning, a scapegoat murder is what the prehumans accomplish. This then leads to unconscious reenactments that preserve the peace that scapegoating brings them again and again. On Girard's account,

> violence escalated until the very end, demanding the founding murder. Starting from this event, peace was spontaneously established, and in order to preserve this peace humans perpetuated both interdictions and sacrifices before the invention of language and other cultural institutions. At this level, the scapegoat mechanism begins to be concealed, for we don't want culture and religion above all to be grounded on a founding murder.[15]

Here, Girard is denying that "language" in the common understanding of the term originates anywhere near the time of the first scapegoating events and rituals. But he is doing so to emphasize his disagreement with Gans (and the remark should not therefore be counted as a disagreement with Sebeok, of whom he appears unaware). Gans, however, does not maintain that any advanced language is suddenly present at this point, but he does insist that a simple gesture, the first human sign, is indeed born somewhere around this "originary scene" of scapegoating. He thus emphasizes language, which begins with simple gestures, to be what is most characteristic of the human. For Girard, rather, it is religion: "men, like animals, have to feed themselves, but it is religion that makes them human."[16]

On the one hand, Girard is correct to see sophisticated products of evolution such as language, cultural institutions, and individual autonomy as anachronistic if projected back on to his scapegoating scene. He sees Gans as proposing such an anachronism. Classifying Gans with other "social contract" theorists, Girard says,

> these people don't see the historicity of concepts such as individualism and choice. They have an ontological understanding of the human mind based on modern presuppositions. It seems evident to me that the human mind has been slowly shaped and trained through prehistory and history by religion and rituals. Modern individualism is nothing but the late result of this process.[17]

But to be fair, it must be noted that Gans proposes no such anachronism. Rather, Gans is simply trying to think the origin of the first human sign *in the gestures and protolanguage* nascent on the scapegoating scene. Where I think Gans goes wrong, however, is in positing the incipient action of signs here as uniquely human. Girard's emphatic point, rather, is that scapegoating first arises in our animality and then only gradually becomes more and more recognizably human. Gans's semiotic hypothesis, however, disconnects the human from the animal by positing an abrupt break in order to define the origin of the human species. As a result, I would argue that this posited break means that Gans's hypothesis is nominalistic, for the reasons that I will now explore, after which, I will conclude with a suggestion about how Girard's gradualist hypothesis may nonetheless still account for a precise point at which the properly human species emerged.

The Nominalism of Eric Gans's "Generative Anthropology"

What does GA have to do with "the disaster of *nominalism*, that infection of speculative thought which blinds the mind to the dependence in understanding of everything the senses yield upon general modes of being insensible as such, yet as independent or more independent of human whim as anything on the order of rocks or stars?"[18] Indeed, with its explicit attempts at a treatment of "transcendence," GA certainly aspires to overcome this disaster. But I argue that in the end it fails to do so, because, in severing "anthropology" and "language" from animal life,[19] GA remains nominalistic, trapped in the modern epistemological paradigm. In the way it conceives of "representation," GA's "originary scene" is as disconnected from the external world as any idea or sense impression of Descartes, Locke, Berkeley, Hume, or Kant.[20] All modern philosophy, from Descartes on, regards sense impressions or ideas as self-representing objects, rather than as other-representing objects (by virtue of being part of the action of signs that in their mode of being transcend subjectivities).[21] The first comprehensive treatment of this nominalism running through modern philosophy seems to be found in Weinberg,[22] but Peirce certainly propounded the thesis,[23] and Deely has recently and definitively established it.[24]

In spite of its pretensions to be "a new way of thinking," GA in fact recapitulates errors characteristic of the modern epistemological paradigm: for example, its semiotic anthropocentrism. With its recurring refrain emphasizing a minimal "anthropology," it repeats the myopic error of Descartes and thus unwittingly adopts a kind of methodical doubt that makes it dogmatically agnostic about anything beyond its own minimal "anthropology." Similar to the approach to language of twentieth-century semiology,[25] GA is not yet properly postmodern but rather merely ultramodern,[26] simply one of the last gasps of modernity's dead-end detour from semiotic consciousness, still mired in "the way of ideas" (to use Leibniz's phrase).

It is best to look at GA as an attempt, similar to that of René Girard, to articulate a complete semiotic theory, one that even dares to include a treatment of the origin of anthroposemiosis. In its thinking of the origin, however, GA's anthropology is a nominalist anthropology.[27] GA omits animality from its definition of the origin of language in the semiotic animal. GA radically fails to account for the nonverbal inlay in linguistic communication,[28] thereby excluding the animality of the semiotic animal. It therefore condemns itself to cling to a dogmatically nominalist position like this:

> GA is founded on the principle that *the uniquely human activity of representation*, including above all language, cannot be understood independently of transcendence. *Nothing in nature is comparable* to the implicit shared agreement as to meaning that grounds the existence of the individual signs (words, morphemes) of language. The analogy between type:token and genotype:phenotype is like that between a circle drawn on a blackboard and the trace of a moving mathematical point. The simple evidence of these truths makes equally evident the ideological nature of the "materialist" refusal of *a distinct ontological status to language and other forms of representation*. Whether or not a sacred being of some sort is *logically necessary* to sustain the community of the sign, the *historical necessity* of the concept of such a being at the origin of this community can hardly be doubted.[29]

In spite of these words, a careful study of Gans shows that he clearly thinks that *only* the "historical necessity" of God may be proven, and *never* the "logical necessity."[30] This dogmatically agnostic position (redolent of modern philosophy's dubious epistemology) is a result of the "distinct ontological status to language and other forms of [human] representation" assumed by Gans, which is the same as that of semiology: that is, language as a self-contained totality, to which "nothing in nature is comparable." But this unwarranted assumption by Gans has now been shown to be fallacious, thanks to the scientific work in the field of biosemiotics, which has developed from the pioneering semiotic work of Thomas Sebeok, who exposed and refuted the *"pars pro toto* fallacy" of semiology.[31] Instead, Sebeok offers a semiotic alternative to semiology.[32]

Briefly, the alternative is this: the human species shares with other animal species the fact that each species brings something species-specific to its generic animal modeling system.[33] Susan Petrilli and Augusto Ponzio explain the unique syntactic role of the primary modeling system within humans, as it has been carefully distinguished in recent decades by biosemiotics: namely, common to all life forms is modeling behavior, and the methodolical framework developed by Sebeok to address this fact is *modeling systems theory* (MST), which came out of Sebeok's research on how semiotics and biology interface; MST approaches semiotic phenomena by distinguishing the various modeling processes at work.[34] Since semiosis (the use of signs) is a capacity common to all life forms, it may be properly understood and defined as "the capacity of a species to produce and comprehend the specific types of models it requires for processing and codifying perceptual input in its own way."[35]

The application of MST to a semiotic phenomenon consists of *systems analysis*, which is the term for engaging in distinguishing between the activity of the primary, secondary, and tertiary modeling systems. Petrilli and Ponzio outline the role of what biosemiotics has now properly distinguished as "language" in the root sense, first by pointing out that the primary modeling system is the innate capacity of a biological species for *simulative* modeling; this why, they explain, Sebeok says that "language" is the species-specifically human primary modeling system. The secondary modeling system, they point out, is where both "indicational" and "extensional" modeling processes occur as forms of indexicality. Various species exhibit a nonverbal form of indicational modeling; but thanks to Sebeok, they say, we can now appreciate that extensional modeling is a uniquely human capacity founded on and presupposing *language*. Thus, Sebeok distinguishes *language* (the primary modeling system) from *speech* (the secondary modeling system species-specific to humans), whereas the Moscow–Tartu School had conflated them and consequently dubbed human cultural systems as "secondary," whereas Sebeok now insists that these abstract and symbol-based processes are the product of the *tertiary* modeling system.[36]

Later on, Petrilli and Ponzio describe the import of this crucial distinction between "language" (or what some, like Augustine of Hippo, have called the "interior word") and "speech" (what some, like Augustine of Hippo, have called the "exterior word"). The semiosis proper to the human species is called anthroposemiosis, and this species-specific activity is enabled by the "modeling device" that Sebeok calls "language" and locates in the primary modeling system. He does this because of the virtual certainty that *Homo habilis* possessed "language" but not "speech."[37] Petrilli and Ponzio explain the significance of this innovation of Sebeok's:

> Sebeok claimed that human verbal language is species-specific. On this basis and often with cutting irony he debated against the enthusiastic supporters of projects which had been developed to teach verbal language to captive primates. Such behavior was based on the false assumption that animals might be able to talk, or even more scandalously, that they are endowed with the capacity for language. The distinction established by Sebeok between *language* and *speech*[38] is not only a response to wrong conclusions regarding animal communication, but it also constitutes a general critique of phonocentrism and the general tendency to base scientific investigation on anthropocentric principles.

The "mute syntax" of "language"—which is what enables the internal modeling that some describe as an "inner word"—thus becomes a scientific marker of the emergence of a distinctively human animal species. On Sebeok's account, language appeared in the evolutionary process as an *adaptation* much earlier than speech, that is, long before *Homo sapiens*. Hence, Sebeok agrees with Noam Chomsky that language is not a communicative device, even though Chomsky fails to distinguish *language* and *speech* as Sebeok does. Petrilli and Ponzio thus rightly credit Sebeok with the insight that while the function of linguistic communication is to transmit messages or to give information, the species-specific function of language does not; on this point, unlike everybody else,[39]

> Sebeok described language as *a primary modeling device*. Every species is endowed with a model that "produces" its own world, and "language" is the name of the model that belongs to human beings. However, as a modeling device, human language is completely different from the modeling devices of other life forms. Its distinctive feature is what the linguists call *syntax*, that is, the capacity to order single elements on the basis of operational rules. But, while for linguists these elements are the words, phrases, and sentences, etc. of historical-natural languages, Sebeok's reference was to a mute syntax. Thanks to syntax, human language, understood not as a historical-natural language but as a modeling device, is similar to Lego building blocks. It can reassemble a limited number of construction pieces in an infinite number of different ways. As a modeling device, language can produce an indefinite number of models; in other words, the same pieces can be taken apart and put together to construct an infinite number of different models.

Therefore, we can see how for Sebeok biosemiotics is the discipline that discerns what is unique to the modeling system of each species (for humans, it is "language," understood in the root sense, as a "mute syntax"), while still appreciating the modeling process of semiosis as a phenomenon common to all living things.

Consequently, one will observe that adaptation to the environment is common to all the diverse species, generating what is bodily "innate" to the biological heritage of each species (e.g., their diverse and peculiar anatomies, which in turn condition their diverse modeling systems). The exaptation of "language" in the human species, however, has brought forth a species-specifically unique manifestation that can be accounted for empirically, without any recourse to innate "ideas" in our biological modeling system. This is because species-specific "exaptation"—not to be confused with the "adaptation" functions of the specific modeling systems—empirically explains that for which some have otiosely postulated the presence of innate "ideas" in our uniquely human cognition. Humans, thanks to language, produce a species-specific worldview common to the species, just as other species do, but the possibilities that this worldview can encompass are endless, because of the precise nature of this unique modeling device that Sebeok calls "language." Sebeok thus insists on making his counterintuitive distinction between speech and language, as Petrilli and Ponzio explain:

> Similarly to language, speech too made its appearance as an adaptation, but *for the sake of communication*, and much later than language, precisely with *Homo sapiens*. Speech organizes and externalizes language. Subsequently, language also ended up becoming a communication device through processes of *exaptation*[40] in the language of evolutionary biologists, enhancing nonverbal capabilities already possessed by human beings; and speech in turn was exapted for (secondary) modeling.

To be precise, then, the exaptation of the biologically underdetermined portion of the primary modeling system—that exapted portion which Sebeok calls "language"—is what at root distinguishes our species across all three modeling systems.[41] The *fact* that it *is* biologically underdetermined (whence its exaptation) is the empiricist answer to the dogmatically semiological theories (such as GA) that see language as a completely separate structural system. Such theories mistakenly make what is properly "human" to be entirely divorced from any bodily animality. But the empirical fact of exaptation demands that all semiologists must now become more semiotic about their view of innate species capacities. That is, they must jettison any inadequate metaphors for the human modeling system, which means to cease defining the human in terms of a dubiously conceived "language" that is entirely and structurally divorced from the semioses of animal life.[42] The better approach is Sebeok's because his distinctions between modeling systems can actually describe how the intersection of semiotics with biology happens.

Therefore, because GA's account of human evolution fails to adequately distinguish adaptation from exaptation,[43] its purported "new way of thinking"[44] is in fact now made obsolete by Sebeok's hypothesis. For Sebeok, understanding language in the root sense as part of a "primary modeling system" (the biologically underdetermined part)[45] is the hypothesis that avoids the error that is characteristic of GA and other merely modern approaches to treating semiosis (the action of signs), approaches that adopt a reductive hypothesis of language, reducing it to what is in fact only "the secondary modeling system" of linguistic communication (which makes possible cultural experience, the tertiary modeling system).[46] As John Deely has explained, this characteristically modern error sees "the semiotic animal as an animal only nominally, by failing to include in the real definition of its metasemiosis the zoösemioses which alone make possible in the first place even the species-specifically human dimension which anthroposemiosis adds to the zoösemioses in which linguistic communication is implicated and upon which it depends for its success, even as it transcends those zoösemioses."[47] Modeling systems theory avoids this error.

GA's conception of the first event of linguistic communication, while extremely improbable (and far from "minimal")[48] as an historical moment of confluence, may still be viewed, however, as *a creative literary composite*, synthesizing a number of true aspects about the later cultural operation of language in the semiotic animal, although these aspects must be better distinguished with respect to their origins, in both structural composition and historical succession.[49] For a number of reasons, the hypothesis of René Girard emerges as the stronger candidate to explain the evolution of the latter,[50] whereas Sebeok's treatment of the former definitively charts the way forward for postmodernity and the truly "new way of thinking" adumbrated now in twenty-first-century semiotics.[51]

Thomas Sebeok and the Significance of Religious Deferral of Violence

Insofar as GA is founded upon its "anthropological" nominalism, which severs language from biology,[52] it remains at a disadvantage when compared to the Girardian approach attempting to delineate the origin of the semiotic animal.[53] As Girard so aptly observes of GA, Gans "impoverishes mimetic theory and lets fall away whole areas of archaic anthropology, depriving us of a whole mass of significant and revealing correspondences that are fully illuminated by that theory. Nothing seems to me to justify his attitude other than that modern allergy to the religious described by Cesareo Bandera."[54] Religion, in other words, is not just a by-product of the evolutionary emergence of linguistic communication, but rather pertains to the meaning of the whole sign system of the living universe.

Religion's evolution can only have unfolded from the full amplitude of semiosis in both verbal and nonverbal communication,[55] even if the mute mental act of "language" (in Sebeok's sense) is what any secondary or tertiary event of origin will have presupposed. On this account, then, *pace* Gans, the truths of semiosis and its logic are able, in principle, to extend to the depths of our animality and even to what sustains it in its very being.[56] We ought to refuse, therefore, to be caged by a mere "anthropology."[57]

More promising is the semiotic bridge to animal semiosis developed by Sebeok. Using his terminology, we can outline Girard's semiotic scene such that we can establish at what point the human must have evolved within the gradualist unfolding of this semiotic scene being repeated again and again on the way from animality to humanity proper. First, the outline (Table 1):

Table 1
The Semiotic Scene of Scapegoating's Sacrificial Logic

(1) SYMPTOM: The fearful contagion of mimetic crisis increases *undifferentiation*.

(2) SIGNAL: Contagion is *dangerous* and therefore comes from a culpable source.

(3) ICON: Anyone still differentiated is *designated* by that stark iconic difference.

(4) INDEX: *Violence* indicates the one victim and, by extension (i.e., via the NAME of the *god*), unanimous community.

(5) SYMBOL: *Reversal* of the mimetic crisis deifies the victim, as a symbol of peace.

My suggestion is that eventually the fourth step within the semiotic scene of scapegoating made the leap from animal to human when *extensional indexicality* entered into animal consciousness. That is, it would have occurred at the point when the animals doing their scapegoating recognized that not only was their violence indexically designating their victim in a productive way that brought them social peace afterward, but *by extension* the scapegoat (who at first, for thousands of years, was deified symbolically, in an unconscious, animal way by them) *was pointing back at them*, that is, designating them as one unified *human* community.

Such would have been the first properly abstract, *human* thought. This thought, of the name of God, as *language's first inner word*, may then have subsequently been externalized, at "food-sharing and 'totem' feasts," as *speech's first outer word*: the name of God as uttered.[58] This evolution, of the species-specific extensional modeling characteristic of humans, marked by the thought of and the naming of God, would have charged the symbolism of the previously animal prohibitions and rituals that had evolved around scapegoating with a now immense new significance, making possible the explosion of human culture that we observe suddenly occurring fifty to sixty thousand years ago.

It is from this origin of human culture—the extension of animal scapegoating rituals into the first word of language, "God," which must also be heard silently, in the mute syntactical separation of sacred and profane in thought, thus marking the very root of the distinctively exapted human modeling system—it is from this origin that human desire was born. Human desire, mimetic as it is, is *distinctively* species-specifically human in that it can transcend all merely animal desire, even though it is rooted in animality and its origin cannot be understood apart from its generation in the violent rituals that incubated (in hunter-gatherers) the syntactic forms of human thought, which our species-specific modeling system exapted as language and speech. Because of this, *human desire is capable of transcendence*. Girard, I believe, is correct to maintain that only the event of a conspecific victim of scapegoating violence would be sufficient, at some point, to effectively motivate the evolution of indexical modeling into extensional modeling. Only the community's conspecific victim needs to be draped behind the name of God. This is the human experience, of the power and peril of human desire, of the animal in every one of us, who drapes the past's hidden victim, craving something more (i.e., transcendence), and remains only dimly aware of the history of human desire, of the things hidden since the foundation of the world.

Perhaps we may reconceive the history of human desire this way, in the following attempt at reading the historical sense of the scriptural account in Genesis: before Adam was Adam, and Eve was Eve (the first *humans*), they were part of a group of hunter-gatherer hominids that had a scapegoating ritual that both concluded the hunt and reenacted it, affecting a social cohesion around the hunt animal, for example, a bison. Violence was regularly discharged on the bison, indexically marked by their blows; but one day Adam became Adam when he realized that the bison was also, by extension, pointing back at its violent attackers: the bison himself was a sign (effectively, a name) for the social cohesion (the divine power) his sacrifice achieved. As a symbol, then, of social peace and order, the bison is consequently able to be named (by extensional modeling) as the god, the totem, of the tribe. Adam and Eve's original sin would then be to have transferred the name of the (bison) god to a conspecific murdered in an analogous scapegoating ritual. They can eat the "fruit" of any "tree," that is, the flesh of any animal, such as a bison; but the flesh of a conspecific is "forbidden" because it then exalts the conspecific (one like them) into the role of the tribal god. Effectively, this would be how they and their fellow species members become "like gods." This power of scapegoating at the root of distinctively human culture (which alone knows of *the name of god*) is "the knowledge of good and evil" that becomes buried in human consciousness, underneath the layers of myth that distort true memory of this cultural origin, the origin of the desire to "be like gods" in the horrified recognition of the murder of a conspecific (not yet human) scapegoat (who becomes transfigured by that same culture into a god).

Perhaps in this way Girard and Sebeok may offer us a path beyond a sanitized version of the original Eden, if we wish to conceive in what sense it may actually be considered as once an historical reality. Note that the biblical text says nothing about what the fruit of the "fruit of the tree of knowledge" is. One can therefore imagine it to be a banana just as well as an apple. In this chapter, I have suggested that we may imagine it as the flesh of a conspecific killed in a scapegoating ritual. Before that event, they ate only the flesh of a totem, until one day a mimetic crisis led to the discovery of the sacred taboo, the taboo being invented as a distorted memory deifying the scapegoated conspecific, giving the deified scapegoat a sacred aura and thus to the taboo its mysterious power as integral to culture. This would be the origin of the truly efficacious power of religion for the human species: namely, the paradox by which, through sacred violence, religion achieves its culturally significant adaptive advantage—the deferral of war.

Notes

1. For the purposes of this chapter, I am adopting the functional definition of religion that is highlighted and adopted by Benedict Ashley, *Choosing a World-View and Value-System* (New York: Alba House, 2000), 10–11.
2. Eric Gans, *The Origin of Language: A Formal Theory of Representation* (Berkeley, CA: University of California Press, 1981); *The End of Culture: Toward a Generative Anthropology* (Berkeley, CA: University of California Press, 1985).
3. René Girard, with Pierpaolo Antonello and João Cezar de Castro Rocha, *Evolution and Conversion: Dialogues on the Origins of Culture* (New York: Continuum Books, 2007), 144.
4. Girard, *Evolution and Conversion*, 143.
5. Ibid., 124.
6. Ibid.
7. Ibid.
8. Sebeok's four key books are *Contributions to the Doctrine of Signs* (1976), *The Play of Musement* (1981), *I Think I Am a Verb: More Contributions to the Doctrine of Signs* (1986), and *The Sign and Its Masters* (1989 [1979]).
9. Thomas A. Sebeok, *Signs: An Introduction to Semiotics*, 2nd ed. (Toronto, ON: University of Toronto Press, 2001 [1994]), 139–49.
10. Girard, *Evolution and Conversion*, 124; in the original text:

    Comment un simple geste, tout « ostensible » qu'il soit, peut-il empêcher les doubles symétriques de s'entretuer ? Comme si, à ce moment-là, la violence n'existait pas ! C'est encore une autre façon de nier la violence. Je crois qu'il s'agit d'une manœuvre de plus pour nier la primauté du religieux dans la culture humaine. Pourquoi pas un « contrat social » au sens traditionnel ? Pour avoir le langage, il faut d'abord une forme embryonnaire de culture, une sorte de protection culturelle contre la violence. À mon avis la solution fondamentale du problème de la violence est forcément religieuse, et, selon moi, ne peut résulter que du mécanisme victimaire, du rassemblement mimétique spontané contre une victime arbitraire. Les rites sacrificiels et l'immolation de victimes viennent en premier. C'est là qu'on doit placer l'origine de tout le reste, à commencer par le langage. . . .

    This passage from Girard, *Les Origines de la Culture* (Descleé de Brouwer, 2004), is also translated by Gans in "René et moi," *Chronicles of Love and Resentment* 307 (September 25, 2004), <http://www.anthropoetics.ucla.edu/views/vw307.htm> as:

    How can a simple gesture, as "ostensible" [sic] as it may be, prevent the symmetrical doubles from killing each other? As if, at that moment, violence no longer existed! This is yet another way of denying violence. I believe it is just one more maneuver to deny the primacy of the religious in human culture. Why not a "social contract" in the traditional sense of the term? To have language, there must first be an embryonic form of culture, a sort of cultural protection against violence. In my opinion, the fundamental solution to the problem of violence is necessarily religious, and, to my mind, can only proceed from the victimary mechanism, the spontaneous mimetic union against an arbitrary victim. Sacrificial rites and the immolation of victims come first. It is there that we should situate the origin of all the rest, beginning with language. . . .

11. Girard, *Les Origines de la Culture* (2004), 181. Girard elaborates on this point later on (in *Evolution and Conversion*, 245):

    . . . I agree with Eric Gans who thinks that globalization is primarily an economic development that produces wealth and helps in stabilizing society, and has no central agency: it's a self-organizing system. Without diminishing the role and the impact of the economy *per se*, for me globalization is mainly the abolition not only of sacrifice, properly speaking, but also of the entire sacrificial order: it is the encompassing spread of Christian ethics and epistemology in relation to every sphere of human activity. Economy itself, as it has developed, would be impossible without the Christian framework.

12. This passage is deleted from the English translation (Girard, *Evolution and Conversion*, 2007); therefore, I quote it from Gans's own reproduction of it and his own translation in Gans, "René et moi" (2004):

    . . . en rétrécissant le rôle du mécanisme victimaire, [Gans] appauvrit la théorie mimétique et il laisse tomber des pans entiers de l'anthropologie archaïque, ce qui nous prive de toute une masse de correspondances significatives et savoureuses, parfaitement éclairées par cette théorie. Rien ne

> me paraît justifier son attitude sinon cette allergie moderne au religieux dont parle Cesareo Bandera. (Girard, *Les Origines de la Culture* [2004], 179–81)

13. Girard, *Evolution and Conversion*, 124.
14. Ibid., 125.
15. Ibid., 126.
16. Ibid., 127.
17. Ibid., 127–28.
18. John Deely, *The Impact of Semiotics on Philosophy* (South Bend, IL: St. Augustine's Press, 2003), 70.
19. In pursuit of "minimality," GA mistakenly makes "the sign" something distinctive only of the human.
20. See John Deely, "Tom Sebeok and the External World," *Semiotica* 150-1/4 (2004): 1–21.
21. John Deely, *Descartes and Poinsot: The Crossroad of Signs and Ideas*, Volume 2 in the "Postmodernity in Philosophy" Poinsot Trilogy: *Contrasting the Way of Signs to the Way of Ideas, Semiotics to Epistemology* (Scranton: University of Scranton Press, 2008).
22. Julius Rudolph Weinberg, *Abstraction, Relation, and Induction: Three Essays in the History of Thought* (Madison, WI: University of Wisconsin Press, 1965), 3–60.
23. Charles Sanders Peirce, *Collected Papers* I: 19.
24. For a brief summary, see Chapter 12 in John Deely, *Augustine and Poinsot: The Protosemiotic Development*, Volume 1 in the "Postmodernity in Philosophy" Poinsot Trilogy: *Determining the Standpoint for a Doctrine of Signs* (Scranton: University of Scranton Press, 2009). For more detail, see John Deely, *Four Ages of Understanding* (Toronto, ON: University of Toronto Press, 2001).
25. See Deely, *Augustine and Poinsot* 91 no. 41, and 205–212.
26. See Deely, *Augustine and Poinsot*, 134–37.
27. C. S. Morrissey, "Original Sin and Generative Anthropology," *Anthropoetics* 13, no. 2 (2007), much too charitably sees nominalism as not necessarily characteristic of GA but rather its main "temptation." But in fact nominalism is not merely a "temptation" for GA that it might hope to avoid, but rather inescapably part of how it mistakenly conceives of the "originary," namely, via the *pars pro toto* fallacy concerning language, which it shares with semiology. Cf. Thomas Sebeok, "Linguistics and Semiotics," in *A Sign Is Just a Sign* (Bloomington, IN: Indiana University Press, 1991), 59–67; see also Deely, *Four Ages*, 669–88.
28. John Deely, "The Nonverbal Inlay in Linguistic Communication," in *The Signifying Animal*, ed. Irmengard Rauch and Gerald F. Carr (Bloomington, IN: Indiana University Press, 1980), 201–17.
29. Eric Gans, "Believing in GA," *Chronicles of Love and Resentment* 358 (May 10, 2008), <http://www.anthropoetics.ucla.edu/views/vw358.htm>. Emphasis in italics is mine.
30. Cf. from the abstract of Eric Gans's Generative Anthropology Summer Conference 2009 talk in Ottawa on transcendence: "The most accessible manifestation of transcendence is not God but *language*. Every aspect of language evolves in time, but the intentional relationship between a sign and its meaning is not subject to mortality. The ontology of the sign is the reverse of that which obtains in nature between a species and its individual members. The species is *our* construct [note Gans's assumption of nominalism here], whereas the sign as an intention or *type* preexists its tokens, just as God preexists his creation. Whether we take *just as* to mean that God created man or that man created God cannot be decided by either logic or empirical discovery. The emergence of transcendence in the world of immanence is the birth of human intentionality, which is necessarily conscious of itself. Humanity cannot have been born unawares; becoming-conscious is an *event*. Natural science ignores this event, yet every religion offers an account of it. Generative anthropology's *originary hypothesis* is the first non-theistic attempt to conceive the origin of transcendence as the event of human language." The denial of mind-independent universals is nominalism. Cf. Deely, *Augustine and Poinsot*, 165 n. 54 and 158 n. 39 for the similarity here with Kant.
31. Thomas A. Sebeok, "'Semiotics' and Its Congeners," in *Frontiers in Semiotics*, ed. John Deely, Brooke Williams, and Felicia E. Kruse (Bloomington, IN: Indiana University Press, 1986), 255–63; see also viii–xvii in the same volume. Cf. Augusto Ponzio and Susan Petrilli, *Thomas Sebeok and the Signs of Life* (London: Icon Books, 2001), 19–20.
32. For the semiotic alternative to GA and other forms of semiology, see Thomas Sebeok, "A Semiotic Perspective on the Sciences: Steps toward a New Paradigm," in *I Think I Am a Verb* (New York and London: Plenum Press, 1986), 17–44.
33. Cf. John Deely, "Semiotics and Jakob von Uexküll's Concept of Umwelt," *Sign System Studies* 32, no. 1/2 (2004): 11–34.
34. Susan Petrilli and Augusto Ponzio, "A Tribute to Thomas Sebeok," *Biosemiotics* 1, no. 1 (2008): 25–39. I am offering an extended paraphrase of their excellent account of Sebeok in the remainder of the section of this chapter.

35. Thomas A. Sebeok and Marcel Danesi, *The Forms of Meaning: Modeling Systems Theory and Semiotic Analysis* (Berlin and New York: Mouton de Gruyter, 2000), 5.
36. For footnotes referencing the work of Sebeok on these points, see Susan Petrilli and Augusto Ponzio, "A Tribute to Thomas Sebeok," *Biosemiotics* 1, no. 1 (2008): 25–39, whose summary account is being paraphrased here.
37. Cf. Thomas A. Sebeok, "Language as a Primary Modeling System?" in *Signs: An Introduction to Semiotics*, 2nd ed. (Toronto, ON: University of Toronto Press, 2001), 139–49.
38. Petrilli and Ponzio, "A Tribute to Thomas Sebeok," here cite Chapter 2 in Thomas Sebeok, *I Think I Am a Verb* (New York and London: Plenum Press, 1986).
39. Petrilli and Ponzio, "A Tribute to Thomas Sebeok."
40. Petrilli and Ponzio, "A Tribute to Thomas Sebeok," here cite Stephen Jay Gould and E. S. Vrba, "Exaptation: A Missing Term in the Science of Form," *Paleobiology* 8 (1982): 4–15.
41. John Deely, "The Primary Modeling System in Animals," in *La filosofia del linguaggio come arte dell'ascolto: sulla ricerca scientifica di Augusto Ponzio/Philosophy of language as the art of listening: on Augusto Ponzio's scientific research*, ed. Susan Petrilli (Bari: Edizione dal Sud, 2007), 161–79.
42. Cf. John Deely, "Umwelt," *Semiotica* 134, nos. 1–4 (2001): 125–35: "But the human modeling system, the *Innenwelt* underlying and correlate with our Umwelt, is, strangely, not wholly tied to our biology. The first effectively to notice this anomaly in the context of semiotics was again Sebeok (e.g., 1984, 1988). When we are born, or, indeed, when our genotype is fixed at fertilization in the zygote from which we develop, what we can see or sense in any direct modality is established and determined, just as is the case with any animal life form. But what language we will speak or what we will say in that language is far from so fixed and determined. Sebeok was the first effectively to point out that failure to grasp the implications of this fact result largely if not entirely from the widespread and long-standing confusion, in learned circles no less than in popular culture, between *language*, which is a matter of an *Innenwelt* or modeling system that is not wholly tied to biological constitution, and *communication*, which is a universal phenomenon that in and of itself has nothing whatever to do with language. Thus zoösemiotics studies the communication systems of animals, both those that are species-specific to each animal form and those that overlap two or more forms, including communicative modalities shared between human animals and other animal species. But language is not first of all a communication system. Language is first of all a way of modeling the world according to possibilities envisioned as alternative to what is given in sensation or experienced in perception. When such a modeling system is exapted for the purpose of communicating it to another, the attempt succeeds, if at all, only when the other to whom one attempts to communicate such a praeter-biological content is a conspecific (that is, only when the prospective receiver likewise has an *Innenwelt* which is not wholly tied *omni ex parte* to biological constitution); and the result of the communication (when and to the extent it succeeds) is the establishment precisely of a *linguistic code*, which will correlate with but in no way reduce to elements accessible through one or another sensory modality of the organism, which is the establishment of a new, species-specific channel of communication, to wit, *linguistic communication*, commonly miscalled and thoroughly confused with language itself. That is why, for communication to be linguistic, it matters not a whit whether it be spoken, written, or gestured: all that matters is the type of *Innenwelt* underlying the communication which makes immediate, non-reductive interpretation of the linguistic code possible in the first place. That is why the 'meaningful world' in which the human animal lives involves postlinguistic structures (Deely 1980) accessible in what is proper to them only by a linguistic animal, whereas all the other animals, even when they employ (as is in fact fairly common) symbolic means of communication, are restricted to the order of prelinguistic, sense-perceptible object domains (including postlinguistic structures in their sense-perceptible aspects of embodiment)."
43. Cf. Augusto Ponzio and Susan Petrilli, *Thomas Sebeok and the Signs of Life* (London: Icon Books, 2001), 37–40.
44. Eric Gans, *A New Way of Thinking: Generative Anthropology in Religion, Philosophy, Art* (Aurora, CO: Davies Group, 2011).
45. Thomas A. Sebeok, "Language as a Primary Modeling System?" in *Signs: An Introduction to Semiotics*, 2nd ed. (Toronto, ON: University of Toronto Press, 2001), 139–49.
46. Cf. Thomas A. Sebeok, "Communication, Language, and Speech: Evolutionary Considerations," in *I Think I Am A Verb*, 10–16; also Thomas A. Sebeok, "The Problem of the Origin of Language in an Evolutionary Frame," *Language Sciences* 8 (1986): 169–76.
47. John Deely, "The Primary Modeling System in Animals," in *La filosofia del linguaggio come arte dell'ascolto: sulla ricerca scientifica di Augusto Ponzio/Philosophy of language as the art of listening: on Augusto Ponzio's scientific research*, ed. Susan Petrilli (Bari: Edizione dal Sud, 2007), 161–79.

48. Far from "minimal," in a fatally deficient way, because it conflates gestures from the primary modeling system with the verbal communication of the secondary modeling system; cf. Sebeok and Danesi, *The Forms of Meaning*, 66–69, 83–90.
49. Cf. Sebeok and Danesi, *The Forms of Meaning*, 171–74.
50. The criticisms of Girard and advocacy of generative anthropology found in C. S. Morrissey, "The Epigenetic Evolution of the Immaterial Intellect on the Originary Scene," in *The Originary Hypothesis: A Minimal Proposal for Humanistic Inquiry*, ed. Adam Katz, Critical Series in the Humanities (Aurora, CO: Davies Group, 2007), 83–109, are ultimately untenable, because they err in failing to take into account modeling systems theory (MST). They therefore view Girard according to the blinders assumed by GA's solipsistic semiological (i.e., "anthropological") perspective. Sebeok and Danesi, however, in *The Forms of Meaning*, 2–44, 158–89, show that the metaphysical terms in which the critique of Girard is attempted (in Morrissey, "Epigenetic Evolution") in fact cannot apply to Girard but would rather *be more appropriately a way to sum up MST's implicit diagnosis of the weakness of GA*: namely, in GA, the formal genesis of the secondary modeling system (the epigenetic formal cause in Gans's "event" scenario) is incoherently disconnected from the biologically underdetermined component of the primary modeling system (the material cause presupposed in Gans's "event" scenario).
51. Cf. John Deely, *The Impact on Philosophy of Semiotics: The Quasi-Error of the External World with a Dialogue between a "Semiotist" and a "Realist"* (South Bend, IN: St. Augustine's Press, 2003), 3–154.
52. Cf. Thomas Sebeok, "Communication," in *A Sign Is Just a Sign* (Bloomington, IN: Indiana University Press, 1991), 22–35.
53. Cf. John Deely, "Defining the Semiotic Animal: A Postmodern Definition Superseding the Modern Definition '*res cogitans*'," *American Catholic Philosophical Quarterly* 79, no. 3 (Summer 2005): 461–81.
54. Translated in Eric Gans, "René et moi," *Chronicles of Love and Resentment* 307 (September 25, 2004), <http://www.anthropoetics.ucla.edu/views/vw307.htm>.
55. Cf. Thomas Sebeok, "The Evolution of Semiosis," in *A Sign Is Just a Sign* (Bloomington, IN: Indiana University Press, 1991), 83–96.
56. Cf. Deely, *Augustine and Poinsot*, 183.
57. Fatal to Gans's entire project of "anthropology" (understood in his special sense, i.e., semiologically) is Gans's glib dismissal of Peirce; see *Signs of Paradox* (Stanford, CA: Stanford University Press, 1997), 13–14. Cf. Deely, *Augustine and Poinsot*, 184; Deely, *Four Ages*, 611–740; and for a detailed treatment, see John Deely, *Basics of Semiotics*, Expanded Fifth Edition, bilingual Estonian/English edition (Tartu: Tartu University Press, 2009), Chapter 3, 26–50—especially the Addendum to Chapter 3 (on "The Interpretant"), 38–50.
58. Cf. René Girard, *The One by Whom Scandal Comes*. Trans. M. B. DeBevoise (East Lansing, MI: Michigan State University Press, 2014), 85–91.

Selected Bibliography

Gans, Eric. "'Scandal to the Jews, Folly to the Pagans.' Review of *Des Choses Cachees Depuis la Fondation du Monde*." *Diacritics* 9, no. 3 (1979): 43–53.

———. *The Origin of Language: A Formal Theory of Representation*. Berkeley, CA: University of California Press, 1981.

———. "Differences." *Modern Language Notes* 96, no. 4 (French Issue May) (1981): 792–808.

———. "The Culture of Resentment." *Philosophy and Literature* 8, no. 1 (1984): 55–66.

———. *The End of Culture: Toward a Generative Anthropology*. Berkeley, CA: University of California Press, 1985.

———. *Science and Faith: The Anthropology of Revelation*. Savage, MD: Rowman & Littlefield, 1990.

———. *Originary Thinking: Elements of Generative Anthropology*. Stanford, CA: Stanford University Press, 1993.

———. *Signs of Paradox: Irony, Resentment, and Other Mimetic Structures*. Stanford, CA: Stanford University Press, 1997.

———. "Form against Content: René Girard's Theory of Tragedy," *Revista Portuguesa de Filosofia* 56, nos. (1–2) (2000): 53–65.

———. "René et moi," *Chronicles of Love and Resentment* 307 (September 25), http://www.anthropoetics.ucla.edu/views/vw307.htm, 2004.

———. *The Scenic Imagination: Originary Thinking from Hobbes to the Present Day*. Stanford, CA: Stanford University Press, 2007.

———. *A New Way of Thinking: Generative Anthropology in Religion, Philosophy, Art*. Aurora, CO: Davies Group, 2011.

Girard, René. *Deceit, Desire, and the Novel: Self and Other in Literary Structure*. Trans. Yvonne Freccero. Baltimore, MD: Johns Hopkins University Press, 1966. (Original edition, *Mensonge romantique et vérité romanesque*, Paris: Grasset, 1961.)

———. *Violence and the Sacred*. Trans. Patrick Gregory. Baltimore, MD: Johns Hopkins University Press, 1977. (Original edition, *La violence et le sacré*, Paris: Grasset, 1972.)

———. *Things Hidden since the Foundation of the World*. Research Undertaken in Collaboration with Jean-Michel Oughourlian and Guy Lefort. Trans. Stephen Bann (Books II and III) and Michael Metteer (Book I). London: Athlone, 1987. (Original edition, *Des choses cachées depuis la fondation du monde*, Paris: B. Grasset, 1978.)

———. "Origins: A View from the Literature." In *Understanding Origins: Contemporary Views on the Origin of Life, Mind and Society*, ed. Francisco J. Varela and Jean-Pierre Dupuy, 27–42. Dordrecht: Kluwer Academic Publishers (Boston Studies in the Philosophy of Science 130), 1992.

———. *The One by Whom Scandal Comes*. Trans. M. B. DeBevoise. East Lansing, MI: Michigan State University Press, 2014.

Girard, René with Pierpaolo Antonello and João Cezar de Castro Rocha. *Les Origines de la Culture*. Descleé de Brouwer [Original text of Girard (2007)], 2004.

Girard, René with Pierpaolo Antonello and João Cezar de Castro Rocha. *Evolution and Conversion: Dialogues on the Origins of Culture* [English Trans. Girard (2004)]. New York: Continuum Books, 2007.

Sebeok, Thomas A. *Contributions to the Doctrine of Signs*. 2nd ed. Lanham, MD: University of America Press, 1976.

———. *The Play of Musement*. Bloomington, IN: Indiana University Press, 1981.

———. "The Evolution of Communication and the Origin of Language," lecture in the June 1–3 ISISSS '84 Colloquium on "Phylogeny and Ontogeny of Communication Systems." Published under the title "Communication, Language, and Speech: Evolutionary Considerations," 1984, in T. Sebeok (1986): 10–16.

———. *I Think I Am a Verb: More Contributions to the Doctrine of Signs*. New York: Plenum Press, 1986.

———. "Language: How Primary a Modeling System?" in *Semiotics 1987*, ed. John Deely, 15–27. Lanham, MD: University Press of America, 1988.

———. *The Sign and Its Masters*. 2nd ed. Austin, TX: University of Texas Press (1st ed: 1979), 1989.

———. "In What Sense Is Language a Primary Modeling System?" In *On Semiotic Modeling*, ed. Myrdene Anderson and Floyd Merrell, 327–39. Berlin: Mouton de Gruyter, 1991.

———. *Signs: An Introduction to Semiotics*. Toronto, ON: University of Toronto Press (2nd ed: 2001), 1994.

———. *Global Semiotics*. Bloomington, IN: Indiana University Press, 2001.

Sebeok, Thomas A., and Marcel Danesi. *The Forms of Meaning: Modeling Systems Theory and Semiotic Analysis*. Berlin and New York: Mouton de Gruyter, 2000.

9

Martyrs of Liberty: Open-Air Preaching and Popular Violence in Victorian Britain and Ireland

Mark Doyle

Street preaching was part of the warp and woof of Victorian outdoor culture. The exhortations and imprecations of street preachers—or open-air preachers, as they were also known—were part of a chorus of hawkers and talkers that enlivened parks, marketplaces, and public squares all over the British Isles. Usually these preachers attracted little opposition, or even much notice, as people chatted and hurried past, but from time to time a group of roughs might come along and start heckling them—sometimes for sport, sometimes in defense of their religion, and often for both reasons at once. The heckling was little different from what went on most nights in the taverns and music halls—insults yelled, food and drink hurled, and crowds mustered—and most street preachers came to accept, indeed to welcome, such intermittent abuse. But sometimes things became more serious: Stones could fly, clothing could tear, and blood could flow.

This chapter is about those rare times when street preaching provoked violence in Victorian Britain and Ireland. It focuses particularly on how the authorities in Ireland responded differently to such episodes, occurring from the 1850s to the 1890s, than the authorities in Britain did. It argues that the British state in Ireland was surprisingly indulgent of evangelical street preachers, putting up with a degree of provocation and disorder that their counterparts in England and Scotland rarely tolerated. As a result, Irish street-preaching confrontations tended to escalate into violence more often than they did in Britain, although serious riots were still quite unusual. I will offer several possible explanations for the state's different responses to street-preaching violence on the two islands, which take us beyond the question of preaching itself and into the very heart of British rule in Ireland. One explanation has to do with the desire of British officials in Ireland to cling to some legitimacy in a country where the state's footing was never secure; another has to do with the centralized nature of British rule in Ireland, which made the Irish state less flexible in handling such outbreaks. Paradoxically, the result of this differential treatment was to create more violence in Ireland, not less, and therefore to confirm in British minds the idea that Ireland was inherently and unusually violent.

First, a few words about the nature and purpose of open-air preaching. The first of the Christian street preachers (as the Victorian preachers liked to say) was Christ himself; the Sermon on the Mount was the model that many evangelical preachers followed in the nineteenth century, as were the subsequent sermons of Christ's apostles.[1] During the Reformation open-air preaching acquired a strong association with evangelical Protestantism when persecuted reformers, particularly Presbyterians and Puritans, took it up.[2] In the eighteenth century John Wesley and his followers had spread Methodism by way of open-air sermons, a practice that continued into the nineteenth century.[3] Meanwhile, as Britain expanded overseas, open-air preaching also became a tool of empire: outdoor sermons were often a necessary, and occasionally a hazardous, occupation for missionaries in Africa, Asia, and the Americas who were trying to reach people where there were as yet no churches. Indeed, it was in a similar missionary spirit that many Victorian British Protestants (usually, but not always, from the smaller dissenting sects) began preaching in Catholic Ireland, which to them was in need of sturdy men, as one preacher put it, "to carry the lamp of truth into its dark places."[4] And it was in that same spirit that open-air preachers traveled into the darkest corners of their own British cities: no less than the savages of Africa or Ireland did the ragged workers of the industrial slums need the light of the Lord.

Sometimes these preachers attracted large crowds, and sometimes they attracted none at all. Violence, when it happened, usually occurred when Protestant preachers deliberately sallied into working-class areas dominated by Catholics.[5] In cities with an especially entrenched tradition of sectarian violence, such as Liverpool or Belfast, preachers could also provoke violence by holding forth in city centers, which were usually neutral areas where neither Protestants nor Catholics held sway. Normally in such cities preaching would be tolerated as long as it was confined to certain socially sanctioned speaking grounds: Speakers' Corner in London's Hyde Park is probably the most famous example, but there were others, such as Glasgow Green and the Belfast Custom House (about which I will say more below). When Protestant preachers did stray into Catholic or disputed areas, they usually knew what they were doing: if a bit of jostling and heckling was the cost of bringing the gospel to poor Catholics, it was a price they were willing to pay.[6] Some went even further and courted actual martyrdom, although martyrdom in these cases usually meant cuts, bruises, and perhaps a night in jail; even the most paranoid antipapal agitators hardly expected to be burned alive for their faith in the nineteenth century.

In taking to the streets these preachers were exercising, often quite consciously, a bundle of cherished political freedoms that they invoked with the phrase "civil and religious liberties." Freedom of religious belief, freedom of expression, and free use of the Queen's highways and other public places—these were cherished British liberties, and whenever somebody tried to curtail them, the preachers were quick to claim the protection of the state in their free exercise thereof. This, perhaps most famously, was the position taken by anti-Catholic agitator William Murphy on his tours through northern England in the 1860s and early 1870s. Though he was not, strictly speaking, an open-air preacher (most of his lectures were indoors, and he once went so far as to build a rough tabernacle on an empty lot in Birmingham when no hall would open its doors to him), the dilemma that he represented was the same one that confronted the authorities who had to deal with street preachers.[7] Where did an individual's right to free expression end and the requirements of public order begin? The authorities answered this question in different ways across Britain and Ireland. In England and Scotland, the Home Office (which was notionally in charge of maintaining law and order nationwide) usually left the decision about whether to protect or suppress a preacher in the hands of the local authorities, sending additional police or troops when needed but otherwise refusing to get involved. In Ireland, as we will see below, the central government pursued quite a different strategy.

In Murphy's case, the central government and most of the municipalities where he appeared (at least for the first few years of his notoriety) decided to permit his lectures and to offer him the protection of the state. On a few occasions local officials (e.g., the mayor of Birmingham in 1867) attempted to prevent Murphy's appearances, but the Home Office, headed for much of this period by the Conservative Gathorne Hardy, held that there was nothing illegal about Murphy's lectures and declined to allow local officials in Britain to prosecute Murphy for breaking the peace.[8] Hardy and another Conservative Home Secretary, Spencer Walpole, agreed that Murphy was a nuisance and that his lectures could "lead to evil,"[9] but they saw no legal way to prevent his preaching and refused to empower local authorities to do so. Thus, for the first few years the Home Office remained resolutely aloof from the controversy, supplying military assistance when asked but otherwise leaving things to the judgment of the local authorities.[10] When soldiers were used, they usually stayed in the background, allowing the unarmed police to develop their own riot-control techniques, which proved to be quite effective in many cases. On only one occasion, in Blackburn in October 1868, did soldiers use weapons against the rioters, and then they used not firearms but cutlasses.[11] This hands-off approach was quite a contrast to the way things were done in Ireland, where the central government was often minutely involved in the policing of riots, soldiers were frequently and ostentatiously deployed, and the police (i.e., the Irish Constabulary) were armed and drilled like soldiers.

The Home Office's laissez-faire approach to Murphy changed in 1869 when a new Liberal Home Secretary, Henry Bruce, in consultation with his law advisors, dug up an eighteenth-century law that could be used to silence Murphy. The Unlawful Societies Act of 1799 was never intended for circumstances such as this—it was enacted during the French Revolution to prohibit seditious organizations, and Murphy's attacks on Romanism were anything but seditious—but it did amount to a statutory limitation on the right of free speech, and London was desperate to avoid further riots. After disturbances in Tynemouth, the Home Office began advising local authorities that they could use this law to prohibit additional lectures by Murphy, which they did. Murphy was outraged and sought an audience with the Home Secretary, but Bruce refused. In the House of Commons the Attorney General, Robert Collier, defended the government's decision to suppress Murphy:

> If ever there were any circumstances in which it was proper to put the Act in force they occurred in the case of Murphy. It was not asserted that he was a housebreaker, or that he went sword in hand, and attacked people; but he went about for the purpose of exciting religious animosity; he used language that was indecent and offensive; and he roused into a violent state of excitement . . . those whose religion he outraged and whose feelings he purposely set at naught. Murphy was rightly described as a firebrand, for wherever he went there were tumult, excitement, and almost insurrection. He was not proceeded against

because he was a Protestant; and if a Roman Catholic or a Presbyterian of a hundred-lecturer power went about the country exciting animosity and ill-will he would have to be dealt with in the same manner.[12]

In June of 1869, when Murphy was scheduled to appear in Birmingham, the police ordered him to stay away. When Murphy refused, he was arrested and jailed for a night. Birmingham's mayor, aware perhaps of the controversy over the use of the Unlawful Societies Act, told the Home Office, "Believing that I can find a justification of my conduct in moral laws, I seek it not in Statute law."[13] Murphy sued, and a Warwickshire jury eventually found in his favor, but they awarded him damages of just forty shillings, thereby affirming that the silencing of Murphy, though technically illegal, was not exactly reprehensible.[14]

Throughout the controversy Murphy and his supporters insisted that he had an absolute right to the protection of the state at all times. This was a frequent theme of Murphy's public and private pronouncements, as when he asked the Home Office to direct the local authorities in Ashton-under-Lyne to protect him and not "to interfere with my rights and liberties as an Englishman[15] so long as I do not transgress the Law"[16] after disturbances there in 1868. Murphy's supporters made similar points in newspaper leaders and letters. Typical was a letter from "A Protestant" to the *Wolverhampton Chronicle* in February 1867, who claimed, "civil and religious liberty is unquestionably the birthright and the pride and boast of the Englishmen, and a most dastardly and determined effort has been made to deprive the greater portion of the inhabitants of this town of this most dearly purchased, highly prized, and never to be sacrificed boon."[17]

Murphy kept speaking despite the ban, and the problem solved itself in 1871 when, prior to a speaking engagement at Whitehaven, a gang of Irishmen delivered him a serious beating that proved fatal. Despite Murphy's violent end, his indoor lectures were, by their nature, considerably less hazardous (for both the preacher and the public) than open-air sermons proper. In the latter cases trouble could erupt in parks, quaysides, village squares, or urban neighborhoods—on Sundays, market days, or really any day at all. Liverpool, with its massive Irish Catholic population, was the English city most prone to this sort of violence, not just because Irish Catholics tended to object to Protestant missionaries in their neighborhoods, but also because Protestant missionaries, tempted by the city's tremendous number of impoverished Catholics, were quite aggressive in their eagerness to preach there.[18] In 1858, for instance, trouble repeatedly broke out during services in the Islington Market and the Old Swan district east of town, occasioning at least one large melee as the police tried to take two preachers to jail after a scuffle.[19] Public evangelism remained a contentious issue in Liverpool into the twentieth century, when, after several years of serious rioting, the authorities finally sought and obtained (via judicial decision and, eventually, Parliamentary action) the power to regulate open-air services.[20]

Western Scotland, also a center of heavy Irish immigration, likewise saw a number of open-air preaching riots in the 1850s and beyond. In 1851 a crowd of Irish Catholics attacked a well-known no-popery agitator in the Clydeside town of Greenock while he spoke on the Custom House steps, prompting local Protestants to wreck Catholic homes and a chapel, and leading frightened Catholics to flee to the hills.[21] That summer a riot nearly broke out in Glasgow as well, when a Protestant minister attempted to preach in the city's heavily Catholic Gorbals neighborhood. Only some energetic politicking by Catholic priests and members of the St. Vincent de Paul Society prevented a disturbance.[22]

Glasgow's street preachers were particularly sophisticated: instead of simply pitching up on a corner and haranguing passersby, they would erect temporary pulpits, raise placards, and display prints showing the horrors of the confessional or the Inquisition. Perhaps the most ambitious open-air mission in Victorian Glasgow began in the summer of 1860, when a Free Kirk minister named McColl started holding sermons in the Catholic neighborhood of Bridgegate from a purpose-built stone pulpit outside his church. After several weeks of mounting confrontations between the Catholics and McColl's Protestant supporters, Sheriff Archibald Alison and two hundred policemen intervened and ended McColl's mission for the year. The following summer McColl was back at it, and Alison again intervened, this time issuing him a legal interdict in the Sheriff's Court. There were, Alison told McColl, "innumerable" places in Glasgow where he might preach—Jail Square, St. Enoch's Square, St. Andrew's Square, George Square, and even in front of the Sherriff's Court itself—but preaching among the Catholics of the Bridgegate was imprudent and dangerous, and it could not be permitted.[23]

As Alison's response to McColl suggests, local authorities in Britain had the legal power to curtail public displays of anti-Catholicism in order to prevent disturbance, and they sometimes did so, even though it often meant incurring (as Alison did) the odium of evangelicals and libertarians. There were many reasons for the authorities not to stop the preachers—they might sympathize with the preachers' missions, they might fear the wrath of their ultra-Protestant constituents, and they might calculate that it was less risky to allow the preaching than to stop it—but it was not uncommon for a mayor or magistrate to deny an especially troublesome orator the use of the roads or even of a public hall. When the rebuffed orators complained to the Home Office, the invariable response was that these were local matters to be dealt with by local officials; even when it felt local officials were overreacting, the Home Office normally refused to interfere with their decisions, especially if there were no criminal charges involved.[24]

Ireland, however, was another matter. Though the legal circumstances were the same (Ireland was fully part of the United Kingdom and subject to the same common law and judicial precedents), the local and central authorities only rarely tried to prohibit open-air preaching or other varieties of public anti-Catholicism. This was so for several reasons. For one thing, in many parts of Ireland (especially the northern province of Ulster) the local authorities were themselves usually Protestants who relied on the support of ultra-Protestant clergymen, newspapers, and voters; those officials who did try to silence the preachers were almost invariably Catholic mayors and magistrates in the south and west. For another thing, the central government in Dublin was anxious to maintain the appearance of religious neutrality in Ireland: few British officials had much sympathy with the preachers (although some did, as we will see), but they understood that preserving these men's right to religious expression was vital to maintaining Protestant morale in the country. A commitment to "civil and religious liberty" was still one of the chief ideological underpinnings of British rule in Ireland, and it was something for which the country's Protestant minority was determined to hold the state accountable, especially since Catholics, ever since obtaining full political rights in 1829, seemed to be gaining more freedom and power by the year. From the perspective of the Irish Executive at Dublin Castle, protecting open-air preachers was a relatively cheap way to forestall Protestant disaffection, and it had the added benefit (or so they thought) of burnishing the state's reputation for impartial, tolerant, and liberal behavior. Finally, as their British counterparts did, many officials in Ireland calculated that interfering with the preachers was likely to cause more trouble than simply letting them proceed. To stop the preaching would be to give in to "the mob," and in Ireland, unlike in Britain, the state could ill-afford such a challenge to its hegemony. British rule was facing enough challenges (from nationalist politicians, agrarian secret societies, and vigilante groups of different shapes and sizes) without also losing control of the country's urban spaces. For these reasons, officials in Ireland were prepared to tolerate a surprising amount of disorder whenever an evangelical preacher decided to preach among Catholics.

Several of the biggest open-air preaching initiatives in Victorian Ireland came from Protestant evangelicals based in Britain.[25] The famine of 1845–1850 created mouthwatering opportunities for evangelicals to spread their missions of material and spiritual uplift into the poorest (and most Catholic) corners of the country, for wasn't this visitation from God a sign that Ireland must abandon the church of Rome and embrace the one true Gospel? During and immediately after the famine groups such as the Irish Church Missions unleashed an all-out *blitzconversion* upon what they felt would be a receptive populace; some of their missions entailed physical relief, but some simply involved preaching the Gospel in the open air.[26] Few, if any, of their services were aggressively anti-Catholic: these were proselytizing sermons meant to entice Catholics, not Murphyesque tirades against the Whore of Babylon. Still, there were plenty of Catholics who failed to appreciate the missionaries' charitable intentions. In 1853 the Evangelical Alliance, an umbrella group encompassing Protestant evangelicals across Britain, sent one hundred preachers to the towns and villages of Ireland to preach in the open air.[27] Within a few weeks of their arrival the preachers were complaining to the Home Office of attacks by bigoted Catholic crowds who, they claimed, were given free rein by the authorities. As in most cases of this sort, the aggrieved preachers deployed the language of British liberty to make their case. A typical letter, from a branch of the Alliance called the Scottish Reformation Society, complained that police interference with their ministers "strikes at the root of that law of toleration on which the constitution of Britain is based" and "is a virtual abrogation of the civil government, and a dissolution of society into its original elements."[28] In a second letter, the Scottish missionaries blamed the attacks on the inherent intolerance of Catholicism and insisted that the government had a duty to defend the liberty of Protestants:

> Your Memorialists submit that these proceedings involve a violation of the first principles of liberty. Any tendency towards a breach of the peace in such perfectly lawful and innocent transactions must arise from the unbridled passions of the Romanists themselves and from that spirit of intolerance which is inseparable from the Romish system, and is so diligently fostered by all Popish priests. This may be a very good reason for keeping Papists under strict control, but it is no reason at all for abridging the liberty of peaceable and well disposed Protestants . . .[29]

Such arguments struck a chord with Lord Palmerston, the Home Secretary at the time, who asked Dublin Castle to prosecute those responsible for the violence. "The Catholics incessantly put forward the principle of religious equality," Palmerston wrote, "and they cannot reasonably refuse equal personal security to persons engaged in explaining & recommending the doctrines of both religions, & blows and stones are not fit arguments to be used in theological discussion."[30] Whether Palmerston was actively sympathetic toward the missionaries is unclear, but it is clear that here, as in other aspects of his religious policies, Palmerston was acting in a manner that was consistent with the ties he had forged with the anti-Catholic lobby. He was, in John Wolffe's words, "ready to exploit anti-Catholicism but wary of being compromised by it."[31] Upholding the rights of evangelical preachers in Ireland was a fairly easy way for Palmerston to keep his ultra-Protestant supporters onside.

Thomas Larcom, the undersecretary at Dublin Castle, responded with equanimity to the missionaries' allegations and Palmerston's concerns. Open-air preaching had been going on for some time in Ireland, he said, and the degree of opposition the preachers encountered rarely rose above "hooting and groaning, accompanied sometimes with insulting gestures." He had seen no evidence that the missionaries had been attacked in the manner they described to Palmerston, and he knew that the police had instituted some prosecutions against the people who had opposed the preachers. "It can scarcely be matter of surprise," Larcom told the Home Office, "that a mission unconnected even with the Established Church should be unpopular in districts where the mass of the people are Roman Catholic." Nevertheless, he said, "every protection which the law and the Government could afford, has been given to these Gentlemen," and every effort to prosecute their assailants had been made.[32] On receiving this information Palmerston suggested that it was probably the Catholic priests, not the people, who were to blame for causing the disturbances, but "whether these riotous proceedings are spontaneous or prompted by the priests they ought equally to be punished."[33]

This three-way exchange involving missionaries, the Home Office, and Dublin Castle followed a pattern that persisted throughout the Victorian period. On one side stood the preachers, who insisted upon their liberty as British subjects to hold open-air services and called upon the protection of the state in the exercise of that liberty. On another side stood the Home Office, not all of whose secretaries were as sympathetic toward the missionaries as Palmerston was, but who all felt that the missionaries should have state protection. On the third side stood the Irish Executive at Dublin Castle (and their appendages, the Resident Magistrates, and Constabulary forces in the towns and villages), who usually tried to strike a pragmatic balance between protecting the preachers and recognizing that their activities might be offensive. There was a fourth party to this discussion, of course. Local Catholics, many of whom saw the preachers as provocateurs, usually kept their distance from the preachers but sometimes offered direct opposition. In 1853 a Limerick crowd hurled a preacher from his platform, in Nenagh Catholics assailed the preachers with mud and manure, and in Clonmel one preacher was hurled down a flight of stairs.[34] In some cases the local authorities (usually Catholics themselves) decided to ban the preachers—the mayor of Limerick personally ordered them to leave town[35]—but in most other cases the police, taking their instructions from Dublin Castle, offered them protection.

Confrontations over street preaching continued throughout the 1850s. In 1855 and 1856 another raft of one hundred preachers arrived from Britain, provoking sixteen different assaults in the town of Kilkenny alone. One frustrated Kilkenny policemen reported, "it is quite impossible to prevent these frequent attacks upon the Scripture-readers, except by actually accompanying them, I might almost say arm-in-arm, on all their peregrinations."[36] The most destructive open-air preaching riot of the Victorian era, in Ireland or anywhere else in the United Kingdom, happened in Belfast in 1857. That city, which was roughly two-thirds Protestant and one-third Catholic, had seen a number of aggressive evangelical initiatives over the preceding decade. The Protestant establishment, anxious to protect Belfast's Protestant identity amidst an influx of poor Catholics seeking work in the linen mills, supported and encouraged aggressively anti-Catholic forms of political and evangelical organizing. Controversial, anti-Catholic lectures and debates formed a vital part of the city's associational culture, and open-air preaching—principally directed at the poor, churchless inhabitants of the inner-city slums—was a longstanding practice that sometimes degenerated into anti-Catholic proselytizing initiatives.[37] "Week after week," wrote the *Ulsterman*, Belfast's Catholic newspaper, in 1854,

> the walls of Belfast and our Northern towns are covered with placards announcing to the ignorant crowd, that some peripatetic preacher will hold forth on the "abominations of Popery." And week after week, in church or meeting house, some one of these firebrands raves by the hour on the inexhaustible theme. He tells how hundreds of millions living upon this fair globe are idolators, criminals, assassins, who hate their Protestant fellow-men, and would burn them all in one common pile. His howlings are accepted as inspired eloquence by ignorant crowds; his statements, mad and wicked as they are, are believed as truths; and the hearers go forth with bitter hatred nursing in their hearts against their countrymen who worship at the altars where their fathers bowed and prayed long centuries ago. Nor is this enough. Preachers go forth upon the highway, as near to the "Popish mass-house" as may be, and to the ignorant mob around them they teach hatred of their fellows, and rancour for the love of God; they tell how base and lawless crowds in America have hunted down their Catholic neighbours, wrecked their houses, and torn down or blown up their chapels; and they laud these murderous wreckers as heroes and saints. Then the breasts of the mob swell with fury, and their eyes rest savagely on the chapel, mirroring their wish to follow the goodly fashion of the transatlantic saints. All which is done in the name of the Christianity Christ preached![38]

The causal link between evangelical preachers and Protestant rioters was more complex than this, of course, but the *Ulsterman*'s characterization of the general no-popery atmosphere in Belfast was accurate enough. Vulnerable and demoralized, the Catholics of Belfast as yet had very few institutional resources by which to resist the onslaught—churches were few, Catholic charities were even fewer, and the Catholic bourgeoisie were rudderless and ineffective—so they tended to respond to Protestant aggression in the same way that their compatriots in industrial Scotland and England did, by either avoiding or attacking their maligners.

The Belfast open-air preaching crisis of September 1857 took place during a tense summer that had already seen rioting between working-class Protestants and Catholics in July. In August a group of local Anglican missionaries began holding services on the steps of the city's new Custom House. Though the services were not especially anti-Catholic in nature, some Catholics, familiar with the proselytizing adventures of open-air preachers elsewhere in the country and their own city, saw them as acts of aggression. A series of escalating confrontations at the Custom House led the Anglicans to abandon their mission after a few weeks, but in early September the young Presbyterian minister Hugh Hanna, who had been gaining notoriety in town for his efforts to lure working-class Catholics to his church, took up the cause. Courting martyrdom like other preachers before and after him, and acting contrary to the urgent pleas of the local magistrates and members of his own denomination, Hanna held a well-publicized open-air service near the Custom House on September 9. As soon as the anticipated Catholic heckling commenced, a group of fifty Protestant shipyard workers, enlisted by Hanna as bodyguards, turned on the Catholics and held a running battle along the quays. This fracas spawned additional fights in working-class neighborhoods on the other side of town, which mostly took the form of violent expulsions of people living in the "wrong" neighborhoods, as well as a few actual battles across patches of waste ground on the edge of town.[39]

The state's initial response to the Belfast crisis was the same as it was throughout this period: while they worked privately to persuade Hanna to desist and the Catholics to forbear, both the local and central authorities accepted that they had no legal grounds to prohibit the preaching and must protect Hanna in the exercise of his right to preach in the open air. In January 1857, before the Belfast crisis broke out, the Earl of Carlisle, Lord Lieutenant of Ireland, had written to Lord Shaftesbury after an open-air preaching riot in Kingston, England:

> I subscribe "toto anims[?]" to the lawfulness of open-air preaching, under proper limitations, of time and place. I equally recognize my full duty as giving protection to all persons lawfully employed against unlawful violence.
>
> I owe it however to truth to add that as far as my personal opinion is concerned, I do not hold the view . . . that the practice of open-air preaching is specially adapted to Ireland, but the reverse. I do so because I think, indeed I know, that it is calculated to provoke a disturbance of the public peace among a people excitable by temperament and the majority of whom are prohibited by actual law from engaging in religious offices, beyond the precincts of their own places of worship, which offices are considered by them at least, to be quite as important as the addresses or sermons of ministers of any denomination.

Thomas Larcom believed that these principles applied equally to open-air preaching in Belfast and in any other place where "the people of a different persuasion [from that of the preacher] predominate," and this was the line Dublin Castle followed in the early stages of the Belfast crisis.[40] When Hanna persisted in holding open-air services even after the violence of September 9, however, Carlisle decided that he had had enough. "It strikes me you should telegraph the Mayor to disperse all assemblages," he telegrammed Larcom just before Hanna's second preaching attempt.[41] Larcom notified the Belfast authorities, and they dutifully, if reluctantly, complied. The mayor of Belfast was, like most of the Belfast government, a staunch Protestant and sympathetic to Hanna's stand for religious freedom, and he protested that in being forced to prevent Hanna's preaching he had acted "unconstitutionally" and would not enforce such orders again.[42] The ultra-Protestant and anti-Catholic *Belfast Newsletter* was livid with indignation, condemning Carlisle's order as "downright and positively, distinctly, actually, and indeed, *illegal*, without warrant in the law or the Constitution of England."[43] There was some justification for this view. Years later, Larcom would remind Carlisle of this "famous telegram," which, he said, the Lord Chancellor had immediately confirmed was "exactly the right thing for the Lord Lieutenant to do, though certainly what no lawyer could have advised!"[44] In fact, Carlisle's order to "disperse all assemblages" foreshadowed the coercion laws that would target nationalist and agrarian movements in Ireland in later decades. Like those laws, Carlisle's order was an emergency measure enacted to prevent disorder, but unlike those laws it lacked the statutory standing of an Act of Parliament and was, indeed, quite illegal.

The Protestant outrage at Carlisle's diktat was just the sort of thing officials in Ireland were trying to avoid when, in most circumstances, they chose to protect street preachers rather than suppressing them. Irish Protestants were already quite disillusioned with the British government, which had spent the last few decades chipping away at their special status in the country, and it took very little to stir them up. In ordinary times the right to public religious expression was hardly a cause for which most Protestants would lay down their lives, but these were not ordinary times: the Catholic Church was undergoing a resurgence in Ireland, and even the slightest capitulation to Catholic "bigotry and intolerance" (as one newspaper put it) threatened to unleash a full-blown anti-Protestant jacquerie.[45] Just as infuriating as the Catholics who objected to street preaching, therefore, was a government that didn't have the nerve to stand up to them. Such fears would be a common theme in ultra-Protestant agitation for the remainder of the century, and they were a topic about which British officials were keenly sensitive. Every concession the government made to Irish Catholics eroded the state's position among Protestants; to be accused of obstructing the "civil and religious liberties" of Protestant street preachers was not a hazard most British officials were willing to face, Carlisle notwithstanding.

After the riots of 1857 there were no more major confrontations in Belfast over the issue of open-air preaching. Whatever damage he might have done to communal relations in town, Hugh Hanna had successfully vindicated the right of public evangelism, and after the hubbub died down the Custom House steps became a popular spot for preachers and other orators (so much so that the recently renovated Custom House Square in Belfast features a statue of a Hanna-like speaker holding forth on its steps). Open-air preaching continued in the rest of Ireland as well, occasionally provoking outrage and disturbance, and throughout the period the state's policy remained the same: the preachers were to be protected, even at the cost of some localized violence, and only in the very last instance were they to be denied the right to free religious expression.

The last significant wave of open-air preaching in Ireland occurred in the 1890s, when the Evangelical Alliance and its Open Air Mission sponsored another preaching campaign in several Irish towns.[46] The political context was different—the famine was a distant memory, and several decades of nationalist agitation had made Irish self-government a very real possibility—but the aims of the preachers were largely the same: to save souls and rescue Ireland from popery. If such work helped to prevent the breakup of the United Kingdom, so much the better, but the aim was primarily religious. As in the 1850s, the policy of the central government was to protect these preachers, but the protection was grudging, and the preachers frequently complained of unlawful interference by the police. After one such complaint by a preacher stationed in Arklow (where disturbances occurred nearly every Sunday from 1890 to 1892) Arthur Balfour, the Chief Secretary of Ireland, testily responded that "large bodies of armed constabulary" had been drafted into Arklow "at a great cost to the public purse and great inconvenience to the officers and men engaged." To the preacher's claim that he was only seeking the same protection he would expect in England, Balfour replied that the situations in the two countries were completely different:

> In Ireland the divisions between different sections of the community, caused by differences of creed, are so deep and far-reaching, religious convictions are so closely interwoven with political passions, that a course which would be innocent, and even praiseworthy, on one side of St. George's Channel, may be morally, if not legally, indefensible on the other.[47]

Balfour was clearly ignoring (or ignorant of) the very deep "divisions between different sections of the community" that existed in British cities such as Liverpool and Glasgow, but his implicit contrast between an essentially tranquil Britain and an incorrigibly turbulent Ireland is a good example of the way British officials thought about violence in the two countries. Violence in Britain could be dismissed as anomalous, reflective not of deep divisions but of temporary circumstances; it could therefore be policed on an *ad hoc* basis, without much reference to general principles. Violence in Ireland, however, was an inevitable consequence of not only religious disputes but also political passions; the state's response had, therefore, to be consistent and scrupulously lawful.

Balfour's handling of the open-air preaching controversy of the 1890s demonstrates how committed even the most conservative officials (Balfour would later be a Tory Prime Minister) were to fundamental liberal values such as free expression and the rule of law. It also demonstrates the dilemmas that these values created for a state that relied heavily on the use of force to maintain order. In a letter to an English sympathizer of the Arklow preachers, Balfour explained the principles guiding his policy. There was a question of law, he said, and another question of morality. It was undeniably legal for a preacher to hold open-air services in hostile territory, and thus the state could not interfere with them. However, it was doubtful that a preacher could be "morally justified in insisting on conducting [services] in the very places and under the very circumstances least calculated to get a hearing for the doctrines he professes, and most calculated to excite irritation and to engender sectarian animosities in the breasts of those whom he desires to convert." There was also a question of expediency: Should the state devote as many resources as it had in protecting the Arklow preachers (some 250 soldiers and policemen) to protecting anybody else, anywhere else, who wanted to exercise their liberties in a similar fashion?

> Would the Executive, for instance, be bound to fill Belfast with troops and constabulary in order to protect a Roman Catholic priest who, though possessed of ample opportunities of worshipping in peace according to his conscience, should insist on celebrating Mass in front of the church door in the most Protestant quarter of the city? And, if not what is the limit of the demands that can legitimately be made upon it?

Balfour declined to directly answer these sticky questions, but he allowed that the maxim of the government's actions in Arklow could not be universalized to the country as a whole. The Arklow preachers' conduct, he said, "if deliberately imitated by all sects and in all places in Ireland, would set the whole country in a blaze of sectarian fury." Here again is the image of Ireland as a dangerous tinderbox of latent violence, an image virtually unchanged since the first wave of disturbances in the 1850s. Balfour went on to assert that his commitment to freedom of conscience was strong, but this was precisely the problem: "It is because I am an earnest supporter of the rights of free religious discussion and of free religious worship that I regret to see these rights abused, even with the best intentions; and it is because that I am a Protestant that I regret that those who abuse them should belong to my own communion."[48] What Balfour was saying was that the preachers were wrong to hold public services in the manner they were doing, but his commitment to the rule of law, the right of free expression—values that were part and parcel of Balfour's own Protestantism—forced him to guard them in their folly.

Over the next few years similar disturbances broke out in Cork, Galway, Athlone, Sligo, and elsewhere. In all cases magistrates and Castle officials scrupulously consulted law advisors and other legal experts to determine how to handle the preachers. Without fail, the Attorney General's office maintained that there was nothing illegal in the preaching, even if violent opposition was anticipated, and it directed Constabulary officers and local officials (many of whom were Catholic and hostile to the preachers) to afford the preachers all necessary protection. In deciding what to do about the preachers the Attorney General's office turned to recent English case law, citing a judgment in the 1882 case of *Beatty v. Gillbanks* concerning Salvation Army processions in England, which found that "An act innocent in itself, and done with innocent intent, does not become criminal because it may provoke, or does provoke, others to break the peace."[49] This judgment was meant to clarify what had long been a murky area of English common law (in whose dark spaces the likes of William Murphy found cover), insofar as it protected potentially offensive speech and placed the onus of good behavior on the shoulders of those who were offended by it, but by focusing on the intent of the speakers, whose "innocence" or otherwise was often open to dispute, it ended up clarifying very little. Indeed, although the application of *Beatty v. Gillbanks* to Ireland indicated that England and Ireland were on the same legal footing in these matters, the ruling left so much discretion in the hands of individual authorities (whose job it was to divine a speaker's intent) that the application of the law could still be radically different in the two countries. In the immediate circumstances, the Irish Attorney General's office did decide that if opposition to the preachers became too violent, the police were permitted to hustle the preachers away and secure them in their lodgings, but they were not allowed to prohibit the preaching outright.[50] The only time the preachers might legally be suppressed and prosecuted was when they caused obstruction to public thoroughfares; this happened on a few occasions, but not often.

Acting on these principles, the Royal Irish Constabulary devoted considerable time and energy to protecting the preachers, in some cases damaging its relations with local Catholics. When crowds gathered to hurl mud, stones, fish, and other items at the preachers, they inevitably hurled them at the police as well. When they hooted and yelled down the preachers, the police caught some of their vitriol too.[51] In Sligo town, which saw large and protracted disturbances from 1895 to 1897, a rumor circulated that the British government was in collusion with the preachers; the evidence for this was not only the massive police protection the preachers were receiving, but also the fact that a government employee named Sampson, the chief clerk in the town post office, was the preachers' principal sponsor.[52] Meanwhile, on the few occasions when the police did interfere with the services, the preachers indignantly alleged that the state was siding with intolerant Catholics and abandoning its responsibility to uphold religious liberty.

Looking at the period as a whole, it seems that, apart from the attacks on the preachers themselves, open-air preaching only rarely provoked widespread communal violence between large numbers of Protestants and Catholics in Ireland (the Belfast riots of 1857 were the exception). In Kilkenny in 1856 a policeman reported that "ill-feeling has been excited and stirred up between two classes of Her Majesty's subjects previously living in harmony and cordiality together," but there was little actual fighting.[53] In Sligo in 1895 Catholics attacked a Protestant journalist and a Congregational Church, as well as a few local Protestants who supported the preachers, but there was no widespread sectarian warfare here.[54] One reason that these open-air services did not provoke more violence was probably that the missionaries were usually (again excepting Belfast) outsiders from small dissenting sects; they had few local Protestant allies or constituents, and they therefore operated outside existing communal networks. Another was that most places in the south and west of Ireland had relatively few Protestants for a Catholic crowd to attack, and relations between the two groups were often cordial, if not always friendly. In most places, in other words, there was simply nobody with whom to have a riot.

More significant than the violence they provoked was the state response these preachers engendered. Scholars are accustomed to thinking of the policing of nineteenth-century Ireland as heavy-handed and repressive.[55] This was undoubtedly the case in many instances, particularly with respect to nationalist agitation, but what stands out about the state's handling of street preaching is, first, the care that officials at all levels took to ensure that their actions remained within the law, and, second, their willingness to tolerate disorder for the sake of preserving the right of street preachers to preach, even when it was clear that they disliked having to do so. In nearly every instance of preaching violence in Ireland, with the significant exception of Hugh Hanna's second attempted open-air service in Belfast in 1857, the central authorities elected to preserve the right of free expression, even at the cost of some disorder. I have suggested some reasons for this: Irish Protestants were already angry over concessions to Catholics in other areas, so state support for public anti-Catholicism was a fairly cheap way of forestalling further Protestant disaffection; Irish officials were often Protestant themselves and sympathetic to the preachers, or at least they knew that their Protestant constituents expected them to be sympathetic; and at least some central government officials (e.g., Lord Palmerston) actively sympathized with the preachers. But the main reason for the discrepancy between the policing of Ireland and Britain may simply be that Ireland was much more centralized than Britain. There were plenty of local Irish authorities who would happily have suppressed the preachers, as many of their English and Scottish counterparts would do, but who were prohibited from doing so by the law mandarins in Dublin and London. Nearly every city and town in Ireland (including Belfast after 1865) was policed by the centrally controlled Constabulary, which took its orders from Dublin Castle, not the local mayors or magistrates. This centralization made the policing of disorder in Ireland much less flexible than in Britain, where municipalities controlled their own police. This centralization, and the consequent emphasis on legality as interpreted by the Attorney General's office, may, in fact, have made street-preaching violence more common in Ireland simply because there was no real chance of local authorities acting on their own initiative to suppress the preachers.

Perversely, then, it may have been the state's scrupulous legality that created the conditions for anti-preacher violence in Ireland and the state's determination to visibly protect the preachers that undermined its reputation for impartiality there. If this was so, then the British state was responsible (albeit with the best of intentions) for creating the very conditions that made open-air preaching violence more common in Ireland, thereby confirming their own stereotype of the Irish as incorrigibly violent and in need of different treatment than the other inhabitants of the United Kingdom. In that way, the street-preaching violence of the era nicely encapsulated the paradoxes and dilemmas of British rule in Victorian Ireland as a whole. If Ireland was more violent than Britain, and there is good reason to think that it was, this may have been because Britain helped make it so.

Notes

1. The Presbyterian Church of Ireland was especially adamant on the point of open-air preaching's apostolic sanction. Beginning in the early 1850s numerous Presbyterian ministers began preaching in the poor rural and industrial districts of Ulster, and when they did, they frequently invoked its apostolic (and Reformation era) roots. In the words of the General Assembly of 1853, "Open-air Preaching had the

sanction of Apostolical practice, was adopted in times of the Reformation, and has been found effectual by several of our ministers, in bringing the Gospel before the minds of many who attend to no place of worship, or none where they hear the truth," *Minutes of the Proceedings of the General Assembly of the Presbyterian Church in Ireland, 1853*, vol. 2, 204.

2. "Open-Air Preaching," *The Irish Presbyterian* (October 1, 1857), 259–60.
3. David Hempton, "Evangelicalism in English and Irish Society, 1780–1840," in *Evangelicalism: Comparative Studies of Popular Protestantism in North America, the British Isles, and Beyond, 1700–1990*, ed. Mark A. Noll, David W. Bebbington, and George A. Rawlyk (Oxford: Oxford University Press, 1994), 156–76 (164–65).
4. Rev. Matthew Kerr, "Our Home Mission—Its Nature and Its Claims," *The Presbyterian Magazine* 1, 12 (December 1859), 265–68 (266).
5. Catholic clergymen seldom, if ever, preached in public spaces. Catholic revivals did sometimes take place in outdoor venues, but these were normally fields or churchyards, and such violence as they attracted tended to target Catholic worshipers traveling to or from a meeting, rather than the meeting itself. Catholic processions, such as the processions of Protestant Orangemen, could also provoke violence. For examples of violence during Catholic revivals in Ireland, see Gerald Hall, *Ulster Liberalism, 1778–1876: The Middle Path* (Dublin: Four Courts Press, 2011), 189–90.
6. Not all Protestant missionary organizations were devoted to proselytism, but a good many of them were, especially in Ireland.
7. Walter L. Arnstein, "The Murphy Riots: A Victorian Dilemma," *Victorian Studies* 19, 1 (September 1975), 51–70.
8. Letters on Murphy riots in Birmingham, 1867, The National Archives of Britain (TNA), Home Office (HO) 45/7991.
9. Letters on Murphy riots in Ashton-under-Lyne, 1868, TNA, HO 45/7991.
10. This was consistent with Home Office practice throughout most of the Victorian period, especially after the establishment of county police forces in 1856. See R. Quinault, "The Warwickshire County Magistracy and Public Order, c. 1830–1870," in *Popular Protest and Public Order: Six Studies in British History, 1790–1920*, ed. R. Quinault and J. Stevenson (London: George Allen & Unwin Ltd., 1974), 181–214; Carolyn Steedman, *Policing the Victorian Community: The Formation of English Provincial Police Forces, 1856–80* (London: Routledge & Kegan Paul, 1984), 32–33.
11. Steedman, *Policing*, 37.
12. *Hansard Parliamentary Debates*, HC 23 July 1869, vol. 198, col. 624. http://millbanksystems.com.
13. Henry Holland to Henry Bruce, June 19, 1869, TNA, HO 45/7991 (no. 63).
14. Walter Arnstein, *Protestant versus Catholic in Mid-Victorian England: Mr. Newdegate and the Nuns* (Columbia, MO: University of Missouri Press, 1982), 101.
15. Murphy was, in fact, Irish.
16. William Murphy to Gathorne Hardy, March 13, 1868, TNA, HO 45/7991.
17. Quoted in R. E. Swift, "Anti-Catholicism and Irish Disturbances: Public Order in Mid-Victorian Wolverhampton," *Midland History* 9 (1984): 87–108 (99).
18. In May 1860, for instance, one Liverpool missionary reported holding thirty-six outdoor lectures and twenty-one indoor ones within the past year, with the former averaging about six hundred hearers, many of them Catholics. John Wolffe, *The Protestant Crusade in Great Britain, 1829–1860* (Oxford: Clarendon Press, 1991), 185.
19. Frank Neal, *Sectarian Violence: The Liverpool Experience, 1819–1914: An Aspect of Anglo-Irish History* (Manchester: Manchester University Press, 1988), 165–67.
20. Frank Neal, *Sectarian Violence: The Liverpool Experience, 1819–1914: An Aspect of Anglo-Irish History* (Manchester: Manchester University Press, 1988), 200–220.
21. Ibid., 200-220.
22. *Glasgow Free Press*, August 2, 1851.
23. Sir Archibald Alison, *Some Account of My Life and Writings*, vol. 2 (Edinburgh: William Blackwood and Sons, 1883), 292–96, 309–13; *Glasgow Daily Herald*, June 6, 1861.
24. For other examples see the descriptions of the riots in Walsall in 1853 and Windsor in 1854, as well as the Cheltenham magistrates' ban on no-popery processions, in D. G. Paz, *Popular Anti-Catholicism in Mid-Victorian England* (Stanford, CA: Stanford University Press, 1992), 99 and 253–54; John Wolffe, *The Protestant Crusade in Great Britain, 1829–1860* (Oxford: Clarendon Press, 1991), 193.
25. Desmond Bowen, *The Protestant Crusade in Ireland, 1800–70* (Dublin: Gill and Macmillan, 1978), 195–256.
26. Desmond Bowen, *Souperism: Myth or Reality* (Cork: The Mercier Press, 1970), 18.

27. Memorial of the Committee of the Executive Council of the British Organization of the Evangelical Alliance to Lord Palmerston, September 8, 1853, TNA, HO 45/5129A (nos. 12–15).
28. Memorial of Scottish Reformation Society to Lord Palmerston, Home Secretary, August 9, 1853, TNA, HO 45/5129A (no. 7).
29. Memorial of Scottish Reformation Society to Lord Palmerston, Home Secretary, November 4, 1853, TNA, HO 45/5129A (no. 3). Among themselves, many evangelicals took a much sterner line, calling for the British state not only to protect the preachers but also to help them sweep Catholicism out of Ireland. Such was the attitude, for instance, of the *Irish Presbyterian* of September 1853 in an article titled "British Evangelical Mission to Ireland," 232–36.
30. Lord Palmerston, internal note, August 12, 1858, TNA, HO 45/5129A (no. 9).
31. Wolffe, *Protestant Crusade*, 277.
32. Thomas Larcom to Home Office, August 23, 1853, TNA, HO 45/5129A.
33. Palmerston memo written on Thomas Larcom's letter to the Home Office, August 23, 1853, TNA, HO 45/5129A.
34. *Limerick Reporter and Tipperary Vindicator*, August 2 and 5, 1853; *The Irish Presbyterian*, September 1853, 132–36.
35. Emmet Larkin and Herman Freudenberger, eds., *A Redemptorist Missionary in Ireland, 1851–1854: Memoirs by Joseph Prost, C. Ss. R.* (Cork: Cork University Press, 1998), 47–48.
36. Returns of the number of convictions for assaults on the agents of the Irish Church Missionary Society, in the city of Kilkenny, for the last twelve months; the number of additional police force lately introduced into Kilkenny; copies of reports and correspondence on the subject of the increased police force; and resolutions of the grand jury to the Lord Lieutenant, and his Excellency's reply (hereafter, *Kilkenny Disturbances Report*), HC 1856 (517) LIII, 2.
37. Mark Doyle, *Fighting Like the Devil for the Sake of God: Protestants, Catholics, and the Origins of Violence in Victorian Belfast* (Manchester: Manchester University Press, 2009), chapter 1.
38. *Ulsterman*, September 13, 1854.
39. For more on the Belfast riots of 1857, see Doyle, *Fighting*, chapter 3; Janice Holmes, "The Role of Open-Air Preaching in the Belfast Riots of 1857," *Proceedings of the Royal Irish Academy*, vol. 102C, 47–66 (2002). As with many Belfast riots, the government held an inquiry into the events of 1857. See *Report of the Commissioners of Inquiry into the Origin and Character of the Riots in Belfast, in July and September, 1857; Together with Minutes of Evidence and Appendix*. HC 1857–58 (2309) XXVI.
40. Lord Carlisle to Lord Shaftesbury, January 25, 1857, National Library of Ireland (NLI), Larcom Papers, 7624/1.
41. Carlisle to Larcom, September 20, 1857, National Archives of Ireland (NAI), Chief Secretary's Office Registered Papers (CSORP) 16743 (1858).
42. Tracy to Larcom, NLI, Larcom Papers, 7624/69. Ten years later, a report on open-air preaching from the Presbyterian Church of Ireland illustrated the active support of local officials for street preaching. At least three of those who subscribed money to the church's Open-Air Mission were Belfast Justices of the Peace: John Lytle, David Drummond, and J. P. Corry. *Seventeenth Annual Report on Open-Air Preaching by Ministers of the General Assembly of the Presbyterian Church in Ireland in the Summer of 1867* (Belfast: D. & J. Allen, 1868), 27.
43. *Belfast Newsletter*, September 21, 1857 (italics in original).
44. Larcom to Carlisle, August 29, 1864, NLI, Larcom Papers, 7626/64.
45. *Banner of Ulster*, September 3, 1857. On the Catholic resurgence of this period, see Emmet Larkin, "The Devotional Revolution in Ireland, 1850–75," *The American Historical Review* 77 (June 1972), 625–52; Emmet Larkin, *The Making of the Roman Catholic Church in Ireland, 1850–1860* (Chapel Hill, NC: University of North Carolina Press, 1980).
46. The only sustained academic study of these episodes is Matthew Kelly, "The Politics of Protestant Street Preaching in 1890s Ireland," *The Historical Journal* 48, no. 1 (2005), 101–25.
47. Arthur James Balfour to Rev. Richard C. Hallowes, February 5, 1891, TNA, Colonial Office (CO) 904/182, 287–88.
48. A. J. Balfour to Rev. W. T. M'Cormack, April 9, 1891, TNA, CO 904/182, 295–97.
49. Memorandum from Attorney General MacDermott, January 18, 1894, TNA, CO 904/182, 312–13.
50. Instructions Issued by Government to Royal Irish Constabulary, August 17 and 27, 1894, TNA, CO 904/182, 344.
51. Kelly ("Politics," 124) claims that preachers' resistance to the police "extend[ed] to the crowd a vague sense of legitimacy as an extra-judicial agency defending rights the officially designated agencies were unable to enforce. . . . In this sense, attacks were not directed against that which the state protected

any more than they were directed against the agents of the state." This may have been true on some occasions, but, as with Orange marches then and now, most of the evidence suggests that Catholic protestors saw the police accompanying these demonstrations as protecting (and thereby tacitly endorsing) the preachers, rather than the other way around.
52. Sampson and his wife were consequently ostracized by the community and ended up transferring to Enniskillen. Reports of Sligo Disturbances, TNA, CO 904/182, 366–82.
53. *Kilkenny Disturbances Report*, 5.
54. Reports of Sligo disturbances, TNA, CO 904/182, 375.
55. Charles Townshend, *Political Violence in Ireland: Government and Resistance since 1848* (Oxford: Clarendon Press, 1983); Elizabeth A. Muenger, *The British Military Dilemma in Ireland: Occupation Politics, 1886–1914* (Lawrence, KS: University Press of Kansas, 1991); Virginia Crossman, *Politics, Law and Order in Nineteenth-Century Ireland* (Dublin: Gill & Macmillan, 1996); Stanley H. Palmer, *Police and Protest in England and Ireland, 1780–1850* (Cambridge: Cambridge University Press, 1988); Elizabeth Malcolm, *The Irish Policeman, 1822–1922: A Life* (Dublin: Four Courts Press, 2006).

10

Moral Injury: A Case Study in the Intersection of Religion and Violence

Kathryn McClymond and Anthony F. Lemieux

It is tempting to simplify the relationship between religion and violence. This tendency is manifest in characterizations of religion as either a "good" force or a "bad" force in its relationship to violence (i.e., religion either reduces or fosters violence). In addition, violence often tends to be imagined solely as explicit physical violence between "us" and "them," with black-and-white demarcations between opposing forces. The reality, of course, is much more complicated. Religion and violence manifest in various and nuanced forms, and they interact with one another in multiple ways, often becoming inextricably intertwined and generating unique dynamics.

Here, we will examine the experience of moral injury as a specific intersection between religion and violence in a military context. We conceptualize moral injury as a form of posttraumatic stress disorder (PTSD) that usually arises as a result of violence done to others (sometimes an enemy, but at other times fellow soldiers or noncombatants). More importantly, we posit that moral injury in itself can be considered a form of violence. In this chapter, we will explore several examples of moral injury in a military context and the various ways in which religion is bound up with this particular form of violence. In doing so, we will note the varied and complex ways in which religion relates to violence in general, including the possibilities of offering healing to those suffering from moral injury.

Building Readiness and Capacity for Violence

A number of mechanisms have been put forth to explain the ways that soldiers are prepared for combat situations. Dave Grossman's *On Killing* is one of the most comprehensive studies to date, documenting the confluence of factors that prepare soldiers to take lethal action against adversaries. Although a thorough review is beyond the scope of this chapter, the kinds of justifications that are used for committing violence, the kinds of obligations that are felt by soldiers, and the kinds of deleterious outcomes and experiences that are potential consequences of such actions have been well documented. The mechanism of moral distancing plays an important role in the process of preparing someone to take lethal action against another and reifies key existential differences between "us" and "them," thereby fortifying the perceived legitimacy of harm.[1]

Albert Bandura proposed that a critically important mechanism allowing people to commit acts of violence against others is moral disengagement.[2] Moral disengagement is posited to result in the suspension of self-sanctioning of behaviors that may be viewed as especially taboo and illegitimate in many contexts (such as inflicting massive harm on another person). Paving the way for moral disengagement are the use of euphemistic language and labeling such as using the term *wasting* someone, redefining the morality of killing, and social comparisons that position killing as righteous and justified. Behaviors that people *know* to be wrong and immoral in many contexts, such as killing, are transformed into something with a moral imperative, and quite often a sense of urgency.

Further, diffusion of responsibility may be a critical factor for our understanding of the scope and potential impact of moral injury. This mechanism may allow the most directly responsible perpetrators to absolve themselves of some aspects of responsibility (i.e., the "just following orders" explanation that is most famously exemplified in Eichmann's Nuremberg defense). However, the other side of the diffusion of responsibility, as Grossman observes, is that there are others who are then positioned to assume more responsibility for the supportive roles that they have played in the context of violence and conflict.[3] Thus, one does not necessarily need to be directly involved in combat or the perpetration of violence to have the potential to experience moral injury. Simply knowing that one's efforts have contributed to the harm and destruction of others may be sufficient.

Thus, perpetrators of violence, broadly construed, may come to know the scope and extent of harm that they have caused and possibly view their actions as illegitimate or unjustified. In cases where expectations and reality are separated by a wide gap, soldiers may come to view a cause as lacking the nobility, legitimacy, or justification that they at one time may have ascribed to it. When the group dynamics and those factors that were initially important in setting the stage for the commission of violence, or when the immediate context that made such actions seem necessary and appropriate start to fade into the background, an individual is left to try to make sense and reassimilate the realities of the consequences of their past actions, the emotional responses that they have, and the memories and visions of their actions, with their present reality. It is in this space where we can search for indicators of moral injury.

Religion and Moral Injury among US Soldiers

US soldiers' struggles with PTSD are well known and well documented.[4] A recent study lists the following facts:

- There are 8.2 million Vietnam era veterans and over 2.3 million American veterans of the Iraq and Afghanistan wars.
- At least 20 percent of Iraq and Afghanistan veterans have PTSD and/or depression. (The authors of this study state that military counselors believe that the percentage is actually significantly higher.)
- Fifty percent of those with PTSD do not seek treatment.
- Of those who seek treatment, only half receive "minimally adequate treatment" according to a RAND Corporation study.[5]

The Department of Defense has reported that between 2003 and 2010, approximately 2,000 active duty service personnel committed suicide. The report goes on to state, "Roughly 50 percent of suicides in 2010 occurred among military members who had deployed to overseas contingency operations."[6] A recent study of Operation Iraqi Freedom veterans suggests that approximately 3 percent of these veterans will consider suicide.[7]

In addition, US spending on PTSD is in the millions. Recent projections suggest that the war waged in Iraq will ultimately cost US$2.2 trillion, including substantial costs for veterans' care through 2053, far exceeding the initial government estimate of $50–$60 billion.[8] The Congressional Budget Office reports that between 2004 and 2009, the Veterans Health Abministration (VHA) spent $2.2 billion on patients experiencing PTSD, traumatic brain injury (TBI), or both. The total spending for PTSD care over these five years was $1.4 billion.[9] The US Government Accounting Office has stated that $24.5 million was spent on PTSD research in fiscal year 2009. From fiscal year 2005 through fiscal year 2009, intramural PTSD research funding ranged from 2.5 percent to 4.8 percent of the Veteran Administration's medical and prosthetic research appropriation.[10]

In recent years, it has become clear that in addition to physical and psychological forms of PTSD, service personnel experience "moral injury," which involves spiritual or moral trauma. Jonathan Shay first introduced the term in his landmark book, *Achilles in Vietnam*, arguing that trauma has a moral dimension that destroys virtue. Brett Litz et al. argued that moral injury involves "an act of transgression that severely and abruptly contradicts an individual's personal or shared expectation about the rules or the code of conduct, either during the event or at some point afterward."[11] The National Center for PTSD currently defines moral injury as an "act of serious transgression that leads to serious inner conflict because the experience is at odds with core ethical and moral beliefs." This "serious inner conflict" is often linked with physical and/or psychological trauma, but moral injury is a distinct form of trauma in and of itself, expressed in expressions of guilt, shame, dishonor, and the violation of personal integrity. All of the definitions of moral injury involve an individual experience of trauma grounded in a perceived rupture of the moral–ethical world the soldier once knew. This rupture originates in specific lived experiences. The lived experience may involve physical or psychological violence perpetrated against an enemy, a military comrade, an innocent victim, or even the soldier herself. The key for our purposes is that the violence at the center of moral injury is violence expressed internally, ethically, spiritually, or morally by the soldier. Moral injury often is accompanied by physical and psychological trauma, but it is distinctive in its expression and origin.

Moral injury also takes the form of despair, driven by the sense that human life has no ultimate value or meaning. Lt. Col. and military chaplain Beth A. Stallinga refers to soldiers encountering "brute facts" that do not conform to their previous understanding of the world.[12] These brute facts—physical atrocities, psychological abuse, and the seeming randomness of life and death—upset soldiers' previous assumptions about the relative goodness or fairness of life. Chaplain William P. Mahedy comments, "Having confronted real radical evil, the veteran is no longer able to accept the cultural assumptions which formed the basis of precombat life. Evil of this magnitude encompasses an almost total immorality into which the soldier is drawn. This creates moral pain on a scale incomprehensible to most noncombatants. The veteran's entire belief system collapses into angry, often lifelong nihilism. This is the most enduring and intractable element of combat."[13]

Sometimes the upheaval is so strong that soldiers state that they wish they had died rather than live the empty existence they currently experience.

It is important to note that although this form of moral injury may occur as a result of participation in combat, research indicates that it also results from experiences in training and other noncombat contexts. Soldiers and caregivers report that as a result of participation in the military, the soldier's "soul may be fundamentally reshaped."[14] The person who leaves the military—or simply returns home from combat—is not the same person who joined the military. Her "self" has been altered. As a result, friends and family often comment that their returning loved ones are not the same people they knew before the war. Relationships are changed, because one of the participants in these relationships has changed. If no one is prepared to help the soldier and her family members negotiate new relationships with the "changed self," destructive patterns can develop. Statistics indicate that soldiers suffering from PTSD engage in behaviors that threaten the physical and psychological well-being of themselves and their loved ones. All of this is to be expected from someone whose "ground of being" has shifted and who has not received appropriate help negotiating this shift.

Up until fairly recently, moral trauma has not been distinguished from psychological trauma. As a result, military personnel suffering from moral injury were treated with traditional psychological techniques. However, in recent decades, it has become clear that moral injury requires a different kind of attention, and that current treatment approaches are inadequate to address this experience of violence. Psychiatrist Georgia Loeffler comments, "neither the diagnosis of posttraumatic stress disorder (PTSD) nor the current trauma-focused psycho-therapies adequately address the ethical dimension of combat trauma."[15] Dr. Edward Tick, a psychotherapist who has worked steadily with US war veterans since 1979, writes, "the traumatic impact of war and violence inflicts wounds so deep we need to address them with extraordinary attention, resources, and methods. Conventional models of medical and psychological functioning and therapeutics are not adequate to explain or treat such wounds. . . . PTSD is not best understood as a stress disorder, as it is now characterized. Rather, it is best understood as an identity disorder and soul wound, affecting the personality at the deepest levels."[16]

Veterans' descriptions of their struggles are in line with Tick's observations. One veteran states simply, "My soul has fled."[17] He elaborates, "You can feel the connection between your body and your soul when it starts to break." Others simply state that "a part of the self has died."[18] Unfortunately, many veterans encounter resistance, dismissal, or simple disbelief when they attempt to describe their trauma in terms of deep ravages to "soul."

However, a growing number of psychologists and other caregivers have begun to view moral injury as a distinct experience that can benefit from distinct treatment plans. Litz, a well-known researcher in this domain, has developed an approach to moral injury based on two common therapeutic techniques: exposure therapy and adaptive disclosure.[19] In this approach the soldier experiencing a violent moral disruption is guided through a reliving of the experience that caused the moral injury. Then she is guided through an imaginary conversation with a "benevolent authority figure" in order to process the experience, with an eye toward "forgiveness-related content."[20]

Thus, we posit that "moral injury" is a distinct kind of violence, involving a violent disruption of one's sense of right and wrong. Moral injury involves a perceived violation or upheaval of a preexisting worldview (which includes a moral, spiritual, religious, or ethical component). For example, one veteran declares, "I went to war to save humanity, but ever since I've felt like a mass murderer."[21] Participating in the military required him to perform acts that he viewed as murder, which completely up-ended his sense of his own moral self. Tick explains, "War survivors commonly report such situations in which they felt forced to betray their moral codes. Afterward, they pass through life without feeling, like wooden puppets on strings."[22]

The "serious inner conflict" associated with moral injury often becomes expressed in terms of guilt, shame, dishonor, and the violation of personal integrity. Tick describes this as "a removal of the center of experience from the living body without completely snapping the connection. . . . The center of experience shifts; the body takes the impact of the trauma but does not register it as deeply as before."[23] This violence often arises from violence that the soldier has seen perpetrated against others or that he has experienced personally, but it is a distinct form of violence, spiritual in nature, which must be addressed as such. Effective treatments must be directed toward the soul, not the psyche. Religious communities and traditions can speak to this upheaval.

Violence and Moral Injury

Given the nature of moral injury, efforts at treatment must involve a recognition that the individual suffering from moral injury is experiencing a particular kind of violence—moral, spiritual, religious, or ethical. This can frequently involve direct challenges to what he understands to be right and wrong, good and evil, human and inhuman. This is important, because typically we understand violence to involve the exercise of power by one party over another party that results in physical, emotional, psychological, or spiritual damage. In most cases, power is brought to bear by one person or group against another person or group, and this power causes trauma. However, research indicates that moral injury often occurs in the absence of an obvious offending party. Instead, moral injury is often the by-product of participating in an act of violence as the aggressor, or even simply while witnessing an act of physical violence perpetrated by and against others. Also, moral injury often results from willing participation in war or military action, so the individual suffering from moral injury cannot neatly be characterized as a victim. Finally, in attempts to address moral injury with acts of moral repair, initial research and anecdotal evidence suggest that it is often imperative to acknowledge that the same violence that prompted an experience of moral injury was necessary or at least appropriate from the perspective of other interested parties.

In addition, therapists have noted that some veterans suffering from moral injury admit to a certain kind of "charge" or "thrill" that accompanies violent action on the battlefield. Without in any way denying the guilt and shame they feel, some soldiers also admit to feeling a perverse kind of intimacy with the enemy, particularly in hand-to-hand combat or close combat situations: "The violence of battle can thus constitute a kind of reverse intimacy."[24] This can be profoundly unsettling, because a soldier may have powerful but negative feelings bound up with experiences of physical intimacy with an enemy. As a result, they are often unable to enjoy healthy intimate physical situations once they return home. To admit this can be shameful, so veterans frequently try to forget or repress these feelings.

Moral Repair

Clearly instances of moral injury and moral repair offer fruitful opportunities for the study of the relationship between religion and violence. If religious or moral worldviews provide the framework out of which moral injury is generated, experienced, and articulated, it only stands to reason that effective responses to moral injury may grow out of religious and moral worldviews. In addition to traditional psychological approaches to PTSD, mental health professionals, chaplains, ethicists, and individual military service personnel have increasingly suggested that moral trauma can be effectively addressed by drawing on the teachings and practices of religious traditions. As Stallinga writes, "Old beliefs about self and world shattered by modern warfare need transforming with the aid of sacred rituals and narratives."[25] Loeffler, a psychiatrist, comments, "we need to reach beyond psychology. . . . Including religion, theology, and spirituality is important as well."[26]

Virtually every religious community includes thoughtful reflection on experiences of violence as well as expertise in sacred practices designed to promote spiritual healing and well-being. However, to date therapists and scholars who have tried to treat moral injury have tended to focus narrowly on religious justifications for war and violence (e.g., just war theory) and ways in which religious language provides rhetoric to authorize and make sense of violence. Scant attention has been paid to the ways in which religious traditions can explain, provide insight into, and express the nature of the violence that occurs in moral injury. Similarly, there has been almost no attempt to identify long-standing religious practices that might offer effective responses to moral injury, apart from chaplain training. Such models draw on centuries-old religious traditions that have effectively addressed feelings of "wrongdoing." We will take these ideas in turn.

First, war is often invested with transcendent significance. There are various reasons for this, including the fact that war draws attention to existential concerns such as life, death, suffering, good versus evil, and humanity's imperfect and finite nature. War theorist Carl von Clausewitz insisted that war universally included the elements of threat, uncertainty, and chance.[27] With these elements come existential questions—reminders of life's uncertainty and fragility raise one's existential awareness. Everyday existence seems to take place on an elevated plane. As Tick writes, "war transforms the mundane into the epic and legendary." However, soldiers comment that war actually involves a tremendous amount of "down" time, time in which they are performing normal, even banal tasks. War, in fact, seems to be a largely mundane experience punctuated by brief moments of violence. In that sense, it can also be said that war couches brief but dramatic moments of violence in long stretches of "normalcy," but a different kind of normal, one shared with military comrades rather than family and friends.

As a result, war creates a new "normal" that is understood as a training ground and existential frame for moments of violence. The violence, although usually comprising a relatively small percentage of soldiers' actual experience, sets the tone and existential framework for all of the mundane experience. Violence thus becomes *the* existential ground for all of lived experience in the military. It becomes the lens through which mundane activity is viewed. War becomes the primary worldview for a soldier in combat. The military becomes her primary community, its priorities become her priorities, its institutions govern her social community, and its values become her values—in effect, the military becomes her religion.

This creates a potential conflict for soldiers who come into the military with strong religious, ethical, or moral codes that conflict with military values. For example, when someone who was raised to believe that killing is morally wrong joins the military, he joins a community in which killing is not only acceptable but, at times, expected and necessary. He is trained to kill and learns to expect that he will be put in situations that require him to kill. However, years of having been taught *not* to hurt or commit murder don't simply disappear overnight. As Stallinga writes, "we ask our warriors to contravene the ethical touchstones we have instilled in them since infancy, those culturally agreed upon moral imperatives which facilitate decency and civility in a normal context."[28] If that soldier eventually does wound or kill, there is a psychological and spiritual toll. As Shay has stated, "what spills blood wounds spirit."[29] A soldier may emerge from combat without a physical wound, but it is highly likely that she will have sustained a massive spiritual wound.

Less obviously, simply being given encouragement to kill can create a moral conflict, even for soldiers who never actually kill anyone. Soldiers who have been raised not to hurt others experience a clash of worldviews when they train for combat. In order to function effectively in the military and to survive in combat, the military worldview *must* prevail in a soldier's thinking and action. However, studies indicate that soldiers struggle with this clash of worldviews internally, even if they behave completely in accordance with military values outwardly.

In order to help military personnel embrace a military worldview, those in leadership (commanders, the government, and even the public) often invoke religious language to invest military activity with authority and significance. For example, soldiers and their families are frequently praised for the "sacrifices" they make. The death of a soldier is considered the ultimate sacrifice, but families are characterized as sacrificing their loved ones simply by being separated from them. For example, in a 2001 national address, the former president George W. Bush referenced a "4th grade girl, with a father in the military. 'As much as I don't want my Dad to fight,' she wrote, 'I'm willing to give him to you.'" Bush declared, "an entire generation of young Americans has gained new understanding of the value of freedom, and its cost in duty and in *sacrifice*."[30] Religious language, such as language of sacrifice, legitimizes the father's absence from his family. Investing war with religious or transcendent importance provides justification for pulling men and women away from their families and putting them in harm's way.

Finally, associating war with religious or cosmic significance gives individuals permission to act in ways that they would not have acted in everyday contexts. The nature of the violence they commit in the context of war differs qualitatively from that of other violence. This occurs as a result of situating that violence in a comprehensive military worldview that values violent acts authorized by the military command.

To be clear, we are not either condoning or criticizing the dynamic in which a military worldview rivals and eventually trumps other religious and moral worldviews. Rather, we are simply noting that such a dynamic occurs. As a result of this dynamic, many soldiers experience a conflict between the religious or moral worldviews that they bring into the military and the moral/ethical worldview of the military itself. This conflict, quite understandably, often gives rise to internal struggles. In some cases, the conflict results in moral injury.

Given the intimate relationship between the military and religious or moral worldviews, it is natural to turn to religious traditions for guidance on how to respond to moral injury. However, up until now, caregivers and scholars have tended to draw somewhat narrowly from religious thought and practice in their attempts to prevent and alleviate moral injury. Specifically, military officials, therapists, and scholars have tended to draw on the "just war" tradition and other schools of thought associated with ethics. The goal behind these strategies has been to reassure (or persuade) veterans that they have not done anything wrong. Renowned ethicists have established programs to train chaplains, unit commanders, and rank-and-file soldiers that war is a special circumstance, and that under certain conditions act that would otherwise be considered wrong are, in actuality, *not* wrong. There's only one problem: the soldiers, by and large, aren't buying it. They feel that they have done wrong, and efforts to persuade them they haven't largely don't work.

Many religious traditions, however, offer an alternative approach. They begin by allowing the soldier to state that he has done something wrong. They take the feelings of guilt and shame seriously. Rather than dismissing these feelings or attempting to finesse them away with abstract theological or ethical explanations, religious communities often offer an alternative approach that addresses guilt and shame associated with wrongdoing head-on. Stallinga refers to this as "bearing witness."[31] We understand this as the act of listening and completely accepting a soldier as she understands her own situation. This requires affirming the fact that she feels guilt, shame, confusion, and despair, and beginning the journey with her at that point, rather than offering excuses, explanations, or contradictions to her story.

Some therapists and chaplains have taken the lead in suggesting approaches to moral injury that draw on religious traditions and practices.[32] Prayer is an obvious example. Many chaplains and other religious leaders offer prayer as a means by which soldiers and veterans can bring their fears, guilt, shame, and brokenness into a moral forum, an existential arena. In that arena they may find forgiveness, healing, and guidance toward some form of restitution or penance. Similarly, every religious tradition has developed traditions for mourning and grieving that can be invoked and that allow individual soldiers to grieve for individuals they have hurt as well as for their own losses. These losses may be physical, psychological, material, or existential. For example, soldiers often express a loss of innocence, and therapists often note a loss of faith in the inherent goodness of humanity. Intangible losses such as these need to be grieved, and religion offers rituals for processing these losses as well as philosophical traditions that can help individuals make sense of these losses.

Thus, some therapists have instituted practices that resonate with religious practices and concepts without realizing that they are doing so. For example, Stallinga, both a chaplain and a military officer, encourages creating "sanctuary," a safe space for a guilty soldier to "flee to." Here she is invoking the biblical notion of "cities of refuge," described in Exodus. In the biblical world, several cities in the Promised Land were to be designated as safe havens for murderers, places where they were safe from punitive execution.[33] In the US military, the chaplain's office offers a metaphorical version of the "city of refuge," a place of utter confidentiality, free from recrimination. It's not clear that Stallinga is consciously referencing these cities of refuge, but her concept of refuge evokes this biblical imagery. Further work on religion and violence can shed light on other models of sanctuary spaces discussed in other religious traditions.

In addition, some individual soldiers have stumbled upon religiously grounded strategies for themselves, perhaps not even realizing that in their attempts to find some meaningful act they can perform in response to the guilt they feel, they are actually performing acts that have long been recognized as confessional or restorative. For example, one veteran posted a home-made video on YouTube, confessing what he understood to be "crimes" he committed against a specific town in Iraq. He determined that one way to redress the wrong he had committed was to raise funds for the town that his unit had attacked, thus providing some kind of restitution for his actions. This strategy of making amends is a long-standing common element in religious traditions around the world.[34]

In addition, many resources available in religious traditions have been ignored entirely, but they offer promising possibilities. Many religious communities include ritual traditions that specifically address wrongdoing, offering specific steps to take to acknowledge morally wrong acts, to make restitution, and to deal with feelings of guilt. For example, the Roman Catholic tradition of confession and repentance is instructive. A soldier need not belong to or believe in all the tenets of the Roman Catholic church in order for him to participate in a ritual modeled after confession, a formalized act in which he describes the actions he has committed and in which he develops, in conjunction with a sympathetic neutral party (a military chaplain, for example), a strategy for making amends.

Finally, certain theoretical work can be helpful as well. For example, it is common for scholars to describe military training in terms of scholar Victor Turner's "rites of passage." According to Turner, rites of passage involve three steps: separation, marginalization or "liminality," and aggregation. According to Turner, these rites "accompany every change of place, state, social position and age."[35] In the military, this involves the separation of an individual from the original group (civilian life, family), a liminal period in which he or she is transformed into a soldier; and finally a period that brings this individual into a stable social place again, but with a newly defined role (as a member of the armed forces). None of this is new.

However, this model does not adequately address a soldier's experience. There are at least two more moments in a soldier's life that should be addressed as full-fledged rites of passage. The first is when the soldier first moves into a combat experience. At this time, she is separated from the social context of training and thrust into a liminal experience in which she participates in and is transformed by combat. Unfortunately, there is no clear process of aggregation, in which the newly transformed soldier—altered from one who has not experienced violence into someone who has experienced violence—is reintegrated into a noncombat military community. Soldiers experience an incomplete rite of passage and they suffer as a result. Most recently this has been noted in military personnel responsible for drone strikes. Typically, someone who performs a drone strike performs this act geographically distant not only from the target, but also from fellow soldiers. After performing his duty, the operator simply returns home to his family. There is no recognition that the act of committing violence, even remotely, is a transformative act, and a rite of aggregation is necessary. As a result, such operators are left hanging between both the realities of combat (life and death consequences of their actions) and the mundane realities of everyday life, with no formal process available to them for aggregating back into society.

More importantly, there is no "rite of passage" for veterans who leave the military. Soldiers are formally discharged, of course, but they simply leave the service. There is no "training" for leaving the military that comes anywhere close to paralleling the process they participate in when they join the military. As a result, a soldier returns home still a soldier, and it is left up to her to figure out how to transition home. Veteran support groups are available, of course, but they are voluntary, not compulsory, and individuals who seek help with the transition are stigmatized. Consequently, our country is filled with former soldiers who were never trained how to be *former* soldiers rather than active duty soldiers.

Again, religious traditions offer models for this transition. For example, it is not unusual for Tibetan monks to set aside their monastic vows and rejoin the lay community after a period of time. When they leave the monastic community, they participate in a kind of "reentry" ritual that transforms them into lay members of society. There is no stigma attached to this reentry, and former monks participate in lay life fully, recognizing that they have left one role behind and now occupy a different role in society.

Some therapists have already begun to draw on religious practices as part of their caregiving. For example, Tick describes a trip that he led to Vietnam with a group of Vietnam veterans. During the course of this trip, one of the veterans participated in a ceremony that offered him a transformative experience: "our group climbed to the Buddhist temple atop Nui Ba Den, Lady Black Mountain, a scene of terrible fighting during the war but today a place of beauty and peace crowned with a Buddhist pagoda. There, with the help of the resident priest, Bob [a Vietnam vet] conducted prayers for the soul of the boy he had slain. . . . Finally, after decades of nightmares, Bob saw the boy's spirit smile at him. The soul of the boy, who would forever be fourteen years old in Bob's mind, offered the aging American veteran peace and the promise that from now on he would be Bob's spiritual ally, his helper and friend."[36] This trip, a spiritual pilgrimage, offered a transformative moment to "Bob," and as a result of that moment, he felt forgiven and freed to move forward in his life.

We are not denying that trips such as this one help veterans by yielding psychological benefits. But it would be wrong to reduce these practices—which can also be understood as religious ritual pilgrimages—to psychological efforts alone. As noted above, many who have experienced and treated moral injury experience guilt, shame, dishonor, and the violation of personal integrity. Effective moral repair addresses these problems, which are distinct from feelings of anxiety and fear. Moral repair that draws on religious thought and practices can be effective in its own distinctive way.

Conclusion: Moral Injury, Religion, and Violence

Until very recently, military commanders and clinicians have been reluctant to acknowledge spiritual/moral wounds as distinct from other forms of psychological trauma. In addition, they have been reluctant to employ therapeutic methods that didn't arise from traditional psychological sources, strategies rooted in religious traditions. This is a result, at least in part, of relatively superficial understanding of religion, violence, and their relationship. Effective moral repair must begin with sophisticated, mature education about the nature of religion, violence, and their relationship in instances of moral injury.

Clinical caregivers are gradually becoming comfortable, acknowledging that traditional psychological approaches to the treatment of PTSD can be augmented with the resources that religious traditions have to offer in preventing and alleviating moral repair. As Shay states, "Religious and cultural therapies are not only appropriate, but may well be superior to what mental health professionals conventionally offer."[37]

Moral injury, as a distinct form of PTSD, is an expression of a distinct form of violence experienced in the military resulting in moral, religious, and ethical wounds. It is grounded in religious, moral, and ethical worldviews, and it arises from a violent conflict between worldviews. As such, it will only be addressed effectively by strategies that recognize spiritual as well as physical and psychological wounds. As Stallinga states, "We treat the full human—body, mind, and spirit—because the whole person went to war."[38] Responsiveness to moral injury affirms that our soldiers are whole people. It affirms that they recognize the cost of war, both to themselves and to others. Feelings of guilt should be addressed directly (rather than attempting to rationalize them away). After all, a soldier who struggles with guilt is a soldier who is still attuned to the moral dimension of the universe, someone who does not hold life lightly.

Scholar and former chair in Ethics at the US Naval Academy Nancy Sherman writes, "Combat is nothing if not existential: it pits an individual against life and its ultimate challenges. It requires seeing the unspeakable and doing the dreaded. It is a role that is immersed and transformative and lingers long after a soldier takes off the uniform."[39] Military service exposes military personnel to a multidimensional experience of violence within a unique metaphysical framework, one that requires that individual soldiers set aside or subordinate previously held religious and moral codes as they embrace the worldview of the US military. As Shay asserts, "the wounds of war are fundamentally a religious issue. Something is lost when we package psychological wounds only as a mental health issue."[40]

Research into the nature, causes, prevention, and treatment for moral injury is in its nascent stage—much is left to be done. Loeffler notes, "While it has long been known that not all combat wounds are physical, the moral dimension of psychological injury remains largely unexplored, at least within mainstream mental health."[41] Early evidence suggests, slim as it may be, that religious thought, ritual practices, and healing strategies may offer effective means for addressing moral injury. In exploring this phenomenon, we are positioned to learn much about the complex nature and relationship between both religion and violence in contemporary military experience.

Notes

1. For a detailed discussion of dehumanization and moral distancing, see also David Livingston Smith, *Less than Human: Why We Demean, Enslave, and Exterminate Others* (New York: St. Martin's Press, 2011).
2. Albert Bandura has written extensively on moral disengagement as it relates to a range of behaviors. See A. Bandura, "Moral Disengagement in the Perpetration of Inhumanities," *Personality and Social Psychology Review* 3 (1999): 193–209; "Mechanisms of Moral Disengagement," in *Origins of Terrorism: Psychologies, Ideologies, Theologies, and States of Mind*, ed. W. Reich (Cambridge: Cambridge University Press, 1990), 161–91; "The Role of Selective Moral Disengagement in Terrorism and Counterterrorism," in *Understanding Terrorism: Psychosocial Roots, Consequences, and Interventions*, ed. F. Moghaddam and A. Marsella (2004), 121–50.
3. Dave Grossman, *On Killing: The Psychological Cost of Learning to Kill in War and Society* (2009), 292. Grossman also draws heavily from Stanley Milgram's classic studies of obedience to authority.

4. For example, John Crawford's *The Last True Story I'll Ever Tell: An Accidental Soldier's Account of the Way in Iraq*, which is a firsthand telling of his experiences both during and after the 2003 war. (New York: Riverhead Books, 2006).
5. "Veterans Statistics: PTSD, Depression, TBI, Suicide." http://www.veteransandptsd.com/PTSD-statistics.html (accessed January 10, 2014).
6. "The Veterans Health Administration's Treatment of PTSD and Traumatic Brain Injury among Recent Combat Veterans," Congressional Budget Office Study, February 2012, 12.
7. S. Maguen, D. D. Luxton, N. A. Skopp, G. A. Gahm, M. Z. Reger, T. J. Metzler, and C. R. Marmar, "Killing in Combat, Mental Health Symptoms, and Suicidal Ideation in Iraq War Veterans," *Journal of Anxiety Disorders* 25, no. 4 (May 2011): 563–67.
8. These numbers appear in a report generated by scholars, according to a new report, with the "Costs of War" project at Brown University's Watson Institute for International Studies (http://news.brown.edu/pressreleases/2013/03/warcosts).
9. "The Veterans Health Administration's Treatment of PTSD and Traumatic Brain Injury among Recent Combat Veterans," Congressional Budget Office Study, February 2012, 17.
10. "VA Spends Millions on Post-Traumatic Stress Disorder Research and Incorporates Research Outcomes into Guidelines and Policy for Post-Traumatic Stress Disorder Services," GAO-11-32, January 24, 2011.
11. Brett Litz, N. Stein, E. Delaney, L. Lebowitz, W. P. Nash, C. Silva, and S. Maguen, "Moral Injury and Moral Repair in War Veterans: A Preliminary Model and Intervention Strategy," *Clinical Psychology Review* 29 (2009): 695–706.
12. Stallinga, 17.
13. Quoted in Marty Mendenhall, "Chaplains in Mental Health: Healing the Spiritual Wounds of War," *Annals of the American Psychotherapy Association* 12, no. 1 (Spring 2009).
14. Edward Tick, *War and the Soul: Healing Our Nation's Veterans from Post-Traumatic Stress Disorder* (Wheaton, IL: Quest Books, 2005), 1.
15. M. D. George Loeffler, "Moral Injury: An Emerging Concept in Combat Trauma," *The Residents' Journal* 8, no. 4 (April 2013), 2.
16. Tick 2005, 2.
17. Tick 2005, 12.
18. Stallinga, 20.
19. See Loeffler, 2.
20. Loeffler, 2.
21. Tick 2005, 17.
22. Tick 2005, 19.
23. Tick 2005, 16.
24. Tick 2005, 20.
25. Beth A. Stallinga, "What Spills Blood Wounds Spirit: Chaplains, Spiritual Care, and Operational Stress Injury," *Reflective Practice: Formation and Supervision in Ministry* X, 13. "A version of this article was submitted in partial fulfillment of the requirements for the degree of Master of Military Studies at the Marine Corps Command and Staff College, Marine Corps University. The Opinions and conclusions expressed herein are those of the individual author and do not necessarily represent the views of the Marine Corps, or any other Governmental Agency"—required statement.
26. Loeffler, 3.
27. Stallinga, 14.
28. Stallinga, 15.
29. Quoted in Stallinga, 14.
30. Bruce Lincoln, 101, my emphasis.
31. Stallinga, 21.
32. See, for example, Dalene C. Fuller Rogers and Harold G. Koenig, *Pastoral Care for Post-Traumatic Stress Disorder: Healing the Shattered Soul* (Routledge, 2002); Rita Nakashima Brock and Gabriella Lettini, *Soul Repair: Recovering from Moral Injury after War* (Beacon Press, 2013); Serene Jones, *Trauma and Grace: Theology in a Ruptured World* (Westminster: John Knox Press, 2009).
33. Note that we have no evidence available indicating whether or not these cities were ever actually established, but this was an ideal presented in the texts.
34. Unfortunately, at the time of this writing this particular YouTube clip is no longer available on YouTube, but many other similar appeals do appear on the site.
35. Victor Turner, *The Forest of Symbols: Aspects of Ndembu Ritual* (Ithaca, NY: Cornell University Press, 1967), 94.
36. Tick 2005, 288.

37. Jonathan Shay, *Odysseus in America: Combat Trauma and the Trials of Homecoming* (New York: Scribner, 2002), 152.
38. Stallinga, 14.
39. Nancy Sherman, *The Untold War: Inside the Hearts, Minds, and Souls of Our Soldiers* (New York: W. W. Norton and Company, 2010), 20.
40. Stallinga, 16, referencing Jonathan Shay, "Healing the Wounds of War."
41. Loeffler, 3.

11

Marshall McLuhan and the Machiavellian Use of Religious Violence

Grant N. Havers

> *As I've tried to point out, the one inexorable consequence of any identity quest generated by environmental upheaval is tremendous violence.*
> —Marshall McLuhan[1]

> *What counts today is the image that authority presents, and not the doctrine that it may want to get across. Christianity is all about transforming the image that we have of ourselves.*
> —Marshall McLuhan[2]

The current revival of interest in the communication theory of Marshall McLuhan has also coincided with a steadily growing interest in the relation between his deeply felt Catholic faith and his study of the mass media. The posthumous publication of his lesser known writings on the role of Catholicism in the age of mass electric media has undoubtedly spurred this interest.[3] It is a challenge to scholars, however, to make sense of this relation since McLuhan himself often disavowed any adherence to a "fixed point of view" that shaped his understanding of media.[4] While it may be tempting to associate his faith with a "fixed point of view," this interpretation may too quickly understate and misunderstand the influence of Catholicism on his communications theory. McLuhan, who converted to Catholicism in the late 1930s as a young man, never abandoned or rejected his early philosophical embrace of Thomism as his studies of the media enjoyed great fame in the 1960s. As he admitted in private correspondence in the early 1970s, his communication theory "is Thomistic to the core. It has the further advantage of being able to explain Aquinas and Aristotle in modern terms."[5] The fact that McLuhan thought it was possible to modernize medieval scholasticism seems to suggest that, in his mind, his Catholic faith and its philosophical buttress Thomism were in no way a "fixed point of view" that hindered the study of media. If anything, Thomism was crucial to making sense of the media. Although McLuhan's rather creative reinvention of Catholic theology does not make him a classic Thomist, and may even counter the criticism that he is offering "Christian Humanism in modern dress,"[6] it is reasonable to spy in McLuhan's thought a political agenda that underlies this reinvention.

Even if it is evident, however, that McLuhan drew a close connection between his faith and his study of the media, it is still not obvious what the substance of that connection happens to be or why it holds importance for our own age. Although his most famous terms and phrases such as "global village" and "the medium is the massage" are part of our everyday modern vocabulary on the media, McLuhan shied away from providing a clear theoretical account of the relation between religion and mass media. His famous aphoristic style, which he commonly employed in his later years as a media theorist, further gives the impression that he was disinterested in providing any type of theory that would ossify into a dogmatic "fixed point of view." Nevertheless, his oeuvre is replete with insights that reveal his recurrent interest in the role of religion as well as its violent use and misuse in the modern era.

One reason that may justify the attempt to read into McLuhan's ideas a coherent and stable account of religion and its role in fostering violence throughout history is his interest in the most famous modern philosopher of realpolitik. If there is one philosopher that intrigued as well as troubled McLuhan, it was Machiavelli. From his earliest writings onward, McLuhan lamented the influence of the Florentine on modern politics. To be sure, that fact by itself does not make McLuhan particularly unique: many politically conservative writers have decried Machiavellianism as one of the greatest evils to be foisted upon the modern age. Most conservatives have opposed Machiavelli's infamous teaching, which is particularly relevant to my discussion, that rulers ought to appear to be pious, charitable, and humane even as their actions are often immoral by necessity.[7] Yet McLuhan's early opposition to a Machiavellian politics is interesting for two related reasons. First, McLuhan particularly opposes the Machiavellian misuse of religion for the purpose of violent change in our time. Second, he laments the fact that so many moderns, including his Christian brethren, fail to understand Machiavelli's influence and even go so far as to unwittingly make the Florentine's ideas more palatable and legitimate than they were intended to be.

McLuhan's moral opposition to Machiavelli may strike more than a few of his readers as counterintuitive, since he often took pains in later years to avoid "moralizing" about the effects of the modern age. Although he admitted that his early work, particularly *The Mechanical Bride* (1951), was characterized by "an extremely moralistic approach to all environmental technology," he came to realize in his later study of the media how "sterile and useless this attitude was"[8] and scrupulously attempted to avoid all judgments that may hinder understanding the impact of mass media. Nevertheless, as a conservative Catholic convert, McLuhan did not avoid making judgments about all phenomena that shaped the modern age. As late as 1977, McLuhan referred to the Industrial Revolution as a "bloodbath" that fragmented society while it fostered atomistic individualism.[9] Moreover, Machiavellianism, or the cynical use of religion for political purposes that may even justify violence, did not escape his judgmental eye. As I shall argue, McLuhan, as a Catholic convert, also never abandoned his view that Protestantism, working alongside Machiavellianism, played a large role in fostering religious and cultural violence in the modern age.

One other potential challenge to the attempt to read into McLuhan's ideas a critique of Machiavellianism may be the fact that, at times, he shows little interest in philosophical ideas apart from their epiphenomenal status in a particular age of media. That is to say, McLuhan often comes across as a technological historicist who reduces all ideas, including philosophical ones, to their historical context. Consistent with his most famous aphorism "the medium is the massage," McLuhan dismissed any implication that ideas can enjoy an influence independent of their original context. Since the media "work us over completely" and "leaves no part of us untouched, unaffected, unaltered," it logically followed that no idea escapes from the deterministic grasp of the media.[10] As a result, the very suggestion that an idea such as Machiavellianism would have any enduring influence beyond its own period of origin would strike McLuhan, the historicist, as absurd. McLuhan himself sometimes arrived at this conclusion with great clarity when he occasionally admitted that Machiavelli's defense of realpolitik as well as the modern nation-state was a product of the print age that was made possible by Gutenberg, and was no more relevant today than the printing press that made his thought possible: "Machiavelli is now as obsolete as Gutenberg from whom he stems."[11]

These extreme historicist judgments are fairly consistent with McLuhan's observations on the role of philosophy in general, as a discipline that both reflects and enhances the media of its age. Consistent with this judgment, McLuhan was inclined to dismiss the philosophy of Plato as a mere epiphenomenon of the great transition from orality to writing in antiquity. Despite his acute awareness of the threat that the new medium of writing poses to human memory, as he argues (through the voice of Socrates) in his dialogue the *Phaedrus* (275a–e), Plato, as McLuhan understood him, helped to advance, unwittingly, the age of writing that put an end to the primacy of oral speech. [Plato's ban on politically unsuitable poetry in his ideal city, which he famously advocates in the *Republic* (377b–e and 607c–608b), arguably contributed to this displacement of orality.] Moreover, Plato belonged to a "tribal" culture that was made obsolete by the print age of Gutenberg. His famous account of philosopher rule in the *Republic* was suited to a population that lived in a small community, a context that was buried by the massifying effects of the print age (although McLuhan left open the possibility that the age of electric media, with its attendant creation of the "global village," might make Plato's political dream a reality).[12] Even if at times McLuhan was willing to admit that Plato's famous description of the "cave," a realm of shadowy images which most human beings ignorantly confuse with reality, paralleled the "dreaming eye of the movie god casting his images on the dark screen,"[13] he never swerved from his position that Platonic philosophy was irrelevant to the more technologically sophisticated modern age. After all, Plato allegedly failed to adequately understand the effects of the new media in his time. Instead, he imposed an artificial order of "nature" on the chaos around him without fully comprehending that "man-made technologies" were far more powerful than anything natural.[14]

Given the pervasive influence of McLuhan's historicist account of philosophy that I have only sketched here, it may seem a daunting task to show that his interest in Machiavelli goes well beyond his observations that the Florentine belonged to a bygone age. For this reason, I divide up McLuhan's work into two stages: his early scholarship from the late 1930s to the late 1950s and his later studies from the 1960s until his death in 1980. At least in his early work, McLuhan ultimately understood that the legacy of Machiavelli is essential to comprehend, since he was the first philosopher in history to brazenly emphasize the eternally violent relation between religion and politics. Not only did Machiavelli seek to understand this relation: he went so far as to present religion as an indispensable way of creating a new politics or identity. Despite his historicist inclinations, McLuhan worried at least at this stage of his thinking that the normalization of Machiavelli's thought in modernity would even infect and adulterate the Christian tradition to which he faithfully adhered. In this stage, McLuhan even went so far as to associate Machiavellianism with Protestantism as the demonic duo that made modernity possible.

Significantly, in his later stage of scholarship in which he enjoyed his greatest fame as a media theorist, McLuhan radically altered his view of Machiavelli by increasingly downplaying and even dismissing the influence of Machiavelli: this shift was based on his shunning of any "moralistic" approach to media as well as his firm embrace of the historicist method. In the process, however, McLuhan ironically (and unwittingly) may have embraced a Machiavellianism of his own making, as he made extensive use of Christian symbolism for the sake of legitimizing his own politics of mass media. Moreover, even if he eventually dismissed the influence of Machiavellianism as historically obsolete, he never abandoned his Catholic suspicion of the role of Protestantism in fostering the violent identity crisis of the modern age. In blaming Protestantism, however, for this crisis, McLuhan was arguably following a Machiavellian logic, which he would otherwise dismiss as immoral and obsolete, that placed far more responsibility for this violence on a single faith tradition than on the agents of cynical realpolitik. To make sense of the twists and turns that characterize McLuhan's understanding of Machiavelli, I shall also draw upon Leo Strauss's famous study of Machiavelli, *Thoughts on Machiavelli* (1958), as well as other writings by Strauss. Throughout this discussion, I shall argue that McLuhan's thought is related to Machiavelli, whether he is an opponent or an imitator of the Florentine.

Machiavelli's Legacy

In the age of electric media, the idea of "identity" becomes both an opportunity and a challenge, since these new mass media encourage the impression that one's identity can be constructed and deconstructed at will. In the 1960s, McLuhan noticed this process with all its violent implications. "From Tokyo to Paris to Columbia, youth mindlessly acts out its identity quest in the theater of the streets, searching not for goals but for roles, striving for an identity that eludes them." Furthermore, "the new integral electronic culture creates a crisis of identity, a vacuum of the self, which generates tremendous violence—violence that is simply an identity quest, private or corporate, social or commercial."[15]

Yet McLuhan always made clear, in both stages of his work, that not only the media fostered this crisis of identity, but religion also played some role. In a 1970 interview "Electric Consciousness and the Church," McLuhan alluded to the eternally powerful nature of religion, particularly Christianity, because of its "mythical" power. "Myth is anything seen at very high speeds; any process seen at a very high speed is a myth. I see myth as the superreal. The Christian myth is not fiction but something more than ordinarily real."[16] This "super-real" myth, which McLuhan identified as the Incarnation, attains even greater influence in the age of electric media precisely because of the "instant awareness of all the varieties of human expression" that "reconstitutes the mythic type of consciousness, of *once-upon-a-time*-ness, which means all-time, out of time."[17] Even if the centralized bureaucracy of the Catholic Church, which was another effect of the now obsolete Gutenberg era, was out of date in this newly mythical time, the universally and infinitely expressible message of Christ would endure and grow in this new age.[18] McLuhan, however, left no doubt that this global dissemination of Christian myth would be in part a violent process. In a 1977 interview, "Our Only Hope is Apocalypse," McLuhan warned that instant awareness in this age would violently transform the Church: "At the speed of light, there is nothing but violence possible, and violence wipes out every boundary. Even territory is violated at the speed of light. There is no place left to hide. The Church becomes a Church of the soul."[19]

In this late stage of his life, was McLuhan claiming that the violence of identity politics, fuelled by the Christian faith, was simply a new product of the electric age of media? It would be too quick to answer in the affirmative here, since McLuhan, in both stages of his work, associated the usage of religion with upheaval. Religion, even before the electric age, was always a source of violence. In his early work in particular, McLuhan squarely blamed this violence on the negative dialectical relationship between Machiavellianism and Protestantism. As far back as his doctoral dissertation on the Elizabethan humanist Thomas Nashe (1941), McLuhan contended that Machiavelli was just as instrumental as Luther and Calvin in violently opposing the Thomistic unity of nature and grace. Machiavelli's repudiation of the Aristotelian teleology that, in its Catholic manifestation, attributed to nature a universal law of morality that all human beings understand by reason, placed the Florentine squarely into a Christian (i.e., Protestant) tradition that similarly rejected any concept of nature as the God-given foundation of the virtues. Both Machiavelli and the early Reformation theologians were practically identical in emphasizing the evil power of nature (particularly human nature) as well as the impotence of reason in saving humanity from the passion that constitutes this utterly fallen nature. McLuhan writes in his dissertation on Nashe:

> Most writers have recognized that his [Machiavelli's] Satanocratism or his violent scission of nature and grace, in which he is at one with Luther and Calvin, is thoroughly Christian. That is, Machiavelli, like Hobbes, Swift or Mandeville, cannot be explained except in terms of Christian culture. There is nothing pagan about his skepticism concerning human nature. He rather looked on nature as shut off from grace and as shut in upon itself, and abandoned to the interplay of its own distorted forces. Within this dying order, however, Machiavelli envisaged the ideal prince as a man devoted to political action, impressing his character upon the flux of events, and living solely for the commonwealth which alone is the expression of the integral laws of our now fallen nature. There is much of the Old Testament attitude in Machiavelli—the attitude of trust in the prince as one who cooperates with God to bring good out of evil, having regard to the passionate and blind violence of men.[20]

Within the two stages of scholarship that constitute his oeuvre, McLuhan never abandoned his perspective that the modern age at a philosophical level had sadly demolished the old medieval Catholic synthesis of reason, nature, and grace. Building on the intellectual antimodernism of Joyce, Eliot, Pound, Chesterton, and Wyndham Lewis, McLuhan in his early work "had prepared himself for the battle of the electric mindset by beginning his studies in that other battle between ancients and moderns that centered on Harvey and Nashe and that set the grounds for an industrial revolution based on the economics of the Protestant ethic and positivistic science."[21] At least in this early stage of scholarship, McLuhan did not hesitate in associating Machiavellianism with Protestantism in violently destroying the virtues of the medieval tradition while making way for the vices of the modern age. Six years after he completed his dissertation on Nashe, McLuhan, in his essay "American Advertising" (1947), wrote of the lingering, destructive legacy that both Machiavelli and Calvin had originally unleashed in the form of corporate capitalism, especially its success in deceiving the masses through advertising. McLuhan felt sorry for the modern intellectual who tries to immunize himself against the effects of modern advertising, which is so saturating in its influence that he must engage "in a perpetual guerilla activity" of critical analysis in a culture that is hostile to this sort of existence. Perhaps worst of all, this intellectual has been deprived of the intellectual resources that could have made sense of the modern age, thanks to the efforts of Machiavelli and Calvin in destroying medieval scholasticism:

> He is a sort of noble savage free-lancing amidst a zombie horde. The dangers attending this mode of existence are obvious. Should he find his energies suddenly depleted or his patience exasperated, he may be tempted to revive them by adopting some lethal myth-mechanism. And at all times he finds it hard to remember the common human nature which persists intact beneath all the modes of mental hysteria rampant from Machiavelli and Calvin until our own day.[22]

It may be tempting to argue here that McLuhan is simply playing the role of a Catholic polemicist who accuses Protestants of "practicing the evil precepts of *The Prince*," an accusation that Protestant polemicists have thrown right back at their Catholic opponents throughout modernity.[23] It may also be tempting to suggest that these ideas represent, by McLuhan's own admission, the "moralistic" stage of his thought. His essay "American Advertising" foreshadows the harsh anticapitalist tones of his first major work *The Mechanical Bride*, which he completed four years after this chapter appeared. Moreover, as I have already noted, McLuhan in his later work as a popular theorist of the media tended to dismiss Machiavelli's influence as obsolete in the new age of electric media.

Yet it would be a mistake to dismiss these early observations as just the obsolete reflections of a younger, more judgmental McLuhan. The "ancient–modern quarrel" that Machiavelli, along with early Protestant theologians, had ushered into being by the time of the Renaissance and the Enlightenment was a fairly recurrent theme in both stages of his thought. In 1946, McLuhan wrote his article "An Ancient Quarrel in Modern America," in which he sharply contrasted the crude capitalist vices of the Yankee North with the noble aristocratic virtues of the old South. In particular, McLuhan, who had spent some time teaching at St. Louis University in Missouri during the late 1930s and early 1940s, admired the South's greater, enduring respect for the old medieval trivium of grammar, rhetoric, and dialectical reason that preserved the last remnant of culture in an increasingly bourgeois America. The modern assault on this trivium, which privileged dialectical reason over grammar and rhetoric, laid the foundation for the ancient–modern quarrel.[24] The coldly calculating power of dialectics now reduced reason to pure instrumentalism, stripped of the leavening influence of natural law philosophy as well as the medieval grammarian's distrust of abstraction. McLuhan never abandoned his early position that the ancients (Isocrates, Cicero, Quintilian, and Augustine, as well as their modern heirs such as Nashe) were intellectually superior to the moderns in holding up the trivium as the true foundation of all learning. In his posthumously published *Laws of Media: The New Science* (1988), which he coauthored with his son Eric, McLuhan returned to the theme of the ancient–modern quarrel. At this time, however, he positioned this conflict in terms of the larger tension between the right and left hemispheres of the brain. Dialectical reasoning appealed to the logical structure of the left hemisphere, whereas rhetoric and grammar appealed to the artistic structure of the right. Only the premodern mind grasped this tension adequately: "with the trivium as a retrieval of the oral logos on the new ground of writing, the conjunction of grammar and rhetoric on the one hand, and dialectic on the other, provided a balance of the hemispheres." Yet the new print age of Gutenberg destroyed this "basis of liberal education and Christian humanism" since the "visual stress of the alphabet gained new ascendancy" and strengthened the rationalistic left hemisphere in the process.[25] Although McLuhan makes no mention of Machiavelli or Calvin in this context, it is evident that he never abandoned his early hope that the medieval trivium would be restored and the ancients would score the final victory over the moderns. In the process, Catholic humanism, aided by the new electric media that would replace the old print media, would reverse the worst effects of Protestantism in modernity.

To fully appreciate McLuhan's insights into the violent role of Machiavellianism and its relation to the use and misuse of religion to foster political change in the modern era, it is worthwhile to compare and contrast his understanding of the Florentine with that of Leo Strauss, arguably the foremost expert in the post–World War II era on Machiavelli's influence on modern political philosophy. Although there is no evidence that Strauss and McLuhan read each other's works, McLuhan perhaps anticipated the need for a scholar such as Strauss to make sense of the Florentine's legacy when he wrote in his dissertation on Nashe that "Machiavelli still awaits the historical scholarship which is necessary to put him in his true perspective."[26] Strauss's major study *Thoughts on Machiavelli* (1958) was considered by many on the postwar American Right to be the definitive work on the Florentine.[27]

Why, however, do I choose Strauss among the myriad of scholars that have written on Machiavelli? There are two related reasons that explain my choice. First, both Strauss and McLuhan were deeply interested in the relation between Machiavelli's legacy and the transformation of Christianity along Machiavellian lines in the modern age. Second, both scholars were troubled by the modern (and often Christian) normalization of Machiavelli's philosophy into a legitimate and defensible discourse. Although Strauss did not write extensively on Christianity and even took pains to distinguish the faith from modern political philosophy, a few Christians have praised him as a source of invaluable teachings on the meaning of the biblical tradition for moderns.[28] Like McLuhan, Strauss also saw the status of Christianity as absolutely central to a proper understanding of the "ancient–modern quarrel."[29] From their shared perspective, Machiavellianism had succeeded in the modern era perhaps beyond the Florentine's wildest dreams because most modern readers had not fully grasped the subtle threats that his thought posed to faith and politics. The post–World War II conservative author James Burnham, who is perhaps Strauss's closest rival as an authority of Machiavelli in this era, argued in his famous study *The Machiavellians: Defenders of Freedom* (1943) that moderns ought to embrace Machiavelli's harsh lessons on realpolitik as simply a common sense approach to statecraft. Yet Burnham is silent on the Machiavellian devaluation of religion as a mere plaything for political rulers.[30] Burnham's lack of interest in the Machiavellian distortion of religion radically sets him apart from the approach and emphasis of Strauss's hermeneutic.

What makes a comparison of Strauss and McLuhan potentially daunting, however, is the fact that McLuhan's historicist method, which I briefly discussed above, would have been absolutely opposed by Strauss. McLuhan was arguably as historicist as Burnham, who in fact praised Machiavelli for his disinterest in "timeless" political questions about the best political order as well as his belief in the relativity of political ideas.[31] As we have seen, McLuhan reduced Plato to the latter's historical context and even went so far as to claim that he understood the age of Plato better than Plato himself. After all, by McLuhan's standards, Plato had a "rearview mirror" understanding of the technological change (especially the transition from orality to writing) that was engulfing his age. Although Plato famously warned of the threat that the new medium of writing posed to human memory in his dialogue the *Phaedrus*, he understood these changes only *after* they were fully entrenched in ancient Greek culture. All this would have struck Strauss as a particularly crude version of historicism that privileges the insight of moderns (such as McLuhan) over ancients (such as Plato).[32] In a sense, Strauss's teaching on the power of philosophical ideas over their historic contexts was exactly the reverse of McLuhan's (and Marx's) historicist teaching.[33] It is quite probable that Strauss would have faulted McLuhan for the same reason that Strauss's Canadian admirer, the Tory political philosopher George Grant, did at the height of McLuhan's fame in the late 1960s. As Grant put it, the "McLuhanite cult" refused to ponder the nihilistic implications of technological change, particularly the danger of surrendering the control of electric media to Nietzsche's "last men" who desire nothing but the power to alter at will both politics and history.[34]

It could be argued that McLuhan has more in common with the political thought of Eric Voegelin, who corresponded with both McLuhan and Strauss in the post–World War II era.[35] McLuhan sounds like Voegelin when he positions Machiavelli into the context of a wider Christian tradition. In fact, Voegelin, in his review of Strauss's study of Xenophon's *Hiero*, took Strauss to task for failing to emphasize the biblical origins of Machiavelli's thought, particularly his praise of Moses as a prophet with the *virtù* necessary to create a new kingdom.[36] In general, both Voegelin and McLuhan believed that the most radical political movements in modernity, which were influenced in part by Machiavelli, have their origins in Protestantism, a faith tradition that both men suspected of encouraging dangerous immoderation and radicalism when it is applied to modern politics.[37]

Yet Strauss, I believe, had a deeper understanding of Machiavelli's influence on the modern Christian tradition than Voegelin did. Strauss always contended that the various allusions that Machiavelli makes to biblical religion should be treated with caution and should not be confused with any sincere indebtedness to any faith tradition on his part.[38] To be sure, Strauss agreed with both McLuhan and Voegelin that the Florentine was not a pagan in any sense, given his disinterest in the classical philosophy of Plato and Aristotle as well as his bold reinvention of virtue to mean *virtù*, the will to create new modes and orders in politics by immoral means if necessary. Strauss chided moderns who called Machiavelli a pagan, based on the false understanding of paganism as simply the desire for power by any means necessary. He also took moderns to task for projecting onto Machiavelli's thought a desire to restore the old pagan order that Christianity had destroyed. Machiavelli's interest in pagan authors, which was largely restricted to historians such as Thucydides and Livy, had nothing to do with the classical pagan belief in a natural teleology that called upon human beings to live a virtuous life. "A man of this sort is not properly called a pagan. Paganism is a kind of piety and one does not find a trace of pagan piety in Machiavelli's work."[39] In short, Machiavelli owed little to "Athens," the great pagan tradition that founded Western civilization.

Strauss was just as convinced that Machiavelli owed nothing substantial to "Jerusalem," that other great founding tradition of the West. At most, Machiavelli's interest in Christianity was confined to the usage of propaganda for rather un-Christian purposes as they were applied in the rough and tumble arena of politics:

> Jesus failed insofar as he was crucified. He did not fail insofar as the new modes and orders found by him have become accepted by many generations of many nations. This victory of Christianity was due to propaganda: the unarmed prophet conquered posthumously by virtue of propaganda. Machiavelli, being himself an unarmed prophet, has no other hope of conquest except through propaganda. The only element of Christianity which Machiavelli took over was the idea of propaganda. This idea is the only link between his thought and Christianity. He attempted to destroy Christianity by the same means by which Christianity was originally established. He desired to imitate, not Moses, the armed prophet, but Jesus.[40]

In his major study of Machiavelli, Strauss emphasized that "the Bible sets forth the demands of morality and religion in their purest and most intransigent form," demands based on charity, humility, and mercy that the Florentine could not realistically accommodate.[41] At best, Machiavelli replaces charity with calculation, since Christianity is simply too otherworldly for the all too worldly context of politics.[42] The biblical teaching on fear as well as love has also led to the most violent religious persecutions in history. The severity of biblical morality, however, did not deter Machiavelli from selectively making use of certain teachings from Scripture that may be politically useful, particularly the biblical validation of absolute rule (monarchy).[43]

Yet Strauss was not content to restate Machiavelli's famous objections to biblical morality and Christianity in particular. Instead, Strauss went so far as to argue that Machiavelli is the true progenitor of what later came to be known as "biblical criticism," or the modern theological attempt to distinguish between what is "mythical" in the Bible and what is "true." Although the honor of inaugurating this tradition usually goes to Spinoza in the Enlightenment period, Strauss argued that Spinoza was simply the heir to the Machiavellian tradition that first articulated this selective biblical hermeneutic. Before Strauss undertook his study of Machiavelli in the late 1950s, he credited (or faulted) Spinoza for persuading modern Christian and Jewish theologians that the Bible is essentially a work with human authorship. In his 1948 lecture "Reason and Revelation," Strauss writes,

> Many present-day theologians subscribe without hesitation to Spinoza's thesis that the Bible is not everywhere truthful and divine. They reject therefore the belief in the verbal inspiration of the Bible and in the historical authenticity of the Biblical records. They reject especially the belief in miracles. They admit that the Bible abounds with mythical notions .... Modern theology stands or falls by the distinction between the central or true and peripheral or mythical elements of the Bible.[44]

As Strauss came round to his mature view that Machiavelli is the true founder of modern political philosophy,[45] the main theme of his *Thoughts on Machiavelli*, he also radically revised his earlier position that Spinoza invented modern biblical criticism. Without Machiavelli's influence, Spinoza could not have articulated his distinction between what is true (e.g., charity) and what is mythical (e.g., miracles) in the biblical text. Moreover, Spinoza argued all this in order to defend the modern regime of liberal democracy on biblical grounds. In brief, if charity is the most central teaching of the Bible, then the Bible did not object to the political equivalent of "love thy neighbor as thyself," which amounted to freedom for all human beings within a liberal democratic regime.[46] Whatever the validity of Spinoza's attempt to democratize the Bible, Strauss was convinced that he was acting as an apt pupil of the Florentine.[47] It was Machiavelli who first made bold distinctions between what is "true" and what is "false" in the Bible: a true teaching is one that encourages Christians to spurn "effeminacy" and take up the manly duties that the political life requires.[48] Spinoza similarly calls upon citizens of a liberal democracy to read the Bible in a manner that commands fidelity to this regime.

No matter how salutary the effects of Spinoza's biblical criticism were, which included the defense of the one regime in history that extended full political rights to Jews, Strauss nevertheless took the hard-line view that any politicization of the Bible's meaning is "blasphemous."[49] The fact that Machiavelli concealed his blasphemous view of Scripture as a politically useful text should not, Strauss believed, conceal his enduring influence over the liberal theology of the modern age. As Strauss writes in *Thoughts on Machiavelli*,

> A liberal theologian once said within my hearing that the traditional judgment on blasphemy is based on too narrow a conception of God's honor. He used the analogy of a very wise and very powerful king who would tolerate and even enjoy jokes about himself however smarting, provided they are graceful and do not create a public scandal. This argument seems to us so patently inappropriate that we may dismiss it without any discussion. We prefer to submit the following consideration. The kinds of unbelief with which we are most familiar today are respectful indifference and such a nostalgia for lost faith as goes with an inability to distinguish between theological truth and myth. Are not these kinds of unbelief much more insulting to belief than is an unbelief like Machiavelli's which takes seriously the claim to truth of revealed religion by regarding the question of its truth as all-important and which therefore is not, at any rate, a lukewarm unbelief? Furthermore, if, as Machiavelli assumes, Biblical religion is not true, if it is of human and not of heavenly origin, if it consists of poetic fables, it becomes inevitable that one should attempt to understand it in merely human terms.[50]

If Strauss is right, one of Machiavelli's greatest successes lies in making a "blasphemous" interpretation of the Bible so respectable that it has been taken up by the liberal theologians of our time who are blissfully unaware of their indebtedness to the Florentine.[51] These theologians as well as modern political scientists have succeeded in giving "Machiavelli's teaching an air of perfect respectability."[52]

McLuhan, at least in the early stage of his scholarship, certainly shared Strauss's worries about the subtle, concealed, and misunderstood legacy of Machiavelli in modernity. In his 1954 lecture "Catholic Humanism and Modern Letters," McLuhan almost sounds like Strauss when he targets the respectability that Machiavelli has achieved in the modern age.

> The positive value in Machiavelli's discovery was that it showed how man's factive intelligence could be turned to artistic use in fashioning cities and states. Machiavelli did not discover that rulers and princes apply perfidy, falsehood, cruelty, and treachery as techniques of power manipulation. Previously in doing these things rulers had felt guilty. By formulating bad faith as a principle of power politics, Machiavelli raised it to a new level of instrumental availability. He enabled men to use this age-old instrument quite impersonally and with a clear conscience. The ultimate receipt for deceit, said Bismarck, is truth.[53]

Even if McLuhan is vastly overstating just how "guilty" pre-Machiavellian rulers felt about their immoral deeds, he is at one with Strauss in targeting the new legitimacy that realpolitik enjoys in modern politics, free of the moral condemnations that the earlier pagan and biblical traditions would have imposed. McLuhan also blames Machiavelli for opening the door to the most violent politics of the modern age, the totalitarian regimes of the twentieth century. "Through this door men have seen a possible path to the totalitarian remaking of human nature. Machiavelli showed us the way to a new circle of the Inferno."[54]

How exactly did this totalitarianism affect the Church in the modern age? In the same lecture, McLuhan associates the liberal theology of John Lindberg with this Machiavellian legacy. Lindberg, a Swedish nobleman who worked for the United Nations in the post–World War II era, argued in his work *Foundations of Social Survival* (1953) that the survival of humanity depended on the world's adoption of Christian brotherly love (charity).[55] Yet Lindberg, as McLuhan read him, was merely echoing the teachings of the Florentine. This nobleman "is not a Christian but he thinks Christianity might be made to work by non-Christians. In short, he proposes practical Christianity as a sort of Machiavellian strategy of culture and power."[56] The moral teachings of the Christian faith would serve "world government." This Christianization of power politics would go far beyond the original intent of Machiavelli:

> We are, then, confronted by this contrast, that with Machiavelli at the beginning of the great secular era which we call the Renaissance and the modern period in history and letters, a lie about man was made the basis of secular prediction and control. And today at the end of the Renaissance a great truth about man is being taken up as the instrument of the totalitarian transformation of man and society. That truth which is our freedom can, neglected by us, become the means of an enslavement of mind and spirit surpassing any tyranny of which history makes mention.[57]

In the same year that he delivered this lecture, McLuhan also penned a full review of Lindberg's book. Here his language was even harsher, questioning both Lindberg's integrity and intent. The Swedish nobleman is described as initially a "Manichean" who was "resigned to the ordinary necessity of rule by myth and lie" who now insists that "the new conditions of global intercommunication compel us to scrap the rationalist Manichean hypothesis in favour of a plunge into faith and the City of Love."[58] Yet Lindberg, according to McLuhan, had not completely abandoned his realpolitik as he called for a return to old Christian mores. Noting his indebtedness to Marx, McLuhan attributed to Lindberg the old Machiavellian view that "reason is the myth-making power which produces the ruler."[59] Given this understanding of reason, it is not a mystery as to what the role of religion ought to be in the new electric age. "Myths are for Lindberg the traditional religions imposed on men. They are products of reason. They are expedient lies." Although Lindberg went on to argue that Christian love, practiced on a global scale through the use of global media, would undermine the "static, myth-built cities of the Western world," Lindberg's "switch" from a politics of fear to one based on love did not persuade his reviewer that Lindberg had abandoned any secret political agenda in the process. "Not belief but necessity urges him to a Christian idea of society and government. It is the same conviction which leads him to abandon the Manichean principles of realpolitik."[60] With as much conviction, McLuhan, in the early stage of his scholarship, was a visceral opponent of the cynical political usage of Christian credos.

McLuhan's Machiavellianism

Why, then, did McLuhan later abandon his suspicion of the Christianized version of realpolitik? The answer to this question is identical to the reason that McLuhan later dismissed the influence of Machiavelli as historically obsolete in the electric age. In the second stage of his scholarship (from the 1960s until his death in 1980), McLuhan often gave the impression that the politics of Machiavellianism, with its emphasis on power, conformity, and secrecy, had no place in the transparent age of electric media in which it was almost impossible to control, much less conceal, the flow of information. (Perhaps for this reason, McLuhan saw the vast bureaucracy of the Catholic Church as *passé* in this age.[61]) In true historicist fashion, McLuhan reduced the influence of Machiavelli to an age that witnessed the transition from the Middle Ages to early modernity. The old communities and kingdoms of the medieval tradition, McLuhan noted with a hint of romanticism, had given way to the harsh nation-states that Machiavelli endorsed. "As the old medieval world of organic coherence fell open, many, like Machiavelli, saw the possibility of dealing with the state as a work of art." This transition was inevitably violent, as politics was reduced to realpolitik and people were forced to become isolated individuals. All this was contrived, similar to a work of art. "All power became a masquerade of fakes and fictions. Loss of the traditional forms of identity and loyalty freed everybody to become an isolated person in somebody's game."[62]

Yet the new age of electric media has ushered in a comparably revolutionary period of transformation. Politics is now participatory, not secretive. Like the Catholic Mass, the new media has closed the gap between rulers and ruled. "On this planet, the entire audience has been rendered active and participant."[63] People, especially youth, no longer wished to conform to the mass individualism of the print age. These youth wanted "roles," not places in an administrative machine. In short, the age of Machiavelli was over. "The young have abandoned all job-holding and specialism in favour of corporate costuming and role-playing. They are in the exact opposite position of Hamlet, who lived in an age when roles were being thrown away, and Machiavelli and individuals were emerging. Today, Machiavelli has been thrown away in favor of role-playing once again."[64] Yet this "tribalistic" world, which encourages corporate identity and role-playing at the expense of private and individualistic identities, would not witness the end of religion. The secret and administrative nature of the Church, we have seen, would give way to the demand for a more involving and participatory faith.[65] New religious identities would be created from below rather than imposed from above. Predictions that religion would disappear with the rise of secularism were dead wrong. As the new technologies of television and the computer extend consciousness, a new age of faith would emerge: "I think that the age we are moving into will probably seem the most religious ever. We are already there."[66]

McLuhan held out the hope that only Christianity can help human beings survive these momentous changes. As old identities are destroyed and new identities are created in equally violent ways, rationalism would be far less effective than faith. "It is not brains or intelligence that is needed to cope with the problems which Plato and Aristotle and all of their successors to the present have failed to confront. What is needed is a readiness to undervalue the world altogether. This is only possible for a Christian." These worldly changes would overwhelm the secular mind (as well as the institutionalized Church), which "struggles to escape from this new pressure," but not the Christian. "Thus war is not only education but also a means of accelerated social revolution. It is these changes that only the Christian can afford to laugh at."[67] How, exactly, though, did the born-again Christian of the electric age withstand these pressures with greater success than anyone else?

McLuhan's surprising answer to this question is that Christians will make bold use of their new power, armed with the electric media, to transform their own faith tradition in a manner that, he believed, was closer to the original (premodern) participatory nature of the Church before it became hopelessly bureaucratized. Far from being the consistent determinist that his critics make him out to be, McLuhan attributed great transformational power to believers in the Church. "In Jesus Christ, there is no distance or separation between the medium and the message: it is the one case where we can say that the medium and the message are fully one and the same." Electric media would fulfill the promise of Christianity at long last:

> In fact, it is only at the level of a lived Christianity that the medium really is the message. It is only at that level that figure and ground meet. And that also applies to the Bible: we often speak of the content of Scripture, all while thinking that this content is the message. It is nothing of the sort. The content is everybody who reads the Bible: so, in reading it, some people "hear" it and others don't. All are users of the Word of God, all are its content, but only a small number of them discern its true message. The words are not the message; the message is the effect on us, and that is conversion.[68]

What, then, would be the most important effect of this transformational fulfillment of the Christian message in the age of television and the computer? McLuhan hoped, and even expected, that the famed "global village" would accomplish what the medieval Church had only imagined: the Christian unity of mankind. This messianism was so rooted in McLuhan's thought that there are even traces of it in his early, "moralistic" phase of writing. In his 1954 lecture, "Catholic Humanism and Modern Letters," he mused that the medium of poetry, as long as it is informed by Catholic humanism, may lead to "the transformation of all common life and politics," which may then provide "the intellectual matrix of a new world society."[69] Ten years later, McLuhan elaborated upon this theme in his famous study *Understanding Media: The Extensions of Man*, in which he emphasized that our electric media had united humanity as never before. "In the electric age we wear all mankind as our skin."[70] Yet in this second stage of his thought, in which he claimed that he had scrapped all his previously obsolete "moralistic" judgments, McLuhan was not reluctant to draw out the religious implications of the new electric age. McLuhan replaced poetry with electric media as the revolutionary force that might fulfill the old Catholic dream of a unified human family: "might not our current translation of our entire lives into the spiritual form of information seem to make of the entire globe, and of the human family, a single consciousness?"[71] In his private correspondence during this later stage of media studies, McLuhan was even more explicit in his emphasis on the electric media's fulfillment of the Christian message:

> Another characteristic of man's humanity is his freedom in community, which the Christian community provides. Christian freedom is found in the corporate freedom in the mystical body of Christ, the Church. The electric age has so involved man with his whole world that he has no individual freedom left. He only has a corporate freedom in the tribal context. The hope of man is that he can be changed sacramentally so that he will eventually come to an awareness of himself in his community and discover individual freedom in the community.[72]

To be sure, McLuhan was not predicting in a Polyannish fashion that the electric age would bring about heaven on earth. In his famous *Playboy* interview (1969), McLuhan starkly warned that the new age of tribalism, which put an end to the bourgeois individualism of the print age, would impose a stern morality on its members and that marriage and the family in particular would become "inviolate institutions," whereas infidelity and divorce would "constitute serious violations of the social bond, not a private deviation but a collective insult and loss of face to the entire tribe."[73] Furthermore, the whole process of change would be a violent one, in which nation-states would disintegrate into tribalist enclaves while peoples search for new identities in a violent global theater of the absurd: "as men not only in the U.S. but throughout the world are united into a single tribe, they will forge a diversity of viable decentralized political and social institutions."[74] Within this new global consciousness, the old medieval dream of global unity may still happen as media such as the computer fulfill the mission of the Church. "In a Christian sense, this is merely a new interpretation of the mystical body of Christ; and Christ, after all, is the ultimate extension of man."[75] Although humanity may build a New Jerusalem of unity amidst disunity, the opposite may also be a distinct possibility: "There are grounds for both optimism and pessimism. The extensions of man's consciousness induced by the electric media could conceivably usher in the millennium, but it also holds the potential for realizing the Anti-Christ—Yeats's rough beast, its hour come round at last, slouching toward Bethlehem to be born."[76]

The grounds for optimism to which McLuhan briefly alludes here not only include the possible hegemony of the Christian message within the new global village. McLuhan also hoped that Protestantism, an old epiphenomenon of the individualistic print age, would gradually disappear in the new tribalistic electric age. As early as his "Catholic Humanism and Modern Letters," McLuhan was confidently predicting that Protestantism, which was historically preoccupied with the purity of the Bible, "was born with printing and seems to be passing with it. There again, the Catholic alone has nothing to fear from the rapidity of the changes in the media of communication."[77] Even late in life, McLuhan never abandoned this expectation. In a 1977 conversation with the Catholic scholar Fr. Pierre Babin, he once again pointed to the historical obsolescence of the Reformation faith tradition. Since "Luther and the first Protestants were 'schoolmen' who were trained in literacy," it followed that their embrace of print and the new visual age of reading would doom their faith to the same future that the book and the newspaper were being consigned.[78] It is not that McLuhan was predicting the total disappearance of Protestantism even though he claimed that Protestants fail to understand the new media due to their tendency to "prefer moral alarm to understanding."[79] He often lamented the fact that a "resurgence" of Protestantism was indirectly influencing the growing tendencies in the Catholic Church to embrace the liberal reforms of Vatican II, which, in his view, diminished and devalued the mystery of the Latin Mass. The Church's embrace of the Protestant custom of having the celebrant face the congregants removed the essential mystery of the Mass. "A continuous confrontation of the audience by the celebrant reduces the occasion to the merely humanistic one. A Catholic priest, in this regard, possesses no more power or mystery than a Protestant padre."[80]

An additional ground for optimism in this age of change lay in his prediction that conservatism may make a comeback in the electric age. This prediction seems particularly counterintuitive, since conservatives have often described themselves as opponents of modern change. McLuhan even concurred with the classic conservative position that this tradition fights a hopeless battle against modern change: "all the conservatism in the world does not afford even a token resistance to the ecological sweep of the new electric media. On a moving highway the vehicle that backs up is accelerating in relation to the highway situation. Such would seem to be the ironical status of the cultural reactionary."[81] Even if conservatives could not control the pace of change (who could?), it did not follow, in McLuhan's view, that conservatism would disappear altogether. If anything, the new tribal order which, as we have seen McLuhan argue, imposes a strict and austere morality on matters of marriage and family, would perhaps create a new type of conservatism that is no longer bourgeois, private, individualistic, or Protestant. Instead, "The world tribe will be essentially conservative, it's true, like all iconic and inclusive societies; a mythic environment lives beyond time and space and thus generates little radical social change ... We can see in our own time how, as we begin to react in depth to the challenges of the global village, we all become reactionaries."[82]

One does not have to be an absolute devotee of Leo Strauss's hermeneutic, as it is applied to Machiavelli, to suspect that there is something amiss in McLuhan's usage of terms such as "Protestant" or "conservative." In associating Protestantism with liberal modernity, McLuhan was portraying this faith tradition, perhaps in a conservative Catholic fashion, as a purely political force with little doctrinal value. At times, he even gave the impression that Protestantism is more of "a political ploy rather than a doctrinal adhesion."[83] It is far from evident, however, that this association is an accurate one. The fact that twentieth-century Protestants embraced liberalism does not justify the conclusion that the entire faith tradition was liberal or unequivocally modern or individualistic. In fact, it has been argued by the evangelical church historian Mark Noll that Vatican II encouraged, rather than imitated, the rise of liberal Protestantism in the 1960s.[84] McLuhan also fails to take into account the degree to which the Enlightenment liberalized Protestantism in a manner that would have surprised Luther and Calvin (whom, we have seen, McLuhan once accused of Machiavellianism). John Lindberg's support of world government as the epitome of Christian love, which McLuhan vigorously decried as Machiavellian, arguably has far more to do with the legacy of the Enlightenment than with that of Protestantism. McLuhan, once again, seems to share Eric Voegelin's view that the modern age has been deeply shaped by the most radical currents in the Protestant tradition. Yet the Enlightenment, particularly the biblical criticism that Spinoza inaugurated, arguably made the Protestant tradition more individualistic than its earliest theologians would have supported. Here Strauss's focus on the need to disentangle the Enlightenment from Protestantism is relevant, since modern philosophers such as Spinoza used quasi-Protestant language in a Machiavellian manner that, directly or indirectly, subverted the strict theology of the Protestant tradition.[85] Strauss arguably would have chided McLuhan for the same reason that he chided Voegelin: in Strauss's view, Voegelin inaccurately conflated the "pseudo-Protestantism" of Spinoza, which bordered on atheism, with the real McCoy. Spinoza denied the authenticity of miracles, after all.[86]

Despite McLuhan's antimodern posturing that was evident in his dismissal of traditional conservatism as obsolete, it is also likely that he himself adhered to a political agenda in his reinvention of conservatism as a tribalist phenomenon in the electric age. McLuhan was arguably reinventing the meaning of conservatism for his own purposes, namely, to justify an anti-individualistic and antibourgeois conservatism in the new age of media.[87] Yet, as Strauss would argue, this version of conservatism barely deserves the appellation of "conservatism," since the most traditionalist conservatives wedded to throne and altar have always been suspicious of a "universalism" that suppresses historical, religious, and cultural particularity. (George Grant, McLuhan's onetime critic, was this type of conservative.)[88] McLuhan never quite explains how these new conservatives, or "reactionaries," could ever conform to the globalizing effects of media that attack the "closed" societies that conservatives cherish: there is nothing "inclusive" about a conservative society, despite McLuhan's reinvention of its meaning to fit the age of the global village.[89] (McLuhan could well respond here, with some justification, that the "conservatism" of today is just the old liberalism, an observation that Strauss would have supported. As McLuhan once quipped, "Novelty causes antiquity."[90])

Was McLuhan, then, a Machiavellian after all in his political reinvention of Protestantism and conservatism? In Strauss's terms, is McLuhan a "lukewarm" Christian who, in a true Machiavellian fashion, prefers to focus on his "earthly fatherland" at the expense of the "heavenly fatherland?"[91] Various readers have suspected McLuhan of harboring a secret political agenda, including Marxist critics who accused him of defending neo-capitalism through his emphasis on the uncontrollable, deterministic effects of technology.[92] Although I will not speculate on whether McLuhan was intentionally Machiavellian his reinvention of Catholic theology as a myth that fits the electric media is remarkably similar to the Machiavellian logic that he decried in Lindberg's theology of world government. In the process, McLuhan ends up sanctioning a version of Catholicism that has more in common with modern historicism than with medieval scholasticism.[93]

In order to fit Catholic theology into the global village, McLuhan, in his second stage of his communication theories, takes pains to show that the fulfillment of the universality of the Christian message was now possible, if not already present, in the new electric age. As we have seen, McLuhan contends that the Gospels are now available to all human beings as never before, who have become the "content" of Scripture. Moreover, the best advice that McLuhan could give to the Catholic Church is to recognize that its hierarchical and secretive structures were an atavism in an age that banished forever the private, individualistic identity. In true historicist fashion, McLuhan even interpreted the truth of Christianity as shaped and determined by the historical age in which it was practiced. Here McLuhan sounded like the Florentine when, in one of his last works, he praised the early Church for understanding the need to spread its "propaganda":

> "Propaganda cannot succeed where people have no trace of Western culture." These words of Jacques Ellul in *Propaganda* draw attention to one of the crucial features of Western history. The Christian church, dedicated to propaganda and propagation, adopted Greco/Roman phonetic literacy from its earliest days. The perpetuation of Greco/Roman literacy and civilization became inseparable from Christian missionary and educational activity. Paradoxically, people are not only unable to receive but are unable to retain doctrinal teaching without a minimum of phonetic or Western culture.[94]

Is McLuhan, then, arguing, as Strauss thought Machiavelli did, that the most powerful tool of Christianity is its propaganda? A couple of pages later, McLuhan observes that the individualism of the Christian faith, which is essential to its practice, is also inseparable from the ancient origins of the faith. It is also inseparable from the medium of the alphabet. "This individualism may be what made Greco/Roman institutions attractive to Christianity, since Christian revelation stresses the private responsibility of all individuals in its doctrine of the resurrection."[95]

If the truth of Christianity, then, is inextricably tied to its classical, individualistic, private, and institutional origins, what happens to this essential truth when the age of the alphabet and print media is succeeded by the age of the television and computer? At times McLuhan often arrived at the conclusion that the old Greco-Roman structure as well as the essential truth of Christian individualism that it fortified could not survive the electric age, which seemed to contradict his optimistic view that the message of Christ was at long last available to all in the global village. In his 1970 interview "Electric Consciousness and the Church," McLuhan urged his brethren to take notice of the historical fact that "Christianity began in Greco-Roman culture," a fact of "enormous significance" that had not been "heeded" by theologians. McLuhan even mused that the "death of God" theology emerged in the 1960s because the Church had held onto its truths as "concepts" that, unlike "percepts," do not encourage mass participation.[96] He went on to observe that Christianity, not simply the Church, "is in for trouble" because it "supports the idea of a private, independent metaphysical substance of the self." This old metaphysics is simply *passé* in the new media age: "Where the technologies supply no cultural basis for this individual, then Christianity is in for trouble. When you have a new tribal culture confronting an individualist religion, there is trouble."[97] Three years later, in his article "Liturgy and Media: Do Americans Go to Church to Be Alone?" McLuhan openly doubted whether the Greco-Roman "inheritance which had been the early cultural matrix of the Church can now be seen in the electric age as a mere expendable husk." Was this inheritance now "a mere political escarpment" that would be overcome by "seas of electric information which now engulf the entire planet?" Did it make any sense for the Church to "transmit the Greco-Roman framework of categories" to tribalist peoples that do not think in individualistic terms? Was it high time to submit "to the electronic pressure to abandon the visual and rational space that began with Plato?"[98]

Whatever the validity of these observations, McLuhan also thought that they provided reason to think that the world was already living through an apocalypse.[99] Even when he sounded optimistic that Christianity alone can transform identity or that the "poetry" of God, "incarnating and uttering the world," can withstand all these changes, McLuhan never abandoned his pessimism on the inevitability of the conflict between individualists and tribalists.[100] The only way to reconcile this contradiction in McLuhan's thought is to distinguish, in a historicist fashion, between the old individualistic Greco-Roman Christianity and the new tribalist participatory Christianity of the new age. McLuhan may have been following the Florentine more closely than he realized when he associated the truth of Christianity with its institutions over time.[101] Yet this distinction between ancient and modern Christianity was not simply based on differentiating political manifestations of the Church from one era to another: it was McLuhan's intent to distinguish between the truth of Christian individualism and the new "myth" of participatory Christianity which is revealed at "high speeds" in the electric age.[102] McLuhan could confidently predict that we are living in the "most religious" age ever precisely because the universal dissemination of the Christian message had become far more transformational than adherence to old, discredited notions such as individualism.

As we have seen, McLuhan sometimes accused Protestants of practicing a political agenda that masqueraded as doctrinal purity. Yet McLuhan shows no reluctance in defending a political agenda of his own, even in that late stage of life in which he supposedly spurned all moralistic judgments. It is hard to avoid the conclusion that he was compelled to reinvent the very meaning of Christianity in order to force the faith to fit the global village, or at least his theory of it. His early defense of Thomistic natural law underwent a massive shift in meaning. In his early stage, McLuhan, in "American Advertising," celebrated the fact that the "common human nature" that had been battered by mass culture still "persists in fact beneath all the modes of mental hysteria rampant from Machiavelli and Calvin until our own day."[103] At the end of the 1960s, however, McLuhan denied that there was an objective human nature altogether, a position that would have shocked both the Florentine and the Reformer. The media now defined nature. "The new media are not bridges between man and nature: they are nature." Moreover, "they are the real world and they reshape what remains of the old world at will."[104] This last statement goes far beyond his attempt to modernize Thomism, which I quoted at the beginning of this essay, since he is denying that there is a "natural law" beyond the control of media today.

McLuhan had no choice but to arrive at this conclusion, since he was absolutely convinced in his second stage of thought that only flexible identities could withstand the violent transformations of the electric media age. We have already seen McLuhan celebrate a new participatory Christianity, which is made possible by the globalization of media; this new movement stands a good chance of replacing the old centralized bureaucracy of the Church. For this reason, McLuhan believed that Christianity, which has always had a universalistic message, would survive and even grow in the new apocalyptic age.[105] McLuhan was similarly optimistic about political identities that may survive and prosper in the new age of electric media. Those identities that are most flexible, or least committed to ideology, would adapt more effectively to the global village. Canada, McLuhan's home and native land, had the advantage of possessing a "low-profile identity" because of its "multiple borderlines." This state of affairs had the effect "of keeping Canadians in a perpetual philosophic mood which nourishes flexibility in the absence of strong commitments or definite goals." The United States, however, "with heavy commitments and sharply defined objectives, is not in a good position to be philosophic or cool or flexible." In general, electronic information "dims down nationalism and private identities."[106]

The flexible identity that, McLuhan believed, is reason for optimism struck Canadian conservatives such as George Grant as a reason for pessimism, since Grant famously lamented the death of the Anglo-Canadian identity that could not withstand the technological changes unleashed in the modern age.[107] Leo Strauss, who was admired by Grant, would have likely spied in McLuhan's defense of flexible identities a political agenda that fit into what Strauss called the "universal homogeneous state." In his debate with Alexandre Kojève, the famous Marxist interpreter of Hegel, over the differences between classical and modern concepts of tyranny, Strauss also lamented what McLuhan celebrated. The universal homogeneous state, which reduces all human beings to the status of passive consumers of goods and technologies, is a new tyranny that forbids the teaching "that there are politically relevant natural differences among men which cannot be abolished or neutralized by progressing scientific technology." Moreover, even those few authentic philosophers that dare to ask such questions will find it hard to go "underground," as they had done so in previous ages. No longer can philosophers engage in esoteric styles of writing in this age in which the "Universal Tyrant" can reach and suppress any philosopher who tries to escape his grasp. Since, in the premodern and early modern periods, "there was no universal state in existence, the philosophers could escape to other countries if life became unbearable in the tyrant's dominion. From the Universal Tyrant however there is no escape. Thanks to the conquest of nature and to the completely unabashed substitution of suspicion and terror for law, the Universal and Final Tyrant has at his disposal practically unlimited means for ferreting out, and for extinguishing, the most modest efforts in the direction of thought." The fateful outcome of this state would be "the end of philosophy on earth."[108] (It is tempting to draw a parallel between Strauss's warnings and recent revelations about the American government's "Prism" program, which facilitates unprecedented statist surveillance over the world's Internet users.)

Strauss also believed that intellectual influences made this great transformation possible. The adulteration, or "secularization," of Christianity, along with classical Greek political philosophy, provided the ideological rationale or impetus that drives this global tyranny. "Classical philosophy created the idea of the universal state. Modern philosophy, which is the secularized form of Christianity, created the idea of the universal and homogeneous state."[109] As long as the strict morality of both Greek philosophy and the Bible, which "made very strict demands on self-restraint," was replaced by a more flexible morality, the victory of the universal homogeneous state was complete. "Kojève's or Hegel's synthesis of classical and Biblical morality effects the miracle of producing an amazingly lax morality," one that allows "all statesmen to try to extend their authority over all men in order to achieve universal recognition."[110] There was no doubt in Strauss's (and Kojève's) mind as to which philosopher had inspired this dream in the first place. It was Machiavelli who indirectly persuaded Hobbes and then Hegel to defend a regime that demands universal recognition (and surveillance).[111] By Strauss's standards, McLuhan's endorsement of the electric age and its transformation of Christian theology into the universal groundwork for such a state is Machiavellian to the core.

If Strauss is right that the universal homogeneous state is the fulfillment of Machiavelli's project of watering down Christian theology for political use, did he provide any countermeasures that could save philosophy from extinction? In *On Tyranny*, Strauss briefly refers to the possibility of revolt: "There will always be men (*andres*) who will revolt against a state which is destructive of humanity or in which there is no longer a possibility of noble action and of great deeds."[112] Strauss also urged the reading of the "Great Works" of political philosophy as the best way to restore the traditional "liberal education" that could remind its readers of the nobility and wisdom that had been almost lost within the universal homogeneous state. Even though Strauss admitted that this "liberal education" will never become universal and will even remain "the obligation and the privilege of a minority," the moderation that stems from the teaching of the Great Works has the best chance of protecting us "against the twin dangers of visionary expectations from politics and unmanly contempt for politics."[113]

The problem here is that Strauss was extremely vague as to how exactly an elite would emerge out of the modern age that could then wield the authority to teach the Great Works to the citizenry in sufficient numbers that may counter the effects of mass culture. Unlike Machiavelli, Strauss did not trouble himself with practical ideas about which institutions are most suited to effecting desired political changes. It is also not hard to imagine McLuhan's historicist response to Strauss's "Great Works" project. McLuhan, who shared Strauss's doubts on whether the modern mind has the wisdom to teach Great

Works,[114] would also likely doubt that the identity-conscious youth that have been raised on tribalist media would even appreciate or understand these works. Despite Strauss's anti-Enlightenment rhetoric, was he indulging in a kind of Enlightenment project that called for at least the selective edification of the people? Could secret writing remain secret in an age in which the most secretive institution in history, the Church, was under pressure to become more open to participatory involvement made possible by media? If McLuhan was correct that only the print age of Gutenberg made possible both the literacy and appreciative reading of the Great Works, then it also tragically followed that the post–print age had rendered these conditions obsolete. Any reading of Plato in the modern age would still contain modern assumptions. Once again, "novelty causes antiquity."[115]

We have seen McLuhan admit, at least in his correspondence, that it is necessary to modernize Thomism to fit the current age. However, there is no reason to think that his version of Thomism is any less vulnerable to a harsh historicist rebuttal than Strauss's teaching of the Great Works. In strict historicist terms, Thomism belonged, after all, to an age of science that was long gone. Even the antihistoricist Strauss, who accepted the triumph of modern science over Aristotelian teleology, would have also doubted the viability of bringing Thomism back to life in the modern age.[116] McLuhan's own dismissal of the Machiavellian influence as obsolete in the modern age, however, was perhaps more historicist than was justified. One of the greatest ironies of McLuhan's later scholarship is that he made the violent transformation of Christian theology for political use far more respectable than it otherwise would have been. In making the shift from condemnation to dismissal of Machiavellianism, McLuhan followed in the footsteps of the Florentine.

Notes

1. Marshall McLuhan, "*Playboy* Interview," in *Essential McLuhan*, ed. Eric McLuhan and Frank Zingrone (Toronto, ON: House of Anansi Press, 1995), 256. McLuhan gave this interview in March 1969.
2. Marshall McLuhan, "Religion and Youth: Second Conversation with Pierre Babin," in *The Medium and the Light: Reflections on Religion*, ed. Eric McLuhan and Jacek Szklarek (Toronto, ON: Stoddart, 1999), 97. This conversation took place in 1977.
3. McLuhan's various writings on religion are now conveniently available in *The Medium and the Light*. In addition, McLuhan's doctoral dissertation on the English Elizabethan humanist Thomas Nashe is now available in print. See *The Classical Trivium: The Place of Thomas Nashe in the Learning of His Time* (Corte Madera, CA: Gingko Press, 2006). In this early work, McLuhan amply displays his adherence to medieval Thomism.
4. McLuhan, "*Playboy* Interview," 236.
5. Marshall McLuhan, *Letters of Marshall McLuhan*, selected and ed. Marie Molinaro, Corinne McLuhan, and William Toye (Oxford: Oxford University Press, 1987), 427. This quote is from a letter (March 8, 1971) to J. M. Davey, advisor to Canadian Prime Minister Pierre Trudeau.
6. Eric McLuhan, "Introduction," *The Medium and the Light*, xix.
7. See Machiavelli, *The Prince*, Chapter 18: "The prince may appear merciful, faithful, humane, religious, upright, and even be so, but he must always keep a mind so disposed that should it become necessary for him not to be so, he will know how to change to the opposite."
8. McLuhan, "*Playboy* Interview," 265. See his *The Mechanical Bride: Folklore of Industrial Man* (New York: The Vanguard Press, 1951).
9. Quoted in Barrington Nevitt and Marshall McLuhan, *Who Was Marshall McLuhan? Exploring a Mosaic of Impressions* (Toronto, ON: Stoddart, 1994), 53.
10. Marshall McLuhan and Quentin Fiore, *The Medium Is the Massage* (New York: Bantam Books, 1967), 26.
11. McLuhan, "Postures and Impostures of Managers Past," in *Essential McLuhan*, 79. See also *Letters*, 397, 401. McLuhan similarly argues that Machiavelli's distinction between public and private morality simply records "the effect and meaning of the printed word in separating writer and reader, producer and consumer, ruler and ruled, into sharply defined categories." These distinctions, along with the relevance

of Machiavelli's philosophy, presumably disappear with the end of the Gutenberg era. See Marshall McLuhan, *The Gutenberg Galaxy: The Making of Typographic Man*, with new essays by W. Terrence Gordon, Elena Lamberti, and Dominique Scheffel-Dunand (Toronto, ON: University of Toronto Press, 2011), 237. In the same work, McLuhan associated the Machiavellian split between the "head" and the "heart" with the print era (193,199).

12. Marshall McLuhan, *Understanding Media: The Extensions of Man*, with a new introduction by Lewis H. Lapham (Cambridge, MA: MIT Press, 1994), 307.
13. McLuhan, "Catholic Humanism and Modern Letters," in *The Medium and the Light*, 165.
14. McLuhan, "Evitable Fate," in *Essential McLuhan*, 361. See also *The Medium and the Light*, 72. McLuhan's reading of Plato was heavily influenced by the classical scholarship of Eric A. Havelock. See note 32.
15. McLuhan, "*Playboy* Interview," 249. See also page 256. McLuhan and his son Eric discuss this theme in *Laws of Media: The New Science* (Toronto, ON: University of Toronto Press, 1988), 97.
16. McLuhan, "Electric Consciousness and the Church," in *The Medium and the Light*, 86. Later in this interview, McLuhan makes clear his view that Christianity is the one true religion and all others are religious only in an "anthropological sense" (87).
17. McLuhan, "Electric Consciousness and the Church," 88. See also *The Medium and the Light*, 50, 169. The fact that Christianity is exposed as myth in the modern secular age did not deter McLuhan from believing that it still held great power.
18. McLuhan, "Electric Consciousness and the Church," 86.
19. McLuhan, "Our Only Hope is Apocalypse," in *The Medium is the Light*, 64. He goes on to refer to the "potential for teaching and learning" that the electric media opens up for the Church. See also page 61.
20. McLuhan, *The Classical Trivium*, 195.
21. Frank Zingrone and Eric McLuhan, "Introduction," in *Essential McLuhan*, 7.
22. McLuhan, "American Advertising," in *Essential McLuhan*, 14. See also "Catholic Humanism and Modern Letters," in which McLuhan associates Machiavelli with the self-improvement ideology of Dale Carnegie (159).
23. James H. Meisel, *The Myth of the Ruling Class: Gaetano Mosca and the Elite* (Ann Arbor, MI: University of Michigan Press, 1962), 282.
24. Marshall McLuhan, "An Ancient Quarrel in Modern America," *The Classical Journal* 41, no. 4 (1946), reprinted in *The Interior Landscape: The Literary Criticism of Marshall McLuhan 1943–1962*, ed. Eugene McNamara (Toronto, ON: McGraw-Hill, 1969), 223–34.
25. McLuhan, *Laws of Media*, 125.
26. McLuhan, *The Classical Trivium*, 195.
27. See Grant Havers, "James Burnham's Elite Theory and the Postwar American Right," *Telos* 154 (Spring 2011): 33–34.
28. George Grant, an Anglican Tory Canadian philosopher who greatly admired Strauss, once wrote, "He [Strauss] is a practicing Jew and I would have no hesitation in saying that he is a better philosopher than any practicing Christian I know on this continent." See "Letter of Resignation (1960)," in *The George Grant Reader*, ed. William Christian and Sheila Grant (Toronto, ON: University of Toronto Press, 1998), 189.
29. In a letter to Karl Löwith (dated August 15, 1946), Strauss observes that the greatest exponents of the "ancient–modern quarrel" in the eighteenth-century Enlightenment recognized "that the real theme of the quarrel is antiquity and Christianity." See Leo Strauss, "Correspondence concerning Modernity: Karl Löwith," *Independent Journal of Philosophy* 4 (1983): 106.
30. James Burnham, *The Machiavellians: Defenders of Freedom* (New York: John Day, 1943). For Burnham's inattention to Machiavelli's treatment of religion, see Havers, "James Burnham's Elite Theory," 40–50.
31. Havers, "James Burnham's Elite Theory," 31–36.
32. For McLuhan's idea of "rearview mirror" thinking, see "*Playboy* Interview," 238. For Strauss's critique of historicism, see Leo Strauss, *Natural Right and History* (Chicago: University of Chicago Press, 1953), Chapter 1; *What Is Political Philosophy? And Other Studies* (Chicago: University of Chicago Press), 56–77. Strauss famously teaches that readers of past philosophers must not assume that they understand these authors better than they understood themselves simply because they lived *after* these thinkers (see *What Is Political Philosophy?*, 67). McLuhan arguably makes this historicist assumption when he claims that "Electric man" understands the age of Plato better than Plato did, since he lives in a modern age that has superior insights into the history of technological change. See McLuhan, "Evitable Fate," in *Essential McLuhan*, 361. In this context, Strauss and McLuhan also radically differed on the historicist scholarship of the classicist Eric A. Havelock, who emphasized the importance of the

transition from orality to writing in the age of Plato; Havelock claimed that Plato's ban on politically inappropriate poetry in the *Republic* accelerated this transition. See Eric A. Havelock, *Preface to Plato* (Cambridge, MA: Harvard University Press, 1963). Whereas McLuhan admired Havelock's study of this historic shift, Strauss dismissed Havelock as a historicist who failed to grasp Plato's original intent. For McLuhan's praise of Havelock as an historian who has a better understanding of the "hidden factors" that lie in ancient history than the ancients had, see "History as Observatory of Change," in *Essential McLuhan*, 76. For Strauss's critique of Havelock's scholarship, see "The Liberalism of Classical Political Philosophy," in Leo Strauss, *Liberalism: Ancient and Modern*, foreword by Allan Bloom (Chicago: University of Chicago Press, 1995), 26–64.

33. See Peter Minowitz, "Machiavellianism Come of Age? Leo Strauss on Modernity and Economics," *Political Science Reviewer* 22 (1993): 178: "Strauss turns Marx on his head, suggesting that there are ruling ideas (but not Hegelian *Geist*), behind the 'ruling class' or the dominant mode of production."
34. George Grant, *Time as History*, edited with an introduction by William Christian (Toronto, ON: University of Toronto Press, 1995), 50. This book was originally published in 1969. For a comparison of Grant's and McLuhan's conservative politics, see Arthur Kroker, *Technology and the Canadian Mind: Innis/McLuhan/Grant* (Montreal: New World Perspectives, 1984), 52–54, 84; Grant Havers, "The Right-Wing Postmodernism of Marshall McLuhan," *Media, Culture, and Society* 25, no. 4 (July 2003): 522.
35. For a small portion of the McLuhan–Voegelin correspondence, see Eric Voegelin, *The Collected Works of Eric Voegelin*, vol. 30: *Selected Correspondence 1950–1984*, translated from the German by Sandy Adler, Thomas A. Hollweck, and William Petropulos (Columbia, MO: University of Missouri Press, 2007), 173–74. In a letter that is dated July 17, 1953, Voegelin responds to McLuhan's interest in "secret cults or societies" in politics and academe. It is not evident that he is referring to the followers of Strauss, who were well known to Voegelin.
36. See Voegelin's review of Strauss's *On Tyranny*, in *Faith and Political Philosophy: The Correspondence between Leo Strauss and Eric Voegelin 1934–1964*, trans. and ed. Peter Emberley and Barry Cooper (University Park, PA: Pennsylvania State University Press, 1993), especially page 48.
37. For an insightful discussion of Voegelin's antipathy toward Protestantism, see John J. Ranieri, *Disturbing Revelation: Leo Strauss, Eric Voegelin, and the Bible* (Columbia, MO: University of Missouri Press, 2009), 153. Ranieri argues that Strauss, who had similar misgivings toward a politics based on Christianity, was far more cautious than Voegelin in expressing them (160).
38. See Strauss's response to Voegelin in *On Tyranny: Including the Strauss-Kojève Correspondence*, ed. Victor Gourevitch and Michael S. Roth (Chicago: University of Chicago Press, 2000), especially 183–84. It is also reprinted in Emberley and Cooper, *Faith and Political Philosophy*, 55–56.
39. Leo Strauss, *Thoughts on Machiavelli* (Chicago: University of Chicago Press, 1958), 175.
40. Leo Strauss, *What Is Political Philosophy?*, 45.
41. Strauss, *Thoughts on Machiavelli*, 133.
42. Strauss, *What Is Political Philosophy?*, 44; *Thoughts on Machiavelli*, 179. See also Clifford Orwin, "Machiavelli's Unchristian Charity," *American Political Science Review* 72 (1978): 1217–28.
43. Strauss, *Thoughts on Machiavelli*, 157, 207. Of course, Machiavelli preferred republicanism to monarchy.
44. Leo Strauss, "Reason and Revelation," in Heinrich Meier, *Leo Strauss and the Theologico-Political Problem*, trans. Marcus Brainard (Cambridge: Cambridge University Press, 2006), 156.
45. Strauss spies within Machiavelli's *Discourses* "the birth of that greatest of all youth movements: modern philosophy." (*Thoughts on Machiavelli*, 127).
46. See Leo Strauss, "How to Study Spinoza's Theologico-Political Treatise," in *Persecution and the Art of Writing* (Chicago: University of Chicago Press, 1952), 147, 163.
47. Strauss describes Spinoza as a thinker who "lifts Machiavellianism to theological heights." See his "Preface to the English Translation," in *Spinoza's Critique of Religion*, trans. E. M. Sinclair (New York: Schocken Books, 1982), 18. Spinoza's library included the complete works of Machiavelli. See Steven Nadler, *A Book Forged in Hell: Spinoza's Scandalous Treatise and the Birth of the Secular Age* (Princeton, NJ: Princeton University Press, 2011), 104.
48. Machiavelli, *Discourses*, Book 2, Chapter 2. See also Strauss, *Thoughts on Machiavelli*, 179.
49. Leo Strauss, "Progress or Return? The Contemporary Crisis in Western Civilization," in *An Introduction to Political Philosophy: Ten Essays by Leo Strauss*, edited with an introduction by Hilail Gildin (Detroit: Wayne State University Press, 1989), 299.
50. Strauss, *Thoughts on Machiavelli*, 50–51.
51. Strauss, in "Reason and Revelation," cites Rudolf Bultmann as a liberal theologian who denied, as Spinoza did, that miracles, including the resurrection of Christ, ever happened." (158).

52. Strauss, *What Is Political Philosophy?*, 43.
53. McLuhan, "Catholic Humanism and Modern Letters," 159–60. In *Thoughts on Machiavelli*, Strauss similarly notes that "Machiavelli does not bring to light a single political phenomenon of any fundamental importance which was not fully known to the classics" (295).
54. McLuhan, "Catholic Humanism and Modern Letters," 160. Strauss similarly contends that Machiavelli's heirs Bacon and Hobbes defended a philosophy that leads directly to Nietzsche's will to power. (*What Is Political Philosophy?*, 172.)
55. John Lindberg, *Foundations of Social Survival* (New York: Columbia University Press, 1953).
56. McLuhan, "Catholic Humanism and Modern Letters," 173.
57. McLuhan, "Catholic Humanism and Modern Letters," 174.
58. McLuhan, "The God-Making Machines of the Modern World," in *The Medium and the Light*, 198.
59. McLuhan, "The God-Making Machines," 199.
60. McLuhan, "The God-Making Machines," 200.
61. McLuhan made this judgment in his 1970 interview, "Electric Consciousness and the Church," 86.
62. McLuhan, "The State as a Work of Art," in *Essential McLuhan*, 81.
63. McLuhan, "Electric Consciousness and the Church," 84. See also page 86.
64. McLuhan, "Electric Consciousness and the Church," 83. See also "*Playboy* Interview," 249.
65. McLuhan, "Electric Consciousness and the Church," 84.
66. McLuhan, "Electric Consciousness and the Church," 88.
67. McLuhan, "'A Peculiar War to Fight': Letter to Robert J. Leuver, C.M.F.," in *The Medium and the Light*, 91–92. This letter is dated July 30, 1969.
68. McLuhan, "Religion and Youth: Second Conversation with Pierre Babin," in *The Medium and the Light*, 104. McLuhan gave this interview in 1977. In *Understanding Media*, McLuhan similarly rejects a "linear" interpretation of the Bible in favor of one that recognizes the relation between God and the world as well as that between man and his neighbor in terms of relations that "subsist together, and act and react upon one another at the same time" (25–26).
69. McLuhan, "Catholic Humanism and Modern Letters," 157.
70. McLuhan, *Understanding Media*, 47.
71. McLuhan, *Understanding Media*, 61.
72. Quoted in Eric McLuhan, "Introduction," in *The Medium and the Light*, xxvii. The quote is from a letter to Allen Maruyama (December 31, 1971).
73. McLuhan, "*Playboy* Interview," 253.
74. McLuhan, "*Playboy* Interview," 258. In the same interview, McLuhan refers to the "Balkanization of the United States" (257).
75. McLuhan, "*Playboy* Interview," 262.
76. McLuhan, "*Playboy* Interview," 268.
77. McLuhan, "Catholic Humanism and Modern Letters," 163.
78. McLuhan, "Keys to the Electronic Revolution: First Conversation with Pierre Babin," in *The Medium and the Light*, 47–48. See also *Letters*, 494.
79. McLuhan, "Communications Media: Makers of the Modern World," in *The Medium and the Light*, 44.
80. McLuhan, "Liturgy and Media: Do Americans Go to Church to Be Alone?," in *The Medium and the Light*, 135. McLuhan published this article in 1973. McLuhan worryingly refers to the rising Protestant influence on the Church on pages 62, 130, and 208.
81. McLuhan, *Understanding Media*, 199.
82. McLuhan, "*Playboy* Interview," 260. See also *Understanding Media*, 34. In a letter to John Culkin (September 17, 1964), McLuhan quotes with approval the historian Richard Hofstadter's view that "the new conservatism has as its content the old liberalism," a phenomenon that, according to McLuhan, had parallels in the realm of technological change. See *Letters*, 310.
83. McLuhan, "Liturgy and Media: Do Americans Go to Church to Be Alone?," in *The Medium and the Light*, 131. See also "Keys to the Electronic Revolution," 51.
84. Mark A. Noll, *What Happened to Christian Canada?* (Vancouver, BC: Regent College Publishing, 2007), 51–53. Noll observes that Vatican II's most enduring impact on liberal Protestants may lie in the fact that it became harder for them to hold a negative image of their old enemy, the Roman Catholic Church.
85. See Strauss, *Spinoza's Critique of Religion*, 193–214. Here Strauss shows the fundamental differences between Spinoza's philosophy and Calvin's theology, despite what he takes to be some superficial resemblances.
86. See Strauss's letter to Voegelin (August 25, 1950), in *Faith and Political Philosophy*, 71. See also their correspondence of Spinoza on pages 60–61, 70, and 73.

87. See Havers, "The Right-Wing Postmodernism of Marshall McLuhan."
88. Leo Strauss, *Liberalism: Ancient and Modern*, viii–ix. See also *What Is Political Philosophy?*, 236–37. For the differences between Grant and McLuhan, see note 34. It should be noted that Grant in the 1970s admired McLuhan's antiabortion activism.
89. McLuhan, "*Playboy* Interview," 260. For Strauss's views on the "closed societies" favored by conservatives, see *Liberalism: Ancient and Modern*, x.
90. Marshall McLuhan and Eric McLuhan, *Media and Formal Cause* (Houston, TX: NeoPoiesis Press, 2011), 29–30. See also note 82. For Strauss's thoughts on conservatism as old-style liberalism, see *Liberalism: Ancient and Modern*, ix–x.
91. Strauss, *What Is Political Philosophy?*, 45–46.
92. For old-style Marxist critiques of McLuhan, see Sidney Finkelstein, *Sense and Nonsense of McLuhan* (New York: International Publishers, 1968); John Fekete, "McLuhanacy: Counterrevolution in Cultural Theory," *Telos* 15 (1973): 75–123. For a discussion of the shift in leftist attitudes toward McLuhan in a more positive direction since his death, see Havers, "The Right-Wing Postmodernism of Marshall McLuhan," 511–15.
93. It is worth noting here that many Catholics saw no relation between their beliefs and McLuhan's writings. See Eric McLuhan, "Introduction," in *The Medium and the Light*, xix.
94. Marshall McLuhan and Bruce R. Powers, *The Global Village: Transformations in World Life and Media in the 21st Century* (Oxford: Oxford University Press, 1989), 60. In a letter to Edward T. Hall (dated July 23, 1969), McLuhan similarly focuses on the role of "process" in Christianity rather than its doctrinal truth. In true Machiavellian fashion, he even admits that he tries to conceal his Christian bias: "I deliberately keep my Christianity out of all these discussions lest perception be diverted from structural processes by doctrinal sectarian passions. My own attitude to Christianity is, itself, awareness of process." See *Letters*, 384.
95. McLuhan and Powers, *The Global Village*, 62.
96. McLuhan, "Electric Consciousness and the Church," 80–81.
97. McLuhan, "Electric Consciousness and the Church," 85.
98. McLuhan, "Liturgy and Media," 131. Once again, McLuhan believed that Plato was irrelevant to the electric age, unless radio was used to duplicate "small and private communities" that "could easily implement the Platonic political dream on a world scale" (*Understanding Media*, 307).
99. McLuhan, "The De-Romanization of the American Catholic Church," in *The Medium and the Light*, 56.
100. McLuhan, "Catholic Humanism and Modern Letters," 169.
101. Strauss blames Machiavelli for shifting attention away from the "formation of character to the trust in institutions." See *What Is Political Philosophy?*, 43.
102. McLuhan, "Electric Consciousness and the Church," 86. Here he remarks that the "Christian myth is not fiction but something more than ordinarily real."
103. McLuhan, "American Advertising," 14.
104. McLuhan, "Media as 'The New Nature,'" in *Essential McLuhan*, 272.
105. McLuhan, "Electric Consciousness and the Church," 87.
106. McLuhan and Powers, *The Global Village*, 165.
107. Grant, *Lament for a Nation: The Defeat of Canadian Nationalism* (Ottawa, ON: Carleton University Press, 1965). For the differences between Grant and McLuhan, see references cited in note 33.
108. Strauss, *On Tyranny*, 211. It is not even obvious that Strauss thought that secret (esoteric) writing was possible after the dawn of liberal modernity. See Catherine and Michael Zuckert, *The Truth about Leo Strauss: Political Philosophy and American Democracy* (Chicago: University of Chicago Press, 2006), 120–36.
109. Strauss, *On Tyranny*, 207.
110. Strauss, *On Tyranny*, 191.
111. Strauss, *On Tyranny*, 186. By contrast, Burnham vehemently disagreed that the wish for a universal regime, as famously articulated by Dante, was compatible with Machiavelli's tough realism. See Burnham, *The Machiavellians*, 3–26.
112. Strauss, *On Tyranny*, 209.
113. Strauss, "Liberal Education and Responsibility," in *Liberalism: Ancient and Modern*, 24. In his essay "What Is Liberal Education?" he describes liberal education as the "counterpoison to mass culture" (*Liberalism: Ancient and Modern*, 5).
114. Commenting on the feature in *Life Magazine* (January 26, 1948) on the new "Great Works" program that Robert Hutchins and Mortimer Adler established at the University of Chicago, McLuhan wondered why the article "should have so mortician-like an air—as though Professor Adler and his associates

had come to bury and not to praise Plato and other great men." He went on to write, "The 'great ideas' whose headstones are alphabetically displayed above the coffin-like filing boxes have been extracted from the great books in order to provide an index tool for manipulating the book themselves." These polemical remarks are from McLuhan, *Mechanical Bride*, 43.

115. Despite Strauss's praise of Greek political philosophy, his modernism often shows through in his support of modern liberal democracy. For extensive analyses of Strauss's modernist tendencies, see Paul Edward Gottfried, *Leo Strauss and the Conservative Movement in America: A Critical Appraisal* (Cambridge: Cambridge University Press, 2012); Grant N. Havers, *Leo Strauss and Anglo-American Democracy: A Conservative Critique* (DeKalb, IL: Northern Illinois University Press, 2013).

116. See McLuhan and McLuhan, Media and Formal Cause, 29-30. For Strauss's acceptance of the triumph of modern science over Aristotelian teleology, see *Natural Right and History*, 7–8. See also Clark A. Merrill, "Leo Strauss's Indictment of Christian Philosophy," *Review of Politics* 62, no. 1 (2000): 77–106. In a letter to S. J. Walter Ong (May 18, 1946), McLuhan complains that "no Thomist has ever faced" the "question of training in sensibility, the education of the passions, the fluid interplay of thought and feeling" in the formation of value judgments, or how such an education could "re-create the total loss of human community in contemporary life." See *Letters*, 187.

12

The Trenches of Capernaum, 1914–1918

Yves Pourcher

Capernaum

What I first see in this place: disorder, chaos, the earth torn up, trees uprooted, objects scattered, dead men, and dead horses. That's how I see it today. But yesterday, a long time ago, the place was delightful. On the shores of the Lake of Gennesaret, in Galilee, a prophet had come. He skirted the shores of Lake Tiberias, climbed the nearby mountains, marched along the plain, visited the small towns. They were called Magdala, Dalmanutha, Bethsaida, Chorazin, and Capernaum. They were surrounded by a lake, shrubs, fields of flowers, and the wind that carried their fragrance.[1]

Fishermen, peasants, and traders lived happily. Jesus had spoken to them and his word had become a religion. But suddenly, on an accursed day in the time of men, horror visited them. Storms of steel! a witness reported, with showers of shells, rockets, bombs, shrapnel from all directions, and clouds of mustard gas. The earth torn up, turned over, pulverized. The trunks of the orange and fig trees cut, the water poisoned, a fetid odor, hell on earth. At the four corners of this canton-sized territory, on its edges, and in the middle, narrow trenches in which, day and night, soldiers waited.

The trenches of Capernaum! That's what I call them and that's how I see them. I recognize them. They're the trenches of another era, one that came much later, during the war called "the War of 14–18" in this corner of France that for four interminable years became an outpost of Capernaum. To describe this time and place, I need to go back to biblical images and to a distant time when a new and great faith was born.

1914–1918: I find places. Marne, Flanders, Éparges, Argonne, Verdun, Chemin des Dames. Vauquois. Côte 304, Mort-Homme, Douaumont, Fort de Vaux. What can those now-mythical names tell us today? My head is full of photos, stories, deafening noises.

On October 26, 1914, General Fayolle, the future Marshal, relates, "... The day before yesterday, Pétain told me, the Senegalese regiment came under fire at Saint-Laurent, near Arras. They lost 20 officers, 38 sergeants, and 800 enlisted men. They lost their nerve and fled. It's butchery: those people are incapable of waging European-style war."[2]

Figure 1
Soldiers in a Trench

And Pétain once again, on November 5, when describing his crackdown: "At the first encounters, I played," he said, "the role of the butcher."

The massacre of the blacks! "Deserters" shot! European war: a huge exercise in butchery. I want to close my eyes and plug my ears. In Verdun in 1995 I sleep at the Hotel du Coq Hardi. The next day, I walk amidst innumerable crosses. In the town, they sell coated almonds as big as pigeon eggs. I flee. I want to forget the War of 14–18, to not speak of it again, ever.

The years go by and I go back. I find the trenches once more. Labyrinths of tunnels zigzagging in the earth with their storehouses of provisions and ammunition. They go deep into the ground, sometimes as far as ten meters. All around are sandbags, barbed wire, stakes strung together with wire, fascines, machine guns, and then the accursed no man's land. One day at the flea market I buy a little painting by the military painter Léon Couturier. I call it "The Hut." In his shelter surrounded by sandbags and stakes, a soldier is looking at the horizon. A little patch of blue toward which his face is turned.

"One is a virgin of horror just as one is a virgin of pleasure," writes Céline in *Journey to the End of the Night*. And in order to forget, I, too, am on a journey. In Seville, at the end of the month of October, 2012, I go into the Fine Arts Museum. A painting by Lucas Cranach attracts my gaze. Christ is on the cross. In front of him, looking at him, is a horseman from another time. His white horse is rearing. I continue my visit and stop in front of a painting by Gustavo Bacarisas. Seville, 1915, it reads. I see three women, their heads covered in mantillas, holding fans. Their dresses are mauve, green, pink, their lips red. Earrings hang from their ears, and white lace covers their arms and shoulders. They are surrounded by bouquets of red and green flowers. The three Andalusian women light up a spring night. They are happy because they are going to dance. The festival is on in Seville. How far the sound of cannons is from here.

Two years later, in 1917, another Spaniard, Ramón Del Valle-Inclán,[3] famous for his tales of the Carlist Wars, visits the trenches. "A stellar vision of a moment in the war," he writes upon his return. Along with hundreds of others—journalists, politicians, rich and influential donors—he was given a tour of this world of troglodytes and iron. After a long march through the tunnels, he did just as the others had, discovering the unknown, the incredible, war as it is. The echo of cannons fills their ears. In the distance, they see the flashes of the bombardments. They leave fast. Back home, they tell their stories, composing texts, poems, and songs. Terrible propaganda! Hatred flows like a spring.

"It is of utmost importance," writes André Suarès,[4] "that the learned men of France invent a method of extermination." And a little further on in his book, on other pages: "In the German mind there is a core of wickedness, un ulcer of nothingness"; "The Boche are butchers (. . .) And they have made the war into a slaughterhouse."

On Christmas day, 2012, after sharing a meal with my family at my brother's house, I look at the dagger that my grandfather brought back from that war, resting on a small piece of furniture. I take it in my hands, draw it from its sheath. At the end of the handle,

Figure 2
Dominique Pourcher, My Paternal Grandfather

there is an inscription: "The avenger of 1870." My nephew—a tall, secretive young man—approaches. He reads, and hesitates. 1870, 1914? What's the connection? He murmurs his failure to comprehend. So I explain. The desire to avenge, the wounds that won't close, the return of war. He listens, nods. But later, I realize that it's he who is right. There was actually just one war, the same one that came back, springing up again like some horrible creature.

Fourteen[5] in 1870, Fourteen in 1914, Fourteen in 1939. Almost a century of war in this part of the world. But Fourteen also in Spain, twenty years after the voyage of Valle-Inclán, in the most terrible of wars, a war of faith and of families. Trenches in Toledo, Teruel, Valencia, and Barcelona. And the evil spreads across the entire world, a filthy epidemic of Fourteen that reaches and infects Leningrad, Stalingrad, Berlin, China, Korea, Vietnam, Eritrea, Iraq, and Syria. Fourteen means war, all wars, gathers them together, qualifies them. It's a global synonym, a number stronger than words. And to add a finishing touch, to express the incomprehension and the mystery one feels when faced with the history of men, a place name, always the same one, the name of a market town in Galilee, where everything began: Capernaum. An image of sadness, death, and desolation.

I am arranging my notes, my library, and almost by chance I find a book that I had forgotten, *The Captain of Capernaum*, by the German writer Ernst Wiechert,[6] a collection of short stories, the first of which gives the book its title. I reread, and at last I understand. Right in the middle of that German civil war, a war after the war, the sign of hope emerges. And with it the other face of the land and people of Capernaum: the message of one who, amid the ruins and the furor, still wanted to believe.

Stupors

The news of war comes as a sound that resonates in all the villages of France on August 1, 1914. The bells ring, slowly, heavily. The alarm bell! I am listening to it on the Internet, the bell of Mont-sur-Lison church, which sits on a hill in the commune of Courcelles-les-Quingey in the department of Doubs. Slow, monotonous, repetitive, oppressive. To go all out, try to understand what this day meant, I should run into a field some distance from there, wait for hours under the sun, and suddenly hear the tolling. But today, who knows the message of the bells? Everything has already been said and written about that sound and that day. "Hallucination in bronze," "rolling thunder," "great blows striking a single note": the bells' echo still haunts collective memory. And what comes afterward, in the heat of late morning or early afternoon, when the grains, the fruit, and the grapes wear the colors of happiness, is even more mysterious.

Stupor! it was said. On the faces and in the bodies of farmers and craftsmen. Those who saw them at that precise moment discerned paralysis, incomprehension, extreme anguish. Rigid torsos, limbs, and neck, trembling, pale cheeks, forehead, hands, as if the blood had gone. Words no longer come, tongues are caught in a vice. This lasts several minutes. Then people get ahold of themselves. The colors come back, arms move. Everyone runs toward one another. Impossible solitude. People touch each other, hold each other. Children cry, and women too. The men steal away. During the night, in the houses, by candlelight and gaslight, bags are packed. The next morning, they leave as a group.

Thus was recounted, with these images and these scenes, the first day of this new calendar just born, the calendar of mobilization time. The film begins with a sound. There follows a freeze-frame and then everything accelerates: gestures, cries, hugs and kisses, tears, singing. A sleepless night, alone in the houses. Mothers, wives, companions, sisters around them. The fathers and the brothers wait in another room. When they come out, the women cling to them, the elderly and the children are a bit farther off. Some of them are men. But others have the air of adolescents. They walk to the stations. They get on board the train cars. Their hands and their arms stick out of the doors. Everyone would like to touch them.

The stupor has been forgotten? And yet a few have kept buried inside them the wound of terror. Over the following days, they wandered. For from the beginning, as soon as war was announced, they felt the irreparable coming, extreme horror. Are they seers? In their mental turmoil, they have touched death. In the face of the event, they feel lost, minuscule, charged and immediately condemned. So they anticipate and commit an irreparable act. One morning or night, in a bedroom or a barn, they are found hung or killed by their own hand. Bodies get caught on branches on the river banks.

These suicides that take place in the first days are particularly interesting to me. Others will follow throughout all these years, even if it is said that in general the number of suicides decreases in wartime. The period after the war will also have its cadavers. But let's come back to the hours that followed the sound of the alarm bell. On August 4, in Avignon, a member of the territorial reserve throws himself from the windows of the town hall. He dies in that city, whose inhabitants drink like fish. Two go completely crazy, while another fires on sentries standing guard on a bridge who fire back and slaughter him. In Bordeaux on August 7, two soldiers are found drowned. Accident or suicide? At the same time, a quartermaster shot himself.

On August 8, in Montauban, a soldier of the 132nd territorial regiment tries to kill himself with his bayonet. In Tulle, on August 9, the body of an adjutant of the hundredth infantry regiment is found. The same day, in Nevers, Lieutenant-Colonel Gaudin of the sixty-fourth territorial puts an end to his days. In a letter, he wrote that the mere idea of commanding an ill-prepared regiment was unbearable to him. In the archives of the army, in Vincennes, I search vainly for his dossier. It seems that it cannot be found.

On August 11, in Troyes, five soldiers go completely crazy. The prefect immediately has them locked up in Saint-Dizier. Fear, panic, alcohol? Perhaps all three. On August 14, in Lyon, a distinguished citizen, the owner of a large silk factory, deputy mayor, the son of a former senator who was the president of the departmental council, a family man—kills himself. In Epinal, the special commissioner of the intelligence services must be urgently transferred to an asylum.

Suicides, madmen. Who are they? What did they see, understand? Frightened, panicked, overwhelmed men, one might answer. But why not simply call them "refusers" or even seers? "Virgins of horror," said Celine. That is perhaps what they were not.

Voyages

They have left. Seated, lying down, packed together in the cars. Some stop at depots. Others head toward the border. The journey is interminable. "To get from Morlaix to the front, it took us three days and four nights," writes Marc Bloch.[7] Throughout this time they talk, sleep, and drink. What strange travelers! Shout, play, eat, piss. The trains are worlds and the stations melting pots. But the war plans took everything into account.

An enormous migration. In the first days of the war, undercover trains, then over the following days, mobilization trains, deployment trains, evacuation trains. And then the innumerable trains bound for the concentration camps.

Trains against trains. This is the new war, its brilliant discovery. For on the German side, the same was done. Starting on July 29, the eighth Bavarian Division landed at Sainte-Marie-aux-Chênes and the sixty-seventh infantry at Amanvillers. The fourth Bavarian Division had already arrived at Malmaison near Gravelotte. Orders are then given to urgently equip the armored Belfort train intended for reconnaissance. The rails became war zones. Starting on July 31, the line toward Batilly is cut off. In Deutsch-Avricourt, a border region, the trains no longer run. On August 1, it is reported that the Germans blocked the Pagny-sur-Moselle line all the way to the border. Germany is inflating little by little like a wineskin ready to explode. Time is suddenly suspended. Millions of men await marching orders.

Of all these departures, I am only interested in one, the one in an image that fascinates me. In Paris, at the Gare de l'Est, I spend hours looking at the immense painting by Albert Herter hung there in 1926. The blue of the greatcoats, the crimson-colored pants, military packs, the women's scarves and shawls, their light-colored dresses, their long hair. Children huddle in the arms of a young father. Baskets of provisions rest on the ground. Ensconced in the train cars, soldiers look out the windows at those who are lingering on the platform. The scenes are heartrending. Hands hold out flowers. Fingers touch and caress. Tender kisses, tears, silences, and looks. The painter put himself at the right of the canvas. He is speaking to a young woman. At the left, his wife, her hands clasped, is looking at children at play. The painter's son, Everit Albert, is in the middle of the work. A rifle in one hand, a kepi in the other, and a blue scarf knotted around his neck, he is saluting the sky. Young, slender, a clear gaze: a voluntary conscript. He will be killed on June 13, 1918, in Bois Belleau near Château-Thierry.

Outbound trains, inbound trains, trains carrying soldiers on leave. Trains for men, for horses, for crews, trains for the immense, gigantic, unequaled, excessive transport of goods: cows, flour, casks, clothing, and letters. Mountains of goods and supplies. Trains for able-bodied soldiers who go and come throughout the years of war. Trains for the wounded, mutilated, amputated, their faces smashed up, their bodies shattered. Their groans can be heard through the doors of the train cars. Day after day the trains roll on. They descend toward the south, head west, come back north. An immense movement. And the delays! To get home, the Corsicans must spend several days. So they protest. But the men from the colonies, from Africa, Indochina, from the other overseas territories of the French empire, are stuck. Suddenly, from all sides, shouts ring out. Perched on the roofs of the train cars and on the footboards, a red flag attached to a stick, men shout: "Down with war!" We're at the Gare de Corbeil in 1917. In Raincy, half-naked soldiers insult women: "Bitches! Piece of trash! Revolt!"

"Fucking war!" "Fucking country!": the anger spreads. It is in the trains, and it bursts forth when they stop. It resounds. Then its echo dies away and silence returns. The chugging of locomotives is a constant accompaniment. Once the war is over, the movement continues nonetheless. New trains circulate. They transport the bodies of the dead to be returned to their families. Trains of death with their multiple stops and their poor passengers. Once they've arrived in their villages, they are buried once more.

"Away! Away! Word of the prodigal!" writes Saint-John Perse in *Winds*.[8] Go away far from the war. Leave the Gare de l'Est in Paris, run, no longer think of those trains, forget them. That war came to an end in a train car. Twenty-two years later, it starts up again. Soldiers climb into the same train car. Then, with time, war becomes a lofty thing. The soldiers climb into airplanes. They are transported through the air. Then they are put on the ground where, as in the past, they march, crawl, and leap. Foot soldiers! Trenches! Capernaum.

In the month of January, 1991, at the Madrid airport, I wait for hours because the first Iraq war has just begun. The sky has suddenly become a military zone. Bombs are being transported. Tons of bombs! In the month of January, 2007, the passenger lounges in the Atlanta airport are full of soldiers. They wear camouflage fatigues the color of sand, leaves, and earth. The colors of autumn. In the past they were khaki, field gray, and forest green. Have they become men of nature and the seasons, these new warriors? Cunning, disguise, spectacle. I sit down next to them and I look. Some have childlike faces. Blacks, whites, Hispanics, a few women. They sleep, dream, and play with their cell phones. Their words are rare. Departing flights are announced over the loudspeakers. Suddenly one of them gets up, gathers his things, loads up his pack, and leaves.

On February 8, 2013, at the airport in Charlotte, North Carolina, I wait for my flight to Germany. Sitting at a table in a Starbucks, I watch the crowd go by. From time to time, soldiers in military garb. Shaved heads, wearing ranger boots, they walk fast. They're points of color, splotches. On their shoulders there is a badge, the star-spangled banner. So dressed, a little woman holds a wheeled cart in her hands. The wheels of the suitcases click on the floor. The soldiers turn right, left, holding telephones. They press on the buttons. In front of me, windows as big as immense portholes. The planes are on the runways.

Little cars transport handicapped people. Their sirens and their flashing lights are tiresome. I feel light-headed, I want to close my eyes. Has war become a voyage in a plane? In the distance, I can make out some brightly lit screens. Arrivals, departures, flight numbers, gates. I see hats, boots, backpacks.

USA, war film. To see it, you just have to be there. I get up, move forward. Beside a bathroom door, an advertisement attracts my gaze. In front of a big American flag, seated in front of a tent, two soldiers with bodies swollen by bullet-proof vests, knee-pads, shoulder-pads, multiple pockets, are looking at me. On the ground there is sand and a few leaves. To their left is a helmet, a backpack, a canteen, and a radio transmitter. They have crew-cuts, one is a redhead, the other has dark hair. They're white-colored mannequins. To the right of the poster, there are tubes of cosmetics and the following slogan: "Show Your Spirit (in brown letters) Military (in black)." I look at the image for a good long time. When I turn around, a young couple goes by. He is very short, in fatigues. She is husky, also in fatigues, and is pushing a baby carriage. Inside there are two babies.

Chestnut

Their hair, their eyes, their mustaches and their skin are the color of grains, fruits, of the sky and of earth. Millions of men. How are they treated? First, several months or years ago, they were called, they were made to undress, they were measured, examined, described. This inventorying has existed since the creation of the armed services. "What recruiting class are you in?" they are asked over and over. The army sees them, their families see them, others see them. And these multiple gazes, with different voices, determine what they are. But the war changes the meaning of this gigantic description. Before, they were just a picture, a photograph before the individual photograph: the identity photo. Afterwards, very often, listing the names of those who haven't aged, mowed down in their youth and dragged too early into the grave, the photograph becomes an obituary item, the trace of a memory.

In their files, I take note of what is called a *signalement*, a physical description. I choose a few, the ones that draw my attention, that intrigue me, interest me, the ones I like.

Robert Walter Hertz, the folklorist, born June 22, 1881 in Saint-Cloud, second-lieutenant in the 330th infantry regiment, killed April 13, 1915 in combat at Marchéville in the Woëvre. I discover his physical features: chestnut hair and eyebrows, blue eyes, high forehead, long nose, medium-sized mouth, round chin, oval face, five feet, eight inches tall.

Another younger one: Roger Allier, born on July 13, 1890 in Paris, second-lieutenant lost in combat at Saint-Dié on or about August 28, 1914. Physical description: chestnut hair, brown eyes. Forehead: receding upward, of medium height and breadth; Nose: straight, raised at the base, long and jutting, wide; Face: oval; five feet, nine inches tall.

Those two are taller than average. "The French race," writes Jean Hugo,[9] "was very small at that time. I was the tallest in the company. The soldiers from Normandy asked me: 'Are you related to Hugo the Giant?'" An art connoisseur, himself a painter, he describes those he sees. A young man named Poirot, nineteen years old, "an angelic face, made up of pink, white, sky blue and gold, without the slightest trace of shadow." A virgin of love, but no longer of war. And another, Avrillier, a handsome fellow from Belleville, with bright eyes and curly hair tumbling over his forehead.

Blond, brown, chestnut: their hair and their eyes. The chestnut color that I love. Perhaps because of the circumflex accent (in French: *châtain*, chestnut), but also because of the tree that inspires the word. The chestnut trees remind me of the Cévennes mountain range and of the trees that, on my paternal grandfather's land, near Marvejols in Lozère, enabled my family to live during the wars. These big trees with saw-toothed leaves cling to the slopes, descend into the valleys, climb to the heights. At the beginning of autumn, the palette of their colors makes for the most beautiful of tableaux. The fruit is enclosed in a cupule bristling with thorns. It protects itself, defends itself, breaks open, and then dries in the sun and in granaries. Poor man's bread, they used to say. This chestnut color became the color of a country, the color of the France whose sons fall like flies. France: chestnut country. France is a fruit, has the chestnut's colors, its taste. Eyes, eyebrows, and hair have the colors of the season, of the clouds, of fire and the night. Chestnut, hazelnut, olive, grape, and grains. Those who go off to war are tree-men, fruits, gifts of nature. They wear the colors of life and those of youth, when gray has yet to come, when hair hasn't fallen off, and the eyes sparkle.

"What color are his eyes?" is the question asked from the first days. "And his hair?" So mothers cut locks of hair that they fold up in handkerchiefs and keep like precious relics. Women, but also men, fathers, brothers, have kept the color from those days of leave taking, the color of eyes and hair. Love will be in such need of these tokens.

The need for specificity. In a schoolboy's notebook kept by a policeman great-uncle after the war, I note the nuances of chestnut: light, soft, ordinary, dark. The redheads were

Figure 3
André-Karl Doumer

bright or mahogany, reddish blond, ordinary red or chestnut red. I take up the army file of another great-uncle, Charles Pourcher, the younger brother of my paternal grandfather, born on the farm in Valadou, in the commune of Montrodat in Lozère, and I find his description: "Black hair and eyes, receding hairline, medium-sized nose, oval face, 5 feet, 7 inches tall." "Can read and count," it is specified. But "doesn't know how to swim." Charles! How many tears his mother, Clémence, spilled for him.

I continue with other descriptions, like those of the sons of Professor Paul Doumer, who would become President of the Republic and would be assassinated in 1932. He taught at the collège (middle school) in Mende. I take them in order of birth, but I could also have gone by order of death.

Marcel-Victor, born in 1886, commander of a squadron, dead in 1918 in aerial combat: blond hair, light chestnut eyebrows, blue eyes.

René-Léon, born in 1887, also a pilot, missing in action in 1917: brown hair and eyebrows, gray eyes.

André-Karl, born in 1889, second-lieutenant in the eighth artillery regiment, fatally wounded on September 22, 1914: chestnut hair and eyebrows, brown eyes.

Armand-Albert, born in 1890, a doctor who died just after the war of tuberculosis: dark chestnut hair, light brown eyes.

Four sons for whom I have the following colors: blond, dark chestnut, light chestnut, eyes blue and gray. But while flipping through their files, though only for André-Karl, I find a little identity photo in black and white stuck on a service record. I photograph it. His features are blurred. I go to the photocopier and increase the size. The face appears. I photograph it once again, and I discover a very young man with a delicate face, his hair, cut short, separated by a parting, wilful eyes and a little mustache. He is wearing a suit with a false collar and a tie. These are his peace-time clothes.

I go back to the dossiers on the other Doumer brothers and compare. By looking at the assessments, the notes, and the reports, I come to understand that André was the most uncontrollable. He was a wayward and happy-go-lucky child, his mother was called Marie Céline Blanche.

I don't know the first names of the mother of Louis Letermelier, a Zouave who died in Reuilly-Sauvigny during the first battle of the Marne. In Tunis, where she was living, this woman received letters telling her that her ailing and abandoned son had been killed by the mayor, who was frightened by the German offensive and the possible reprisals. "I'm pretty sure," one of them said, "that he had blue eyes though I only saw them half-closed, a very light, sparse and rather short blond beard, twenty-three years old, as for the height I don't know having only seen him lying in bed." At the time of the inquest, and when the body was exhumed, the mother took a lock of hair. Over the following months, caressing her son's hair, she found some sand, incontrovertible proof for her that her son had been drowned. The case was eventually dismissed. But, she had insinuated herself in my brain. To free myself, I wrote a novel, to express the color of those eyes and the air of he who remained a child.

Another book, and a magnificent, important one, one that touched me deeply, especially when you know what happened afterwards and take note of the passage that describes the moment when François goes into the house of one of his great aunts whose children are dead. He sees the walls covered in old diplomas, in portraits of the deceased, and in lockets in curls of dead hair. In the work's[10] frontispiece, I find a black-and-white photo of the author, Alain-Fournier, in suit and tie, very young, his hands leaning on a little table, his head turned to one side. I want to know. What color was his parted hair, his little mustache, his eyes? At the army archives, I write to ask for the dossier of lieutenant Henri-Alban Fournier. But when I go in person on Tuesday, December 11, 2012, I am told by an official that unfortunately the archive could not be found.

How many mothers kept locks of hair in secret hiding places? I am well aware that for my brother and me, those locks of hair also exist. On the evening of February 22, 2013, in Mende, during a bitter stretch of cold in this winter that keeps sky and earth ceaselessly in its grip, I gently put the question to my mother. She tells me to follow her. In her room, she opens her armoire, a drawer, lifts up some papers, some photos, and, suddenly, hands me an envelope and a little package. I take it delicately. On the envelope, there is my first and last name. I open it and find a long lock of hair. In my older brother's case, the hair was inserted in tissue paper. It looks the same as mine. Light chestnut, almost blond. My mother tells me to go get an envelope. I take one and, on it, I write the last and first name of my brother.

Two Doctors in the Snow

It must still have been very cold on March 9, 1882, when, in Javols in the mountainous regions of Lozère, Pierre-Jean-Joseph Allanche was born. I know nothing about the childhood and adolescence of this farm owner's son. But that's not very serious since I am mostly interested in him because of the war. On November 15, 1904, Allanche joined the 142nd infantry regiment based in Mende and Lodève, and was released from service because of his plans to get a doctorate in medicine. In 1909, he was named reserve auxiliary doctor and, in 1912, he was moved to the mobile portion of the 342nd. Mobilized in August, 1914, he had left with the 142nd. Jean-Pierre-Casimir-Calixte Remize was a little younger than him, born on March 10, 1885, in Saint-Chély-d'Aubrac in Aveyron, the son of a farmer. On the day of the draft board examination, he measured five feet, six-and-half inches, and Remize, five feet seven inches. Both had chestnut hair and eyes. But Remize knew how to ride a horse. He enlisted as a volunteer for three years on October 6, 1905, at the town hall in Rodez, and had been sent to the eighty-first before being put on reserve a year later. A military nurse, he had been transferred to Perpignan in 1910. On April 8, 1914, he was placed in the mobile portion of the Mende reserve regiment and, on the following August 10, he marched with the 342nd. Jean Remize studied medicine in Toulouse and had been a doctor since 1912. Pierre Allanche would defend his thesis at the University of Montpellier on November 16, 1916.

The two doctors march with their respective regiments in August 1914. The 342nd then numbers thirty-six officers, 110 noncommissioned officers, 2,026 corporals and soldiers and 129 horses. For the 142nd I have no figures because, for the first months of the war, the diary doesn't exist. I know only that on June 15, 1916, at the time of his departure from the subsector of Fort de Vaux, besides the colonel and the battalion and squadron chiefs, the unit had five captains, twelve lieutenants, twelve second-lieutenants and 1,639 troops. But long months of war had methodically decimated its ranks.

The 142nd was attached to the thirty-first division and the 342nd to the thirty-second, which belonged to the sixteenth corps of the Second Army, then commanded by General Taverna. Whatever became of the general? I dig a little. Nothing, no biographical note, just a photo of him when he was a colonel. Perhaps he was swept away by the great purge of autumn 1914 implacably carried out by Joffre? Between the lines of the logbooks and the chronicles, I look for the days they've lived, the places they went. What can I do to reach them, to follow and understand them? I find formulas, coded messages, useless declarations.

Sometimes, too, lightning flashes and confessions. Across these pages parade villages, rivers, roads, and ponds. These narratives are maps and calendars. I see ascents, descents, and immense flat stretches. Charged like beasts, men advance beneath the sun. At headquarters, they stop for a moment, then set off again. After having formed clusters, they sleep in fields or in barns. Suddenly, I am in their midst, and I too became one of the troops. I hear orders, I follow in the footsteps of the person in front of me. My feet are wounds. Sweat soaks my undershirt and boxer shorts. Marching like that, without quite knowing where one is headed—I hadn't done it since maneuvers years ago. "The border," I hear from my comrades here and there. "We're getting close." In the distance, the noise of cannon fire. It doesn't frighten us.

On August 14, the farms burn on the plain. Herds without masters trample the ripe grains. The 142nd reaches Maizières and billets in Desseling. On August 18, the order is given to seize the villages of Loudrefing and Mittersheim while ensuring that the Salines canal is unblocked. The first and third battalions cross the forest of Mühlwald and march on Angviller. Fearsome is the German artillery barrage. Shells, machinegun bullets: the bodies pile up. The living get stuck in the swamps of the Vape-Wiser tarn. Despite the adversity, a few individuals reach Loudrefing where the enemy bombardment pulverizes them. When night falls, the retreat has begun.

How many dead on August 18? The lieutenant-colonel and his second in command, twenty-seven officers and 1,150 men. On August 19 and 20, the 142nd decamps all the way to Lunéville.

I change texts and sectors. Once again, I read, discover. The same story unfolds. On August 12, the 342nd set out from Mirecourt. On August 18, it reaches Maizières where it is put on reserve for the thirty-second division. The next day, the regiment receives the order to follow the fifty-third through Languimberg, Fribourg, Bisping. It finally reaches Angviller. On August 20, two of its companies penetrate into the forest of Mühlwald. But fire from the German infantry pins them down. On all sides, the troops of the sixteenth corps withdraw. They fly toward Angviller. Around 13:30, the 342nd finally receives the order to retreat. The German bombardment pounds the companies. The men manage to reach Cote No. 260, located 1,600 meters southwest of Bisping.

I climb upwards to reach the Main Headquarters. What do we see here? The maps of Lorraine are spread out, and the telephone never stops ringing. Starting on August 19, despite the advance, it was understood here that the retreat of the Bavarian army corps was strategic. The men were exhausted. At 8:00 in the morning, General Taverna, who disappeared from the history books, decides to have the thirty-second division pass in front of the thirty-first, which is utterly spent. At dawn on August 20, mist covers a part of the battlefield. Suddenly, at sunrise, the Germans go on the attack. They charge toward the Mühlwald woods, infiltrate toward Angviller. The sixteenth corps floods back toward the forest. The Major of the Second Army, General Castelnau, orders a withdrawal. In the vicinity of Guermange, Angviller, and Bisping, the situation is very troubling. The losses are considerable. The trains, vehicle fleets, and convoys are pushed to the left bank of the Meurthe. On the morning of August 21, the sixteenth corps arrives in the region of Igney, Avricourt, Moussey.

These narratives are contour lines. As I follow them, I rise, descend, and listen. Voices speak. They say what they've seen, what they've been told, what they've been commanded to write. What I retain from all of that are the place names: the forest of Mühlwald, Angviller, Loudrefing. I dig around in my library and find the volume that Victor-Eugène Ardouin-Dumazet, in his Voyage en France, devoted to the "Lost Provinces."[11] In 1906 he came to this part of Lorraine, the land of great ponds where, with the changing years and seasons, wheat and fish were harvested. Winding his way through the bodies of water, he followed in the footsteps of an author who was very famous at the time. "The sad pool of Lindre," writes Maurice Barrès in Au service de l'Allemagne. Then in the train that carried him toward other discoveries, on the Metz-Strasbourg line, Ardouin-Dumazet rode along the Mittersheim pond, which was surrounded by forests. In the middle of the Angviller ponds the Mühlwald woods appeared, those woods where, in August 1914, the war would rush in like a fury, downing both French and German men.

Guermange isn't far, right on the edge of the Lindre pond. But Lunéville, on the French side of the 1871 border? Ardouin-Dumazet had already spoken of it. The countryside surrounding the town appeared banal to him. Long, rounded knolls with barren hillsides, wooded at the summit, then when one has finally reached the little Amezale river, isolated mounts on which vines, oaks, orchards, and fields are spread out.

These are precious places for me. I want to roam across them, touch them, listen to their stories. At Guermange, on August 20, 1914, my two doctors, Pierre Allanche and

Jean Remize, left the stage. The logbook of the 342nd tells how: "The regiment's medical service (personnel and equipment) disappeared this very day under unexplained circumstances (Medical Officer Jouffreau, Assistant Medical Officer Bec, auxiliary doctors and nurses). Everything points to the fact that personnel and equipment that left their post to the west of Bisping before the withdrawal of the regiment, owe their disappearance to having gone in the wrong direction."

Allanche and Remize were thus together. Where are they now? Dead, disappeared? That's not enough for me. I hasten toward Lunéville where the 142nd continued to fight. And I learn that on August 22, in a sector that I can't locate, my great-uncle Charles Pourcher, younger brother of my paternal grandfather, conscripted in 1909, registration number 221, black hair and eyes, was gravely wounded by a bullet in the chest. Two scars described in his medical record would remain on his mutilated body: "the entry wound, in the upper part of the thorax, above the left breast, and the exit wound, on the external edge of the left shoulder blade." The bullet had missed the heart. And my great-uncle Charles, lying there on that day and perhaps night of August 22, 1914, losing blood, without the aid of the vanished doctors and nurses of his regiment, calling out to his parents, his brothers and sisters. Suddenly he hears footsteps. Are his eyes open? Hands slide under his coat, searching, they take his papers, touch his identity tag. Suddenly he is seized, and carried away.

Time is suspended. Three men have exited this story. At their homes, in Lozère, their loved ones wait in anguish. Interminable days, weeks on end without any news. In Aumont, Dr. Allanche's young wife, Marie Anastasie Eulalie, no longer knows what to think. They had been married some months before, on February 22 to be exact. But Eulalie still wants to hope. In Nasbinals sur l'Aubrac, where Dr. Remize had settled, his wife Marie-Thérèse, a native of Ariège, writes:

September 3, 1914

My dear friend,
I'm very, very, very worried, still no news. But tell me what can be happening to prevent you from taking a moment to write? Or else correspondence has been stopped in some places. Well, let's be patient a little longer. Kisses from your little wife who is miserable far from you and above all without knowing what has happened to you.

Love,
Thérèse.

The next day, she takes up her pen once more.

My dear friend,
Truly, I don't know what to think not having any news from you here in Nasbinals. I've been writing to you every day for five weeks without any reply. I dare to think that you're in good health all the same. As for me, I'm doing pretty well. Your little wife, who hasn't forgotten you, sends you her softest caresses.

Love,
Thérèse.

At the end of the month, Marie-Thérèse receives a letter from a woman living in Poitiers. She tells her that her husband, head doctor of the 325th line regiment, is a prisoner in Bavaria. Thanks to a Swiss doctor, he was able to write to her and gave her a list of his companions in captivity. Among them is Marie-Thérèse's husband, Jean Remize. On October 9, a card finally arrives. Jean says that for a month he has been held with his friend Allanche at Ingolstadt fort number 8. Captured on August 20, they tended to French and German wounded men. Then they were taken to the fort. Jean adds that he has been treated well. Over the following months, he is transferred. Through the Red Cross, Marie-Thérèse learns that he is now at Dachau, the only Frenchman and the only doctor for thousands of Russian prisoners. The winter is harsh, and snow covers the camp. But no more than it does Aubrac! Jean doesn't complain. "I conclude, ma grande amie," he writes at the end of one of his letters, "by kissing you with you all my heart and telling you not to worry because I am in no way unhappy."

Jean Remize is repatriated in France on October 4, 1916. Pierre Allanche comes back two days later. Assigned to the ward for German officers taken prisoner at Maugères, Remize then goes to Bar-sur-Aube, then to Bossancourt and Saint-Dizier in the civilian ward. Allanche stays near his home, in Sévérac-le-Château, until July 11, 1917. He then goes to Ramerupt in Aube. And it is here that the tragedy occurs. On October 29, 1918, at nine in the evening, he is called urgently to a farm to minister to a soldier wounded by a rifle shot. Allanche arrives. But a "Moroccan rebel," as the report specifies, raises his weapon and fires two bullets. Allanche dies instantly. For France! On September 9, 1919, his little girl, Thérésia Maria Noémie, born on October 1, 1917, is officially adopted as a Ward of the French Nation.

Jean Remize goes back to Nasbinals. On the village's monument to the dead, seventy-nine names are engraved. The doctor resumes his house calls and roams the high plain of Aubrac. In winter, the snow accumulates. The north wind forms snowdrifts. Everything comes to a halt, the dead are no longer buried. The earth is as hard as iron. But at night, there is knocking at the doctor's door. It opens. Voices murmur. It's for a birth, a hemorrhage, a suffocating child. Horses are waiting. Jean Remize puts on his big hooded cape. He goes out and climbs onto his beautiful chestnut named Voïna, a Russian name that he learned in Germany, and they go. The snow is up to the stirrups. They sink into the powder, scramble onto the drifts. The wind burns their cheeks and foreheads. Their eyes can no longer see. Suddenly they arrive. The doctor enters the farm. He tends to the sick patient. Then they depart, slowly. But on the night of February 22, 1927, an ordinary night, lost in his thoughts, the doctor suddenly perceived an immense glowing light. He sees cadavers, hundreds of soldiers' cadavers and, in their midst, his friend Allanche whose uniform is stained with blood. The wounded man reaches out his hand, his lips move. A little farther on, another man whom he doesn't know, my great-uncle Charles Pourcher, lying in a ditch, calls out and shouts that he wants to live. The doctor returns home. But that night, worn out with fatigue, Jean Remize remains for hours in front of the fire burning in the granite fireplace.

"*The world is a white whirlwind*," affirms Drieu La Rochelle, in État civil (Civil Status). But I'm more interested in the Signalement, the physical status. And so I start over again: "Black hair and eyes, receding hairline, oval face, 5 feet, 7 inches tall." And I think of the man I loved. When did they gather up my great-uncle's body? Charles, the son of farmers, a farmer himself. Cared for by the Germans. But perhaps, after all, it was those two doctors, Allanche or Remize? For him, captivity was awful. I recall that he said he was sent to work on a farm where the son had been killed in the war. The people of the household were not welcoming. But they fed him. I often see him in my thoughts, my bachelor great-uncle. Very thin, his cheeks hollow, always working. He had a very nice cow that he called Marquise, a name which amused and delighted us. At the end of his days he became senile and was placed in Saint-Alban's, in that place which, later on, would cause me such suffering. We went to see him on certain Sundays. One day while I was standing right behind him, he went to the window. Suddenly, his features drawn, he extended his right hand. "The Germans!" he cried. And, completely lost, like an idiot, I looked out and searched for shadows in the grove of trees.

Jonston

Jonston is the little horse that belonged to my paternal great-grandfather. On the farm in the village of Valadou, in the commune of Montrodat near Marvejols, the war turned life upside down. In this family of mine, besides my parents and a bachelor uncle, I count the children. My grandfather, Dominique, the first-born, in 1887. Then comes Hélène, born in 1888, Charles in 1889, Victor in 1891, Anne-Marie in 1896, and Casimir in 1902. Two other children listed in the family birth register died. In 1914, the father is seventy-two and the mother fifty-five. Because he was the eldest in a large family, my grandfather was not immediately mobilized. But his two brothers went away and, on August 22, Charles was gravely wounded near Lunéville.

In Valadou, the family's land was scattered. Fields, meadows, some woods and heaths. The main house was located above the village, right beside the school. The farm wasn't very large. But it made it possible to earn a living. My great-aunt, Hélène, was adopted by an uncle and aunt who lived some distance away, on the Margeride, on the lovely property of Coulagnettes which stretched over nearly one hundred hectares. On the banks of the Colagne, the master's house, made entirely of granite, had a beautiful bell tower. The meadow, which was irrigated, was vast and the herd was large. My great-aunt had become "Mademoiselle Hélène," and thus she would remain until her death. I see her in her youth in a photo that I have placed on the wall next to my desk. Tall, with a round face, wearing a long dress tied at the waist, she is holding the horn of an Easter ox. Other photos are there. One of my grandfather, Dominique, in uniform. He holds himself upright on his horse. His mustache is long.

I am in possession of letters about this period, most of which were sent to the prisoner. "My dear brother," writes Hélène one April 30, "thank you for taking the trouble to write us from time to time. We so love to read your letters. The news that you give us is fairly good. So you've come back from Stuttgart from a lazaretto where you were at first. It must be really quite different from a camp. Fortunately the nice weather has come, which is reassuring, and then we're always hearing about happy events."

Hélène sends news of the other members of the family. Then she speaks to him of their work. "The weather," she says, "is superb. The grass is growing before our eyes, our animals have been grazing outside for what will soon be three weeks. Dominiquou will bring over the young filly. Here the pastures are big, she'll have more space. This year, we won't have any foals. Nothing but our two mares and a horse from last year."

The same images and the same expressions are found in the cards and letters. The sisters write. In the brothers' absence, they've taken charge of daily tasks. Plowing,

Figure 4
The Landlord of Coulagnettes between Two Servants

Figure 5
My Great Uncle with Fellow Prisoners in Bavaria

sowing, scything, harvesting. To Charles, held captive in Bavaria, they send packages and postal orders. On June 25, 1915, Hélène announces that two jars of preserves have been sent. "As for the bread," she adds, "with the heat we're having, it's obvious that it's going moldy. We'll do as you say, two very thin dry baguettes which will always keep, better dry than moldy."

The brothers, Dominique and Victor, are at war. They come back from time to time on leave and work nonstop. They write little cards to their brother Charles. The latter replies by sending a photo, proof that he's alive, that he's doing well. Among all the snapshots that he sent, I find the ones where he appears in the midst of others. In the street of a German town lined with tall houses with steeply pitched roofs, a line of prisoners follows a hearse. In front of them, soldiers in pointed helmets. Other photos show a group in front of a tomb. On the cross, I read a name, then another in another snapshot. I search in the immense virtual cemetery formed by the website Mémoire des hommes and, among the 1.3 million files, I find the ones that interest me. Émile Marius ABEL, a soldier in the 157th infantry regiment, who died for France on October 31, 1918, in Hunsinger (Wurtenberg) and Pierre CROZET, a soldier in the thirty-eighth infantry regiment, who died November 4, 1918, in Hermuthausen. Type of death: illness in captivity. The first, born in Barcelonnette in the Basses-Alpes, was thirty-five years old. The second, born in Saint-Rambert, in the department of Loire, was twenty-six years old.

On November 30, 1917, the last of the Valadou children, Casimir, who was then fifteen, a student at the little seminary of Marvejols, tells his brother everything he's doing at the house. "Jonston walked well, but at Vallons (that was the last field that we harvested), the little wheel split somewhat. The machine couldn't make it all the way to the house. (. . .) This year, there was a lot of fruit. I wish you could have seen the trees! The branches were bent all the way down to the ground. We picked them all up. There were chestnuts, but the cold froze them."

The strong little horse pulls the plow, pulls carts of hay, bundles of vegetables, and sacks before being able at last, in the evening, to gallop freely in the meadows. In Coulagnettes, in the springtime, the meadows are white with narcissus. It looks like snow or sea foam. On the banks of the river, some lines have been cast to catch trout. When I was a child, my great-aunt Anne-Marie spoke to me of the happy days she had known on this land, which she loved so. In the evening, by the fireplace, she sang songs of her youth. "Lorraine, Lorraine chérie," I can still hear like a murmur, "au coeur de la France meurtrie. Aux trois couleurs, aux trois couleurs." Sometimes my paternal grandfather Dominique told us about the war. These were always extraordinary stories that fascinated and frightened us. After that conflict, from which he returned gassed, he married. Then he abandoned the Valadou property, which he had received as an inheritance, and left for the south of France with his wife and his three children. After the other war, the second of that century, and during the German occupation, he returned to his land to live as a farmer.

But one day, I wondered why I knew nothing of my other grandfather, my mother's father, Alphonse Delmas. I have a photo of him that I enlarged. I often look at it. In the foreground there is an anvil set on a log. "Class 1908" is written on the back in chalk. Eight soldiers stare at the lens. In the middle of them, my grandfather, a little man with short, thick, perhaps black hair, a cigarette in his mouth, a ribbon tied around his neck.

Figure 6
Alphonse Delmas, My Maternal Grandfather, Blacksmith

He is slender, solidly planted on his legs, with a strong-willed, frank air about him. I am able to interpret because I knew him a little and because my mother often described him to me. Under his left arm he is holding the leg and the hoof of a horse. He and the others wear the aprons and have the hands of blacksmith farriers. My grandfather indeed belonged to the 1909 class.

Physical description—I can give one thanks to this photo. But on this Sunday, January 20, 2013, in Mende, as snowflakes hover around the window, I put the question to my mother and her brother, who is younger than her by a few years: "Did he talk to you about the war?" "Yes!" says my uncle, and my mother agrees with him. Yet she doesn't know much. It was a man's affair, stories one told to one's sons. My grandfather told them at the forge. My uncle tells me that his father belonged to the baggage train. The number of horses he shod! One enormous gallop. They drool, cry. Their hindquarters and legs tremble. Some fall down exhausted. But others replace them. They are shod. Metal becomes rare. Metal is recuperated, melted down, diverted. Now there are new shoes. But as I listen, an image keeps coming back. The image that I have of my grandfather. The goodness of his gaze, and then the enormous bruise on his thigh that he showed me one day. A blow from a nasty beast.

Figure 7
Charles Pourcher, My Great Uncle, Grievously Wounded August 22, 1914

Massacre

There are moments where one has to go very fast; to say in a few words what happened. Then come back to the unknown, to mystery, horror, to try to see. I begin, then, with this avowal. It springs up in the hollow of a paragraph that I want to relate. It's October 4, 1916, in the middle of the Battle of the Somme, and General Fayolle writes: "The 1st corps took 35 prisoners and 9 eighty-eights. It seems the 8th I.R. massacred the Boches, thus the small number of prisoners. It has been raining for three days. Regarding troop morale and the soul of the race. Our men feel that victory is truly nigh."

They massacred!

How did they come to that?

"It's the war of men," responds André Suarès, petrified by hatred. But for me, grandson of a farmer and a blacksmith farrier, that's not enough. So I scrape at the earth and the hoofs of horses. To comprehend the incomprehensible. To get to the unspeakable, the inexpressible. And I recall that distant television program where, on the set, after the usual historians had finished their perorations, an old man, one of the last witnesses, mumbled a dreadful sentence: "To think what these hands have done!"

Where are the traces of what really happened on October 4, 1916?

I take up the logbook of the eighth infantry regiment, which then belongs to the first army corps, second division, fourth brigade. On August 1, 1914, it numbered 210 non-commissioned officers, 3,062 troops, and 184 horses and mules. Its soldiers came from the north, in the region of Saint-Omer, Boulogne, Calais. Since July 1, 1916, the great butchery of the Somme was underway. Marching slowly or released in waves, English and French regiments advanced in front of the German trenches. They were ravaged, pulverized. At the beginning of autumn, little has changed. I turn the pages and count the days. On September 12, the order is given to attack with the 110th toward the Anderla wood, the trenches of Hôpital and Trentin, the Le Priez farm. Outcome: one hundred prisoners from the Guards Regiments (Franz regiment and Augusta regiment). The other defenders were killed where they were. The eighth has eighteen officers hors de combat, five of which were killed, and five hundred thirty-five men. But during the night, the Germans counterattack.

On September 13, there is a fresh assault. The units leap into the Hôpital trench which they empty and mop up all the way to the Le Priez Farm-Anderla wood path. Sixty prisoners are taken. The Hôpital trench is strewn with cadavers. On September 15, there is tremendous chaos in the tunnels. The eleventh company of the regiment arrives to find a shattered terrain where there is no longer any trace whatsoever of the trenches.

Replaced on September 19, the eighth infantry regiment goes back to the front lines on the twenty-fifth. It replaces the English troops. On October 1, it receives the order to attack the Morval trench, the Haie wood and the Prilip trench. The fighting is fierce. The men find intact barbed wire, machine guns, and grenades. Ground is won little by little. On October 2 and 3, the enemy bombardment is enormous. On October 4, Lieutenant-Colonel Roubert, the Major of the regiment, decides once again to attack. The artillery pounds away through the night. At 6 o'clock in the morning, the assault is launched. The sixth and seventh companies move forward grenade by grenade. Men jump into the Prilip trench and kill the German defenders. But enemy fire pins them down in the ravine. Cadavers! At the same time, in the Morval trench, a mop-up operation.

Relief forces come on the night of the October 4 and 5. The men bivouac around the Bronfay farm in the commune of Maricourt. On October 6, the regiment is taken by automobile toward Loeuilly where a reinforcement of five hundred twenty-six men, including twenty-three noncommissioned officers, arrives. On October 9, there are reinforcements: two sergeants and forty-eight men. The regiment leaves Conty for an unknown destination.

Chaos in the tunnels.

Mop-up. Have to mop-up. An immense butchery.

How many prisoners? And how many bodies?

Silence

On October 21, the eighth infantry regiment is recognized by the Army for its "irresistible momentum and indomitable tenacity." It has the right to wear the fourragère on its uniform. The fourragère—a gold braid stapled to the shoulder. It encircles the arm and is ornamented with metal aiglets. The men of the eighth infantry regiment parade about with their fourragère. But during the night, while having horrible nightmares, some are afraid of their hands.

Crosses

Wood, iron, war. Décor, decoration, parade. A red and green ribbon on the left side of the chest. They wear a cross in Florentine bronze, thirty-seven millimeters in diameter, a Maltese cross with two crossed swords in between the branches. This cross serves as a reward and a distinction. You find them sometimes at the flea markets. They are bought, sold, passed from hand to hand. Strange collection!

Were all of those who fought crusaders? "Ah, Boches!" writes Suarès. "You'll have to ask for forgiveness and get down on your knees." But he was drunk with vengeance. Wars seen as crusades, works of those wearing Crosses, wars of religion. Believers battling with other believers. Yet "the world is not so old that it shouldn't suddenly laugh" responds a poet.[12]

The great leaders parade. In Metz, on November 19, 1918, General Mangin, the inflexible Mangin, proponent of attack rather than defense and of la force noire, the black African forces, falls from his horse. Had my grandfather shod the animal? Unseated! says Pascal Quignard.[13] I prefer: Fallen from his horse. The beasts rear up, neigh, go crazy. They've come from so far. In the tenth dragoons, based at Montauban, in February 1915, American horses are trained. A month later, they arrive from Canada and Argentina. Their muzzles fill up with the odor of war. In Strasbourg, at the parade on November 25, 1918, Pétain, a prudent man, proceeds on foot. In Metz, on December 8, he receives his Marshal's baton. "Maréchal, nous voilà!" That's another story.

Figure 8
Sarasota's War Memorial, Dedicated November 12, 1928, on the Tenth Anniversary of the Armistice of World War I

They fell from their horses, fell beneath bullets, grenades, shells, poison gas. Fallen soldiers,[14] the English and Americans say. We, the French, prefer Dead for France, in the imaginary territories we see as Fields of honor.

They stretch on, these "Shadows of Honor," says Céline,[15] going from East to West, contaminating the world. In the American cemetery of Saint-James, located on the Channel, white crosses are lined up in the green grass. The names are inscribed, "Connu de Dieu," "Known but to God," is the inscription for those without an identity.

In Sarasota, Florida, located on the Gulf of Mexico, where I have been going regularly every January for more than ten years, I stop in front of the monument to the dead near the ocean. Perched on a granite tablet, a foot soldier, a rifle in his left hand, a grenade in the other, valiantly advances. Affixed to the stone, gray metal plaques give the names of the dead. For World War I, I read: Mink, Horace W. I look for his file and I find it. He was born in Bee Ridge on June 30, 1891 in a family of seven children. Died in France, May 28, 1918, of pneumonia.

Lungs, the organ for breathing.

Horace W. Mink died of an illness.

I walk around the little monument and I count: ninety-five dead in the course of the Second World War, ten in Korea and forty-two in Vietnam. At the monument's base, another plaque has been added. "Global war on terrorism," is the inscription, followed by three names. Just in front, at ground level, I see in January 2011 a little American flag on which the following words are written: "Pete, we love u and we miss you. Merry Christmas, son, in haven [sic]. We love u always & forever. Mama & family."

In 2013, a photo was left with the same message of love.

Peter Woodall, who died in Iraq on May 1, 2007, was twenty-five. He was the father of a little boy named Jacob, who was three years old at the time.

Translated by Trevor Merrill.

Notes

1. Ernest Renan, *Vie de Jésus* (Paris: Michel Lévy Frères, Libraires Éditeurs, 1863).
2. Maréchal Fayolle, *Cahiers Secrets de la Grande Guerre* (Paris: Plon, 1964), 49–50.
3. Ramón Del Valle-Inclán, *Flor de Santidad. La Media Noche* (Madrid: Espasa Calpe, 1978).
4. André Suarès, *C'est la Guerre* (Paris: Émile-Paul Frères Éditeurs, 1915).
5. As in, the War of 14–18.
6. Ernst Wiechert, *Le Capitaine de Capharnaüm* (Paris: Calmann-Lévy, 1967).
7. M. Bloch, *Souvenirs de Guerre 1914–1915*, Cahiers des Annales 26 (Paris: A. Colin), 54.
8. "S'en aller! S'en aller! Parole du prodigue!"
9. Jean Hugo, *Le Regard de la Mémoire* (Arles: Actes Sud, 1983).
10. Alain-Fournier, *Le Grand Meaulnes* (Paris: Éditions Émile-Paul Frères, 1913).
11. Ardouin-Dumazet, *Voyage en France. Les Provinces Perdues, III Lorraine (50° Série)* (Paris, Nancy: Berger-Levrault et Cie, Éditeurs, 1907).
12. Saint-John Perse, *Éloges, . . . le monde n'est pas si vieux que soudain il n'ait ri* (Paris: Gallimard, 1960).
13. P. Quignard, *Les Désarçonnés* (Paris: Garsset, 2012).
14. In English in the original.
15. Céline, *Féérie Pour une Autre Fois* (Paris: Gallimard, 1995).

Contributors

Darrell Cole is associate professor of religion at Drew University and chair of the Department of Comparative Religion. He teaches courses in professional ethics, religious ethics, and warfare and ethics. He is the author of "Torture and Just War," *The Journal of Religious Ethics* 40.1 (March 2012). His forthcoming works include "Questions Posed by Nuclear and Other Weapons of Mass Destruction," in *Ashgate Research Companion to Military Ethics*, edited by James Turner Johnson and Eric Patterson, Ashgate Publications, Surrey. He has just completed a manuscript on the ethics of spying to be titled *Whether Spies, Too, Can Be Saved*.

Mark Doyle received his PhD in 2006 from Boston College. He held postdoctoral fellowships at the University of Pennsylvania and Amherst College and is currently an assistant professor of history at Middle Tennessee State University. He is the author of *Fighting Like the Devil for the Sake of God: Protestants, Catholics, and the Origins of Violence in Victorian Belfast* (Manchester University Press, 2009), as well as several articles on communal violence and policing in the British Empire. He is working on a book about the Victorian British state's handling of communal violence across the British Empire.

Jonathan Fine lectures at the Lauder School of government at the IDC (the interdisciplinary center) Herzlyia, Israel, where he also serves as the undergraduate academic advisor of the international and Israeli programs in Government, Diplomacy, and Strategy. He received his PhD at the Hebrew University of Jerusalem, and is a graduate of the Executive program in Counter Terrorism at the International Institute for Counter-Terrorism (ICT), and programs in Intelligence services and security studies at the universities of Cartagena and Alicante in Spain. He has a wide background in history, comparative religion, political science, and international relations. His major interest focuses on the transition from secular to religious political violence, with special emphasis on the phenomena of fundamentalism in Judaism, Christianity, and Islam. He is also a member of the ICSR (The International Center for Study of Radicalization and Political Science) in London, and ICTAC (The International Counter—Terrorism Academic Community). One book is forthcoming soon in the United States (SUNY Press): *The Israeli Governmental System: The Establishment of a Sovereign State. 1947–1951*. He has also published articles in books and academic journals such as: the *Middle East Quarterly* (Washington, DC) and *Middle Eastern Studies* (London).

Nicholas F. Gier taught in the philosophy department at the University of Idaho from 1972 to 2003. He was also a coordinator of religious studies from 1980 to 2003. He has published five books: *Wittgenstein and Phenomenology* (SUNY Press, 1981), *God, Reason, and the Evangelicals* (University Press of America, 1987), *Spiritual Titanism: Indian, Chinese, and Western Perspectives* (SUNY Press, 2000), *The Virtue of Non-Violence: From Gautama to Gandhi* (SUNY Press, 2004), and *The Origins of Religious Violence: An Asian Perspective* (Lexington Books, 2014).

Grant N. Havers is professor of philosophy and chair of the Department of Philosophy (with a cross-appointment in the Department of Political Studies) at Trinity Western University (Canada). He has published and lectured widely on political philosophy, especially the conservative tradition. His most recently published book is *Leo Strauss and Anglo-American Democracy: A Conservative Critique* (Northern Illinois University Press, 2013).

Anthony (Tony) F. Lemieux earned his PhD and MA in social psychology at the University of Connecticut and his BA in psychology and sociology at Boston College. He is an associate professor of communication at Georgia State University, where he is a lead researcher in a newly established interdisciplinary Second Century Initiative on transcultural conflict and violence. He is also an investigator with the National Consortium for the Study of Terrorism and Responses to Terrorism (START), a US Department of Homeland Security Center of Excellence based at the University of Maryland. Dr. Lemieux has a blog at *Psychology Today* on the motivations and methods of terrorism. Prior to moving to Atlanta, he was an associate professor of psychology at Purchase College, State University of New York, where he chaired the university's Strategic Planning Committee.

Dr. Asaf Maliach holds a BA in Islamic and Middle Eastern studies from the Hebrew University in Jerusalem. He obtained both MA and PhD in Middle Eastern studies at Bar-Ilan University, Ramat Gan. His PhD dissertation deals with "'Abdallah 'Azzam and the Ideological Origins of Usama Bin Ladens' Worldwide Islamic Terrorism." Dr. Maliach was a researcher in the political science department at Bar-Ilan University, Israel. He was also a senior researcher in the Institute for Policy and Strategy (IPS) and in the International Institute for Counter-Terrorism (ICT), both at the IDC, Herzliya, Israel. Dr. Maliach is now a lecturer and consultant to public and private institutes and organizations on the Middle East issues and Global Islamic Terrorism. He also teaches the Arabic language at the Ministry of Education (Israel). He has published a book titled *From Kabul to Jerusalem— Al-Qa'ida's, the Worldwide Islamic Jihad and the Israeli-Palestinian Conflict* (Tel Aviv: Matar Publication, 2009) and has written many articles for the ICT Internet website.

Kathryn McClymond received her BA from Harvard University and her MA and PhD in religious studies from the University of California, Santa Barbara. She is professor and chair in the Department of Religious Studies at Georgia State University. Her research focuses on religion and violence, especially ritualized violence. Her recent work examines how understanding violence as "sacrifice" shapes individual and community responses to violence they themselves have perpetrated, and how individuals deal with moral injury through drawing on world cultures's narrative and ritual traditions. She has authored *Beyond Sacred Violence* (Johns Hopkins University Press, 2008) and *Ritual Gone Wrong: What We Learn from Ritual Disruption* (Oxford University Press, now in production), as well as several articles and chapters on religion, sacrifice, and violence. She has held multiple offices in the American Academy of Religion, and she was recently invited to join the American Society for the Study of Religion.

Christopher S. Morrissey is associate professor of philosophy at Redeemer Pacific College. He is the author of *Hesiod: Theogony/Works and Days* and the managing editor of *The American Journal of Semiotics*.

Yves Pourcher is professor of political anthropology at the Institut d'études politiques de Toulouse in the Laboratoire des Sciences Sociales du Politique, LASSP research group. His work focuses on local power and elections and on the history of World War I and the occupation in France. He is the author of several works of history and anthropology—*Les Maîtres de granit* (Orban, 1987; Plon, 1995), *Les Jours de guerre* (Plon, 1994), *Pierre Laval vu par sa fille* (Le Cherche Midi, 2002), and *Votez tous pour moi!* (Presses de Sciences po, 2004)—and three novels, including *Le Rêveur d'étoiles* (Le Cherche Midi, 2004).

Oliver Rafferty, SJ is a Jesuit priest and a historian, and has taught at colleges and universities in Britain, Ireland, and the United States. Currently he is visiting scholar in history and Irish studies at Boston College. Among his many publications is the edited collection *Irish Catholic Identities* (Manchester University Press, 2013). At present he is researching a book on *The Catholic Church in Ireland and the 1916 Rising*.

Gabriel R. Ricci is associate professor of humanities at Elizabethtown College where he teaches philosophy and history. He is the editor of the book series *Culture & Civilization* (Transaction Publishers) and has been the editor of *Religion and Public Life* (Transaction Publishers) since 1999. He has written extensively on time consciousness in the German historical tradition and he is currently researching the legacy of Edmund Husserl in the quarterly journal *Philosophy and Phenomenological Research* founded by Marvin Farber in 1940.

Rebecca Rist is a lecturer for the Graduate Centre for Medieval Studies at the University of Reading. Her research interests include the history of crusading, Jewish-Christian relations, the medieval Church, the papacy, religious belief and political ideas in the Central Middle Ages. Her book *The Papacy and Crusading in Europe, 1198–1245* (Continuum 2009) examines the papacy's authorization of crusades against heretics and political enemies in Europe during the first half of the thirteenth century. Her recent work has explored aspects of papal policy with regard to crusading and the papacy's treatment of heretics and Jews in the High Middle Ages. She is currently writing a book on the papacy and the Jews in the Central Middle Ages.

Brian Sandberg is associate professor of history at Northern Illinois University. His research focuses on intersections of religion, violence, and political culture in early modern history, especially during the European wars of religion. His first book, *Warrior Pursuits: Noble Culture and Civil Conflict in Early Modern France* (Baltimore, MD: Johns Hopkins University Press, 2010), analyzes provincial nobles's orchestration of civil warfare in southern France. He has served as a National Endowment for the Humanities Fellow at the Medici Archive Project and held a Jean Monnet Fellowship at the European University Institute. He has published several articles on religious violence, gender, and noble culture during the French wars of religion, and he is currently revising a monograph entitled *Heroic Souls: French Nobles and Religious Conflict after the Edict of Nantes, 1598–1629.*

Lightning Source UK Ltd.
Milton Keynes UK
UKHW032024181019
351894UK00007B/82/P